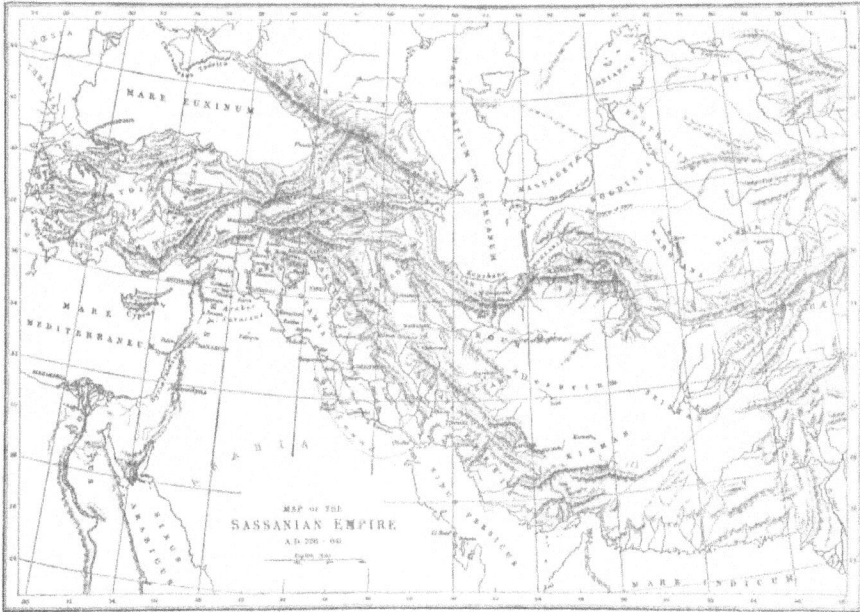

[MAP]

## PREFACE TO SEVENTH MONARCHY

This work completes the Ancient History of the East, to which the author has devoted his main attention during the last eighteen years. It is a sequel to his "Parthians," published in 1873; and carries down the History of Western Asia from the third century of our era to the middle of the seventh. So far as the present writer is aware, no European author has previously treated this period from the Oriental stand-point, in any work aspiring to be more than a mere sketch or outline.

Very many such sketches have been published; but they have been scanty in the extreme, and the greater number of them have been based on the authority of a single class of writers. It has been the present author's aim to combine the various classes of authorities which are now accessible to the historical student, and to give their due weight to each of them. The labors of M. C. Muller, of the Abbe Gregoire Kabaragy Garabed, and of M. J. St. Martin have opened to us the stores of ancient Armenian literature, which were previously a sealed volume to all but a small class of students. The early Arab historians have been translated or analyzed by Kosegarten, Zotenberg, M. Jules Mohl, and others. The coinage of the Sassanians has been elaborately—almost exhaustively—treated by Mordtmann and Thomas. Mr. Fergusson has applied his acute and practised powers to the elucidation of the Sassanian architecture. By combining the results thus obtained with the old sources of information—the classical, especially the Byzantine writers—it has become possible to compose a history of the Sassanian Empire which is at once consecutive, and not absolutely meagre. How the author has performed his task, he must leave it to the public to judge; he will only venture to say that he has spared no labor, but has gone carefully through the entire series of the Byzantine writers who treat of the time, besides availing himself of the various modern works to which reference has been made above. If he has been sometimes obliged to draw conclusions from his authorities other than those drawn by Gibbon, and has deemed it right, in the interests of historic truth, to express occasionally his dissent from that writer's views, he must not be thought blind to the many and great excellencies which render the "Decline and Fall" one of the best, if not the best, of our histories. The mistakes of a writer less eminent and less popular might have been left unnoticed without ill results. Those of an historian generally regarded as an authority from whom there is no appeal could not be so lightly treated.

The author begs to acknowledge his great obligations, especially, to the following living writers: M. Patkanian, M. Jules Mohl, Dr. Haug, Herr Spiegel, Herr Windischmann, Herr Mordtmann, Canon Tristram, Mr. James Fergusson, and Mr. E. Thomas. He is also largely beholden to the works of M. Texier and of MM. Flandin and Coste for the illustrations, which he has been able to give, of Sassanian sculpture and architecture. The photographic illustrations of the newly-discovered palace at Mashita are due to the liberality of Mr. R. C. Johnson (the amateur artist who accompanied Canon Tristram in his exploration of the "Land of Moab"), who, with Canon Tristram's kind consent, has allowed them to appear in the present volume. The numismatic illustrations are chiefly derived from Longperier; but one or two have been borrowed from other sources. For his frontispiece the author is indebted to his brother, Sir Henry Rawlinson, who has permitted it to be taken from an original drawing in his possession, which he believed to be a truthful representation of the great Sassanian building.

*CANTERBURY: December 1875.*

CHAPTER I

*Condition of the Persians under the Successors of Alexander—under the Arsacidce. Favor shown them by the latter—allowed to have Kings of their own. Their Religion at first held in honor. Power of their Priests. Gradual Change of Policy on the part of the Parthian Monarchs, and final Oppression of the Magi. Causes which produced the Insurrection of Artaxerxes.*

*"The Parthians had been barbarians; they had ruled over a nation far more civilized than themselves, and had oppressed them and their religion."*
*Niebuhr, Lectures on Roman History, vol. iii. p. 270.*

# The Seven Great Monarchies of the Ancient Eastern World by George Rawlinson

**Volume VII (of VII) The Seventh Monarchy: The Sassanian or New Persian Empire**

George Rawlinson was born on 23rd November 1812 at Chadlington, Oxfordshire. He was the younger brother to the eminent Assyriologist, Sir Henry Rawlinson.

Rawlinson took his degree at Trinity College, Oxford in 1838. Here he also enjoyed playing cricket and was considered to have been a rare talent at the sport. In 1840 he was elected to a fellowship at Exeter College, Oxford. After being ordained in 1841 he became, from 1842 to 1846, a tutor there as well.

In 1846 Rawlinson married Louisa, the daughter of Sir RA Chermside.

His progress continued to be rapid and varied in acknowledgement of his undoubted talents. In 1859 he was made a Bampton lecturer, and was Camden Professor of Ancient History from 1861 to 1889.

By 1872 Rawlinson was appointed canon of Canterbury, and after 1888 he was rector of All Hallows, Lombard Street.

In 1873, he was made proctor in Convocation for the Chapter of Canterbury.

As a scholar he produced, either on his own or in collaboration, several works which are greatly thought of even to this day. His translation of the History of Herodotus (in collaboration with Sir Henry Rawlinson and Sir John Gardiner Wilkinson), 1858–60; The Five Great Monarchies of the Ancient Eastern World, 1862–67; which was later expanded to include The Sixth Great Oriental Monarchy (Parthian), 1873; and The Seventh Great Oriental Monarchy (Sassanian), 1875. Among his other works were Manual of Ancient History, 1869; Historical Illustrations of the Old Testament, 1871; The Origin of Nations, 1877; History of Ancient Egypt, 1881; Egypt and Babylon, 1885; History of Phoenicia, 1889; Parthia, 1893; Memoir of Major-General Sir HC Rawlinson, 1898.

His lectures to an audience at Oxford University on the topic of the accuracy of the Bible in 1859 were published as the apologetic work The Historical Evidences of the Truth of the Scripture Records Stated Anew in later years.

Despite this somewhat prodigious output and alongside his other clerical and family duties he contributed to the Speaker's Commentary, the Pulpit Commentary, Smith's Dictionary of the Bible, and various similar publications.

George Rawlinson died on 7th October, 1902 in Canterbury.

## Index of Contents

## Index of Illustrations

When the great Empire of the Persians, founded by Cyrus, collapsed under the attack of Alexander the Great, the dominant race of Western Asia did not feel itself at the first reduced to an intolerable condition. It was the benevolent design of Alexander to fuse into one the two leading peoples of Europe and Asia, and to establish himself at the head of a Perso-Hellenic State, the capital of which was to have been Babylon. Had this idea been carried out, the Persians would, it is evident, have lost but little by their subjugation. Placed on a par with the Greeks, united with them in marriage bonds, and equally favored by their common ruler, they could scarcely have uttered a murmur, or have been seriously discontented with their position. But when the successors of the great Macedonian, unable to rise to the height of his grand conception, took lower ground, and, giving up the idea of a fusion, fell back upon the ordinary status, and proceeded to enact the ordinary role, of conquerors, the feelings of the late lords of Asia, the countrymen of Cyrus and Darius, must have undergone a complete change. It had been the intention of Alexander to conciliate and elevate the leading Asiatics by uniting them with the Macedonians and the Greeks, by promoting social intercourse between the two classes of his subjects and encouraging them to intermarry, by opening his court to Asiatics, by educating then in Greek ideas and in Greek schools, by promoting them to high employments, and making them feel that they were as much valued and as well cared for as the people of the conquering race: it was the plan of the Seleucidae to govern wholly by means of European officials, Greek or Macedonian, and to regard and treat the entire mass of their Asiatic subjects as mere slaves. Alexander had placed Persian satraps over most of the provinces, attaching to them Greek or Macedonian commandants as checks. Seloucus divided his empire into seventy-two satrapies; but among his satraps not one was an Asiatic—all were either Macedonians or Greeks. Asiatics, indeed, formed the bulk of his standing army, and so far were admitted to employment; they might also, no doubt, be tax-gatherers, couriers, scribes, constables, and officials of that mean stamp; but they were as carefully excluded from all honorable and lucrative offices as the natives of Hindustan under the rule of the East India Company. The standing army of the Seleucidae was wholly officered, just as was that of our own Sepoys, by Europeans; Europeans thronged the court, and filled every important post under the government. There cannot be a doubt that such a high-spirited and indeed arrogant people as the Persians must have fretted and chafed under this treatment, and have detested the nation and dynasty which had thrust them down from their pre-eminence and converted them from masters into slaves. It would scarcely much tend to mitigate the painfulness of their feelings that they could not but confess their conquerors to be a civilized people—as civilized, perhaps more civilized than themselves—since the civilization was of a type and character which did not please them or command their approval. There is an essential antagonism between European and Asiatic ideas and modes of thought, such as seemingly to preclude the possibility of Asiatics appreciating a European civilization. The Persians must have felt towards the Greco-Macedonians much as the Mohammedans of India feel towards ourselves—they may have feared and even respected them—but they must have very bitterly hated them. Nor was the rule of the Seleucidae such as to overcome by its justice or its wisdom the original antipathy of the dispossessed lords of Asia towards those by whom they had been ousted. The satrapial system, which these monarchs lazily adopted from their predecessors, the Achaemenians, is one always open to great abuses, and needs the strictest superintendence and supervision. There is no reason to believe that any sufficient watch was kept over their satraps by the Seleucid kings, or even any system of checks established, such as the Achaemenidae had, at least in theory, set up and maintained. The Greco-Macedonian governors of provinces seem to have been left to themselves almost entirely, and to have been only controlled in the exercise of their authority by their own notions of what was right or expedient. Under these circumstances, abuses were sure to creep in; and it is not improbable that gross outrages were sometimes perpetrated by those in power—outrages calculated to make the blood of a nation boil, and to produce a keen longing for vengeance. We have no direct evidence that the Persians of the time did actually suffer from such a misuse of satrapial authority; but it is unlikely that they entirely escaped the miseries which are incidental to the system in question. Public opinion ascribed the grossest acts of tyranny and oppression to some of the Seleucid satraps; probably the Persians were not exempt from the common lot of the subject races.

Moreover, the Seleucid monarchs themselves were occasionally guilty of acts of tyranny, which must have intensified the dislike wherewith they were regarded by their Asiatic subjects. The reckless conduct of Antiochus Epiphanes towards the Jews is well known; but it is not perhaps generally recognized that intolerance and impious cupidity formed a portion of the system on which he governed. There seems, however, to be good reason to believe that, having exhausted his treasury by his wars and his extravagances, Epiphanes formed a general design of recruiting it by means of the plunder of his subjects. The temples of the Asiatics had hitherto been for the most part respected by their European conquerors, and large stores of the precious metals were accumulated in them. Epiphanes saw in these hoards the means of relieving his own necessities, and determined to seize and confiscate them. Besides plundering the Temple of Jehovah at Jerusalem, he made a journey into the southeastern portion of his empire, about B.C. 165, for the express purpose of conducting in person the collection of the sacred treasures. It was while he was engaged in this unpopular work that a spirit of disaffection showed itself; the East took arms no less than the West; and in Persia, or upon its borders, the avaricious monarch was forced to retire before the opposition which his ill-judged measures had provoked, and to allow one of the doomed temples to escape him. When he soon afterwards sickened and died, the natives of this part of Asia saw in his death a judgment upon him for his attempted sacrilege.

It was within twenty years of this unfortunate attempt that the dominion of the Seleucidae over Persia and the adjacent countries came to an end. The Parthian Empire had for nearly a century been gradually growing in power and extending itself at the expense of the Syro-Macedonian; and, about B.C. 163, an energetic prince, Mithridates I., commenced a series of conquests towards the West, which terminated (about B.C. 150) in the transference from the Syro-Macedonian to the Parthian rule of Media Magna, Susiana, Persia, Babylonia, and Assyria Proper. It would seem that the Persians offered no resistance to the progress of the new conqueror. The Seleucidae had not tried to conciliate their attachment, and it was impossible that they should dislike the rupture of ties which had only galled hitherto. Perhaps their feeling, in prospect of the change, was one of simple indifference. Perhaps it was not without some stir of satisfaction and complacency that they saw the pride of the hated Europeans abased, and a race, which, however much it might differ from their own, was at least Asiatic, installed in power. The Parthia system, moreover, was one which allowed greater liberty to the subject races than the Macedonian, as it had been understood and carried out by the Seleucidae; and so far some real gain was to be expected from the change. Religious motives must also have conspired to make the Persians sympathize with the new power, rather than with that which for centuries had despised their faith and had recently insulted it.

The treatment of the Persians by their Parthian lords seems, on the whole, to have been marked by moderation. Mithridates indeed, the original conqueror, is accused of having alienated his new subjects by the harshness of his rule; and in the struggle which occurred between him and the Seleucid king, Demetrius II., Persians, as well as Elymseans and Bactrians, are said to have fought on the side of the Syro-Macedonian. But this is the only occasion in Parthian history, between the submission of Persia and the great revolt under Artaxerxes, where there is any appearance of the Persians regarding their masters with hostile feelings. In general they show themselves submissive and contented with their position, which was certainly, on the whole, a less irksome one than they had occupied under the Seleucidae.

It was a principle of the Parthian governmental system to allow the subject peoples, to a large extent, to govern themselves. These peoples generally, and notably the Persians, were ruled by native kings, who succeeded to the throne by hereditary right, had the full power of life and death, and ruled very much as they pleased, so long as they paid regularly the tribute imposed upon them by the "King of Kings," and sent him a respectable contingent when he was about to engage in a military expedition. Such a system implies that the conquered peoples have the enjoyment of their own laws and institutions, are exempt from troublesome interference, and possess a sort of semi-independence. Oriental nations, having once assumed this position, are usually contented with it, and rarely make any effort to better themselves. It would seem that, thus far at any rate, the Persians could not complain of the Parthian rule, but must have been fairly satisfied with their condition.

Again, the Greco-Macedonians had tolerated, but they had not viewed with much respect, the religion which they had found established in Persia. Alexander, indeed, with the enlightened curiosity which characterised him, had made inquiries concerning, the tenets of the Magi, and endeavored to collect in one the writings of Zoroaster. But the later monarchs, and still more their subjects, had held the system in contempt. and, as we have seen, Epiphanes had openly insulted the religious feelings of his Asiatic subjects. The Parthians, on the other hand, began at any rate with a treatment of the Persian religion which was respectful and gratifying. Though perhaps at no time very sincere Zoroastrians, they had conformed to the State religion under the Achaemenian kings; and when the period came that they had themselves to establish a system of government, they gave to the Magian hierarchy a distinct and important place in their governmental machinery. The council, which advised the monarch, and which helped to elect and (if need were) depose him, was composed of two elements—the Sophi, or wise men, who were civilians; and the Magi, or priests of the Zoroastrian religion. The Magi had thus an important political status in Parthia, during the early period of the Empire; but they seem gradually to have declined in favor, and ultimately to have fallen into disrepute. The Zoroastrian creed was, little by little, superseded among the Parthians by a complex idolatry, which, beginning with an image-worship of the Sun and Moon, proceeded to an association with those deities of the deceased kings of the nation, and finally added to both a worship of ancestral idols, which formed the most cherished possession of each family, and practically monopolized the religious sentiment. All the old Zoroastrian practices were by degrees laid aside. In Armenia the Arsacid monarchs allowed the sacred fire of Ormazd to become extinguished; and in their own territories the Parthian Arsacidae introduced the practice, hateful to Zoroastrians, of burning the dead. The ultimate religion of these monarchs seems in fact to have been a syncretism wherein Sabaism, Confucianism, Greco-Macedonian notions, and an inveterate primitive idolatry were mixed together. It is not impossible that the very names of Ormazd and Ahriman had ceased to be known at the Parthian Court, or were regarded as those of exploded deities, whose dominion over men's minds had passed away.

On the other hand, in Persia itself, and to some extent doubtless among the neighboring countries, Zoroastrianism (or what went by the name) had a firm hold on the religious sentiments of the multitude, who viewed with disfavor the tolerant and eclectic spirit which animated the Court of Ctesiphon. The perpetual fire, kindled, as it was, from heaven, was carefully tended and preserved on the fire-altars of the Persian holy places; the Magian hierarchy was held in the highest repute, the kings themselves (as it would seem) not disdaining to be Magi; the ideas—even perhaps the forms—of Ormazd and Ahriman were familiar to all; image-worship was abhorred the sacred writings in the Zend or most ancient Iranian language were diligently preserved and multiplied; a pompous ritual was kept up; the old national religion, the religion of the Achaemenians, of the glorious period of Persian ascendency in Asia, was with the utmost strictness maintained, probably the more zealously as it fell more and more into disfavor with the Parthians.

The consequence of this divergence of religious opinion between the Persians and their feudal lords must undoubtedly have been a certain amount of alienation and discontent. The Persian Magi must have been especially dissatisfied with the position of their brethren at Court; and they would doubtless use their influence to arouse the indignation of their countrymen generally. But it is scarcely probable that this cause alone would have produced any striking result. Religious sympathy rarely leads men to engage in important wars, unless it has the support of other concurrent motives. To account for the revolt of the Persians against their Parthian lords under Artaxerxes, something more is needed than the consideration of the religious differences which separated the two peoples.

First, then, it should be borne in mind that the Parthian rule must have been from the beginning distasteful to the Persians, owing to the rude and coarse character of the people. At the moment of Mithridates's successes, the Persians might experience a sentiment of satisfaction that the European invader was at last thrust back, and that Asia had re-asserted herself; but a very little experience of Parthian rule was sufficient to call forth different feelings. There can be no doubt that the Parthians, whether they were actually Turanians or no, were, in comparison with the Persians, unpolished and uncivilized. They showed their own sense of this inferiority by an affectation of Persian manners. But this affectation was not very successful. It is evident that in art, in architecture, in manners, in habits of life, the Parthian race reached only a low standard; they stood to their Hellenic and Iranian subjects in much the same relation that the Turks of the present day stand to the modern Greeks; they made themselves respected by their strength and their talent for organization; but in all that adorns and beautifies life they were deficient. The Persians must, during the whole time of their subjection to Parthia, have been sensible of a feeling of shame at the want of refinement and of a high type of civilization in their masters.

Again, the later sovereigns of the Arsacid dynasty were for the most part of weak and contemptible character. From the time of Volagases I. to that of Artabanus IV., the last king, the military reputation of Parthia had declined. Foreign enemies ravaged the territories of Parthian vassal kings, and retired when they chose, unpunished. Provinces revolted and established their independence. Rome was entreated to lend assistance to her distressed and afflicted rival, and met the entreaties with a refusal. In the wars which still from time to time were waged between the two empires Parthia was almost uniformly worsted. Three times her capital was occupied, and once her monarch's summer palace was burned. Province after province had to be ceded to Rome. The golden throne which symbolized her glory and magnificence was carried off. Meanwhile feuds raged between the different branches of the Arsacid family; civil wars were frequent; two or three monarchs at a time claimed the throne, or actually ruled in different portions of the Empire. It is not surprising that under these circumstances the bonds were loosened between Parthia and her vassal kingdoms, or that the Persian tributary monarchs began to despise their suzerains, and to contemplate without alarm the prospect of a rebellion which should place them in an independent position.

While the general weakness of the Arsacid monarchs was thus a cause naturally leading to a renunciation of their allegiance on the part of the Persians, a special influence upon the decision taken by Artaxerxes is probably to be assigned to one, in particular, of the results of that weakness. When provinces long subject to Parthian rule revolted, and revolted successfully, as seems to have been the case with Hyrcania, and partially with Bactria, Persia could scarcely for very shame continue submissive. Of all the races subject to Parthia, the Persians were the one which had held the most brilliant position in the past, and which retained the liveliest remembrance of its ancient glories. This is evidenced not only by the grand claims which Artaxorxes put forward in his early negotiations with the Romans, but by the whole course of Persian literature, which has fundamentally an historic character, and exhibits the people as attached, almost more than any other Oriental nation, to the memory of its great men and of their noble achievements. The countrymen of Cyrus, of Darius, of Xerxes, of Ochus, of the conquerors of Media, Bactria, Babylon, Syria, Asia Minor, Egypt, of the invaders of Scythia and Greece, aware that they had once borne sway over the whole region between Tunis and the Indian Desert, between the Caucasus and the

Cataracts, when they saw a petty mountain clan, like the Hyrcanians, establish and maintain their independence despite the efforts of Parthia to coerce them, could not very well remain quiet. If so weak and small a race could defy the power of the Arsacid monarchs, much more might the far more numerous and at least equally courageous Persians expect to succeed, if they made a resolute attempt to recover their freedom.

It is probable that Artaxerxes, in his capacity of vassal, served personally in the army with which the Parthian monarch Artabanus carried on the struggle against Rome, and thus acquired the power of estimating correctly the military strength still possessed by the Arsacidae, and of measuring it against that which he knew to belong to his nation. It is not unlikely that he formed his plans during the earlier period of Artabanus's reign, when that monarch allowed himself to be imposed upon by Caracallus, and suffered calamities and indignities in consequence of his folly. When the Parthian monarch atoned for his indiscretion and wiped out the memory of his disgraces by the brilliant victory of Nisibis and the glorious peace which he made with Macrinus, Artaxerxes may have found that he had gone too far to recede; or, undazzled by the splendor of these successes, he may still have judged that he might with prudence persevere in his enterprise. Artabanus had suffered great losses in his two campaigns against Rome, and especially in the three days' battle of Nisibis. He was at variance with several princes of his family, one of whom certainly maintained himself during his whole reign with the State and title of "King of Parthia." Though he had fought well at Nisibis, he had not given any indications of remarkable military talent. Artaxerxes, having taken the measure of his antagonist during the course of the Roman war, having estimated his resources and formed a decided opinion on the relative strength of Persia and Parthia, deliberately resolved, a few years after the Roman war had come to an end, to revolt and accept the consequences. He was no doubt convinced that his nation would throw itself enthusiastically into the struggle, and he believed that he could conduct it to a successful issue. He felt himself the champion of a depressed, if not an oppressed, nationality, and had faith in his power to raise it into a lofty position. Iran, at any rate, should no longer, he resolved, submit patiently to be the slave of Turan; the keen, intelligent, art-loving Aryan people should no longer bear submissively the yoke of the rude, coarse, clumsy Scyths. An effort after freedom should be made. He had little doubt of the result. The Persians, by the strength of their own right arms and the blessing of Ahuramazda, the "All-bounteous," would triumph over their impious masters, and become once more a great and independent people. At the worst, if he had miscalculated, there would be the alternative of a glorious death upon the battle-field in one of the noblest of all causes, the assertion of a nation's freedom.

CHAPTER II

*Situation and Size of Persia. General Character of the Country and Climate. Chief Products. Characteristics of the Persian People, physical and moral. Differences observable in the Race at different periods.*

Persia Proper was a tract of country lying on the Gulf to which it has given name, and extending about 450 miles from north-west to south-east, with an average breadth of about 250 miles. Its entire area may be estimated at about a hundred thousand square miles. It was thus larger than Great Britain, about the size of Italy, and rather less than half the size of France. The boundaries were, on the west, Elymais or Susiana (which, however, was sometimes reckoned a part of Persia); on the north, Media; on the east, Carmania; and on the south, the sea. It is nearly represented in modern times by the two Persian provinces of Farsistan and Laristan, the former of which retains, but slightly changed, the ancient appellation. The Hindyan or Tab (ancient Oroatis) seems towards its mouth to have formed the western limit. Eastward, Persia extended to about the site of the modern

Bunder Kongo. Inland, the northern boundary ran probably a little south of the thirty-second parallel, from long. 50° to 55°. The line dividing Persia Proper from Carmania (now Kerman) was somewhat uncertain.

The character of the tract is extremely diversified. Ancient writers divided the country into three strongly contrasted regions. The first, or coast tract, was (they said) a sandy desert, producing nothing but a few dates, owing to the intensity of the heat. Above this was a fertile region, grassy, with well-watered meadows and numerous vineyards, enjoying a delicious climate, producing almost every fruit but the olive, containing pleasant parks or "paradises," watered by a number of limpid streams and clear lakes, well wooded in places, affording an excellent pasture for horses and for all sorts of cattle, abounding in water-fowl and game of every kind, and altogether a most delightful abode. Beyond this fertile region, towards the north, was a rugged mountain tract, cold and mostly covered with snow, of which they did not profess to know much.

In this description there is no doubt a certain amount of truth; but it is mixed probably with a good deal of exaggeration. There is no reason to believe that the climate or character of the country has undergone any important alteration between the time of Nearchus or Strabo and the present day. At present it is certain that the tract in question answers but very incompletely to the description which those writers give of it. Three regions may indeed be distinguished, though the natives seem now to speak of only two; but none of them corresponds at all exactly to the accounts of the Greeks. The coast tract is represented with the nearest approach to correctness. This is, in fact, a region of arid plain, often impregnated with salt, ill-watered, with a poor soil, consisting either of sand or clay, and productive of little besides dates and a few other fruits. A modern historian says of it that "it bears a greater resemblance in soil and climate to Arabia than to the rest of Persia." It is very hot and unhealthy, and can at no time have supported more than a sparse and scanty population. Above this, towards the north, is the best and most fertile portion of the territory. A mountain tract, the continuation of Zagros, succeeds to the flat and sandy coast region, occupying the greater portion of Persia Proper. It is about two hundred miles in width, and consists of an alternation of mountain, plain, and narrow valley, curiously intermixed, and hitherto mapped very imperfectly. In places this district answers fully to the description of Nearchus, being, "richly fertile, picturesque, and romantic almost beyond imagination, with lovely wooded dells, green mountain sides, and broad plains, suited for the production of almost any crops." But it is only to the smaller moiety of the region that such a character attaches; more than half the mountain tract is sterile and barren; the supply of water is almost everywhere scanty; the rivers are few, and have not much volume; many of them, after short courses, end in the sand, or in small salt lakes, from which the superfluous water is evaporated. Much of the country is absolutely without streams, and would be uninhabitable were it not for the kanats or kareezes—subterranean channels made by art for the conveyance of spring water to be used in irrigation. The most desolate portion of the mountain tract is towards the north and north-east, where it adjoins upon the third region, which is the worst of the three. This is a portion of the high tableland of Iran, the great desert which stretches from the eastern skirts of Zagros to the Hamoon, the Helmend, and the river of Subzawur. It is a dry and hard plain, intersected at intervals by ranges of rocky hills, with a climate extremely hot in summer and extremely cold in winter, incapable of cultivation, excepting so far as water can be conveyed by kanats, which is, of course, only a short distance. The fox, the jackal, the antelope, and the wild ass possess this sterile and desolate tract, where "all is dry and cheerless," and verdure is almost unknown.

Perhaps the two most peculiar districts of. Persia are the lake basins of Neyriz and Deriah-i-Nemek. The rivers given off from the northern side of the great mountain chain between the twenty-ninth and thirty-first parallels, being unable to penetrate the mountains, flow eastward towards the desert; and their waters gradually collect into two streams, which end in two lakes, the Deriah-i-

Nemek and that of Neyriz, or Lake Bakhtigan. The basin of Lake Neyriz lies towards the north. Here the famous Bendamir, and the Pulwar or Kur-ab, flowing respectively from the north-east and the north, unite in one near the ruins of the ancient Persepolis, and, after fertilizing the plain of Merdasht, run eastward down a rich vale for a distance of some forty miles into the salt lake which swallows them up. This lake, when full, has a length of fifty or sixty miles, with a breadth of from three to six. In summer, however, it is often quite dry, the water of the Bendamir being expended in irrigation before reaching its natural terminus. The valley and plain of the Bendamir, and its tributaries, are among the most fertile portions of Persia, as well as among those of most historic interest.

The basin of the Deriah-i-Nemek is smaller than that of the Neyriz, but it is even more productive. Numerous brooks and streams, rising not far from Shiraz, run on all sides into the Nemek lake, which has a length of about fifteen and a breadth of three or three and a half miles. Among the streams is the celebrated brook of Hafiz, the Rockrabad, which still retains "its singular transparency and softness to the taste." Other rills and fountains of extreme clearness abound, and a verdure is the result, very unusual in Persia. The vines grown in the basin produce the famous Shiraz wine, the only good wine which is manufactured in the East. The orchards are magnificent. In the autumn "the earth is covered with the gathered harvest, flowers, and fruits; melons, peaches, pears, nectarines, cherries, grapes, pomegranates; all is a garden, abundant in sweets and refreshment."

But, notwithstanding the exceptional fertility of the Shiraz plain and of a few other places, Persia Proper seems to have been rightly characterized in ancient times as "a scant land and a rugged." Its area was less than a fifth of the area of modern Persia; and of this space nearly one half was uninhabitable, consisting either of barren stony mountain or of scorching sandy plain, ill supplied with water and often impregnated with salt. Its products, consequently, can have been at no time either very abundant or very varied. Anciently, the low coast tract seems to have been cultivated to a small extent in corn, and to have produced good dates and a few other fruits. The mountain region was, as we have seen, celebrated for its excellent pastures, for its abundant fruits, and especially for its grapes. Within the mountains, on the high plateau, assafoetida (silphium) was found, and probably some other medicinal herbs. Corn, no doubt, could be grown largely in the plains and valleys of the mountain tract, as well as on the plateau, so far as the kanats carried the water. There must have been, on the whole, a deficiency of timber, though the palms of the low tract, and the oaks, planes, chenars or sycamores, poplars, and willows of the mountain regions sufficed for the wants of the natives. Not much fuel was required, and stone was the general material used for building. Among the fruits for which Persia was famous are especially noted the peach, the walnut, and the citron. The walnut bore among the Romans the appellation of "royal."

Persia, like Media, was a good nursery for horses. Fine grazing grounds existed in many parts of the mountain region, and for horses of the Arab breed even the Deshtistan was not unsuited. Camels were reared in some places, and sheep and goats were numerous. Horned cattle were probably not so abundant, as the character of the country is not favorable for them. Game existed in large quantities, the lakes abounding with water-fowl, such as ducks, teal, heron, snipe, etc.; and the wooded portions of the mountain tract giving shelter to the stag, the wild goat, the wild boar, the hare, the pheasant, and the heathcock, fish were also plentiful. Whales visited the Persian Gulf, and were sometimes stranded upon the shores, where their carcases furnished a mine of wealth to the inhabitants. Dolphins abounded, as well as many smaller kinds; and shell-fish, particularly oysters, could always be obtained without difficulty. The rivers, too, were capable of furnishing fresh-water fish in good quantity, though we cannot say if this source of supply was utilized in antiquity.

The mineral treasures of Persia were fairly numerous. Good salt was yielded by the lakes of the middle region, and was also obtainable upon the plateau. Bitumen and naphtha were produced by sources in the low country. The mountains contained most of the important metals and a certain number of valuable gems. The pearls of the Gulf acquired early a great reputation, and a regular fishery was established for them before the time of Alexander.

EARLIER COINS OF ARTAXERXES I.

ANCIENT PERSIANS (from a bas-relief at Persepolis).

PLATE XI

But the most celebrated of all the products of Persia were its men. The "scant and rugged country" gave birth, as Cyrus the Great is said to have observed, to a race brave, hardy, and enduring, calculated not only to hold its own against aggressors, but to extend its sway and exercise dominion over the Western Asiatics generally. The Aryan family is the one which, of all the races of mankind, is the most self-asserting, and has the greatest strength, physical, moral, and intellectual. The Iranian branch of it, whereto the Persians belonged, is not perhaps so gifted as some others; but it has qualities which place it above most of those by which Western Asia was anciently peopled. In the primitive times, from Cyrus the Great to Darius Hystaspis, the Persians seem to have been rude mountaineers, probably not very unlike the modern Kurds and Lurs, who inhabit portions of the same chain which forms the heart of the Persian country. Their physiognomy was handsome. A high straight forehead, a long slightly aquiline nose, a short and curved upper lip, a well-rounded chin, characterized the Persian. The expression of his face was grave and noble. He had abundant hair, which he wore very artificially arranged. Above and round the brow it was made to stand away from the face in short crisp curls; on the top of the head it was worn smooth; at the back of the head it was again trained into curls, which followed each other in several rows from the level of the forehead to the nape of the neck. The moustache was always cultivated, and curved in a gentle sweep. A beard and whiskers were worn, the former sometimes long and pendent, like the Assyrian, but more often clustering around the chin in short close curls. The figure was well-formed, but somewhat stout; the carriage was dignified and simple. [PLATE XI, Fig. 1.]

Simplicity of manners prevailed during this period. At the court there was some luxury; but the bulk of the nation, living in their mountain territory, and attached to agriculture and hunting, maintained the habits of their ancestors, and were a somewhat rude though not a coarse people. The dress commonly worn was a close-fitting shirt or tunic of leather, descending to the knee, and with sleeves that reached down to the wrist. Round the tunic was worn a belt or sash, which was tied in front. The head was protected by a loose felt cap and the feet by a sort of high shoe or low boot. The ordinary diet was bread and cress-seed, while the sole beverage was water. In the higher ranks, of course, a different style of living prevailed; the elegant and flowing "Median robe" was worn; flesh of various kinds was eaten; much wine was consumed; and meals were extended to a great length; The Persians, however, maintained during this period a general hardihood and bravery which made them the most dreaded adversaries of the Greeks, and enabled them to maintain an unquestioned dominion over the other native races of Western Asia.

As time went on, and their monarchs became less warlike, and wealth accumulated, and national spirit decayed, the Persian character by degrees deteriorated, and sank, even under the Achaemenian kings, to a level not much superior to that of the ordinary Asiatic. The Persian antagonists of Alexander were pretty nearly upon a par with the races which in Hindustan have yielded to the British power; they occasionally fought with gallantry, but they were deficient in resolution, in endurance, in all the elements of solid strength; and they were quite unable to stand their ground against the vigor and dash of the Macedonians and the Greeks. Whether physically they were very different from the soldiers of Cyrus may be doubted, but morally they had fallen far below the ancient standard; their self-respect their love of country, their attachment to their monarch had diminished; no one showed any great devotion to the cause for which he fought; after two defeats the empire wholly collapsed; and the Persians submitted, apparently without much reluctance, to the Helleno-Macedonian yoke.

Five centuries and a half of servitude could not much improve or elevate the character of the people. Their fall from power, their loss of wealth and of dominion did indeed advantage them in one way: it but an end to that continually advancing sloth and luxury which had sapped the virtue of the nation, depriving it of energy, endurance, and almost every manly excellence. It dashed the

Persians back upon the ground whence they had sprung, and whence, Antseus-like, they proceeded to derive fresh vigor and vital force. In their "scant and rugged" fatherland, the people of Cyrus once more recovered to a great extent their ancient prowess and hardihood—their habits became simplified, their old patriotism revived, their self-respect grew greater. But while adversity thus in some respects proved its "sweet uses" upon them, there were other respects in which submission to the yoke of the Greeks, and still more to that of the Parthians, seems to have altered them for the worse rather than for the better. There is a coarseness and rudeness about the Sassanian Persians which we do not observe in Achaemenian times. The physique of the nation is not indeed much altered. Nearly the same countenance meets us in the sculptures of Artaxerxes, the son of Babek, of Sapor, and of their successors, with which we are familiar from the bas-reliefs of Darius Hystapis and Xerxes. There is the same straight forehead, the same aquiline nose, the same well-shaped mouth, the same abundant hair. The form is, however, coarser and clumsier; the expression is less refined; and the general effect produced is that the people have, even physically, deteriorated. The mental and aesthetic standard seems still more to have sunk. There is no evidence that the Persians of Sassanian times possessed the governmental and administrative ability of Darius Hystapis or Artaxerxes Ochus. Their art, though remarkable, considering the almost entire disappearance of art from Western Asia under the Parthians, is, compared with that of Achaemenian times, rude and grotesque. In architecture, indeed, they are not without merit though even here the extent to which they were indebted to the Parthians, which cannot be exactly determined, must lessen our estimation of them; but their mimetic art, while not wanting in spirit, is remarkably coarse and unrefined. As a later chapter will be devoted to this subject, no more need be said upon it here. It is sufficient for our present purpose to note that the impression which we obtain from the monumental remains of the Sassanian Persians accords with what is to be gathered of them from the accounts of the Romans and the Greeks. The great Asiatic revolution of the year A.D. 226 marks a revival of the Iranic nationality from the depressed state into which it had sunk for more than five hundred years; but the revival is not full or complete. The Persians of the Sassanian kingdom are not equal to those of the time between Cyrus the Great and Darius Codomannus; they have ruder manners, a grosser taste, less capacity for government and organization; they have, in fact, been coarsened by centuries of Tartar rule; they are vigorous, active, energetic, proud, brave; but in civilization and refinement they do not rank much above their Parthian predecessors. Western Asia gained, perhaps, something, but it did not gain much, from the substitution of the Persians for the Parthians as the dominant power. The change is the least marked among the revolutions which the East underwent between the accession of Cyrus and the conquests of Timour. But it is a change, on the whole, for the better. It is accompanied by a revival of art, by improvements in architecture; it inaugurates a religious revolution which has advantages. Above all, it saves the East from stagnation. It is one among many of those salutary shocks which, in the political as in the natural world, are needed from time to time to stimulate action and prevent torpor and apathy.


CHAPTER III

*Reign of Artaxerxes I. Stories told of him. Most probable account of his Descent, Rank, and Parentage. His Contest with Artabanus. First War with Chosroes of Armenia. Contest with Alexander Severus. Second War with Chosroes and conquest of Armenia. Religious Reforms. Internal Administration and Government. Art. Coinage. Inscriptions.*

Around the cradle of an Oriental sovereign who founds a dynasty there cluster commonly a number of traditions, which have, more or less, a mythical character. The tales told of the Great, which even Herodotus set aside as incredible, have their parallels in narratives that were current within one or two centuries with respect to the founder of the Second Persian Empire, which would not have disgraced the mythologers of Achaemenian times. Artaxerxes, according to some, was the son of a common soldier who had an illicit connection with the wife of a Persian cobbler and astrologer, a certain Babek or Papak, an inhabitant of the Cadusian country and a man of the lowest class. Papak, knowing by his art that the soldier's son would attain a lofty position, voluntarily ceded his rights as husband to the favorite of fortune, and bred up as his own the issue of this illegitimate commerce, who, when he attained to manhood, justified Papak's foresight by successfully revolting from Artabanus and establishing the new Persian monarchy. Others said that the founder of the new kingdom was a Parthian satrap, the son of a noble, and that, having long meditated revolt, he took the final plunge in consequence of a prophecy uttered by Artabanus, who was well skilled in magical arts, and saw in the stars that the Parthian empire was threatened with destruction. Artabanus, on a certain occasion, when he communicated this prophetic knowledge to his wife, was overheard by one of her attendants, a noble damsel named Artaducta, already affianced to Artaxerxes and a sharer in his secret counsels. At her instigation he hastened his plans, raised the standard of revolt, and upon the successful issue of his enterprise made her his queen. Miraculous circumstances were freely interwoven with these narratives, and a result was produced which staggered the faith even of such a writer as Moses of Chorene, who, desiring to confine himself to what was strictly true and certain, could find no more to say of Artaxerxes's birth and origin than that he was the son of a certain Sasan, and a native of Istakr, or Persepolis.

Even, however, the two facts thus selected as beyond criticism by Moses are far from being entitled to implicit credence. Artaxerxes, the son of Sasan according to Agathangelus and Moses, is the same as Papak (or Babek) in his own and his son's inscriptions. The Persian writers generally take the same view, and declare that Sasan was a remoter ancestor of Artaxerxes, the acknowledged founder of the family, and not Artaxerxes' father. In the extant records of the new Persian Kingdom, the coins and the inscriptions, neither Sasan nor the gentilitial term derived from it, Sasanidae, has any place; and though it would perhaps be rash to question on this account the employment of the term Sasanidae by the dynasty, yet we may regard it as really "certain" that the father of Artaxerxes was named, not Sasan, but Papak; and that, if the term Sasanian was in reality a patronymic, it was derived, like the term "Achaemenian," from some remote progenitor whom the royal family of the new empire believed to have been their founder.

The native country of Artaxerxes is also variously stated by the authorities. Agathangelus calls him an Assyrian, and makes the Assyrians play an important part in his rebellion. Agathias says that he was born in the Cadusian country, or the low tract south-west of the Caspian, which belonged to Media rather than to Assyria or Persia. Dio Cassus, and Herodian, the contemporaries of Artaxerxes, call him a Persian; and there can be no reasonable doubt that they are correct in so doing. Agathangelus allows the predominantly Persian character of his revolt, and Agathias is apparently unaware that the Cadusian country was no part of Persia. The statement that he was a native of Persepolis (Istakr) is first found in Moses of Chorene. It may be true, but it is uncertain; for it may have grown out of the earlier statement of Agathangelus, that he held the government of the province of Istakr. We can only affirm with confidence that the founder of the new Persian monarchy was a genuine Persian, without attempting to determine positively what Persian city or province had the honor of producing him.

A more interesting question, and one which will be found perhaps to admit of a more definite answer, is that of the rank and station in which Artaxerxes was born. We have seen that Agathias (writing ab. A.D. 580) called him the supposititious son of a cobbler. Others spoke of him as the child of a shepherd; while some said that his father was "an inferior officer in the service of the government." But on the other hand, in the inscriptions which Artaxerxes himself setup in the neighborhood of Persepolis, he gives his father, Papak, the title of "King." Agathangelus calls him a "noble" and "satrap of Persepolitan government;" while Herodian seems to speak of him as "king of the Persians," before his victories over Artabanus. On the whole, it is perhaps most probable that, like Cyrus, he was the hereditary monarch of the subject kingdom of Persia, which had always its own princes under the Parthians, and that thus he naturally and without effort took the leadership of the revolt when circumstances induced his nation to rebel and seek to establish its independence. The stories told of his humble origin, which are contradictory and improbable, are to be paralleled with those which made Cyrus the son of a Persian of moderate rank, and the foster-child of a herdsman. There is always in the East a tendency towards romance and exaggeration; and when a great monarch emerges from a comparatively humble position, the humility and obscurity of his first condition are intensified, to make the contrast more striking between his original low estate and his ultimate splendor and dignity.

The circumstances of the struggle between Artaxerxes and. Artabanus are briefly sketched by Dio Cassius and Agathangelus, while they are related more at large by the Persian writers. It is probable that the contest occupied a space of four or five years. At first, we are told, Artabanus neglected to arouse himself, and took no steps towards crushing the rebellion, which was limited to an assertion of the independence of Persia Proper, or the province of Fars. After a time the revolted vassal, finding himself unmolested, was induced to raise his thoughts higher, and commenced a career of conquest. Turning his arms eastward, he attacked Kerman (Carmania), and easily succeeded in reducing that scantily-peopled tract under his dominion. He then proceeded to menace the north, and, making war in that quarter, overran and attached to his kingdom some of the outlying provinces of Media. Roused by these aggressions, the Parthian monarch at length took the field, collected an army consisting in part of Parthians, in part of the Persians who continued faithful to him, against his vassal, and, invading Persia, soon brought his adversary to a battle. A long and bloody contest followed, both sides suffering great losses; but victory finally declared itself in favor of Artaxerxes, through the desertion to him, during the engagement, of a portion of his enemy's forces. A second conflict ensued within a short period, in which the insurgents were even more completely successful; the carnage on the side of the Parthians was great, the loss of the Persians small; and the great king fled precipitately from the field. Still the resources of Parthia were equal to a third trial of arms. After a brief pause, Artabanus made a final effort to reduce his revolted vassal; and a last engagement took place in the plain of Hormuz, which was a portion of the Jerahi valley, in the beautiful country between Bebahan and Shuster. Here, after a desperate conflict, the Parthian monarch suffered a third and signal defeat; his army was scattered; and he himself lost his life in the combat. According to some, his death was the result of a hand-to-hand conflict with his great antagonist, who, pretending to fly, drew him on, and then pierced his heart with an arrow.

The victory of Hormuz gave to Artaxerxes the dominion of the East; but it did not secure him this result at once, or without further struggle. Artabanus had left sons; and both in Bactria and Armenia there were powerful branches of the Arsacid family, which could not see unmoved the downfall of their kindred in Parthia. Chosroes, the Armenian monarch, was a prince of considerable ability, and is said to have been set upon his throne by Artabanus, whose brother he was, according to some writers. At any rate he was an Arsacid; and he felt keenly the diminution of his own influence involved in the transfer to an alien race of the sovereignty wielded for five centuries by the descendants of the first Arsaces. He had set his forces in motion, while the contest between Artabanus and Artaxerxes was still in progress, in the hope of affording substantial help to his relative. But the march of events was too rapid for him; and, ere he could strike a blow, he found that the time for effectual action had gone by, that Artabanus was no more, and that the dominion of Artaxerxes was established over most of the countries which had previously formed portions of the Parthian Empire. Still, he resolved to continue the struggle; he was on friendly terms with Rome, and might count on an imperial contingent; he had some hope that the Bactrian Arsacidae would join him; at the worst, he regarded his own power as firmly fixed and as sufficient to enable him to maintain an equal contest with the new monarchy. Accordingly he took the Parthian Arsacids under his protection, and gave them a refuge in the Armenian territory. At the same time he negotiated with both Balkh and Rome, made arrangements with the barbarians upon his northern frontier to lend him aid, and, having collected a large army, invaded the new kingdom on the north-west, and gained certain not unimportant successes. According to the Armenian historians, Artaxerxes lost Assyria and the adjacent regions; Bactria wavered; and, after the struggle had continued for a year or two, the founder of the second Persian empire was obliged to fly ignominiously to India! But this entire narrative seems to be deeply tinged with the vitiating stain of intense national vanity, a fault which markedly characterizes the Armenian writers, and renders them, when unconfirmed by other authorities, almost worthless. The general course of events, and the position which Artaxerxes takes in his dealings with Rome (A.D. 229-230), sufficiently indicate that any reverses which he sustained at this time in his struggle with Chosroes and the unsubmitted Arsacidae must have been trivial, and that they certainly had no greater result than to establish the independence of Armenia, which, by dint of leaning upon Rome, was able to maintain itself against the Persian monarch and to check the advance of the Persians in North-Western Asia.

Artaxerxes, however, resisted in this quarter, and unable to overcome the resistance, which he may have regarded as deriving its effectiveness (in part at least) from the support lent it by Rome, determined (ab. A.D. 229) to challenge the empire to an encounter. Aware that Artabanus, his late rival, against whom he had measured himself, and whose power he had completely overthrown, had been successful in his war with Macrinus, had gained the great battle of Nisibis, and forced the Imperial State to purchase an ignominious peace by a payment equal to nearly two millions of our money, he may naturally have thought that a facile triumph was open to his arms in this direction. Alexander Severus, the occupant of the imperial throne, was a young man of a weak character, controlled in a great measure by his mother, Julia Mamaea, and as yet quite undistinguished as a general. The Roman forces in the East were known to be licentious and insubordinate; corrupted by the softness of the climate and the seductions of Oriental manners, they disregarded the restraints of discipline, indulged in the vices which at once enervate the frame and lower the moral character, had scant respect for their leaders, and seemed a defence which it would be easy to overpower and sweep away. Artaxerxes, like other founders of great empires, entertained lofty views of his abilities and his destinies; the monarchy which he had built up in the space of some five or six years was far from contenting him; well read in the ancient history of his nation, he sighed after the glorious days of Cyrus the Great and Darius Hystaspis, when all Western Asia from the shores of the AEgean to the Indian desert, and portions of Europe and Africa, had acknowledged the sway of the Persian king. The territories which these princes had ruled he regarded as his own by right of inheritance; and we are told that he not only entertained, but boldly published, these views. His emissaries everywhere declared that their master claimed the dominion of Asia as far as the AEgean Sea and the Propontis. It was his duty and his mission to recover to the Persians their pristine empire. What Cyrus had conquered, what the Persian kings had held from that time until the defeat of Codomannus by Alexander, was his by indefeasible right, and he was about to take possession of it.

Nor were these brave words a mere brutum fulmen. Simultaneously with the putting forth of such lofty pretensions the troops of the Persian monarch crossed the Tigris and spread themselves over the entire Roman province of Mesopotamia, which was rapidly overrun and offered scarcely any resistance. Severus learned at the same moment the demands of his adversary and the loss of one of his best provinces. He heard that his strong posts upon the Euphrates, the old defences of the empire in this quarter, were being attacked, and that Syria daily expected the passage of the invaders. The crisis was one requiring prompt action; but the weak and inexperienced youth was content to meet it with diplomacy, and, instead of sending an army to the East, despatched ambassadors to his rival with a letter. "Artaxerxes," he said, "ought to confine himself to his own territories and not seek to revolutionize Asia; it was unsafe, on the strength of mere unsubstantial hopes, to commence a great war. Every one should be content with keeping what belonged to him.

Artaxerxes would find war with Rome a very different thing from the contests in which he had been hitherto engaged with barbarous races like his own. He should call to mind the successes of Augustus and Trajan, and the trophies carried off from the East by Lucius Verus and by Septimius Severus."

The counsels of moderation have rarely much effect in restraining princely ambition. Artaxerxes replied by an embassy in which he ostentatiously displayed the wealth and magnificence of Persia; but, so far from making any deduction from his original demands, he now distinctly formulated them, and required their immediate acceptance. "Artaxerxes, the Great King," he said, "ordered the Romans and their ruler to take their departure forthwith from Syria and the rest of Western Asia, and to allow the Persians to exercise dominion over Ionia and Caria and the other countries within the AEgean and the Euxine, since these countries belonged to Persia by right of inheritance." A Roman emperor had seldom received such a message; and Alexander, mild and gentle as he was by nature, seems to have had his equanimity disturbed by the insolence of the mandate. Disregarding the sacredness of the ambassadorial character, he stripped the envoys of their splendid apparel, treated them as prisoners of war, and settled them as agricultural colonists in Phrygia. If we may believe Herodian, he even took credit to himself for sparing their lives, which he regarded as justly forfeit to the offended majesty of the empire.

Meantime the angry prince, convinced at last against his will that negotiations with such an enemy were futile, collected an army and began his march towards the East. Taking troops from the various provinces through which he passed, he conducted to Antioch, in the autumn of A.D. 231, a considerable force, which was there augmented by the legions of the East and by troops drawn from Egypt and other quarters. Artaxerxes, on his part, was not idle. According to Soverus himself, the army brought into the field by the Persian monarch consisted of one hundred and twenty thousand mailed horsemen, of eighteen hundred scythed chariots, and of seven hundred trained elephants, bearing on their backs towers filled with archers; and though this pretended host has been truly characterized as one "the like of which is not to be found in Eastern history, and has scarcely been imagined in Eastern romance," yet, allowing much for exaggeration, we may still safely conclude that great exertions had been made on the Persian side, that their forces consisted of the three arms mentioned, and that the numbers of each were large beyond ordinary precedent. The two adversaries were thus not ill-matched; each brought the flower of his troops to the conflict; each commanded the army, on which his dependence was placed, in person; each looked to obtain from the contest not only an increase of military glory, but substantial fruits of victory in the shape of plunder or territory.

It might have been expected that the Persian monarch, after the high tone which he had taken, would have maintained an aggressive attitude, have crossed the Euphrates, and spread the hordes at his disposal over Syria, Cappadocia, and Asia Minor. But it seems to be certain that he did not do so, and that the initiative was taken by the other side. Probably the Persian arms, as inefficient in sieges as the Parthian, were unable to overcome the resistance offered by the Roman forts upon the great river; and Artaxerxes was too good a general to throw his forces into the heart of an enemy's country without having first secured a safe retreat. The Euphrates was therefore crossed by his adversary in the spring of A.D. 232; the Roman province of Mesopotamia was easily recovered; and arrangements were made by which it was hoped to deal the new monarchy a heavy blow, if not actually to crush and conquer it.

Alexander divided his troops into three bodies. One division was to act towards the north, to take advantage of the friendly disposition of Chosroes, king of Armenia, and, traversing his strong mountain territory, to direct its attack upon Media, into which Armenia gave a ready entrance. Another was to take a southern line, and to threaten Persia Proper from the marshy tract about the junction of the Euphrates with the Tigris, a portion of the Babylonian territory. The third and main division, which was to be commanded by the emperor in person, was to act on a line intermediate between the other two, which would conduct it to the very heart of the enemy's territory, and at the same time allow of its giving effective support to either of the two other divisions if they should need it.

The plan of operations appears to have been judiciously constructed, and should perhaps be ascribed rather to the friends whom the youthful emperor consulted than to his own unassisted wisdom. But the best designed plans may be frustrated by unskilfulness or timidity in the execution; and it was here, if we may trust the author who alone gives us any detailed account of the campaign, that the weakness of Alexander's character showed itself. The northern army successfully traversed Armenia, and, invading Media, proved itself in numerous small actions superior to the Persian force opposed to it, and was able to plunder and ravage the entire country at its pleasure. The southern division crossed Mesopotamia in safety, and threatened to invade Persia Proper. Had Alexander with the third and main division kept faith with the two secondary armies, had he marched briskly and combined his movements with theirs, the triumph of the Roman arms would have been assured. But, either from personal timidity or from an amiable regard for the anxieties of his mother Mamsea, he hung back while his right and left wings made their advance, and so allowed the enemy to concentrate their efforts on these two isolated bodies. The army in Media, favored by the rugged character of the country, was able to maintain its ground without much difficulty; but that which had advanced by the line of the Euphrates and Tigris, and which was still marching through the boundless plains of the great alluvium, found itself suddenly beset by a countless host, commanded by Artaxerxes in person, and, though it struggled gallantly, was overwhelmed and utterly destroyed by the arrows of the terrible Persian bowmen. Herodian says, no doubt with some exaggeration, that this was the greatest calamity which had ever befallen the Romans. It certainly cannot compare with Cannae, with the disaster of Varus, or even with the similar defeat of Crassus in a not very distant region. But it was (if rightly represented by Herodian) a terrible blow. It absolutely determined the campaign. A Caesar or a Trajan might have retrieved such a loss. An Alexander Severus was not likely even to make an attempt to do so. Already weakened in body by the heat of the climate and the unwonted fatigues of war, he was utterly prostrated in spirit by the intelligence when it reached him. The signal was at once given for retreat. Orders were sent to the corps d' armee which occupied Media to evacuate its conquests and to retire forthwith upon the Euphrates. These orders were executed, but with difficulty. Winter had already set in throughout the high regions; and in its retreat the army of Media suffered great losses through the inclemency of the climate, so that those who reached Syria were but a small proportion of the original force. Alexander himself, and the army which he led, experienced less difficulty; but disease dogged the steps of this division, and when its columns reached Antioch it was found to be greatly reduced in numbers by sickness, though it had never confronted an enemy. The three armies of Severus suffered not indeed equally, but still in every case considerably, from three distinct causes—sickness, severe weather, and marked inferiority to the enemy. The last-named cause had annihilated the southern division; the northern had succumbed to climate; the main army, led by Severus himself, was (comparatively speaking) intact, but even this had been decimated by sickness, and was not in a condition to carry on the war with vigor. The result of the campaign had thus been altogether favorable to the Persians, but yet it had convinced Artaxerxes that Rome was more powerful than he had thought. It had shown him that in imagining the time had arrived when they might be easily driven out of Asia—he had made a mistake. The imperial power had proved itself strong enough to penetrate deeply within his territory, to ravage some of his best provinces, and to threaten his capital. The grand ideas with which he had entered upon the contest had consequently to be abandoned; and it had to be recognized that the struggle with Rome was one in which the two parties were very evenly matched, one in which it was not to be supposed that either side would very soon obtain any decided preponderance. Under these circumstances the grand ideas were quietly dropped; the army which had been gathered together to enforce them was allowed to disperse, and was not required within any given time to reassemble; it is not unlikely that (as Niebuhr conjectures) a peace was made, though whether Rome ceded any of her territory by its terms is exceedingly doubtful. Probably the general principle of the arrangement was a return to the status quo ante bellum, or, in other words, the acceptance by either side, as the true territorial limits between Rome and Persia, of those boundaries which had been previously held to divide the imperial possessions from the dominions of the Arsacidse.

The issue of the struggle was no doubt disappointing to Artaxerxes; but if, on the one hand, it dispelled some illusions and proved to him that the Roman State, though verging to its decline, nevertheless still possessed a vigor and a life which he had been far from anticipating, on the other hand it left him free to concentrate his efforts on the reduction of Armenia, which was really of more importance to him, from Armenia being the great stronghold of the Arsacid power, than the nominal attachment to the empire of half-a-dozen Roman provinces. So long as Arsacidae maintained themselves in a position of independence and substantial power so near the Persian borders, and in a country of such extent and such vast natural strength as Armenia, there could not but be a danger of reaction, of the nations again reverting to the yoke whereto they had by long use become accustomed, and of the star of the Sasanidae paling before that of the former masters of Asia. It was essential to the consolidation of the new Persian Empire that Armenia should be subjugated, or at any rate that Arsacidae should cease to govern it; and the fact that the peace which appears to have been made between Rome and Persia, A.D. 232, set Artaxerxes at liberty to direct all his endeavors to the establishment of such relations between his own state and Armenia as he deemed required by public policy and necessary for the security of his own power, must be regarded as one of paramount importance, and as probably one of the causes mainly actuating him in the negotiations and inclining him to consent to peace on any fair and equitable terms. Consequently, the immediate result of hostilities ceasing between Persia and Rome was their renewal between Persia and Armenia. The war had indeed, in one sense, never ceased; for Chosroes had been an ally of the Romans during the campaign of Severus, and had no doubt played a part in the invasion and devastation of Media which have been described above. But, the Romans having withdrawn, he was left wholly dependent on his own resources; and the entire strength of Persia was now doubtless brought into the field against him. Still he defended himself with such success, and caused Artaxerxes so much alarm, that after a time that monarch began to despair of ever conquering his adversary by fair means, and cast about for some other mode of accomplishing his purpose. Summoning an assembly of all the vassal kings, the governors, and the commandants throughout the empire, he besought them to find some cure for the existing distress, at the same time promising a rich reward to the man who should contrive an effectual remedy. The second place in the kingdom should be his; he should have dominion over one half of the Arians; nay, he should share the Persian throne with Artaxerxes himself, and hold a rank and dignity only slightly inferior. We are told that these offers prevailed with a noble of the empire, named Anak, a man who had Arsacid blood in his veins, and belonged to that one of the three branches of the old royal stock which had long been settled at Bactria (Balkh), and that he was induced thereby to come forward and undertake the assassination of Chosroes, who was his near relative and would not be likely to suspect him of an ill intent. Artaxerxes warmly encouraged him in his design, and in a little time it was successfully carried out. Anak, with his wife, his children, his brother, and a train of attendants, pretended to take refuge in Armenia from the threatened vengeance of his sovereign, who caused his troops to pursue him, as a rebel and deserter, to the very borders of Armenia. Unsuspicious of any evil design, Ohosroes received the exiles with favor, discussed with them his plans for the subjugation of Persia, and, having sheltered them during the whole of the autumn and winter, proposed to them in the spring that they should accompany him and take part in the year's campaign. Anak, forced by this proposal to precipitate his designs, contrived a meeting between himself, his brother, and Chosroes, without attendants, on the pretext of discussing plans of attack, and, having thus got the Armenian monarch at a disadvantage, drew sword upon him, together with his brother, and easily put him to death. The crime which he had undertaken was thus accomplished; but he did not live to receive the reward promised him for it. Armenia rose in arms on learning the foul deed wrought upon its king; the bridges and the few practicable outlets by which the capital could be quitted were occupied by armed men; and the murderers, driven to desperation, lost their lives in an attempt to make their escape by swimming the river Araxes. Thus Artaxerxes obtained his object without having to pay the price that he had agreed upon; his dreaded rival was removed; Armenia lay at his mercy; and he had not to weaken his power at home by sharing it with an Arsacid partner.

The Persian monarch allowed the Armenians no time to recover from the blow which he had treacherously dealt them. His armies at once entered their territory and carried everything before them. Chosroes seems to have had no son of sufficient age to succeed him, and the defence of the country fell upon the satraps, or governors of the several provinces. These chiefs implored the aid of the Roman emperor, and received a contingent; but neither were their own exertions nor was the valor of their allies of any avail. Artaxerxes easily defeated the confederate army, and forced the satraps to take refuge in Roman territory. Armenia submitted to his arms, and became an integral portion of his empire. It probably did not greatly trouble him that Artavasdes, one of the satraps, succeeded in carrying off one of the sons of Chosroes, a boy named Tiridates, whom he conveyed to Rome, and placed under the protection of the reigning emperor.

Such were the chief military successes of Artaxerxes. The greatest of our historians, Gibbon, ventures indeed to assign to him, in addition, "some easy victories over the wild Scythians and the effeminate Indians." But there is no good authority for this statement; and on the whole it is unlikely that he came into contact with either nation. His coins are not found in Afghanistan; and it may be doubted whether he ever made any eastern expedition. His reign was not long; and it was sufficiently occupied by the Roman and Armenian wars, and by the greatest of all his works, the reformation of religion.

The religious aspect of the insurrection which transferred the headship of Western Asia from the Parthians to the Persians, from Artabanus to Artaxerxes, has been already noticed; but we have now to trace, so far as we can, the steps by which the religious revolution was accomplished, and the faith of Zoroaster, or what was believed to be such, established as the religion of the State throughout the new empire. Artaxerxes, himself (if we may believe Agathias) a Magus, was resolved from the first that, if his efforts to shake off the Parthian yoke succeeded, he would use his best endeavors to overthrow the Parthian idolatry and install in its stead the ancestral religion of the Persians. This religion consisted of a combination of Dualism with a qualified creature-worship, and a special reverence for the elements, earth, air, water, and fire. Zoroastrianism, in the earliest form which is historically known to us, postulated two independent and contending principles—a principle of good, Ahura-Mazda, and a principle of evil, Angro-Mainyus. These beings, who were coeternal and coequal, were engaged in a perpetual struggle for supremacy; and the world was the battle-field wherein the strife was carried on. Each had called into existence numerous inferior beings, through whose agency they waged their interminable conflict. Ahura-Mazda (Oromazdos, Ormazd) had created thousands of angel beings to perform his will and fight on his side against the Evil One; and Alngro-Mainyus (Arimanius, Ahriman) had equally on his part called into being thousands of malignant spirits to be his emissaries in the world, to do his work, and fight his battles. The greater of the powers called into being by Ahura-Mazda were proper objects of the worship of man, though, of course, his main worship was to be given to Ahura-Mazda. Angro-Mainyus was not to be worshipped, but to be hated and feared. With this dualistic belief had been combined, at a time not much later than that of Darius Hystaspis, an entirely separate system, the worship of the elements. Fire, air, earth, and water were regarded as essentially holy, and to pollute any of them was a crime. Fire was especially to be held in honor; and it became an essential part of the Persian religion to maintain perpetually upon the fire-altars the sacred flame, supposed to have been originally kindled from heaven, and to see that it never went out. Together with this elemental worship was introduced into the religion a profound regard for an order of priests called Magians, who interposed themselves between the deity and the worshipper, and claimed to possess prophetic powers. This Magian order was a priest-caste, and exercised vast influence, being internally organized into a hierarchy containing many ranks, and claiming a sanctity far above that of the best laymen.

Artaxerxes found the Magian order depressed by the systematic action of the later Parthian princes, who had practically fallen away from the Zoroastrian faith and become mere idolaters. He found the fire-altars in ruins, the sacred flame extinguished, the most essential of the Magian ceremonies and practices disregarded. Everywhere, except perhaps in his own province of Persia Proper, he found idolatry established. Temples of the sun abounded, where images of Mithra were the object of worship, and the Mithraic cult was carried out with a variety of imposing ceremonies. Similar temples to the moon existed in many places; and the images of the Arsacidae were associated with those of the sun and moon gods, in the sanctuaries dedicated to them. The precepts of Zoroaster were forgotten. The sacred compositions which bore that sage's name, and had been handed down from a remote antiquity, were still indeed preserved, if not in a written form, yet in the memory of the faithful few who clung to the old creed; but they had ceased to be regarded as binding upon their consciences by the great mass of the Western Asiatics. Western Asia was a seething-pot, in which were mixed up a score of contradictory creeds, old and new, rational and irrational, Sabaism, Magism, Zoroastrianism, Grecian polytheism, teraphim-worship, Judaism, Chaldae mysticism, Christianity. Artaxerxes conceived it to be his mission to evoke order out of this confusion, to establish in lieu of this extreme diversity an absolute uniformity of religion.

The steps which he took to effect his purpose seem to have been the following. He put down idolatry by a general destruction of the images, which he overthrew and broke to pieces. He raised the Magian hierarchy to a position of honor and dignity such as they had scarcely enjoyed even under the later Achaemenian princes, securing them in a condition of pecuniary independence by assignments of lands, and also by allowing their title to claim from the faithful the tithe of all their possessions. He caused the sacred fire to be rekindled on the altars where it was extinguished, and assigned to certain bodies of priests the charge of maintaining the fire in each locality. He then proceeded to collect the supposed precepts of Zoroaster into a volume, in order to establish a standard of orthodoxy whereto he might require all to conform. He found the Zoroastrians themselves divided into a number of sects. Among these he established uniformity by means of a "general council," which was attended by Magi from all parts of the empire, and which settled what was to be regarded as the true Zoroastrian faith. According to the Oriental writers, this was effected in the following way: Forty thousand, or, according to others, eighty thousand Magi having assembled, they were successively reduced by their own act to four thousand, to four hundred, to forty, and finally to seven, the most highly respected for their piety and learning. Of these seven there was one, a young but holy priest, whom the universal consent of his brethren recognized as pre-eminent. His name was Arda-Viraf. "Having passed through the strictest ablutions, and drunk a powerful opiate, he was covered with a white linen and laid to sleep. Watched by seven of the nobles, including the king, he slept for seven days and nights; and, on his reawaking, the whole nation listened with believing wonder to his exposition of the faith of Ormazd, which was carefully written down by an attendant scribe for the benefit of posterity."

The result, however brought about, which must always remain doubtful, was the authoritative issue of a volume which the learned of Europe have now possessed for some quarter of a century, and which has recently been made accessible to the general reader by the labors of Spiegel. This work, the Zendavesta, while it may contain fragments of a very ancient literature, took its present shape in the time of Artaxerxes, and was probably then first collected from the mouths of the Zoroastrian priests and published by Arda-Viraf. Certain additions may since have been made to it; but we are assured that "their number is small," and that we "have no reason to doubt" that the text of the Avesta, in the days of Arda-Viraf, was on the whole exactly the same as at present. The religious system of the new Persian monarchy is thus completely known to us, and will be described minutely in a later chapter. At present we have to consider, not what the exact tenets of the Zoroastrians were, but only the mode in which Artaxerxes imposed them upon his subjects.

The next step, after settling the true text of the sacred volume, was to agree upon its interpretation. The language of the Avesta, though pure Persian, was of so archaic a type that none but the most learned of the Magi understood it; to the common people, even to the ordinary priest, it was a dead letter. Artaxerxes seems to have recognized the necessity of accompanying the Zend text with a translation and a commentary in the language of his own time, the Pehlevi or Huzvaresh. Such a translation and commentary exist; and though in part belonging to later Sassanian times, they reach back probably in their earlier portions to the era of Artaxerxes, who may fairly be credited with the desire to make the sacred book "understanded of the people."

Further, it was necessary, in order to secure permanent uniformity of belief, to give to the Magian priesthood, the keepers and interpreters of the sacred book, very extensive powers. The Magian hierarchy was therefore associated with the monarch in the government and administration of the State. It was declared that the altar and the throne were inseparable, and must always sustain each other. The Magi were made to form the great council of the nation. While they lent their support to the crown, the crown upheld them against all impugners, and enforced by pains and penalties their decisions. Persecution was adopted and asserted as a principle of action without any disguise. By an edict of Artaxerxes, all places of worship were closed except the temples of the fire-worshippers. If no violent outbreak of fanaticism followed, it was because the various sectaries and schismatics succumbed to the decree without resistance. Christian, and Jew, and Greek, and Parthian, and Arab allowed their sanctuaries to be closed without striking a blow to prevent it; and the non-Zoroastrians of the empire, the votaries of foreign religions, were shortly reckoned at the insignificant number of 80,000.

Of the internal administration and government of his extensive empire by Artaxerxes, but little is known. That little seems, however, to show that while in general type and character it conformed to the usual Oriental model, in its practical working it was such as to obtain the approval of the bulk of his subjects. Artaxerxes governed his provinces either through native kings, or else through Persian satraps. At the same time, like the Achaemenian monarchs, he kept the armed force under his own control by the appointment of "generals" or "commandants" distinct from the satraps. Discarding the Parthian plan of intrusting the military defence of the empire and the preservation of domestic order to a mere militia, he maintained on a war footing a considerable force, regularly paid and drilled. "There can be no power," he remarked, "without an army, no army without money, no money without agriculture, and no agriculture without justice." To administer strict justice was therefore among his chief endeavors. Daily reports were made to him of all that passed not only in his capital, but in every province of his vast empire; and his knowledge extended even to the private actions of his subjects. It was his earnest desire that all well-deposed persons should feel an absolute assurance of security with respect to their lives, their property, and their honor. At the same time he punished crimes with severity, and even visited upon entire families the transgression of one of their members. It is said to have been one of his maxims, that "kings should never use the sword where the cane would answer;" but, if the Armenian historians are to be trusted, in practice he certainly did not err on the side of clemency.

Artaxerxes was, of course, an absolute monarch, having the entire power of life or death, and entitled, if he chose, to decide all matters at his own mere will and pleasure. But, in practice, he, like most Oriental despots, was wont to summon and take the advice of counsellors. It is perhaps doubtful whether any regular "Council of State" existed under him. Such an institution had prevailed under the Parthians, where the monarchs were elected and might be deposed by the Megistanes; but there is no evidence that Artaxerxes continued it, or did more than call on each occasion for the advice of such persons among his subjects as he thought most capable. In matters affecting his relations towards foreign powers he consulted with the subject kings, the satraps, and the generals; in religious affairs he no doubt took counsel with the chief Magi. The general principles which guided his conduct both in religious and other matters may perhaps be best gathered from the words of that "testament," or "dying speech," which he is said to have addressed to his son Sapor. "Never forget," he said, "that, as a king, you are at once the protector of religion and of your country. Consider the altar and the throne as inseparable; they must always sustain each other. A sovereign without religion is a tyrant; and a people who have none may be deemed the most monstrous of all societies. Religion may exist without a state; but a state cannot exist without religion; and it is by holy laws that a political association can alone be bound. You should be to your people an example of piety and of virtue, but without pride or ostentation.... Remember, my son, that it is the prosperity or adversity of the ruler which forms the happiness or misery of his subjects, and that the fate of the nation depends on the conduct of the individual who fills the throne. The world is exposed to constant vicissitudes; learn, therefore, to meet the frowns of fortune with courage and fortitude, and to receive her smiles with moderation and wisdom. To sum up all—may your administration be such as to bring, at a future day, the blessings of those whom God has confided to our parental care upon both your memory and mine!"

PLATE XII

There is reason to believe that Artaxerxes, some short time before his death, invested Sapor with the emblems of sovereignty, and either associated him in the empire, or wholly ceded to him his own place. The Arabian writer, Macoudi, declares that, sated with glory and with power, he withdrew altogether from the government, and, making over the administration of affairs to his favorite son, devoted himself to religious contemplation. Tabari knows nothing of the religious motive, but relates that towards the close of his life Artaxerxes "made Sapor regent, appointed him formally to be his successor, and with his own hands placed the .crown on his head." [PLATE XII.] These notices would, by themselves, have been of small importance; but force is lent to them by the facts that Artaxerxes is found to have placed the effigy of Sapor on his later coins, and that in one of his bas-reliefs he seems to be represented as investing Sapor with the diadem. This tablet, which is at Takht-i-Bostan, has been variously explained, and, as it is unaccompanied by any inscription, no certain account can be given of it; but, on the whole the opinion of those most competent to judge seems to be that the intention of the artist was to represent Artaxerxes (who wears the cap and inflated ball) as handing the diadem to Sapor—distinguished by the mural crown of his own tablets and coins—while Ormazd, marked by his customary baton, and further indicated by a halo of glory around his head, looks on, sanctioning and approving the transaction. A prostrate figure under the feet of the two Sassanian kings represents either Artabanus or the extinct Parthian monarchy, probably the former; while the sunflower upon which Ormazd stands, together with the rays that stream from his head, denote an intention to present him under a Mithraitic aspect, suggestive to the beholder of a real latent identity between the two great objects of Persian worship.

The coins of Artaxerxes present five different types. [PLATE XI., Fig. 1.] In the earliest his effigy appears on the obverse, front-faced, with the simple legend AETaHsnaTE (Artaxerxes), or sometimes with the longer one, BaGi ARTaiiSHaTR MaLKA, "Divine Artaxerxes, King;" while the reverse bears the profile of his father, Papak, looking to the left, with the legend BaGi PAPaKi MaLKA, "Divine Papak, King;" or BaBI BaGi PAPaKi MaLKA, 'Son of Divine Papak, King." Both heads wear the ordinary Parthian diadem and tiara; and the head of Artaxerxes much resembles that of Volagases V., one of the later Parthian kings. The coins of the next period have a head on one side only. This is in profile, looking to the right, and bears a highly ornamental tiara, exactly like that of Mithridates I. of Parthia, the great conqueror. It is usually accompanied by the legend MaZDiSN BaGi ARTaHSHaTR MaLKA (or MaLKAN MaLKA) aiean, i.e. "The Ormazd-worshipping Divine Artaxerxes, King of Iran," or "King of the Kings of Iran." The reverse of these coins bears a fire-altar, with the legend ARTaHSHaTR nuvazi, a phrase of doubtful import. In the third period, while the reverse remains unchanged, on the obverse the Parthian costume is entirely given up; and the king takes, instead of the Parthian tiara, a low cap surmounted by the inflated ball, which thenceforth becomes the almost universal badge of a Sassanian monarch. The legend is now longer, being commonly MaZDiSN BaGi ARTaiisi-iaTR MaLKAN MaLKA airanMiNUCHiTRi iniN YazDAN, or "The Ormazd-worshipping Divine Artaxerxes, King of the Kings of Iran, heaven-descended of (the race of) the Gods." The fourth period is marked by the assumption of the mural crown, which in the sculptures of Artaxerxes is given only to Ormazd, but which was afterwards adopted by Sapor I. and many later kings, in combination with the ball, as their usual head-dress. The legend on these coins remains as in the third period, and the reverse is likewise unchanged. Finally, there are a few coins of Artaxerxes, belonging to the very close of his reign, where he is represented with the tiara of the third period, looking to the right; while in front of him, and looking towards him, is another profile, that of a boy, in whom numismatists recognize his eldest son and successor, Sapor.

Vol. III.    Fig. 1.              Fig. 3.        Plate XV.

LATER COINS OF ARTAXERXES I.        COIN OF HORMISDAS I.

Fig 2.

COINS OF SAPOR I.

Fig 4.        Fig. 5.              Fig. 6.

COIN OF VARAHRAN I.              COIN OF VARAHRAN II.

HEAD OF SAPOR I.
(from a gem).

Fig. 7.

COIN OF SAPOR I.

PLATE XV

It is remarkable that with the accession of Artaxerxes there is at once a revival of art. Art had sunk under the Parthians, despite their Grecian leanings, to the lowest ebb which it had known in Western Asia since the accession of Asshur-izir-pal to the throne of Assyria (B.C. 886). Parthian attempts at art were few and far between, and when made were unhappy, not to say ridiculous. The coins of Artaxerxes, compared with those of the later Parthian monarchs, show at once a renaissance. The head is well cut; the features have individuality and expression; the epigraph is sufficiently legible. Still more is his sculpture calculated to surprise us. Artaxerxes represents himself as receiving the Persian diadem from the hands of Ormazd; both he and the god are mounted upon chargers of a stout breed, which are spiritedly portrayed; Artabanus lies prostrate under the feet of the king's steed, while under those of the deity's we observe the form of Ahriman, also prostrate, and indeed seemingly dead. Though the tablet has not really any great artistic merit, it is far better than anything that remains to us of the Parthians; it has energy and vigor; the physiognomies are carefully rendered; and the only flagrant fault is a certain over-robustness in the figures, which has an effect that is not altogether pleasing. Still, we cannot but see in the new Persian art—even at its very beginning—a movement towards life after a long period of stagnation; an evidence of that general stir of mind which the downfall of Tartar oppression rendered possible; a token that Aryan intelligence was beginning to recover and reassert itself in all the various fields in which it had formerly won its triumphs.

The coinage of Artaxerxes, and of the other Sassanian monarchs, is based, in part upon Roman, in part upon Parthian, models. The Roman aureus furnishes the type which is reproduced in the Sassanian gold coins, while the silver coins follow the standard long established in Western Asia, first under the Seleucid, and then under the Arsacid princes. This standard is based upon the Attic drachm, which was adopted by Alexander as the basis of his monetary system. The curious occurrence of a completely different standard for gold and silver in Persia during this period is accounted for by the circumstances of the time at which the coinage took its rise. The Arsacidae had employed no gold coins, but had been content with a silver currency; any gold coin that may have been in use among their subjects for purposes of trade during the continuance of their empire must have been foreign money—Roman, Bactrian, or Indian; but the quantity had probably for the most part been very small. But, about ten years before the accession of Artaxerxes there had been a sudden influx into Western Asia of Roman gold, in consequence of the terms of the treaty concluded between Artabanus and Macrinus (A.D. 217), whereby Rome undertook to pay to Parthia an indemnity of above a million and a half of our money. It is probable that the payment was mostly made in aurei. Artaxerxes thus found current in the countries, which he overran and formed into an empire, two coinages—a gold and a silver—coming from different sources and possessing no common measure. It was simpler and easier to retain what existed, and what had sufficiently adjusted itself through the working of commercial needs, than to invent something new; and hence the anomalous character of the New Persian monetary system.

The remarkable bas-relief of Artaxerxes described above and figured below in the chapter on the Art of the Sassanians, is accompanied by a bilingual inscription, or perhaps we should say by two bilingual inscriptions, which possess much antiquarian and some historic interest. The longer of the two runs as follows:—"Pathkar zani mazdisn bagi Artahshatr, malkan malka Airan, minuchitri min Ydztan, bari bagi Pap-aki malka;" while the Greek version of it is—

ΤΟΥΤΟΤΟⅡΡΟCΟΠΟΝΜΑCΔΑCΝΟΥ

ΘΕΟΥΑΡΤΑΞΑΡΟΥΒΑCΙΛΕωCΒΑCΙΛΕωΝ

ΑΡΙΑΝωΝΕΚΓΕΝΟΥCΘΕωΝΥΙΟΥ

ΘΕΟΥΠΑΠΑΚΟΥΒΑCΙΛΕωC.

The shorter inscription runs—" *Pathkar zani Ahuramazda bagi*, the Greek being

ΤΟΥΤΟΤΟΠΡΟCωΠΟΝΔΙΟCΘΕΟΥ.

The inscriptions are interesting, first, as proving the continued use of the Greek character and language by a dynasty that was intensely national and that wished to drive the Greeks out of Asia. Secondly, they are interesting as showing the character of the native language, and letters, employed by the Persians, when they came suddenly into notice as the ruling people of Western Asia. Thirdly, they have an historic interest in what they tell us of the relationship of Artaxerxes to Babek (Papak), of the rank of Babek, and of the religious sympathies of the Sassanians. In this last respect they do indeed, in themselves, little but confirm the evidence of the coins and the general voice of antiquity on the subject. Coupled, however, with the reliefs to which they are appended, they do more. They prove to us that the Persians of the earliest Sassanian times were not averse to exhibiting the great personages of their theology in sculptured forms; nay, they reveal to us the actual forms then considered appropriate to Ahura-Mazda (Ormazd) and Angro-Mainyus (Ahriman); for we can scarcely be mistaken in regarding the prostrate figure under the hoofs of Ahura-Mazda's steed as the antagonist Spirit of Evil. Finally, the inscriptions show that, from the commencement of their sovereignty, the Sassanian princes claimed for themselves a qualified divinity, assuming the title of BAG and ALHA, "god," and taking, in the Greek version of their legends, the correspondent epithet of OEOE

## CHAPTER IV

*Death of Artaxerxes I. and Accession of Sapor I. War of Sapor with Manizen. His first War with Rome. Invasion of Mesopotamia, A.D. 241. Occupation of Antioch. Expedition of Gordian to the East. Recovery by Rome of her lost Territory. Peace made between Rome and Persia. Obscure Interval. Second War with Rome. Mesopotamia again invaded, A.D. 258. Valerian takes the Command in the East. Struggle between him and Sapor. Defeat and Capture of Valerian, A.D. 260. Sapor invests Miriades with the Purple. He takes Syria and Southern Cappadocia, but is shortly afterwards attacked by Odenathus. Successes of Odenathus. Treatment of Valerian. Further successes of Odenathus. Period of Tranquillity. Great Works of Sapor. His Scriptures. His Dyke. His Inscriptions. His Coins. His Religion. Religious Condition of the East in his Time. Rise into Notice of Mani. His Rejection by Sapor. Sapor's Death. His Character.*

Διαδέχεται τὸ κράτος Σαπώρης ἐκεῖνος ὁ ἐναγέστατος, καὶ διεβίω πρὸς τῷ ἑνὶ τριάκοντα τοὺς πάντας ἐνιαυτοὺς, πλεῖστα ὅσα τοὺς Ῥωμαίους λυμαινόμενος.—AGATHIAS, iv. p. 134, B.

Artaxerxes appears to have died in A.D. 240. He was succeeded by his son, Shahpuhri, or Sapor, the first Sassanian prince of that name. According to the Persian historians, the mother of Sapor was a daughter of the last Parthian king, Artabanus, whom Artaxerxes had taken to wife after his conquest of her father. But the facts known of Sapor throw doubt on this story, which has too many parallels in Oriental romance to claim implicit credence. Nothing authentic has come down to us respecting Sapor during his father's lifetime; but from the moment that he mounted the throne, we find him engaged in a series of wars, which show him to have been of a most active and energetic character. Armenia, which Artaxerxes had subjected, attempted (it would seem) to regain its independence at the commencement of the new reign; but Sapor easily crushed the nascent insurrection, and the Armenians made no further effort to free themselves till several years after his death. Contemporaneously with this revolt in the mountain region of the north, a danger showed itself in the plain country of the south, where Manizen, king of Hatra, or El Hadhr, not only declared himself independent, but assumed dominion over the entire tract between the Euphrates and the Tigris, the Jezireh of the Arabian geographers. The strength of Hatra was great, as had been proved by Trajan and Severus; its thick walls and valiant inhabitants would probably have defied every attempt of the

Persian prince to make himself master of it by force. He therefore condescended to stratagem. Manizen had a daughter who cherished ambitious views. On obtaining a promise from Sapor that if she gave Hatra into his power he would make her his queen, this unnatural child turned against her father, betrayed him into Sapor's hands, and thus brought the war to an end. Sapor recovered his lost territory; but he did not fulfil his bargain. Instead of marrying the traitress, he handed her over to an executioner, to receive the death that she had deserved, though scarcely at his hands. Encouraged by his success in these two lesser contests, Sapor resolved (apparently in A.D. 241) to resume the bold projects of his father, and engage in a great war with Rome. The confusion and troubles which afflicted the Roman Empire at this time were such as might well give him hopes of obtaining a decided advantage. Alexander, his father's adversary, had been murdered in A.D. 235 by Maximin, who from the condition of a Thracian peasant had risen into the higher ranks of the army. The upstart had ruled like the savage that he was; and, after three years of misery, the whole Roman world had risen against him. Two emperors had been proclaimed in Africa; on their fall, two others had been elected by the Senate; a third, a mere boy, had been added at the demand of the Roman populace. All the pretenders except the last had met with violent deaths; and, after the shocks of a year unparalleled since A.D. 69, the administration of the greatest kingdom in the world was in the hands of a youth of fifteen. Sapor, no doubt, thought he saw in this condition of things an opportunity that he ought not to miss, and rapidly matured his plans lest the favorable moment should pass away.

Crossing the middle Tigris into Mesopotamia, the bands of Sapor first attacked the important city of Nisibis. Nisibis, at this time a Roman colony, was strongly situated on the outskirts of the mountain range which traverses Northern Mesopotamia between the 37th and 38th parallels. The place was well fortified and well defended; it offered a prolonged resistance; but at last the Avails were breached, and it was forced to yield itself. The advance was then made along the southern flank of the mountains, by Carrhae (Harran) and Edessa to the Euphrates, which was probably reached in the neighborhood of Birehjik, The hordes then poured into Syria, and, spreading themselves over that fertile region, surprised and took the metropolis of the Roman East, the rich and luxurious city of Antioch. But meantime the Romans had shown a spirit which had not been expected from them. Gordian, young as he was, had quitted Rome and marched through Mossia and Thrace into Asia, accompanied by a formidable army, and by at least one good general. Timesitheus, whose daughter Gordian had recently married, though his life had hitherto been that of a civilian, exhibited, on his elevation to the dignity of Praetorian prefect, considerable military ability. The army, nominally commanded by Gordian, really acted under his orders. With it Timesitheus attacked and beat the bands of Sapor in a number of engagements, recovered Antioch, crossed the Euphrates, retook Carrhae, defeated the Persian monarch in a pitched battle near Resaina (Ras-el-Ain), recovered Nisibis, and once more planted the Roman standards on the banks of the Tigris. Sapor hastily evacuated most of his conquests, and retired first across the Euphrates and then across the more eastern river; while the Romans advanced as he retreated, placed garrisons in the various Mesopotamian towns, and even threatened the great city of Ctesiphon. Gordian was confident that his general would gain further triumphs, and wrote to the Senate to that effect; but either disease or the arts of a rival cut short the career of the victor, and from the time of his death the Romans ceased to be successful. The legions had, it would seem, invaded Southern Mesopotamia when the Praetorian prefect who had succeeded Timesitheus brought them intentionally into difficulties by his mismanagement of the commissariat; and at last retreat was determined on. The young emperor was approaching the Khabour, and had almost reached his own frontier, when the discontent of the army, fomented by the prefect, Philip, came to a head. Gordian was murdered at a place called Zaitha, about twenty miles south of Circesium, and was buried where he fell, the soldiers raising a tumulus in his honor. His successor, Philip, was glad to make peace on any tolerable terms with the Persians; he felt himself insecure upon his throne, and was anxious to obtain the Senate's sanction of his usurpation. He therefore quitted the East in A.D. 244, having concluded a treaty with Sapor, by which Armenia seems to have been left to the Persians, while Mesopotamia returned to its old condition of a Roman province.

The peace made between Philip and Sapor was followed by an interval of fourteen years, during which scarcely anything is known of the condition of Persia. We may suspect that troubles in the north-east of his empire occupied Sapor during this period, for at the end of it we find Bactria, which was certainly subject to Persia during the earlier years of the monarchy, occupying an independent position, and even assuming an attitude of hostility towards the Persian monarch. Bactria had, from a remote antiquity, claims to pre-eminence among the Aryan nations. She was more than once inclined to revolt from the Achaemenidae; and during the later Parthian period she had enjoyed a sort of semi-independence. It would seem that she now succeeded in detaching herself altogether from her southern neighbor, and becoming a distinct and separate power. To strengthen her position she entered into relations with Rome, which gladly welcomed any adhesions to her cause in this remote region.

Sapor's second war with Rome was, like his first, provoked by himself. After concluding his peace with Philip, he had seen the Roman world governed successively by six weak emperors, of whom four had died violent deaths, while at the same time there had been a continued series of attacks upon the northern frontiers of the empire by Alemanni, Goths, and Franks, who had ravaged at their will a number of the finest provinces, and threatened the absolute destruction of the great monarchy of the West. It was natural that the chief kingdom of Western Asia should note these events, and should seek to promote its own interests by taking advantage of the circumstances of the time. Sapor, in A.D. 258, determined on a fresh invasion of the Roman provinces, and, once more entering Mesopotamia, carried all before him, became master of Nisibis, Carrhae, and Edessa, and, crossing the Euphrates, surprised Antioch, which was wrapped in the enjoyment of theatrical and other representations, and only knew its fate on the exclamation of a couple of actors "that the Persians were in possession of the town." The aged emperor, Valerian, hastened to the protection of his more eastern territories, and at first gained some successes, retaking Antioch, and making that city his headquarters during his stay in the East. But, after this, the tide turned. Valerian entrusted the whole conduct of the war to Macrianus, his Praetorian prefect, whose talents he admired, and of whose fidelity he did not entertain a suspicion. Macrianus, however, aspired to the empire, and intentionally brought Valerian into difficulties, in the hope of disgracing or removing him. His tactics were successful. The Roman army in Mesopotamia was betrayed into a situation whence escape was impossible, and where its capitulation was only a question of time. A bold attempt' made to force a way through the enemy's lines failed utterly, after which famine and pestilence began to do their work. In vain did the aged emperor send envoys to propose a peace, and offer to purchase escape by the payment of an immense sum in gold. Sapor, confident of victory, refused the overture, and, waiting patiently till his adversary was at the last gasp, invited him to a conference, and then treacherously seized his person. The army surrendered or dispersed. Macrianus, the Praetorian prefect, shortly assumed the title of emperor, and marched against Gallienus, the son and colleague of Valerian, who had been left to direct affairs in the West. But another rival started up in the East. Sapor conceived the idea of complicating the Roman affairs by himself putting forward a pretender; and an obscure citizen of Antioch, a certain Miriades or Cyriades, a refugee in his camp, was invested with the purple, and assumed the title of Caesar.

Plate XIII

No. III.

SAPOR I. PRESENTING CYRIADES TO THE ROMAN TROOPS AS THEIR EMPEROR.

PLATE XIII

The blow struck at Edessa laid the whole of Roman Asia open to attack, and the Persian monarch was not slow to seize the occasion. His troops crossed the Euphrates in force, and, marching on Antioch, once more captured that unfortunate town, from which the more prudent citizens had withdrawn, but where the bulk of the people, not displeased at the turn of affairs, remained and welcomed the conqueror. Miriades was installed in power, while Sapor himself, at the head of his irresistible squadrons, pressed forward, bursting "like a mountain torrent" into Cilicia and thence into Cappadocia. Tarsus, the birthplace of St. Paul, at once a famous seat of learning and a great emporium of commerce, fell; Cilicia Campestris was overrun; and the passes of Taurus, deserted or weakly defended by the Romans, came into Sapor's hands. Penetrating through them and entering the champaign country beyond, his bands soon formed the siege of Caesarea Mazaca, the greatest city of these parts, estimated, at this time to have contained a population of four hundred thousand souls. Demosthenes, the governor of Caesarea, defended it bravely, and, had force only been used against him, might have prevailed; but Sapor found friends within the walls, and by their help made himself master of the place, while its bold defender was obliged to content himself with escaping by cutting his way through the victorious host. All Asia Minor now seemed open to the conqueror; and it is difficult to understand why he did not at any rate attempt a permanent occupation of the territory which he had so easily overrun. But it seems certain that he entertained no such idea. Devastation and plunder, revenge and gain, not permanent conquest, were his objects; and hence his course was everywhere marked by ruin and carnage, by smoking towns, ravaged fields, and heaps of slain. His cruelties have no doubt been exaggerated; but when we hear that he filled the ravines and valleys of Cappadocia with dead bodies, and so led his cavalry across them; that he depopulated Antioch, killing or carrying off into slavery almost the whole population; that he suffered his prisoners in many cases to perish of hunger, and that he drove them to water once a day like beasts, we may be sure that the guise in which he showed himself to the Romans was that of a merciless scourge—an avenger bent on spreading the terror of his name—not of one who really sought to enlarge the limits of his empire.

During the whole course of this plundering expedition, until the retreat began, we hear but of one check that the bands of Sapor received. It had been determined to attack Emesa (now Hems), one of the most important of the Syrian towns, where the temple of Venus was known to contain a vast treasure. The invaders approached, scarcely expecting to be resisted; but the high priest of the temple, having collected a large body of peasants, appeared, in his sacerdotal robes, at the head of a fanatic multitude armed with slings, and succeeded in beating off the assailants. Emesa, its temple, and its treasure, escaped the rapacity of the Persians; and an example of resistance was set, which was not perhaps without important consequences.

For it seems certain that the return of Sapor across the Euphrates was not effected without considerable loss and difficulty. On his advance into Syria he had received an embassy from a certain Odenathus, a Syrian or Arab chief, who occupied a position of semi-independence at Palmyra, which, through the advantages of its situation, had lately become a flourishing commercial town. Odenathus sent a long train of camels laden with gifts, consisting in part of rare and precious merchandise, to the Persian monarch, begging him to accept them, and claiming his favorable regard on the ground that he had hitherto refrained from all acts of hostility against the Persians. It appears that Sapor took offence at the tone of the communication, which was not sufficiently humble to please him. Tearing the letter to fragments and trampling it beneath his feet, he exclaimed—"Who is this Odenathus, and of what country, that he ventures thus to address his lord? Let him now, if he would lighten his punishment, come here and fall prostrate before me with his hands tied behind his back. Should he refuse, let him be well assured that I will destroy himself, his race, and his land." At the same time he ordered his servants to cast the costly presents of the Palmyrene prince into the Euphrates.

This arrogant and offensive behavior naturally turned the willing friend into an enemy. Odenathus, finding himself forced into a hostile position, took arms and watched his opportunity. So long as Sapor continued to advance, he kept aloof. As soon, however, as the retreat commenced, and the Persian army, encumbered with its spoil and captives, proceeded to make its way back slowly and painfully to the Euphrates, Odenathus, who had collected a large force, in part from the Syrian villages, in part from the wild tribes of Arabia, made his appearance in the field. His light and agile horsemen hovered about the Persian host, cut off their stragglers, made prize of much of their spoil, and even captured a portion of the seraglio of the Great King. The harassed troops were glad when they had placed the Euphrates between themselves and their pursuer, and congratulated each other on their escape. So much had they suffered, and so little did they feel equal to further conflicts, that on their march through Mesopotamia they consented to purchase the neutrality of the people of Edessa by making over to them all the coined money that they had carried off in their Syrian raid. After this it would seem that the retreat was unmolested, and Sapor succeeded in conveying the greater part of his army, together with his illustrious prisoner, to his own country.

With regard to the treatment that Valerian received at the hands of his conqueror, it is difficult to form a decided opinion. The writers nearest to the time speak vaguely and moderately, merely telling us that he grew old in his captivity, and was kept in the condition of a slave. It is reserved for authors of the next generation to inform us that he was exposed to the constant gaze of the multitude, fettered, but clad in the imperial purple; and that Sapor, whenever he mounted on horseback, placed his foot upon his prisoner's neck. Some add that, when the unhappy captive died, about the year A.D. 265 or 266, his body was flayed, and the skin inflated and hung up to view in one of the most frequented temples of Persia, where it was seen by Roman envoys on their visits to the Great King's court.

It is impossible to deny that Oriental barbarism may conceivably have gone to these lengths; and it is in favor of the truth of the details that Roman vanity would naturally have been opposed to their invention. But, on the other hand, we have to remember that in the East the person of a king is generally regarded as sacred, and that self-interest restrains the conquering monarch from dishonoring one of his own class. We have also to give due weight to the fact that the earlier authorities are silent with respect to any such atrocities and that they are first related half a century after the time when they are said to have occurred. Under these circumstances the scepticism of Gibbon with respect to them is perhaps more worthy of commendation than the ready faith of a recent French writer.

It may be added that Oriental monarchs, when they are cruel, do not show themselves ashamed of their cruelties, but usually relate them openly in their inscriptions, or represent them in their bas-reliefs. The remains ascribed on good grounds to Sapor do not, however, contain anything confirmatory of the stories which we are considering. Valerian is represented on them in a humble attitude, but not fettered, and never in the posture of extreme degradation commonly associated with his name. He bends his knee, as no doubt he would be required to do, on being brought into the Great King's presence; but otherwise he does not appear to be subjected to any indignity. It seems thus to be on the whole most probable that the Roman emperor was not more severely treated than the generalty of captive princes, and that Sapor has been unjustly taxed with abusing the rights of conquest.

The hostile feeling of Odenathus against Sapor did not cease with the retreat of the latter across the Euphrates. The Palmyrene prince was bent on taking advantage of the general confusion of the times to carve out for himself a considerable kingdom, of which Palmyra should be the capital. Syria and Palestine on the one hand, Mesopotamia on the other, were the provinces that lay most conveniently near to him, and that he especially coveted. But Mesopotamia had remained in the possession of the Persians as the prize of their victory over Valerian, and could only be obtained by wresting it from the hands into which it had fallen. Odenathus did not shrink from this contest. It had been with some reason conjectured that Sapor must have been at this time occupied with troubles which had broken out on the eastern side of his empire. At any rate, it appears that Odenathus, after a short contest with Macriarius and his son, Quietus, turned his arms once more, about A.D. 263, against the Persians, crossed the Euphrates into Mesopotamia, took Oarrhee and Nisibis, defeated Sapor and some of his sons in a battle, and drove the entire Persian host in confusion to the gates of Ctesiphon. He even ventured to form the siege of that city; but it was not long before effectual relief arrived; from all the provinces flocked in contingents for the defence of the Western capital; several engagements were fought, in some of which Odenathus was defeated; and at last he found himself involved in difficulties through his ignorance of the localities, and so thought it best to retire. Apparently his retreat was undisturbed; he succeeded in carrying off his booty and his prisoners, among whom were several satraps, and he retained possession of Mesopotamia, which continued to form a part of the Palmyrene kingdom until the capture of Zenobia by Aurelian (A.D. 273).

The successes of Odenathus in A.D. 263 were followed by a period of comparative tranquillity. That ambitious prince seems to have been content with ruling from the Tigris to the Mediterranean, and with the titles of "Augustus," which he received from the Roman emperor, Gallienus, and "king of kings," which he assumed upon his coins. He did not press further upon Sapor; nor did the Roman emperor make any serious attempt to recover his father's person or revenge his defeat upon the Persians. An expedition which he sent out to the East, professedly with this object, in the year A.D. 267, failed utterly, its commander, Heraclianus, being completely defeated by Zenobia, the widow and successor of Odenathus. Odenathus himself was murdered by a kinsman three or four years after his great successes; and, though Zenobia ruled his kingdom almost with a man's vigor, the removal of his powerful adversary must have been felt as a relief by the Persian monarch. It is evident, too, that from the time of the accession of Zenobia, the relations between Rome and Palmyra had become unfriendly; the old empire grew jealous of the new kingdom which had sprung up upon its borders; and the effect of this jealousy, while it lasted, was to secure Persia from any attack on the part of either.

It appears that Sapor, relieved from any further necessity of defending his empire in arms, employed the remaining years of his life in the construction of great works, and especially in the erection and ornamentation of a new capital. The ruins of Shahpur, which still exist near Kazerun, in the province of Fars, commemorate the name, and afford some indication of the grandeur, of the second Persian monarch. Besides remains of buildings, they comprise a number of bas-reliefs and rock inscriptions, some of which were beyond a doubt set up by Sapor I. In one of the most remarkable the Persian monarch is represented on horseback, wearing the crown usual upon his coins, and holding by the hand a tunicked figure, probably Miriades, whom he is presenting to the captured Romans as their sovereign. Foremost to do him homage is the kneeling figure of a chieftain, probably Valerian, behind whom are arranged in a double line seventeen persons, representing apparently the different corps of the Roman army.

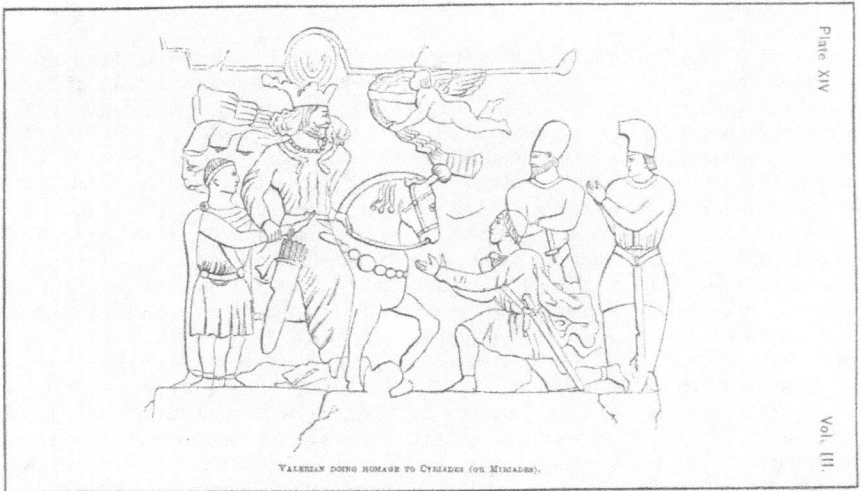

VALERIAN DOING HOMAGE TO CYRIADES (OR MIRIADES).

PLATE XIV

All these persons are on foot, while in contrast with them are arranged behind Sapor ten guards on horseback, who represent his irresistible cavalry. Another bas-relief at the same place gives us a general view of the triumph of Sapor on his return to Persia with his illustrious prisoner. Here fifty-seven guards are ranged behind him, while in front are thirty-three tribute-bearers, having with them an elephant and a chariot. In the centre is a group of seven figures, comprising Sapor, who is on horseback in his usual costume; Valerian, who is under the horse's feet; Miriades, who stands by Sapor's side; three principal tribute-bearers in front of the main figure; and a Victory which floats in the sky.

ΤΟΠΡΟΣΩΠΟΝΤΟΥΤΟΜΑΣΔΑΣΝΟΥΘΕΟΥ

ΣΑΠΩΡΟΥΒΑCΙΛΕΩCΒΑCΙΛΕΩΝΑΡΙΑΝΩΝ

ΚΑΙΑΝΑΡΙΑΝΩΝΕΚΓΕΝΟΥCΘΕΩΝΥΙΟΥ

ΜΑCΔΑCΝΟΥΘΕΟΥΑΡΤΑΞΑΡΟΥΒΑCΙΛΕΩΟ

ΒΑCΙΛΕΩΝΑΡΙΑΝΩΝΕΚΓΕΝΟΥCΘΕΩΝ

ΕΚΓΟΝΟΥΘΕΟΥΠΑΠΑΚΟΥΒΑCΙΛΕΩC

Illustration: PLATE XIV

Another important work, assigned by tradition to Sapor I., is the great dyke at Shuster. This is a dam across the river Karun, formed of cut stones, cemented by lime, and fastened together by clamps of iron; it is twenty feet broad, and no less than twelve hundred feet in length. The whole is a solid mass excepting in the centre, where two small arches have been constructed for the purpose of allowing a part of the stream to flow in its natural bed. The greater portion of the water is directed eastward into a canal cut for it; and the town of Shuster is thus defended on both sides by a water barrier, whereby the position becomes one of great strength. Tradition says that Sapor used his power over Valerian to obtain Roman engineers for this work; and the great dam is still known as the Bund-i-Kaisar, or "dam of Caesar," to the inhabitants of the neighboring country.

Besides his works at Shahpur and Shuster, Sapor set up memorials of himself at Haji-abad, Nakhsh-i-Rajab, and Nakhsh-i-Rustam, near Persepolis, at Darabgerd in South-eastern Persia, and elsewhere; most of which still exist and have been described by various travellers. At Nakhsh-i-Rustam Valerian is seen making his submission in one tablet, while another exhibits the glories of Sapor's court. The sculptures are in some instances accompanied by inscriptions. One of these is, like those of Artaxerxes, bilingual, Greek and Persian. The Greek inscription runs as follows:

Τεθνηκότος τοῦ Σαπώρου, Ὁρμισδάτης, ὁ τούτου παῖς, τὴν βασιλείαν παραλαμβάνει.
AGATH. iv. p. 134, C.

In the main, Sapor, it will be seen, follows the phrases of his father Artaxerxes; but he claims a wider dominion. Artaxerxes is content to rule over Ariana (or Iran) only; his son calls himself lord both of the Arians and the non-Arians, or of Iran and Turan. We may conclude from this as probable that he held some Scythic tribes under his sway, probably in Segestan, or Seistan, the country south and east of the Hamoon, or lake in which the Helmend is swallowed up. Scythians had been settled in these parts, and in portions of Afghanistan and India, since the great invasion of the Yue-chi, about B.C. 200; and it is not unlikely that some of them may have passed under the Persian rule during the reign of Sapor, but we have no particulars of these conquests.

Sapor's coins resemble those of Artaxerxes in general type, but may be distinguished from them, first, by the head-dress, which is either a cap terminating in the head of an eagle, or else a mural crown surmounted by an inflated ball; and, secondly, by the emblem on the reverse, which is almost always a fire-altar between two supporters [PLATE XV., Fig. 2.] The ordinary legend on the coins is "Mazdisn bag Shahpuhri, malkan malka Airan, minuchitri minyazdan," on the obverse; and on the reverse "Shahpuhri nuvazi."

It appears from these legends, and from the inscription above given, that Sapor was, like his father, a zealous Zoroastrian. His faith was exposed to considerable trial. Never was there a time of greater religious ferment in the East, or a crisis which more shook men's belief in ancestral creeds. The absurd idolatry which had generally prevailed through Western Asia for two thousand years—a nature-worship which gave the sanction of religion to the gratification of men's lowest propensities—was shaken to its foundation; and everywhere men were striving after something higher, nobler, and truer than had satisfied previous generations for twenty centuries. The sudden revivification of Zoroastrianism, after it had been depressed and almost forgotten for five hundred years, was one result of this stir of men's minds. Another result was the rapid progress of Christianity, which in the course of the third century overspread large portions of the East, rooting itself with great firmness in Armenia, and obtaining a hold to some extent on Babylonia, Bactria, and perhaps even on India. Judaism, also, which had long had a footing in Mesopotamia, and which after the time of Hadrian may be regarded as having its headquarters at Babylon—Judaism itself, usually so immovable, at this time showed signs of life and change, taking something like a new form in the schools wherein was compiled the vast and strange work known as "the Babylonian Talmud."

Amid the strife and jar of so many conflicting systems, each having a root in the past, and each able to appeal with more or less of force to noble examples of virtue and constancy among its professors in the present, we cannot be surprised that in some minds the idea grew up that, while all the systems possessed some truth, no one of them was perfect or indeed much superior to its fellows. Eclectic or syncretic views are always congenial to some intellects; and in times when religious thought is deeply stirred, and antagonistic creeds are brought into direct collision, the amiable feeling of a desire for peace comes in to strengthen the inclination for reconciling opponents by means of a fusion, and producing harmony by a happy combination of discords. It was in Persia, and in the reign of Sapor, that one of the most remarkable of these well-meaning attempts at fusion and reconciliation that the whole of history can show was made, and with results which ought to be a lasting warning to the apostles of comprehension. A certain Mani (or Manes, as the ecclesiastical writers call him), born in Persia about A.D. 240, grew to manhood under Sapor, exposed to the various religious influences of which we have spoken. With a mind free from prejudice and open to conviction, he studied the various systems of belief which he found established in Western Asia—the Cabalism of the Babylonian Jews, the Dualism of the Magi, the mysterious doctrines of the Christians, and even the Buddhism of India. At first he inclined to Christianity, and is said to have been admitted to priest's orders and to have ministered to a congregation; but after a time he thought that he saw his way to the formation of a new creed, which should combine all that was best in the religious systems which he was acquainted with, and omit what was superfluous or objectionable. He adopted the Dualism of the Zoroastrians, the metempsychosis of India, the angelism and demonism of the Talmud, and the Trinitarianism of the Gospel of Christ. Christ himself he identified with Mithra, and gave Him his dwelling in the sun. He assumed to be the Paraclete promised by Christ, who should guide men into all truth, and claimed that his "Ertang," a sacred book illustrated by pictures of his own painting, should supersede the New Testament. Such pretensions were not likely to be tolerated by the Christian community; and Manes had not put them forward very long when he was expelled from the church and forced to carry his teaching elsewhere. Under these circumstances he is said to have addressed himself to Sapor, who was at first inclined to show him some favor; but when he found out what the doctrines of the new teacher actually were, his feelings underwent a change, and Manes, proscribed, or at any rate threatened with penalties, had to retire into a foreign country.

The Zoroastrian faith was thus maintained in its purity by the Persian monarch, who did not allow himself to be imposed upon by the specious eloquence of the new teacher, but ultimately rejected the strange amalgamation that was offered to his acceptance. It is scarcely to be regretted that he so determined. Though the morality of the Manichees was pure, and though their religion is regarded by some as a sort of Christianity, there were but few points in which it was an improvement on Zoroastrianism. Its Dualism was pronounced and decided; its Trinitarianism was questionable; its teaching with respect to Christ destroyed the doctrines of the incarnation and atonement; its "Ertang " was a poor substitute for Holy Scripture. Even its morality, being deeply penetrated with asceticism, was of a wrong type and infer or to that preached by Zoroaster. Had the creed of Manes been accepted by the Persian monarch, the progress of real Christianity in the East would, it is probable, have been impeded rather than forwarded—the general currency of the debased amalgam would have checked the introduction of the pure metal.

It must have been shortly after his rejection of the teaching of Manes that Sapor died, having reigned thirty-one years, from A.D. 240 to A.D. 271. He was undoubtedly one of the most remarkable princes of the Sassanian series. In military talent, indeed, he may not have equalled his father; for though he defeated Valerian, he had to confess himself inferior to Odenathus. But in general governmental ability he is among the foremost of the Neo-Persian monarchs, and may compare favorably with almost any prince of the series. He baffled Odenathus, when he was not able to defeat him, by placing himself behind walls, and by bringing into play those advantages which naturally belonged to the position of a monarch attacked in his own country. He maintained, if he did not permanently advance, the power of Persia in the west; while in the east it is probable that he considerably extended the bounds of his dominion. In the internal administration of his empire he united works of usefulness with the construction of memorial which had only a sentimental and aesthetic value. He was a liberal patron of art, and is thought not to have confined his patronage to the encouragement of native talent. On the subject of religion he did not suffer himself to be permanently led away by the enthusiasm of a young and bold freethinker. He decided to maintain the religious system that had descended to him from his ancestors, and turned a deaf ear to persuasions that would have led him to revolutionize the religious opinion of the East without placing it upon a satisfactory footing. The Orientals add to these commendable features of character, that he was a man of remarkable beauty, of great personal courage, and of a noble and princely liberality. According to them, "he only desired wealth that he might use it for good and great purposes."

## CHAPTER V

**Short Reign of Hormisdas I. His dealings with Manes. Accession of Varahran I. He puts Manes to Death. Persecutes the Manichaeans and the Christians. His Relations with Zenobia. He is threatened by Aurelian. His Death. Reign of Varahran II. His Tyrannical Conduct. His Conquest of Seistan, and War with India. His war with the Roman Emperors Cams and Diocletian. His Loss of Armenia. His Death. Short Reign of Varahran III.**

Τεθνηκότος τοῦ Σαπώρου, Ὁρμισδάτης, ὁ τούτου παῖς, τὴν βασιλείαν παραλαμβάνει.
AGATH. iv. p. 134, C.

The first and second kings of the Neo-Persian Empire were men of mark and renown. Their successors for several generations were, comparatively speaking, feeble and insignificant. The first burst of vigor and freshness which commonly attends the advent to power of a new race in the East, or the recovery of its former position by an old one, had passed away, and was succeeded, as so often happens, by reaction and exhaustion, the monarchs becoming luxurious and inert, while the people willingly acquiesced in a policy of which the principle was "Rest and be thankful." It helped to keep matters in this quiescent state, that the kings who ruled during this period had, in almost every instance, short reigns, four monarchs coming to the throne and dying within the space of a little more than twenty-one years. The first of these four was Hormisdates, Hormisdas, or Hormuz, the son of Sapor, who succeeded his father in A.D. 271. His reign lasted no more than a year and ten days, and was distinguished by only a single event of any importance. Mani, who had fled from Sapor, ventured to return to Persia on the accession of his son, and was received with respect and favor. Whether Hormisdas was inclined to accept his religious teaching or no, we are not told; but at any rate he treated him kindly, allowed him to propagate his doctrines, and even assigned him as his residence a castle named Arabion. From this place Mani proceeded to spread his views among the Christians of Mesopotamia, and in a short time succeeded in founding the sect which, under the name of Manichaeans or Manichaes, gave so much trouble to the Church for several centuries. Hormisdas, who, according to some founded the city of Ram-Hormuz in Eastern Persia, died in A.D.272, and was succeeded by his son or brother, Vararanes or Varahran. He left no inscriptions, and it is doubted whether we possess any of his coins.

Varahran I., whose reign lasted three years only, from A.D. 272 to 275, is declared by the native historians to have been a mild and amiable prince; but the little that is positively known of him does not bear out this testimony. It seems certain that he put Mani to death, and probable that he enticed him to leave the shelter of his castle by artifice, thus showing himself not only harsh but treacherous towards the unfortunate heresiarch. If it be true that he caused him to be flayed alive, we can scarcely exonerate him from the charge of actual cruelty, unless indeed we regard the punishment as an ordinary mode of execution in Persia. Perhaps, however, in this case, as in other similar ones, there is no sufficient evidence that the process of flaying took place until the culprit was dead, the real object of the excoriation being, not the infliction of pain, but the preservation of a memorial which could be used as a warning and a terror to others. The skin of Mani, stuffed with straw, was no doubt suspended for some time after his execution over one of the gates of the great city of Shahpur; and it is possible that this fact may have been the sole ground of the belief (which, it is to be remembered, was not universal) that he actually suffered death by flaying.

The death of the leader was followed by the persecution of his disciples. Mani had organized a hierarchy, consisting of twelve apostles, seventy-two bishops, and a numerous priesthood; and his sect was widely established at the time of his execution. Varahran handed over these unfortunates, or at any rate such of them as he was able to seize, to the tender mercies of the Magians, who put to death great numbers of Manichseans. Many Christians at the same time perished, either because they were confounded with the followers of Mani, or because the spirit of persecution, once let loose, could not be restrained, but passed on from victims of one class to those of another, the Magian priesthood seizing the opportunity of devoting all heretics to a common destruction.

Thus unhappy in his domestic administration, Varahran was not much more fortunate in his wars. Zenobia, the queen of the East, held for some time to the policy of her illustrious husband, maintaining a position inimical alike to Rome and Persia from the death of Odenathus in A.D. 267 to Aurelian's expedition against her in A.D. 272. When, however, in this year, Aurelian marched to attack her with the full forces of the empire, she recognized the necessity of calling to her aid other troops besides her own. It was at this time that she made overtures to the Persians, which were favorably received; and, in the year A.D. 273, Persian troops are mentioned among those with whom Aurelian contended in the vicinity of Palmyra. But the succors sent were inconsiderable, and were easily overpowered by the arts or arms of the emperor. The young king had not the courage to throw himself boldly into the war. He allowed Zenobia to be defeated and reduced to extremities without making anything like an earnest or determined effort to save her. He continued her ally, indeed, to the end, and probably offered her an asylum at his court, if she were compelled to quit her capital; but even this poor boon he was prevented from conferring by the capture of the unfortunate princess just as she reached the banks of the Euphrates.

In the aid which he lent Zenobia, Varahran, while he had done too little to affect in any degree the issue of the struggle, had done quite enough to provoke Rome and draw down upon him the vengeance of the Empire, It seems that he quite realized the position in which circumstances had placed him. Feeling that he had thrown out a challenge to Rome, and yet shrinking from the impending conflict, he sent an embassy to the conqueror, deprecating his anger and seeking to propitiate him by rare and costly gifts. Among these were a purple robe from Cashmere, or some other remote province of India, of so brilliant a hue that the ordinary purple of the imperial robes could not compare with it, and a chariot like to those in which the Persian monarch was himself wont to be carried. Aurelian accepted these gifts; and it would seem to follow that he condoned Varahran's conduct, and granted him terms of peace. Hence, in the triumph which Aurelian celebrated at Rome in the year A.D. 274, no Persian captives appeared in the procession, but Persian envoys were exhibited instead, who bore with them the presents wherewith their master had appeased the anger of the emperor.

A full year, however, had not elapsed from the time of the triumph when the master of the Roman world thought fit to change his policy, and, suddenly declaring war against the Persians, commenced his march towards the East. We are not told that he discovered, or even sought to discover, any fresh ground of complaint. His talents were best suited for employment in the field, and he regarded it as expedient to "exercise the restless temper of the legions in some foreign war." Thus it was desirable to find or make an enemy; and the Persians presented themselves as the foe which could be attacked most conveniently. There was no doubt a general desire to efface the memory of Valerian's disaster by some considerable success; and war with Persia was therefore likely to be popular at once with the Senate, with the army, and with the mixed multitude which was dignified with the title of "the Roman people."

Aurelian, therefore, set out for Persia at the head of a numerous, but still a manageable, force. He proceeded through Illyricum and Macedonia towards Byzantium, and had almost reached the straits, when a conspiracy, fomented by one of his secretaries, cut short his career, and saved the Persian empire from invasion. Aurelian was murdered in the spring of A.D. 275, at Coenophrurium, a small station between Heraclea (Perinthus) and Byzantium. The adversary with whom he had hoped to contend, Varahran, cannot have survived him long, since he died (of disease as it would seem) in the course of the year, leaving his crown to a young son who bore the same name with himself, and is known in history as Varahran the Second.

PLATE XVI

Varahran II. is said to have ruled at first tyrannically, and to have greatly disgusted all his principal nobles, who went so far as to form a conspiracy against him, and intended to put him to death. The chief of the Magians, however, interposed, and, having effectually alarmed the king, brought him to acknowledge himself wrong and to promise an entire change of conduct. The nobles upon this returned to their allegiance; and Varahran, during the remainder of his reign, is said to have been distinguished for wisdom and moderation, and to have rendered himself popular with every class of his subjects.

It appears that this prince was not without military ambition. He engaged in a war with the Segestani (or Sacastani), the inhabitants of Segestan or Seistan, a people of Scythic origin, and after a time reduced them to subjection [PLATE XVII]. He then became involved in a quarrel with some of the natives of Afghanistan, who were at this time regarded as "Indians." A long and desultory contest followed without definite result, which was not concluded by the year A.D. 283, when he found himself suddenly engaged in hostilities on the opposite side of the empire.

VARAHRAN II.—RECEIVING THE SUBMISSION OF THE SEGESTANI.

PLATE XVII

Rome, in the latter part of the third century, had experienced one of those reactions which mark her later history, and which alone enabled her to complete her predestined term of twelve centuries. Between the years A.D. 274 and 282, under Aurelian, Tacitus, Probus, and Carus, she showed herself once more very decidedly the first military power in the world, drove back the barbarians on all sides, and even ventured to indulge in an aggressive policy. Aurelian, as we have seen, was on the point of invading Persia when a domestic conspiracy brought his reign and life to an end. Tacitus, his successor, scarcely obtained such a firm hold upon the throne as to feel that he could with any prudence provoke a war. But Probus, the next emperor, revived the project of a Persian expedition, and would probably have led the Roman armies into Mesopotamia, had not his career been cut short by the revolt of the legions in Illyria (A.D. 282). Carus, who had been his praetorian prefect, and who became emperor at his death, adhered steadily to his policy. It was the first act of his reign to march the forces of the empire to the extreme east, and to commence in earnest the war which had so long been threatened. Led by the Emperor in person, the legions once more crossed the Euphrates.

Mesopotamia was rapidly overrun, since the Persians (we are told) were at variance among themselves, and a civil war was raging. The bulk of their forces, moreover, were engaged on the opposite side of the empire in a struggle with the Indians, probably those of Afghanistan. Under these circumstances, no effectual resistance was possible; and, if we may believe the Roman writers, not only was the Roman province of Mesopotamia recovered, but the entire tract between the rivers as far south as the latitude of Bagdad was ravaged, and even the two great cities of Seleucia and Ctesiphon were taken without the slightest difficulty. Persia Proper seemed to lie open to the invader, and Carus was preparing to penetrate still further to the east, when again an opportune death checked the progress of the Roman arms, and perhaps saved the Persian monarchy from destruction. Carus had announced his intention of continuing his march; some discontent had shown itself; and an oracle had been quoted which declared that a Roman emperor would never proceed victoriously beyond Ctesiphon, Carus was not convinced, but he fell sick, and his projects were delayed; he was still in his camp near Ctesiphon, when a terrible thunderstorm broke over the ground occupied by the Roman army. A weird darkness was spread around, amid which flash followed flash at brief intervals, and peal upon peal terrified the superstitious soldiery. Suddenly, after the most violent clap of all, the cry arose that the Emperor was dead. Some said that his tent had been struck by lightning, and that his death was owing to this cause; others believed that he had simply happened to succumb to his malady at the exact moment of the last thunder-clap; a third theory was that his attendants had taken advantage of the general confusion to assassinate him, and that he merely added another to the long list of Roman emperors murdered by those who hoped to profit by their removal. It is not likely that the problem of what really caused the death of Carus will ever be solved. That he died very late in A.D. 283, or within the first fortnight of A.D. 284, is certain; and it is no less certain that his death was most fortunate for Persia, since it brought the war to an end when it had reached a point at which any further reverses would have been disastrous, and gave the Persians a breathing-space during which they might, at least partially, recover from their prostration.

Upon the death of Carus, the Romans at once determined on retreat. It was generally believed that the imperial tent had been struck by lightning; and it was concluded that the decision of the gods against the further advance of the invading army had been thereby unmistakably declared. The army considered that it had done enough, and was anxious to return home; the feeble successor of Carus, his son Numerian, if he possessed the will, was at any rate without the power to resist the wishes of the troops; and the result was that the legions quitted the East without further fighting, and without securing, by the conclusion of formal terms of peace, any permanent advantage from their victories.

A pause of two years now occurred, during which Varahran had the opportunity of strengthening his position while Rome was occupied by civil wars and distracted between the claims of pretenders. No great use seems, however, to have been made of this interval. When, in A.D. 286, the celebrated Diocletian determined to resume the war with Persia, and, embracing the cause of Tiridates, son of Chosroes, directed his efforts to the establishment of that prince, as a Roman feudatory, on his father's throne. Varahran found himself once more overmatched, and could offer no effectual resistance. Armenia had now been a province of Persia for the space of twenty-six (or perhaps forty-six) years; but it had in no degree been conciliated or united with the rest of the empire. The people had been distrusted and oppressed; the nobles had been deprived of employment; a heavy tribute had been laid on the land; and a religious revolution had been violently effected. It is not surprising that when Tiridates, supported by a Roman corps d'armee, appeared upon the frontiers, the whole population received him with transports of loyalty and joy. All the nobles flocked to his standard, and at once acknowledged him for their king. The people everywhere welcomed him with acclamations. A native prince of the Arsacid dynasty united the suffrages of all; and the nation threw itself with enthusiastic zeal into a struggle which was viewed as a war of independence. It was forgotten that Tiridates was in fact only a puppet in the hand of the Roman emperor, and that, whatever the result of the contest, Armenia would remain at its close, as she had been at its commencement, a dependant upon a foreign power.

The success of Tiridates at the first was such as might have been expected from the forces arrayed in his favor. He defeated two Persian armies in the open field, drove out the garrisons which held the more important of the fortified towns, and became undisputed master of Armenia. He even crossed the border which separated Armenia from Persia, and gained signal victories on admitted Persian ground. According to the native writers, his personal exploits were extraordinary; he defeated singly a corps of giants, and routed on foot a large detachment mounted on elephants! The narrative is here, no doubt, tinged with exaggeration; but the general result is correctly stated. Tiridates, within a year of his invasion, was complete master of the entire Armenian highland, and was in a position to carry his arms beyond his own frontiers.

Such seems to have been the position of things, when Varahran II. suddenly died, after a reign of seventeen years,52 A.D. 292. He is generally said to have left behind him two sons, Varahran and Narsehi, or Narses, of whom the elder, Varahran, was proclaimed king. This prince was of an amiable temper, but apparently of a weakly constitution. He was with difficulty persuaded to accept the throne, and anticipated from the first an early demise. No events are assigned to his short reign, which (according to the best authorities) did not exceed the length of four months. It is evident that he must have been powerless to offer any effectual opposition to Tiridates, whose forces continued to ravage, year after year, the north-western provinces of the Persian empire. Had Tiridates been a prince of real military talent, it could scarcely have been difficult for him to obtain still greater advantages. But he was content with annual raids, which left the substantial power of Persia untouched. He allowed the occasion of the throne's being occupied by a weak and invalid prince to slip by. The consequences of this negligence will appear in the next chapter. Persia, permitted to escape serious attack in her time of weakness, was able shortly to take the offensive and to make the Armenian prince regret his indolence or want of ambition. The son of Chosroes became a second time a fugitive; and once more the Romans were called in to settle the affairs of the East. We have now to trace the circumstances of this struggle, and to show how Rome under able leaders succeeded in revenging the defeat and captivity of Valerian, and in inflicting, in her turn, a grievous humiliation upon her adversary.

## CHAPTER VI

*Civil War of Narses and his Brother Hormisdas. Narses victorious. He attacks and expels Tiridates. War declared against him by Diocletian. First Campaign of Galerius, A.D. 297. Second Campaign, A.D. 298. Defeat suffered by Narses. Negotiations. Conditions of Peace. Abdication and Death of Narses.*

It appears that on the death of Varahran III., probably without issue, there was a contention for the crown between two brothers, Narses and Hormisdas. We are not informed which of them was the elder, nor on what grounds they respectively rested their claims; but it seems that Narses was from the first preferred by the Persians, and that his rival relied mainly for success on the arms of foreign barbarians. Worsted in encounters wherein none but Persians fought on either side, Hormisdas summoned to his aid the hordes of the north—Gelli from the shores of the Caspian, Scyths from the Oxus or the regions beyond, and Russians, now first mentioned by a classical writer. But the perilous attempt to settle a domestic struggle by the swords of foreigners was not destined on this occasion to prosper. Hormisdas failed in his endeavor to obtain the throne; and, as we hear no more of him, we may regard it as probable that he was defeated and slain. At any rate Narses was, within a year or two of his accession, so firmly settled in his kingdom that he was able to turn his thoughts to the external affairs of the empire, and to engage in a great war. All danger from internal disorder must have been pretty certainly removed before Narses could venture to affront, as he did, the strongest of existing military powers. [PLATE XVIII.]

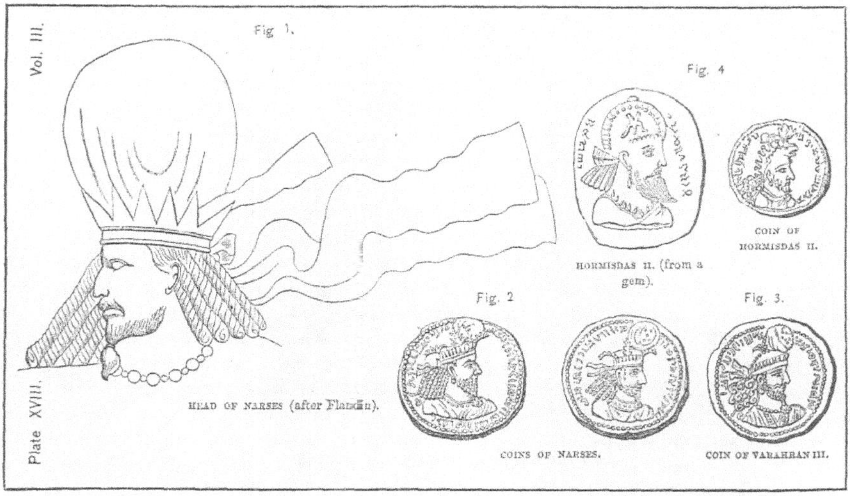

PLATE XVIII

Narses ascended the throne in A.D. 292 or 293. It was at least as early as A.D. 296 that he challenged Rome to an encounter by attacking in force the vassal monarch whom her arms had established in Armenia. Tiridates had, it is evident, done much to provoke the attack by his constant raids into Persian territory, which were sometimes carried even to the south of Ctesiphon. He was probably surprised by the sudden march and vigorous assault of an enemy whom he had learned to despise; and, feeling himself unable to organize an effectual resistance, he had recourse to flight, gave up Armenia to the Persians, and for a second time placed himself under the protection of the Roman emperor. The monarch who held this proud position was still Diocletian, the greatest emperor that had occupied the Roman throne since Trajan, and the prince to whom Tiridates was indebted for his restoration to his kingdom. It was impossible that Diocletian should submit to the affront put upon him without an earnest effort to avenge it. His own power rested, in a great measure, on his military prestige; and the unpunished insolence of a foreign king would have seriously endangered an authority not very firmly established. The position of Diocletian compelled him to declare war against Narses in the year A.D. 296, and to address himself to a struggle of which he is not likely to have misconceived the importance. It might have been expected that he would have undertaken the conduct of the war in person; but the internal condition of the empire was far from satisfactory, and the chief of the State seems to have felt that he could not conveniently quit his dominions to engage in war beyond his borders. He therefore committed the task of reinstating Tiridates and punishing Narses to his favorite and son-in-law, Galerius, while he himself took up a position within the limits of the empire, which at once enabled him to overawe his domestic adversaries and to support and countenance his lieutenant.

The first attempts of Galerius were unfortunate. Summoned suddenly from the Danube to the Euphrates, and placed at the head of an army composed chiefly of the levies of Asia, ill-disciplined, and unacquainted with their commander, he had to meet an adversary of whom he knew little or nothing, in a region the character of which was adverse to his own troops and favorable to those of the enemy. Narses had invaded the Roman province of Mesopotamia, had penetrated to the Khabour, and was threatening to cross the Euphrates into Syria. Galerius had no choice but to encounter him on the ground which he had chosen. Now, though Western Mesopotamia is ill-described as a smooth and barren surface of sandy desert, without a hillock, without a tree, and without a spring of fresh water, it is undoubtedly an open country, possessing numerous plains, where, in a battle, the advantage of numbers is likely to be felt, and where there is abundant room for the evolutions of cavalry. The Persians, like their predecessors the Parthians, were especially strong in horse; and the host which Narses had brought into the field greatly outnumbered the troops which Diocletian had placed at the disposal of Galerius. Yet Galerius took the offensive. Fighting under the eye of a somewhat stern master, he was scarcely free to choose his plan of campaign. Diocletian expected him to drive the Persians from Mesopotamia, and he was therefore bound to make the attempt. He accordingly sought out his adversary in this region, and engaged him in three great battles. The first and second appear to have been indecisive; but in the third the Roman general suffered a complete defeat. The catastrophe of Crassus was repeated almost upon the same battle-field, and probably almost by the same means. But, personally, Galerius was more fortunate than his predecessor. He escaped from the carnage, and, recrossing the Euphrates, rejoined his father-in-law in Syria. A conjecture, not altogether destitute of probability, makes Tiridates share both the calamity and the good fortune of the Roman Caesar. Like Galerius, he escaped from the battle-field, and reached the banks of the Euphrates. But his horse, which had received a wound, could not be trusted to pass the river. In this emergency the Armenian prince dismounted, and, armed as he was, plunged into the stream. The river was both wide and deep; the current was rapid; but the hardy adventurer, inured to danger and accustomed to every athletic exercise, swam across and reached the opposite bank in safety.

Thus, while the rank and file perished ignominiously, the two personages of most importance on the Roman side were saved. Galerius hastened towards Antioch, to rejoin his colleague and sovereign. The latter came out to meet him, but, instead of congratulating him on his escape, assumed the air of an offended master, and, declining to speak to him or to stop his chariot, forced the Caesar to follow him on foot for nearly a mile before he would condescend to receive his explanations and apologies for defeat. The disgrace was keenly felt, and was ultimately revenged upon the prince who had contrived it. But, at the time, its main effect doubtless was to awake in the young Caesar the strongest desire of retrieving his honor, and wiping out the memory of his great reverse by a yet more signal victory. Galerius did not cease through the winter of A.D. 297 to importune his father-in-law for an opportunity of redeeming the past and recovering his lost laurels.

The emperor, having sufficiently indulged his resentment, acceded to the wishes of his favorite. Galerius was continued in his command. A new army was collected during the winter, to replace that which had been lost; and the greatest care was taken that its material should be of good quality, and that it should be employed where it had the best chance of success. The veterans of Illyria and Moesia constituted the flower of the force now enrolled; and it was further strengthened by the addition of a body of Gothic auxiliaries. It was determined, moreover, that the attack should this time be made on the side of Armenia, where it was felt that the Romans would have the double advantage of a friendly country, and of one far more favorable for the movements of infantry than for those of an army whose strength lay in its horse. The number of the troops employed was still small. Galerius entered Armenia at the head of only 25,000 men; but they were a picked force, and they might be augmented, almost to any extent, by the national militia of the Armenians. He was now, moreover, as cautious as he had previously been rash; he advanced slowly, feeling his way; he even personally made reconnaissances, accompanied by only one or two horsemen, and, under the shelter of a flag of truce, explored the position of his adversary. Narses found himself overmatched alike in art and in force. He allowed himself to be surprised in his camp by his active enemy, and suffered a defeat by which he more than lost all the fruits of his former victory. Most of his army was destroyed; he himself received a wound, and with difficulty escaped by a hasty flight. Galerius pursued, and, though he did not succeed in taking the monarch himself, made prize of his wives, his sisters, and a number of his children, besides capturing his military chest. He also took many of the most illustrious Persians prisoners. How far he followed his flying adversary is uncertain; but it is scarcely probable that he proceeded much southward of the Armenian frontier. He had to reinstate Tiridates in his dominions, to recover Eastern Mesopotamia, and to lay his laurels at the feet of his colleague and master. It seems probable that having driven Narses from Armenia, and left Tiridates there to administer the government, he hastened to rejoin Diocletian before attempting any further conquests.

The Persian monarch, on his side, having recovered from his wound, which could have been but slight, set himself to collect another army, but at the same time sent an ambassador to to the camp of Galerius, requesting to know the terms on which Rome would consent to make peace. A writer of good authority has left us an account of the interview which followed between the envoy of the Persian monarch and the victorious Roman. Apharban (so was the envoy named) opened the negotiations with the following speech:

"The whole human race knows," he said, "that the Roman and Persian kingdoms resemble two great luminaries, and that, like a man's two eyes, they ought mutually to adorn and illustrate each other, and not in the extremity of their wrath to seek rather each other's destruction. So to act is not to act manfully, but is indicative rather of levity and weakness; for it is to suppose that our inferiors can never be of any service to us, and that therefore we had bettor get rid of them. Narses, moreover, ought not to be accounted a weaker prince than other Persian kings; thou hast indeed conquered him, but then thou surpassest all other monarchs; and thus Narses has of course been worsted by thee, though he is no whit inferior in merit to the best of his ancestors. The orders which my master has given me are to entrust all the rights of Persia to the clemency of Rome; and I therefore do not even bring with me any conditions of peace, since it is for the emperor to determine everything. I have only to pray, on my master's behalf, for the restoration of his wives and male children; if he receives them at your hands, he will be forever beholden to you, and will be better pleased than if he recovered them by force of arms. Even now my master cannot sufficiently thank you for the kind treatment which he hears you have vouchsafed them, in that you have offered them no insult, but have behaved towards them as though on the point of giving them back to their kith and kin. He sees herein that you bear in mind the changes of fortune and the instability of all human affairs."

At this point Galerius, who had listened with impatience to the long harangue, burst in with a movement of anger that shook his whole frame—"What? Do the Persians dare to remind us of the vicissitudes of fortune, as though we could forget how they behave when victory inclines to them? Is it not their wont to push their advantage to the uttermost and press as heavily as may be on the unfortunate? How charmingly they showed the moderation that becomes a victor in Valerian's time! They vanquished him by fraud; they kept him a prisoner to advanced old age; they let him die in dishonor; and then when he was dead they stripped off his skin, and with diabolical ingenuity made of a perishable human body an imperishable monument of our shame. Verily, if we follow this envoy's advice, and look to the changes of human affairs, we shall not be moved to clemency, but to anger, when we consider the past conduct of the Persians. If pity be shown them, if their requests be granted, it will not be for what they have urged, but because it is a principle of action with us—a principle handed down to us from our ancestors—to spare the humble and chastise the proud."

Apharban, therefore, was dismissed with no definite answer to his question, what terms of peace Rome would require; but he was told to assure his master that Rome's clemency equalled her valor, and that it would not be long before he would receive a Roman envoy authorized to signify the Imperial pleasure, and to conclude a treaty with him.

Having held this interview with Apharban, Galerius hastened to meet and consult his colleague. Diocletian had remained in Syria, at the head of an army of observation, while Galerius penetrated into Armenia and engaged the forces of Persia. When he heard of his son-in-law's great victory he crossed the Euphrates, and advancing through Western Mesopotamia, from which the Persians probably retired, took up his residence at Nisibis, now the chief town of these parts. It is perhaps true that his object was "to moderate, by his presence and counsels, the pride of Galarius." That prince was bold to rashness, and nourished an excessive ambition. He is said to have at this time entertained a design of grasping at the conquest of the East, and to have even proposed to himself to reduce the Persian Empire into the form of a Roman province. But the views of Diocletian were humbler and more prudent. He held to the opinion of Augustus and Hadrian, that Rome did not need any enlargement of her territory, and that the absorption of the East was especially undesirable. When he and his son-in-law met and interchanged ideas at Nisibis, the views of the elder ruler naturally prevailed; and it was resolved to offer to the Persians tolerable terms of peace. A civilian of importance, Sicorius Probus, was selected for the delicate office of envoy, and was sent, with a train of attendants, into Media, where Narses had fixed his headquarters. We are told that the Persian monarch received him with all honor, but, under pretence of allowing him to rest and refresh himself after his long journey, deferred his audience from day to day; while he employed the time thus gained in collecting from various quarters such a number of detachments and garrisons as might constitute a respectable army. He had no intention of renewing the war, but he knew the weight which military preparation ever lends to the representations of diplomacy. Accordingly it was not until he had brought under the notice of Sicorius a force of no inconsiderable size that he at last admitted him to an interview. The Roman ambassador was introduced into an inner chamber of the royal palace in Media, where he found only the king and three others—Apharban, the envoy sent to Galerius, Archapetes, the captain of the guard, and Barsaborsus, the governor of a province on the Armenian frontier. He was asked to unfold the particulars of his message, and say what were the terms on which Rome would make peace. Sicorius complied. The emperors, he said, required five things:—(i.) The cession to Rome of five provinces beyond the river Tigris, which are given by one writer as Intilene, Sophene, Arzanene, Carduene, and Zabdicene; by another as Arzanene, Moxoene, Zabdicene, Rehimene, and Corduene; (ii.) the recognition of the Tigris, as the general boundary between the two empires; (iii.) the extension of Armenia to the fortress of Zintha, in Media; (iv.) the relinquishment by Persia to Rome of her protectorate over Iberia, including the right of giving investiture to the Iberian kings; and (v.) the recognition of Nisibis as the place at which alone commercial dealings could take place between the two nations.

It would seem that the Persians were surprised at the moderation of these demands. Their exact value and force will require some discussion; but at any rate it is clear that, under the circumstances, they were not felt to be excessive. Narses did not dispute any of them except the last: and it seems to have been rather because he did not wish it to be said that he had yielded everything, than because the condition was really very onerous, that he made objection in this instance. Sicorius was fortunately at liberty to yield the point. He at once withdrew the fifth article of the treaty, and, the other four being accepted, a formal peace was concluded between the two nations.

To understand the real character of the peace now made, and to appreciate properly the relations thereby established between Rome and Persia, it will be necessary to examine at some length the several conditions of the treaty, and to see exactly what was imported by each of them. There is scarcely one out of the whole number that carries its meaning plainly upon its face; and on the more important very various interpretations have been put, so that a discussion and settlement of some rather intricate points is here necessary.

(i.) There is a considerable difference of opinion as to the five provinces ceded to Rome by the first article of the treaty, as to their position and extent, and consequently as to their importance. By some they are put on the right, by others on the left, bank of the Tigris; while of those who assign them this latter position some place them in a cluster about the sources of the river, while others extend them very much further to the southward. Of the five provinces three only can be certainly named, since the authorities differ as to the two others. These three are Arzanene, Cordyene, and Zabdicene, which occur in that order in Patricius. If we can determine the position of these three, that of the others will follow, at least within certain limits.

Now Arzanene was certainly on the left bank of the Tigris. It adjoined Armenia, and is reasonably identified with the modern district of Kherzan, which lies between Lake Van and the Tigris, to the west of the Bitlis river. All the notices of Arzanene suit this locality; and the name "Kherzan" may be regarded as representing the ancient appellation.

Zabdicene was a little south and a little east of this position. It was the tract about a town known as Bezabda (perhaps a corruption of Beit-Zaoda), which had been anciently called Phoenica. This town is almost certainly represented by the modern Fynyk, on the left bank of the Tigris, a little above Jezireh. The province whereof it was the capital may perhaps have adjoined Arzanene, reaching as far north as the Bitlis river.

If these two tracts are rightly placed, Cordyene must also be sought on the left bank of the Tigris. The word is no doubt the ancient representative of the modern Kurdistan, and means a country in which Kurds dwelt. Now Kurds seem to have been at one time the chief inhabitants of the Mons Masius, the modern Jebel Kara j ah Dagh and Jebel Tur, which was thence called Oordyene, Gordyene, or the Gordisean mountain chain. But there was another and a more important Cordyene on the opposite side of the river. The tract to this day known as Kurdistan, the high mountain region south and south-east of Lake Van between Persia and Mesopotamia, was in the possession of Kurds from before the time of Xenophon, and was known as the country of the Carduchi, as Cardyene, and as Cordyene. This tract, which was contiguous to Arzanene and Zabdicene, if we have rightly placed those regions, must almost certainly have been the Cordyene of the treaty, which, if it corresponded at all nearly in extent with the modern Kurdistan, must have been by far the largest and most important of the five provinces.

The two remaining tracts, whatever their names, must undoubtedly have lain on the same side of the Tigris with these three. As they are otherwise unknown to us (for Sophene, which had long been Roman, cannot have been one of them), it is impossible that they should have been of much importance. No doubt they helped to round off the Roman dominion in this quarter; but the great value of the entire cession lay in the acquisition of the large and fruitful province of Cordyene, inhabited by a brave and hardy population, and afterwards the seat of fifteen fortresses which brought the Roman dominion to the very edge of Adiabene, made them masters of the passes into Media, and laid the whole of Southern Mesopotamia open to their incursions. It is probable that the hold of Persia on the territory had never been strong; and in relinquishing it she may have imagined that she gave up no very great advantage; but in the hands of Rome Kurdistan became a standing menace to the Persian power, and we shall find that on the first opportunity the false step now taken was retrieved, Cordyene with its adjoining districts was pertinaciously demanded of the Romans, was grudgingly surrendered, and was then firmly re-attached to the Sassanian dominions.

(ii.) The Tigris is said by Patricius and Festus to have been made the boundary of the two empires. Gibbon here boldly substitutes the Western Khabour and maintains that "the Roman frontier traversed, but never followed, the course of the Tigris." He appears not to be able to understand how the Tigris could be the frontier, when five provinces across the Tigris were Roman. But the intention of the article probably was, first, to mark the complete cession to Rome of Eastern as well as Western Mesopotamia, and, secondly, to establish the Tigris as the line separating the empires below the point down to which the Romans held both banks. Cordyene may not have touch the Tigris at all, or may have touched it only about the 37th parallel. From this point southwards, as far as Mosul, or Nimrud, or possibly Kileh Sherghat, the Tigris was probably now recognized as the dividing line between the empires. By the letter of the treaty the whole Euphrates valley might indeed have been claimed by Rome; but practically she did not push her occupation of Mesopotamia below Circesium. The real frontier from this point was the Mesopotamian desert, which extends from Kerkesiyeh to Nimrud, a distance of 150 miles. Above this it was the Tigris, as far probably as Feshapoor; after which it followed the line, whatever it was, which divided Oordyene from Assyria and Media.

(iii.) The extension of Armenia to the fortress of Zintha, in Media, seems to have imported much more than would at first sight appear from the words. Gibbon interprets it as implying the cession of all Media Atropatene, which certainly appears a little later to be in the possession of the Armenian monarch, Tiridates. A large addition to the Armenian territory out of the Median is doubtless intended; but it is quite impossible to determine definitely the extent or exact character of the cession.

(iv.) The fourth article of the treaty is sufficiently intelligible. So long as Armenia had been a fief of the Persian empire, it naturally belonged to Persia to exercise influence over the neighboring Iberia, which corresponded closely to the modern Georgia, intervening between Armenia and the Caucasus. Now, when Armenia had become a dependency of Rome, the protectorate hitherto exercised by the Sassanian princes passed naturally to the Caesars; and with the protectorate was bound up the right of granting investiture to the kingdom, whereby the protecting power was secured against the establishment on the throne of an unfriendly person. Iberia was not herself a state of much strength; but her power of opening or shutting the passes of the Caucasus gave her considerable importance, since by the admission of the Tatar hordes, which were always ready to pour in from the plains of the North, she could suddenly change the whole face of affairs in North-Western Asia, and inflict a terrible revenge on any enemy that had provoked her. It is true that she might also bring suffering on her friends, or even on herself, for the hordes, once admitted, were apt to make little distinction between friend and foe; but prudential considerations did not always prevail over the promptings of passion, and there had been occasions when, in spite of them, the gates had been thrown open and the barbarians invited to enter. It was well for Rome to have it in her power to check this peril. Her own strength and the tranquillity of her eastern provinces were confirmed and secured by the right which she (practically) obtained of nominating the Iberian monarchs.

(v.) The fifth article of the treaty, having been rejected by Narses and then withdrawn by Sicorius, need not detain us long. By limiting the commercial intercourse of the two nations to a single city, and that a city within their own dominions, the Romans would have obtained enormous commercial advantages. While their own merchants remained quietly at home, the foreign merchants would have had the trouble and expense of bringing their commodities to market a distance of sixty miles from the Persian frontier and of above a hundred from any considerable town; they would of course have been liable to market dues, which would have fallen wholly into Roman hands; and they would further have been chargeable with any duty, protective or even prohibitive, which Rome chose to impose. It is not surprising that Narses here made a stand, and insisted on commerce being left to flow in the broader channels which it had formed for itself in the course of ages.

Rome thus terminated her first period of struggle with the newly revived monarchy of Persia by a great victory and a great diplomatic success. If Narses regarded the terms—and by his conduct he would seem to have done so—as moderate under the circumstances, our conclusion must be that the disaster which he had suffered was extreme, and that he knew the strength of Persia to be, for the time, exhausted. Forced to relinquish his suzerainty over Armenia and Iberia, he saw those countries not merely wrested from himself, but placed under the protectorate, and so made to minister to the strength, of his rival. Nor was this all. Rome had gradually been advancing across Mesopotamia and working her way from the Euphrates to the Tigris. Narses had to acknowledge, in so many words, that the Tigris, and not the Euphrates, was to be regarded as her true boundary, and that nothing consequently was to be considered as Persian beyond the more eastern of the two rivers. Even this concession was not the last or the worst. Narses had finally to submit to see his empire dismembered, a portion of Media attached to Armenia, and five provinces, never hitherto in dispute, torn from Persia and added to the dominion of Rome. He had to allow Rome to establish herself in force on the left bank of the Tigris, and so to lay open to her assaults a great portion of his northern besides all his western frontier. He had to see her brought to the very edge of the Iranic plateau, and within a fortnight's march of Persia Proper. The ambition to rival his ancestor Sapor, if really entertained, was severely punished: and the defeated prince must have felt that he had been most ill-advised in making the venture.

Narses did not long continue on the throne after the conclusion of this disgraceful, though, it may be, necessary, treaty. It was made in A.D. 297. He abdicated in A.D. 301. It may have been disgust at his ill-success, it may have been mere weariness of absolute power, which caused him to descend from his high position and retire into private life. He was so fortunate as to have a son of full age in whose favor he could resign, so that there was no difficulty about the succession. His ministers seem to have thought it necessary to offer some opposition to his project; but their resistance was feeble, perhaps because they hoped that a young prince would be more entirely guided by their counsels. Narses was allowed to complete his act of self-renunciation, and, after crowning his son Hormisdas with his own hand, to spend the remainder of his days in retirement. According to the native writers, his main object was to contemplate death and prepare himself for it. In his youth he had evinced some levity of character, and had been noted for his devotion to games and to the chase; in his middle age he laid aside these pursuits, and, applying himself actively to business, was a good administrator, as well as a brave soldier. But at last it seemed to him that the only life worth living was the contemplative, and that the happiness of the hunter and the statesman must yield to that of the philosopher. It is doubtful how long he survived his resignation of the throne, but tolerably certain that he did not outlive his son and successor, who reigned less than eight years.

## CHAPTER VII

*Reign of Hormisdas II. His Disposition. General Character of his Reign. His Taste for Building. His new Court of Justice. His Marriage with a Princess of Cabul. Story of his Son Hormisdas. Death of Hormisdas II., and Imprisonment of his Son Hormisdas. Interregnum. Crown assigned to Sapor II. before his Birth. Long Reign of Sapor. First Period of his Reign, from A.D. 309 to A.D. 337. Persia plundered by the Arabs and the Turks. Victories of Sapor over the Arabs. Persecution of the Christians. Escape of Hormisdas. Feelings and Conduct of Sapor.*

Hormisdas II., who became king on the abdication of his father, Narses, had, like his father, a short reign. He ascended the throne A.D. 301; he died A.D. 309, not quite eight years later. To this period historians assign scarcely any events. The personal appearance of Hormisdas, if we may judge by a gem, was pleasing; [PLATE XVIII., Fig. 4.] he is said, however, to have been of a harsh temper by nature, but to have controlled his evil inclinations after he became king, and in fact to have then neglected nothing that could contribute to the welfare of his subjects. He engaged in no wars; and his reign was thus one of those quiet and uneventful intervals which, furnishing no materials for history, indicate thereby the happiness of a nation. We are told that he had a strong taste for building, and could never see a crumbling edifice without instantly setting to work to restore it. Ruined towns and villages, so common throughout the East in all ages, ceased to be seen in Persia while he filled the throne. An army of masons always followed him in his frequent journeys throughout his empire, and repaired dilapidated homesteads and cottages with as much care and diligence as edifices of a public character. According to some writers he founded several entirely new towns in Khuzistan or Susiana, while, according to others, he built the important city of Hormuz, or (as it is sometimes called) Ram-Aormuz, in the province of Kerman, which is still a flourishing place. Other authorities ascribe this city, however, to the first Hormisdas, the son of Sapor I. and grandson of Artaxerxes.

Among the means devised by Hormisdas II. for bettering the condition of his people the most remarkable was his establishment of a new Court of Justice. In the East the oppression of the weak by the powerful is the most inveterate and universal of all evils, and the one that well-intentioned monarchs have to be most careful in checking and repressing. Hormisdas, in his anxiety to root out this evil, is said to have set up a court expressly for the hearing of causes where complaint was made by the poor of wrongs done to them by the rich. The duty of the judges was at once to punish the oppressors, and to see that ample reparation was made to those whom they had wronged. To increase the authority of the court, and to secure the impartiality of its sentences, the monarch made a point of often presiding over it himself, of hearing the causes, and pronouncing the judgments in person. The most powerful nobles were thus made to feel that, if they offended, they would be likely to receive adequate punishment; and the weakest and poorest of the people were encouraged to come forward and make complaint if they had suffered injury.

Among his other wives, Hormisdas, we are told, married a daughter of the king of Cabul. It was natural that, after the conquest of Seistan by Varahran II., about A.D. 280, the Persian monarchs should establish relations with the chieftains ruling in Afghanistan. That country seems, from the first to the fourth century of our era, to have been under the government of princes of Scythian descent and of considerable wealth and power. Kadphises, Kanerki, Kenorano. Ooerki, Baraoro, had the main seat of their empire in the region about Cabul and Jellalabad; but from this centre they exercised an extensive sway, which at times probably reached Candahar on the one hand, and the Punjab region on the other. Their large gold coinage proves them to have been monarchs of great wealth, while their use of the Greek letters and language indicates a certain amount of civilization. The marriage of Hormisdas with a princess of Cabul implies that the hostile relations existing under Varahran II. had been superseded by friendly ones. Persian aggression had ceased to be feared. The reigning Indo-Scythic monarch felt no reluctance to give his daughter in marriage to his Western neighbor, and sent her to his court (we are told) with a wardrobe and ornaments of the utmost magnificence and costliness.

Hormisdas II. appears to have had a son, of the same name with himself, who attained to manhood while his father was still reigning. This prince, who was generally regarded, and who, of course, viewed himself, as the heir-apparent, was no favorite with the Persian nobles, whom he had perhaps offended by an inclination towards the literature and civilization of the Greeks. It must have been upon previous consultation and agreement that the entire body of the chief men resolved to vent their spite by insulting the prince in the most open and public way at the table of his father. The king was keeping his birthday, which was always, in Persia, the greatest festival of the year, and so the most public occasion possible. All the nobles of the realm were invited to the banquet; and all came and took their several places. The prince was absent at the first, but shortly arrived, bringing with him, as the excuse for his late appearance, a quantity of game, the produce of the morning's chase. Such an entrance must have created some disturbance and have drawn general attention; but the nobles, who were bound by etiquette to rise from their seats, remained firmly fixed in them, and took not the slightest notice of the prince's arrival. This behavior was an indignity which naturally aroused his resentment. In the heat of the moment he exclaimed aloud that "those who had insulted him should one day suffer for it—their fate should be the fate of Marsyas." At first the threat was not understood; but one chieftain, more learned than his fellows, explained to the rest that, according to the Greek myth, Marsyas was flayed alive. Now, flaying alive was a punishment not unknown to the Persian law; and the nobles, fearing that the prince really entertained the intention which he had expressed, became thoroughly alienated from him, and made up their minds that they would not allow him to reign. During his father's lifetime, they could, of course, do nothing; but they laid up the dread threat in their memory, and patiently waited for the moment when the throne would become vacant, and their enemy would assert his right to it.

Apparently, their patience was not very severely taxed. Hormisdas II. died within a few years; and Prince Hormisdas, as the only son whom he had left behind him, thought to succeed as a matter of course. But the nobles rose in insurrection, seized his person, and threw him into a dungeon, intending that he should remain there for the rest of his life. They themselves took the direction of affairs, and finding that, though King Hormisdas had left behind him no other son, yet one of his wives was pregnant, they proclaimed the unborn infant king, and even with the utmost ceremony proceeded to crown the embryo by suspending the royal diadem over the womb of the mother. A real interregnum must have followed; but it did not extend beyond a few months. The pregnant widow of Hormisdas fortunately gave birth to a boy, and the difficulties of the succession were thereby ended. All classes acquiesced in the rule of the infant monarch, who received the name of Sapor—whether simply to mark the fact that he was believed to be the late king's son, or in the hope that he would rival the glories of the first Sapor, is uncertain.

The reign of Sapor II. is estimated variously, at 69, 70, 71, and 72 years; but the balance of authority is in favor of seventy. He was born in the course of the year A.D. 309, and he seems to have died in the year after the Roman emperor Valens, or A.D. 379. He thus reigned nearly three-quarters of a century, being contemporary with the Roman emperors, Galerius, Constantine, Constantius and Constans, Julian, Jovian, Valentinian I., Valens, Gratian, and Valentinian II.

This long reign is best divided into periods. The first period of it extended from A.D. 309 to A.D. 337, or a space of twenty-eight years. This was the time anterior to Sapor's wars with the Romans. It included the sixteen years of his minority and a space of twelve years during which he waged successful wars with the Arabs. The minority of Sapor was a period of severe trial to Persia. On every side the bordering nations endeavored to take advantage of the weakness incident to the rule of a minor, and attacked and ravaged the empire at their pleasure. The Arabs were especially aggressive, and made continual raids into Babylonia, Khuzistan, and the adjoining regions, which desolated these provinces and carried the horrors of war into the very heart of the empire. The tribes of Beni-Ayar and Abdul-Kais, which dwelt on the southern shores of the Persian Gulf, took the lead in these incursions, and though not attempting any permanent conquests, inflicted terrible sufferings on the inhabitants of the tracts which they invaded. At the same time a Mesopotamian. chieftain, called Tayer or Thair, made an attack upon Otesiphon, took the city by storm, and captured a sister or aunt of the Persian monarch. The nobles, who, during Sapor's minority, guided the helm of the State, were quite incompetent to make head against these numerous enemies. For sixteen years the marauding bands had the advantage, and Persia found herself continually weaker, more impoverished, and less able to recover herself. The young prince is said to have shown extraordinary discretion and intelligence. He diligently trained himself in all manly exercises, and prepared both his mind and body for the important duties of his station. But his tender years forbade him as yet taking the field; and it is not unlikely that his ministers prolonged the period of his tutelage in order to retain, to the latest possible moment, the power whereto they had become accustomed. At any rate, it was not till he was sixteen, a later age than Oriental ideas require, that Sapor's minority ceased—that he asserted his manhood, and, placing himself at the head of his army, took the entire direction of affairs, civil and military, into his own hands.

From this moment the fortunes of Persia began to rise. Content at first to meet and chastise the marauding bands on his own territory, Sapor, after a time, grew bolder, and ventured to take the offensive. Having collected a fleet of considerable size, he placed his troops on board, and conveyed them to the city of El-Katif, an important place on the south coast of the Persian Gulf, where he disembarked and proceeded to carry fire and sword through the adjacent region. Either on this occasion, or more probably in a long series of expeditions, he ravaged the whole district of the Hejer, gaining numerous victories over the tribes of the Temanites, the Beni-Wa'iel, the Abdul-Kais, and others, which had taken a leading part in the invasion of Persia. His military genius and his valor were everywhere conspicuous; but unfortunately these excellent qualities were unaccompanied by the humanity which has been the crowning virtue o£ many a conqueror. Sapor, exasperated by the sufferings of his countrymen during so many years, thought that he could not too severely punish those who had inflicted them. He put to the sword the greater part of every tribe that he conquered; and, when his soldiers were weary of slaying, he made them pierce the shoulders of their prisoners, and insert in the wound a string or thong by which to drag them into captivity. The barbarity of the age and nation approved these atrocities; and the monarch who had commanded them was, in consequence, saluted as Dhoulacta, or "Lord of the Shoulders," by an admiring people. Cruelties almost as great, but of a different character, were at the same time sanctioned by Sapor in regard to one class of his own subjects—viz., those who had made profession of Christianity. The Zoroastrian zeal of this king was great, and he regarded it as incumbent on him to check the advance which Christianity was now making in his territories. He issued severe edicts against the Christians soon after attaining his majority; and when they sought the protection of the Roman emperor, he punished their disloyalty by imposing upon them a fresh tax, the weight of which was oppressive. When Symeon, Archbishop of Seleucia, complained of this additional burden in an offensive manner, Sapor retaliated by closing the Christian churches, confiscating the ecclesiastical property, and putting the complainant to death. Accounts of these severities reached Constantine, the Roman emperor, who had recently embraced the new religion (which, in spite of constant persecution, had gradually overspread the empire), and had assumed the character of a sort of general protector of the Christians throughout the world. He remonstrated with Sapor, but to no purpose. Sapor had formed the resolution to renew the contest terminated so unfavorably forty years earlier by his grandfather. He made the emperor's interference with Persian affairs, and encouragement of his Christian subjects in their perversity, a ground of complaint, and began to threaten hostilities. Some negotiations, which are not very clearly narrated, followed. Both sides, apparently, had determined on war, but both wished to gain time. It is uncertain what would have been the result had Constantine lived. But the death of that monarch in the early summer of A.D. 337, on his way to the eastern frontier, dispelled the last chance of peace by relieving Sapor from the wholesome fear which had hitherto restrained his ambition. The military fame of Constantine was great, and naturally inspired respect; his power was firmly fixed, and he was without competitor or rival. By his removal the whole face of affairs was changed; and Sapor, who had almost brought himself to venture on a rupture with Rome during Constantine's life, no longer hesitated on receiving news of his death, but at once commenced hostilities.

It is probable that among the motives which determined the somewhat wavering conduct of Sapor at this juncture was a reasonable fear of the internal troubles which it seemed to be in the power of the Romans to excite among the Persians, if from friends they became enemies. Having tested his own military capacity in his Arab wars, and formed an army on whose courage, endurance, and attachment he could rely, he was not afraid of measuring his strength with that of Rome in the open field; but he may well have dreaded the arts which the Imperial State was in the habit of employing, to supplement her military shortcomings, in wars with her neighbors. There was now at the court of Constantinople a Persian refugee of such rank and importance that Constantine had, as it were, a pretender ready made to his hand, and could reckon on creating dissension among the Persians whenever he pleased, by simply proclaiming himself this person's ally and patron. Prince Hormisdas, the elder brother of Sapor, and rightful king of Persia, had, after a long imprisonment, contrived, by the help of his wife, to escape from his dungeon, and had fled to the court of Constantine as early as A.D. 323. He had been received by the emperor with every mark of honor and distinction, had been given a maintenance suited to his rank, and had enjoyed other favors. Sapor must have felt himself deeply aggrieved by the undue attention paid to his rival; and though he pretended to make light of the matter, and even generously sent Hormisdas the wife to whom his escape was due, he cannot but have been uneasy at the possession, by the Roman emperor, of his brother's person. In weighing the reasons for and against war he cannot but have assigned considerable importance to this circumstance. It did not ultimately prevent him from challenging Rome to the combat; but it may help to account for the hesitation, the delay, and the fluctuations of purpose, which we remark in his conduct during the four or five years which immediately preceded the death of Constantine.

CHAPTER VIII

*Position of Affairs on the Death of Constantine. First War of Sapor with Rome, A.D. 337-350. First Siege of Nisibis. Obscure Interval. Troubles in Armenia, and Recovery of Armenia by the Persians. Sapor's Second Siege of Nisibis. Its Failure. Great Battle of Singara. Sapor's Son made Prisoner and murdered in cold blood. Third Siege of Nisibis. Sapor called away by an Invasion of the Massagatae.*

Καβάδης δὲ ὁ τοῦ Περόζου ὕστατας υἱός, τῆς βασιλείας δραξάμενος, ἐπὶ τὸ βιαιότερον τῇ ἀρχῇ ἐχρᾶτο καὶ κοινὰς τὰς γυναῖκας ἐνομοθέτησεν ἔχειν.—Cedrenus, p. 356, B, C.

"Constantius adversus Persas et Saporem, qui Mesopotamiam vastaverant, novem prasliis parum prospere decertavit."—Orosius, Hist. vii. 39.

The death of Constantine was followed by the division of the Roman world among his sons. The vast empire with which Sapor had almost made up his mind to contend was partitioned out into three moderate-sized kingdoms. In place of the late brave and experienced emperor, a raw youth, who had given no signs of superior ability, had the government of the Roman provinces of the East, of Thrace, Asia Minor, Syria, Mesopotamia, and Egypt. Master of one third of the empire only, and of the least warlike portion, Constantius was a foe whom the Persian monarch might well despise, and whom he might expect to defeat without much difficulty. Moreover, there was much in the circumstances of the time that seemed to promise success to the Persian arms in a struggle with Rome. The removal of Constantine had been followed by an outburst of licentiousness and violence among the Roman soldiery in the capital; and throughout the East the army had cast off the restraints of discipline, and given indications of a turbulent and seditious spirit. The condition of Armenia was also such as to encourage Sapor in his ambitious projects. Tiridates, though a persecutor of the Christians in the early part of his reign, had been converted by Gregory the Illuminator, and had then enforced Christianity on his subjects by fire and sword. A sanguinary conflict had followed. A large portion of the Armenians, firmly attached to the old national idolatry, had resisted determinedly. Nobles, priests, and people had fought desperately in defence of their temples, images, and altars; and, though the persistent will of the king overbore all opposition, yet the result was the formation of a discontented faction, which rose up from time to time against its rulers, and was constantly tempted to ally itself with any foreign power from which it could hope the re-establishment of the old religion. Armenia had also, after the death of Tiridates (in A.D. 314), fallen under the government of weak princes. Persia had recovered from it the portion of Media Atropatene ceded by the treaty between Galerius and Narses. Sapor, therefore, had nothing to fear on this side; and he might reasonably expect to find friends among the Armenians themselves, should the general position of his affairs allow him to make an effort to extend Persian influence once more over the Armenian highland.

The bands of Sapor crossed the Roman frontier soon after, if not even before, the death of Constantine; and after an interval of forty years the two great powers of the world were once more engaged in a bloody conflict. Constantius, having paid the last honors to his father's remains, hastened to the eastern frontier, where he found the Roman army weak in numbers, badly armed and badly provided, ill-disposed towards himself, and almost ready to mutiny. It was necessary, before anything could be done to resist the advance of Sapor, that the insubordination of the troops should be checked, their wants supplied, and their good-will conciliated. Constantius applied himself to effect these changes. Meanwhile Sapor set the Arabs and Armenians in motion, inducing the Pagan party among the latter to rise in insurrection, deliver their king, Tiranus, into his power, and make incursions into the Roman territory, while the latter infested with their armed bands the provinces of Mesopotamia and Syria. He himself was content, during the first year of the war, A.D. 337, with moderate successes, and appeared to the Romans to avoid rather than seek a pitched battle. Constantius was able, under these circumstances, not only to maintain his ground, but to gain certain advantages. He restored the direction of affairs in Armenia to the Roman party, detached some of the Mesopotamian Arabs from the side of his adversary, and attached them to his own, and even built forts in the Persian territory on the further side of the Tigris. But the gains made were slight; and in the ensuing year (A.D. 338) Sapor took the field in greater force than before, and addressed himself to an important enterprise. He aimed, it is evident, from the first, at the recovery of Mesopotamia, and at thrusting back the Romans from the Tigris to the Euphrates. He found it easy to overrun the open country, to ravage the crops, drive off the cattle, and burn the villages and homesteads. But the region could not be regarded as conquered, it could not be permanently held, unless the strongly fortified posts which commanded it, and which were in the hands of Rome, could be captured. Of all these the most important was Nisibis. This ancient town, known to the Assyrians as Nazibina, was, at any rate from the time of Lucullus, the most important city of Mesopotamia. It was situated at the distance of about sixty miles from the Tigris, at the edge of the Mons Masius, in a broad and fertile plain, watered by one of the affluents of the river Khabour, or Aborrhas. The Romans, after their occupation of Mesopotamia, had raised it to the rank of a colony; and its defences, which were of great strength, had always been maintained by the emperors in a state of efficiency. Sapor regarded it as the key of the Roman position in the tract between the rivers, and, as early as A.D. 338, sought to make himself master of it.

The first siege of Nisibis by Sapor lasted, we are told, sixty-three days. Few particulars of it have come down to us. Sapor had attacked the city, apparently, in the absence of Constantius, who had been called off to Pannonia to hold a conference with his brothers. It was defended, not only by its garrison and inhabitants, but by the prayers and exhortations of its bishop, St. James, who, if he did not work miracles for the deliverance of his countrymen, at any rate sustained and animated their resistance. The result was that the bands of Sapor were repelled with loss, and he was forced, after wasting two months before the walls, to raise the siege and own himself baffled.

After this, for some years the Persian war with Rome languished. It is difficult to extract from the brief statements of epitomizers, and the loose invectives or panegyrics of orators, the real circumstances of the struggle; but apparently the general condition of things was this. The Persians were constantly victorious in the open field; Constantius was again and again defeated; but no permanent gain was effected by these successes. A weakness inherited by the Persians from the Parthians—an inability to conduct sieges to a prosperous issue—showed itself; and their failures against the fortified posts which Rome had taken care to establish in the disputed regions were continual. Up to the close of A.D. 340 Sapor had made no important gain, had struck no decisive blow, but stood nearly in the same position which he had occupied at the commencement of the conflict.

But the year A.D. 341 saw a change. Sapor, after obtaining possession of the person of Tiranus, had sought to make himself master of Armenia, and had even attempted to set up one of his own relatives as king. But the indomitable spirit of the inhabitants, and their firm attachment to their Arsacid princes, caused his attempts to fail of any good result, and tended on the whole to throw Armenia into the arms of Rome. Sapor, after a while, became convinced of the folly of his proceedings, and resolved on the adoption of a wholly new policy. He would relinquish the idea of conquering, and would endeavor instead to conciliate the Armenians, in the hope of obtaining from their gratitude what he had been unable to extort from their fears. Tiranus was still living; and Sapor, we are told, offered to replace him upon the Armenian throne; but, as he had been blinded by his captors, and as Oriental notions did not allow a person thus mutilated to exercise royal power, Tiranus declined the offer made him, and suggested the substitution of his son, Arsaces, who was, like himself, a prisoner in Persia. Sapor readily consented; and the young prince, released from captivity, returned to his country, and was installed as king by the Persians, with the good-will of the natives, who were satisfied so long as they could feel that they had at their head a monarch of the ancient stock. The arrangement, of course, placed Armenia on the Persian side, and gave Sapor for many years a powerful ally in his struggle with Rome.

Thus Sapor had, by the, year A.D. 341, made a very considerable gain. He had placed a friendly sovereign on the Armenian throne, had bound him to his cause by oaths, and had thereby established his influence, not only over Armenia itself, but over the whole tract which lay between Armenia and the Caucasus. But he was far from content with these successes. It was still his great object to drive the Romans from Mesopotamia; and with that object in view it continued to be his first wish to obtain possession of Nisibis. Accordingly, having settled Armenian affairs to his liking, he made, in A.D. 346, a second attack on the great city of Northern Mesopotamia, again investing it with a large body of troops, and this time pressing the siege during the space of nearly three months. Again, however, the strength of the walls and the endurance of the garrison baffled him. Sapor was once more obliged to withdraw from, before the place, having suffered greater loss than those whom he had assailed, and forfeited much of the prestige which he had acquired by his many victories.

It was, perhaps, on account of the repulse from Nisibis, and in the hope of recovering his lost laurels, that Sapor, in the next year but one, A.D. 348, made an unusual effort. Calling out the entire military force of the empire, and augmenting it by large bodies of allies and mercenaries, the Persian king, towards the middle of summer, crossed the Tigris by three bridges, and with a numerous and well-appointed army invaded Central Mesopotamia, probably from Adiabene, or the region near and a little south of Nineveh. Constantius, with the Roman army, was posted on and about the Sinjax range of hills, in the vicinity of the town of Singara, which is represented by the modern village of Sinjar. The Roman emperor did not venture to dispute the passage of the river, or to meet his adversary in the broad plain which, intervenes between the Tigris and the mountain range, but clung to the skirts of the hills, and commanded his troops to remain wholly on the defensive. Sapor was thus enabled to choose his position, to establish a fortified camp at a convenient distance from the enemy, and to occupy the hills in its vicinity—some portion of the Sinjar range—with his archers. It is uncertain whether, in making these dispositions, he was merely providing for his own safety, or whether he was laying a trap into which he hoped to entice the Roman army. Perhaps his mind was wide enough to embrace both contingencies. At any rate, having thus established a point d'appui in his rear, he advanced boldly and challenged the legions to an encounter. The challenge was at once accepted, and the battle commenced about midday; but now the Persians, having just crossed swords with the enemy, almost immediately began to give ground, and retreating hastily drew their adversaries along, across the thirsty plain, to the vicinity of their fortified camp, where a strong body of horse and the flower of the Persian archers were posted. The horse charged, but the legionaries easily defeated them, and elated with their success burst into the camp, despite the warnings of their leader, who strove vainly to check their ardor and to induce them to put off the completion of their victory till the next day. A small detachment found within the ramparts was put to the sword; and the soldiers scattered themselves among the tents, some in quest of booty, others only anxious for some means of quenching their raging thirst. Meantime the sun had gone down, and the shades of night fell rapidly. Regarding the battle as over, and the victory as assured, the Romans gave themselves up to sleep or feasting. But now Sapor saw his opportunity—the opportunity for which he had perhaps planned and waited. His light troops on the adjacent hills commanded the camp, and, advancing on every side, surrounded it. They were fresh and eager for the fray; they fought in the security afforded by the darkness; while the fires of the camp showed them their enemies, worn out with fatigue, sleepy, or drunken. The result, as might have been expected, was a terrible carnage. The Persians overwhelmed the legionaries with showers of darts and arrows; flight, under the circumstances, was impossible; and the Roman soldiers mostly perished where they stood. They took, however, ere they died, an atrocious revenge. Sapor's son had been made prisoner in the course of the day; in their desperation the legionaries turned their fury against this innocent youth; they beat him with whips, wounded him with the points of their weapons, and finally rushed upon him and killed him with a hundred blows.

The battle of Singara, though thus disastrous to the Romans, had not any great effect in determining the course or issue of the war. Sapor did not take advantage of his victory to attack the rest of the Roman forces in Mesopotamia, or even to attempt the siege of any large town. Perhaps he had really suffered large losses in the earlier part of the day; perhaps he was too much affected by the miserable death of his son to care, till time had dulled the edge of his grief, for military glory. At any rate, we hear of his undertaking no further enterprise till the second year after the battle, A.D. 350, when he made his third and most desperate attempt to capture Nisibis.

The rise of a civil war in the West, and the departure of Constantius for Europe with the flower of his troops early in the year no doubt encouraged the Persian monarch to make one more effort against the place which had twice repulsed him with ignominy. He collected a numerous native army, and strengthened it by the addition of a body of Indian allies, who brought a large troop of elephants into the field. With this force he crossed the Tigris in the early summer, and, after taking several fortified posts, march northwards and invested Nisibis. The Roman commander in the place was the Count Lucilianus, afterwards the father-in-law of Jovian, a man of resource and determination. He is said to have taken the best advantage of every favorable turn of fortune in the course of the siege, and to have prolonged the resistance by various subtle stratagems. But the real animating spirit of the defence was once more the bishop, St. James, who raised the enthusiasm of the inhabitants to the highest pitch by his exhortations, guided them by his counsels, and was thought to work miracles for them by his prayers. Sapor tried at first the ordinary methods of attack; he battered the walls with his rams, and sapped them with mines. But finding that by these means he made no satisfactory progress, he had recourse shortly to wholly novel proceedings. The river Mygdonius (now the Jerujer), swollen by the melting of the snows in the Mons Masius, had overflowed its banks and covered with an inundation the plain in which Nisibis stands. Sapor saw that the forces of nature might be employed to advance his ends, and so embanked the lower part of the plain that the water could not run off, but formed a deep lake round the town, gradually creeping up the walls till it had almost reached the battlements. Having thus created an artificial sea, the energetic monarch rapidly collected, or constructed, a fleet of vessels, and, placing his military engines on board, launched the ships upon the waters, and so attacked the walls of the city at great advantage. But the defenders resisted stoutly, setting the engines on fire with torches, and either lifting the ships from the water by means of cranes, or else shattering them with the huge stones which they could discharge from their balistics. Still, therefore, no impression was made; but at last an unforeseen circumstance brought the besieged into the greatest peril, and almost gave Nisibis into the enemy's hands. The inundation, confined by the mounds of the Persians, which prevented it from running off, pressed with continually increasing force against the defences of the city, till at last the wall, in one part, proved too weak to withstand the tremendous weight which bore upon it, and gave way suddenly for the space of a hundred and fifty feet. What further damage was done to the town we know not; but a breach was opened through which the Persians at once made ready to pour into the place, regarding it as impossible that so huge a gap should be either repaired or effectually defended. Sapor took up his position on an artificial eminence, while his troops rushed to the assault. First of all marched the heavy cavalry, accompanied by the horse-archers; next came the elephants, bearing iron towers upon their backs, and in each tower a number of bowmen; intermixed with the elephants were a certain amount of heavy-armed foot. It was a strange column with which to attack a breach; and its composition does not say much for Persian siege tactics, which were always poor and ineffective, and which now, as usual, resulted in failure. The horses became quickly entangled in the ooze and mud which the waters had left behind them as they subsided; the elephants were even less able to overcome these difficulties, and as soon as they received a wound sank down—never to rise again—in the swamp. Sapor hastily gave orders for the assailing column to retreat and seek the friendly shelter of the Persian camp, while he essayed to maintain his advantage in a different way. His light archers were ordered to the front, and, being formed into divisions which were to act as reliefs, received orders to prevent the restoration of the ruined wall by directing an incessant storm of arrows into the gap made by the waters. But the firmness and activity of the garrison and inhabitants defeated this well-imagined proceeding. While the heavy-armed troops stood in the gap receiving the flights of arrows and defending themselves as they best could, the unarmed multitude raised a new wall in their rear, which, by the morning of the next day, was six feet in height. This last proof of his enemies' resolution and resource seems to have finally convinced Sapor of the hopelessness of his enterprise. Though he still continued the siege for a while, he made no other grand attack, and at length drew off his forces, having lost twenty thousand men before the walls, and wasted a hundred days, or more than three months.

Perhaps he would not have departed so soon, but would have turned the siege into a blockade, and endeavored to starve the garrison into submission, had not alarming tidings reached him from his north-eastern frontier. Then, as now, the low flat sandy region east of the Caspian was in the possession of nomadic hordes, whose whole life was spent in war and plunder. The Oxus might be nominally the boundary of the empire in this quarter; but the nomads were really dominant over the entire desert to the foot of the Hyrcanian and Parthian hills. Petty plundering forays into the fertile region south and east of the desert were no doubt constant, and were not greatly regarded; but from time to time some tribe or chieftain bolder than the rest made a deeper inroad and a more sustained attack than usual, spreading consternation around, and terrifying the court for its safety. Such an attack seems to have occurred towards the autumn of A.D. 350. The invading horde is said to have consisted of Massagatae; but we can hardly be mistaken in regarding them as, in the main, of Tatar, or Turkoman blood, akin to the Usbegs and other Turanian tribes which still inhabit the sandy steppe. Sapor considered the crisis such as to require his own presence; and thus, while civil war summoned one of the two rivals from Mesopotamia to the far West, where he had to contend with the self-styled emperors, Magnentius and Vetranio, the other was called away to the extreme East to repel a Tatar invasion. A tacit truce was thus established between the great belligerents—a truce which lasted for seven or eight years. The unfortunate Mesopotamians, harassed by constant war for above twenty years, had now a breathing-space during which to recover from the ruin and desolation that had overwhelmed them. Rome and Persia for a time suspended their conflict. Rivalry, indeed, did not cease; but it was transferred from the battlefield to the cabinet, and the Roman emperor sought and found in diplomatic triumphs a compensation for the ill-success which had attended his efforts in the field.

## CHAPTER IX

*Revolt of Armenia and Acceptance by Arsaces of the Position of a Roman Feudatory. Character and Issue of Sapor's Eastern Wars. His negotiations with Constantius. His Extreme Demands. Circumstances under which he determines to renew the War. His Preparations. Desertion to him of Antoninus. Great Invasion of Sapor. Siege of Amida. Sapor's Severities. Siege and Capture of Singara; of Bezabde. Attack on Virtu fails. Aggressive Movement of Constantius. He attacks Bezabde, but fails Campaign of A.D. 361. Death of Constantius.*

*Evenerat . . . quasi fatali constellatione . . . ut Constantium dimicantem cum Persis fortuna semper sequeretur afflictior.—Amm. Marc. xx. 9, ad fin.*

It seems to have been soon after the close of Sapor's first war with Constantius that events took place in Armenia which once more replaced that country under Roman influence. Arsaces, the son of Tiranus, had been, as we have seen, established as monarch, by Sapor, in the year A.D. 341, under the notion that, in return for the favor shown him, he would administer Armenia in the Persian interest. But gratitude is an unsafe basis for the friendships of monarchs. Arsaces, after a time, began to chafe against the obligations under which Sapor had laid him, and to wish, by taking independent action, to show himself a real king, and not a mere feudatory. He was also, perhaps, tired of aiding Sapor in his Roman war, and may have found that he suffered more than he gained by having Rome for an enemy. At any rate, in the interval between A.D. 351 and 359, probably while Sapor was engaged in the far East, Arsaces sent envoys to Constantinople with a request to Constantius that he would give him in marriage a member of the Imperial house. Constantius was charmed with the application made to him, and at once accepted the proposal. He selected for the proffered honor a certain Olympias, the daughter of Ablabius, a Praetorian prefect, and lately the betrothed bride of his own brother, Constans; and sent her to Armenia, where Arsaces welcomed her, and made her (as it would seem) his chief wife, provoking thereby the jealousy and aversion of his previous sultana, a native Armenian, named Pharandzem. The engagement thus entered into led on, naturally, to the conclusion of a formal alliance between Rome and Armenia—an alliance which Sapor made fruitless efforts to disturb, and which continued unimpaired down to the time A.D. 359 when hostilities once more broke out between Rome and Persia.

Of Sapor's Eastern wars we have no detailed account. They seem to have occupied him from A.D. 350 to A.D. 357, and to have been, on the whole, successful. They were certainly terminated by a peace in the last-named year—a peace of which it must have been a condition that his late enemies should lend him aid in the struggle which he was about to renew with Rome. Who these enemies exactly were, and what exact region they inhabited, is doubtful. They comprised certainly the Chionites and Gelani, probably the Euseni and the Vertse. The Chionites are thought to have been Hiongnu or Huns; and the Euseni are probably the Usiun, who, as early as B.C. 200, are found among the nomadic hordes pressing towards the Oxus. The Vertse are wholly unknown. The Gelani should, by their name, be the inhabitants of Ghilan, or the coast tract south-west of the Caspian; but this locality seems too remote from the probable seats of the Chionites and Euseni to be the one intended. The general scene of the wars was undoubtedly east of the Caspian, either in the Oxus region, or still further eastward, on the confines of India and Scythia. The result of the wars, though not a conquest, was an extension of Persian influence and power. Troublesome enemies were converted into friends and allies. The loss of a predominating influence over Armenia was thus compensated, or more than compensated, within a few years, by a gain of a similar kind in another quarter.

While Sapor was thus engaged in the far East, he received letters from the officer whom he had left in charge of his western frontier, informing him that the Romans were anxious to exchange the precarious truce which Mesopotamia had been allowed to enjoy during the last five or six years for a more settled and formal peace. Two great Roman officials, Cassianus, duke of Mesopotamia, and Musonianus, Praetorian prefect, understanding that Sapor was entangled in a bloody and difficult war at the eastern extremity of his empire, and knowing that Constantius was fully occupied with the troubles caused by the inroads of the barbarians into the more western of the Roman provinces, had thought that the time was favorable for terminating the provisional state of affairs in the Mesopotamian region by an actual treaty. They had accordingly opened negotiations with Tamsapor, satrap of Adiabene, and suggested to him that he should sound his master on the subject of making peace with Rome. Tamsapor appears to have misunderstood the character of these overtures, or to have misrepresented them to Sapor; in his despatch he made Constantius himself the mover in the matter, and spoke of him as humbly supplicating the great king to grant him conditions. It happened that the message reached Sapor just as he had come to terms with his eastern enemies, and had succeeded in inducing them to become his allies. He was naturally elated at his success, and regarded the Roman overture as a simple acknowledgment of weakness. Accordingly he answered in the most haughty style. His letter, which was conveyed to the Roman emperor at Sirmium by an ambassador named Narses, was conceived in the following terms:

"Sapor, king of kings, brother of the sun and moon, and companion of the stars, sends salutation to his brother, Constantius Caesar. It glads me to see that thou art at last returned to the right way, and art ready to do what is just and fair, having learned by experience that inordinate greed is oft-times punished by defeat and disaster. As then the voice of truth ought to speak with all openness, and the more illustrious of mankind should make their words mirror their thoughts, I will briefly declare to thee what I propose, not forgetting that I have often said the same things before. Your own authors are witness that the entire tract within the river Strymon and the borders of Macedon was once held by my ancestors; if I required you to restore all this, it would not ill become me (excuse the boast), inasmuch as I excel in virtue and in the splendor of my achievements the whole line of our ancient monarchs. But as moderation delights me, and has always been the rule of my conduct—wherefore from my youth up I have had no occasion to repent of any action—I will be content to receive Mesopotamia and Armenia, which was fraudulently extorted from my grandfather. We Persians have never admitted the principle, which you proclaim with such effrontery, that success in war is always glorious, whether it be the fruit of courage or trickery. In conclusion, if you will take the advice of one who speaks for your good, sacrifice a small tract of territory, one always in dispute and causing continual bloodshed, in order that you may rule the remainder securely. Physicians, remember, often cut and burn, and even amputate portions of the body, that the patient may have the healthy use of what is left to him; and there are animals which, understanding why the hunters chase them, deprive themselves of the thing coveted, to live thenceforth without fear. I warn you, that, if my ambassador returns in vain, I will take the field against you, so soon as the winter is past, with all my forces, confiding in my good fortune and in the fairness of the conditions which I have now offered."

It must have been a severe blow to Imperial pride to receive such a letter; and the sense of insult can scarcely have been much mitigated by the fact that the missive was enveloped in a silken covering, or by the circumstance that the bearer, Narses, endeavored by his conciliating manners to atone for his master's rudeness. Constantius replied, however, in a dignified and calm tone. "The Roman emperor," he said, "victorious by land and sea, saluted his brother, King Sapor. His lieutenant in Mesopotamia had meant well in opening a negotiation with a Persian governor; but he had acted without orders, and could not bind his master. Nevertheless, he (Constantius) would not disclaim what had been done, since he did not object to a peace, provided it were fair and honorable. But to ask the master of the whole Roman world to surrender territories which he had successfully defended when he ruled only over the provinces of the East was plainly indecent and absurd. He must add that the employment of threats was futile, and too common an artifice; more especially as the Persians themselves must know that Rome always defended herself when attacked, and that, if occasionally she was vanquished in a battle, yet she never failed to have the advantage in the event of every war." Three envoys were entrusted with the delivery of this reply—Prosper, a count of the empire; Spectatus, a tribune and notary; and Eustathius, an orator and philosopher, a pupil of the celebrated Neo-Platonist, Jamblichus, and a friend of St. Basil. Constantius was most anxious for peace, as a dangerous war threatened with the Alemanni, one of the most powerful tribes of Germany. He seems to have hoped that, if the unadorned language of the two statesmen failed to move Sapor, he might be won over by the persuasive eloquence of the professor of rhetoric.

But Sapor was bent on war. He had concluded arrangements with the natives so long his adversaries in the East, by which they had pledged themselves to join his standard with all their forces in the ensuing spring. He was well aware of the position of Constantius in the West, of the internal corruption of his court, and of the perils constantly threatening him from external enemies. A Roman official of importance, bearing the once honored name of Antoninus, had recently taken refuge with him from the claims of pretended creditors, and had been received into high favor on account of the information which he was able to communicate with respect to the disposition of the Roman forces and the condition of their magazines. This individual, ennobled by the royal authority, and given a place at the royal table, gained great influence over his new master, whom he stimulated by alternately reproaching him with his backwardness in the past, and putting before him the prospect of easy triumphs over Rome in the future. He pointed out that the emperor, with the bulk of his troops and treasures, was detained in the regions adjoining the Danube, and that the East was left almost undefended; he magnified the services which he was himself competent to render; he exhorted Sapor to bestir himself, and to put confidence in his good fortune. He recommended that the old plan of sitting down before walled towns should be given up, and that the Persian monarch, leaving the strongholds of Mesopotamia in his rear, should press forward to the Euphrates, pour his troops across it, and overrun the rich province of Syria, which he would find unguarded, and which had not been invaded by an enemy for nearly a century. The views of Antoninus were adopted; but, in practice, they were overruled by the exigencies of the situation. A Roman army occupied Mesopotamia, and advanced to the banks of the Tigris. When the Persians in full force crossed the river, accompanied by Chionite and Albanian allies, they found a considerable body of troops prepared to resist them. Their opponents did not, indeed offer battle, but they laid waste the country as the Persians took possession of it; they destroyed the forage, evacuated the indefensible towns (which fell, of course, into the enemy's hands), and fortified the line of the Euphrates with castles, military engines, and palisades. Still the programme of Antoninus would probably have been carried out, had not the swell of the Euphrates exceeded the average, and rendered it impossible for the Persian troops to ford the river at the usual point of passage into Syria. On discovering this obstacle, Antoninus suggested that, by a march to the north-east through a fertile country, the "Upper Euphrates" might be reached, and easily crossed, before its waters had attained any considerable volume. Sapor agreed to adopt this suggestion. He marched from Zeugma across the Mons Masius towards the Upper Euphrates, defeated the Romans in an important battle near Arnida, took, by a sudden assault, two castles which defended the town, and then somewhat hastily resolved that he would attack the place, which he did not imagine capable of making much resistance.

Amida, now Diarbekr, was situated on the right bank of the Upper Tigris, in a fertile plain, and was washed along the whole of its western side by a semi-circular bend of the river. It had been a place of considerable importance from a very ancient date, and had recently been much strengthened by Constantius, who had made it an arsenal for military engines, and had repaired its towers and walls. The town contained within it a copious fountain of water, which was liable, however, to acquire a disagreeable odor in the summer time. Seven legions, of the moderate strength to which legions had been reduced by Constantine, defended it; and the garrison included also a body of horse-archers, composed chiefly or entirely of noble foreigners. Sapor hoped in the first instance to terrify it into submission by his mere appearance, and boldly rode up to the gates with a small body of his followers, expecting that they would be opened to him. But the defenders were more courageous than he had imagined. They received him with a shower of darts and arrows that were directed specially against his person, which was conspicuous from its ornaments; and they aimed their weapons so well that one of them passed through a portion of his dress and was nearly wounding him. Persuaded by his followers, Sapor upon this withdrew, and committed the further prosecution of the attack to Grumbates, the king of the Chionites, who assaulted the walls on the next day with a body of picked troops, but was repulsed with great loss, his only son, a youth of great promise, being killed at his side by a dart from a balista. The death of this prince spread dismay through the camp, and was followed by a general mourning; but it now became a point of honor to take the town which had so injured one of the great king's royal allies; and Grumbates was promised that Amida should become the funeral pile of his lost darling.

The town was now regularly invested. Each nation was assigned its place. The Chionites, burning with the desire to avenge their late defeat, were on the east; the Vertae on the south; the Albanians, warriors from the Caspian region, on the north; the Segestans, who were reckoned the bravest soldiers of all, and who brought into the field a large body of elephants, held the west. A continuous line of Persians, five ranks deep, surrounded the entire city, and supported the auxiliary detachments. The entire besieging army was estimated at a hundred thousand men; the besieged, including the unarmed multitude, were under 30,000. After the pause of an entire day, the first general attack was made. Grumbates gave the signal for the assault by hurling a bloody spear into the space before the walls, after the fashion of a Roman fetialis. A cloud of darts and arrows from every side followed the flight of this weapon, and did severe damage to the besieged, who were at the same time galled with discharges from Roman military engines, taken by the Persians in some capture of Singara, and now employed against their former owners. Still a vigorous resistance continued to be made, and the besiegers, in their exposed positions, suffered even more than the garrison; so that after two days the attempt to carry the city by general assault was abandoned, and the slow process of a regular siege was adopted. Trenches were opened at the usual distance from the walls, along which the troops advanced under the cover of hurdles towards the ditch, which they proceeded to fill up in places. Mounds were then thrown up against the walls; and movable towers were constructed and brought into play, guarded externally with iron, and each mounting a balista. It was impossible long to withstand these various weapons of attack. The hopes of the besieged lay, primarily, in their receiving relief from without by the advance of an army capable of engaging their assailants and harassing them or driving them off; secondarily, in successful sallies, by means of which they might destroy the enemy's works and induce him to retire from before the place.

There existed, in the neighborhood of Amida, the elements of a relieving army, under the command of the new prefect of the East, Sabinianus. Had this officer possessed an energetic and enterprising character, he might, without much difficulty, have collected a force of light and active soldiers, which might have hung upon the rear of the Persians, intercepted their convoys, cut off their stragglers, and have even made an occasional dash upon their lines. Such was the course of conduct recommended by Ursicinus, the second in command, whom Sabinianus had recently superseded; but the latter was jealous of his subordinate, and had orders from the Byzantine court to keep him unemployed. He was himself old and rich, alike disinclined to and unfit for military enterprise; he therefore absolutely rejected the advice of Ursicinus, and determined on making no effort. He had positive orders, he said, from the court to keep on the defensive and not endanger his troops by engaging them in hazardous adventures. Amida must protect itself, or at any rate not look to him for succor. Ursicinus chafed terribly, it is said, against this decision, but was forced to submit to it. His messengers conveyed the dispiriting intelligence to the devoted city, which learned thereby that it must rely wholly upon its own exertions.

Nothing now remained but to organize sallies on a large scale and attack the besieger's works. Such attempts were made from time to time with some success; and on one occasion two Gaulish legions, banished to the East for their adherence to the cause of Magnentius, penetrated, by night, into the heart of the besieging camp, and brought the person of the monarch into danger. This peril was, however, escaped; the legions were repulsed with the loss of a sixth of their number; and nothing was gained by the audacious enterprise beyond a truce of three days, during which each side mourned its dead, and sought to repair its losses.

The fate of the doomed city drew on. Pestilence was added to the calamities which the besieged had to endure. Desertion and treachery were arrayed against them. One of the natives of Amida, going over to the Persians, informed them that on the southern side of the city a neglected staircase led up from the margin of the Tigris through underground corridors to one of the principal bastions; and under his guidance seventy archers of the Persian guard, picked men, ascended the dark passage at dead of night, occupied the tower, and when morning broke displayed from it a scarlet flag, as a sign to their countrymen that a portion of the wall was taken. The Persians were upon the alert, and an instant assault was made. But the garrison, by extraordinary efforts, succeeded in recapturing the tower before any support reached its occupants; and then, directing their artillery and missiles against the assailing columns, inflicted on them tremendous losses, and soon compelled them to return hastily to the shelter of their camp. The Verte, who maintained the siege on the south side of the city, were the chief sufferers in this abortive attempt.

Sapor had now spent seventy days before the place, and had made no perceptible impression. Autumn was already far advanced, and the season for military operations would, soon be over. It was necessary, therefore, either to take the city speedily or to give up the siege and retire. Under these circumstances Sapor resolved on a last effort. He had constructed towers of such a height that they overtopped the wall, and poured their discharges on the defenders from a superior elevation. He had brought his mounds in places to a level with the ramparts, and had compelled the garrison to raise countermounds within the walls for their protection. He now determined on pressing the assault day after day, until he either carried the town or found all his resources exhausted. His artillery, his foot, and his elephants were all employed in turn or together; he allowed the garrison no rest. Not content with directing the operations, he himself took part in the supreme struggle, exposing his own person freely to the enemy's weapons, and losing many of his attendants. After the contest had lasted three continuous days from morn to night, fortune at last favored him. One of the inner mounds, raised by the besieged behind their wall, suddenly gave way, involving its defenders in its fall, and at the same time filling up the entire space between the wall and the mound raised outside by the Persians. A way into the town was thus laid open, and the besiegers instantly occupied it. It was in vain that the flower of the garrison threw itself across the path of the entering columns—nothing could withstand the ardor of the Persian troops. In a little time all resistance was at an end; those who could quitted the city and fled—the remainder, whatever their sex, age, or calling, whether armed or unarmed, were slaughtered like sheep by the conquerors.

Thus fell Amida after a siege of seventy-three days. Sapor, who on other occasions showed himself not deficient in clemency, was exasperated by the prolonged resistance and the losses which he had sustained in the course of it. Thirty thousand of his best soldiers had fallen; the son of his chief ally had perished; he himself had been brought into imminent danger. Such audacity on the part of a petty town seemed no doubt to him to deserve a severe retribution. The place was therefore given over to the infuriated soldiery, who were allowed to slay and plunder at their pleasure. Of the captives taken, all belonging to the five provinces across the Tigris, claimed as his own by Sapor, though ceded to Rome by his grandfather, were massacred in cold blood. The Count Elian, and the commanders of the legions who had conducted the gallant defence, were barbarously crucified. Many other Romans of high rank were subjected to the indignity of being manacled, and were dragged into Persia as slaves rather than as prisoners.

The campaign of A.D. 359 terminated with this dearly bought victory. The season was too far advanced for any fresh enterprise of importance; and Sapor was probably glad to give his army a rest after the toils and perils of the last three months. Accordingly he retired across the Tigris, without leaving (so far as appears) any garrisons in Mesopotamia, and began preparations for the campaign of A.D. 360. Stores of all kinds were accumulated during the winter; and, when the spring came, the indefatigable monarch once more invaded the enemy's country, pouring into Mesopotamia an army even more numerous and better appointed than that which he had led against Amida in the preceding year. His first object now was to capture Singara, a town of some consequence, which was, however, defended by only two Roman legions and a certain number of native soldiers. After a vain attempt to persuade the garrison to a surrender, the attack was made in the usual way, chiefly by scaling parties with ladders, and by battering parties which shook the walls with the ram. The defenders kept the scalers at bay by a constant discharge of stones and darts from their artillery, arrows from their bows, and leaden bullets from their slings. They met the assaults of the ram by attempts to fire the wooden covering which protected it and those who worked it. For some days these efforts sufficed; but after a while the besiegers found a weak point in the defences of the place—a tower so recently built that the mortar in which the stones were laid was still moist, and which consequently crumbled rapidly before the blows of a strong and heavy battering-ram, and in a short time fell to the ground. The Persians poured in through the gap, and were at once masters of the entire town, which ceased to resist after the catastrophe. This easy victory allowed Sapor to exhibit the better side of his character; he forbade the further shedding of blood, and ordered that as many as possible of the garrisons and citizens should be taken alive. Reviving a favorite policy of Oriental rulers from very remote times, he transported these captives to the extreme eastern parts of his empire, where they might be of the greatest service to him in defending his frontier against the Scythians and Indians.

It is not really surprising, though the historian of the war regards it as needing explanation, that no attempt was made to relieve Singara by the Romans. The siege was short; the place was considered strong; the nearest point held by a powerful Roman force was Nisibis, which was at least sixty miles distant from Singara. The neighborhood of Singara was, moreover, ill supplied with water; and a relieving army would probably have soon found itself in difficulties. Singara, on the verge of the desert, was always perilously situated. Rome valued it as an outpost from which her enemy might be watched, and which might advertise her of a sudden danger, but could not venture to undertake its defence in case of an attack in force, and was prepared to hear of its capture with equanimity.

From Singara Sapor directed his march almost due northwards, and, leaving Nisibis unassailed upon his left, proceeded to attack the strong fort known indifferently as Phoenica or Bezabde. This was a position on the east bank of the Tigris, near the point where that river quits the mountains and debouches upon the plain; though not on the site, it may be considered the representative of the modern Jezireh, which commands the passes from the low country into the Kurdish mountains. Bezabde was the chief city of the province, called after it Zabdicene, one of the five ceded by Narses and greatly coveted by his grandson. It was much valued by Rome, was fortified in places with a double wall, and was guarded by three legions and a large body of Kurdish archers. Sapor, having reconnoitred the place, and, with his usual hardihood, exposed himself to danger in doing so, sent a flag of truce to demand a surrender, joining with the messengers some prisoners of high rank taken at Singara, lest the enemy should open fire upon his envoys. The device was successful; but the garrison proved stanch, and determined on resisting to the last. Once more all the known resources of attack and defence were brought into play; and after a long siege, of which the most important incident was an attempt made by the bishop of the place to induce Sapor to withdraw, the wall was at last breached, the city taken, and its defenders indiscriminately massacred. Regarding the position as one of first-rate importance, Sapor, who had destroyed Singara, carefully repaired the defences of Bezabde, provisioned it abundantly, and garrisoned it with some of his best troops. He was well aware that the Romans would feel keenly the loss of so important a post, and expected that it would not be long before they made an effort to recover possession of it.

The winter was now approaching, but the Persian monarch still kept the field. The capture of Bezabde was followed by that of many other less important strongholds, which offered little resistance. At last, towards the close of the year, an attack was made upon a place called Virta, said to have been a fortress of great strength, and by some moderns identified with Tekrit, an important city upon the Tigris between Mosul and Bagdad. Here the career of the conqueror was at last arrested. Persuasion and force proved alike unavailing to induce or compel a surrender; and, after wasting the small remainder of the year, and suffering considerable loss, the Persian monarch reluctantly gave up the siege, and returned to his own country.

Meanwhile the movements of the Roman emperor had been slow and uncertain. Distracted between a jealous fear of his cousin Julian's proceedings in the West, and a desire of checking the advance of his rival Sapor in the East, he had left Constantinople in the early spring, but had journeyed leisurely through Cappadocia and Armenia Minor to Samosata, whence, after crossing the Euphrates, he had proceeded to Edessa, and there fixed himself. While in Cappadocia he had summoned to his presence Arsaces, the tributary king of Armenia, had reminded him of his engagements, and had endeavored to quicken his gratitude by bestowing on him liberal presents. At Edessa he employed himself during the whole of the summer in collecting troops and stores; nor was it till the autumnal equinox was past that he took the field, and, after weeping over the smoking ruins of Amida, marched to Bezabde, and, when the defenders rejected his overtures of peace, formed the siege of the place. Sapor was, we must suppose, now engaged before Virta, and it is probable that he thought Bezabde strong enough to defend itself. At any rate, he made no effort to afford it any relief; and the Roman emperor was allowed to employ all the resources at his disposal in reiterated assaults upon the walls. The defence, however, proved stronger than the attack. Time after time the bold sallies of the besieged destroyed the Roman works. At last the rainy season set in, and the low ground outside the town became a glutinous and adhesive marsh. It was no longer possible to continue the siege; and the disappointed emperor reluctantly drew off his troops, recrossed the Euphrates, and retired into winter quarters at Antioch.

The successes of Sapor in the campaigns of A.D. 359 and 360, his captures of Amida, Singara, and Bezabde, together with the unfortunate issue of the expedition made by Constantius against the last-named place, had a tendency to shake the fidelity of the Roman vassal-kings, Arsaces of Armenia, and Meribanes of Iberia. Constantius, therefore, during the winter of A.D. 360-1, which he passed at Antioch, sent emissaries to the courts of these monarchs, and endeavored to secure their fidelity by loading them with costly presents. His policy seems to have been so far successful that no revolt of these kingdoms took place; they did not as yet desert the Romans or make their submission to Sapor. Their monarchs seem to have simply watched events, prepared to declare themselves distinctly on the winning side so soon as fortune should incline unmistakably to one or the other combatant. Meanwhile they maintained the fiction of a nominal dependence upon Rome.

It might have been expected that the year A.D. 361 would have been a turning-point in the war, and that, if Rome did not by a great effort assert herself and recover her prestige, the advance of Persia would have been marked and rapid. But the actual course of events was far different. Hesitation and diffidence characterize the movements of both parties to the contest, and the year is signalized by no important enterprise on the part of either monarch. Constantius reoccupied Edessa, and had (we are told) some thoughts of renewing the siege of Bezabde; actually, however, he did not advance further, but contented himself with sending a part of his army to watch Sapor, giving them strict orders not to risk an engagement. Sapor, on his side, began the year with demonstrations which were taken to mean that he was about to pass the Euphrates; but in reality he never even brought his troops across the Tigris, or once set foot in Mesopotamia. After wasting weeks or months in a futile display of his armed strength upon the eastern bank of the river, and violently alarming the officers sent by Constantius to observe his movements, he suddenly, towards autumn, withdrew his troops, having attempted nothing, and quietly returned to his capital! It is by no means difficult to understand the motives which actuated Constantius. He was, month after month, receiving intelligence from the West of steps taken by Julian which amounted to open rebellion, and challenged him to engage in civil war. So long as Sapor threatened invasion he did not like to quit Mesopotamia, lest he might appear to have sacrificed the interests of his country to his own private quarrels; but he must have been anxious to return to the seat of empire from the first moment that intelligence reached him of Julian's assumption of the imperial name and dignity; and when Sapor's retreat was announced he naturally made all haste to reach his capital. Meanwhile the desire of keeping his army intact caused him to refrain from any movement which involved the slightest risk of bringing on a battle, and, in fact, reduced him to inaction. So much is readily intelligible. But what at this time withheld Sapor, when he had so grand an opportunity of making an impression upon Rome—what paralyzed his arm when it might have struck with such effect it is far from easy to understand, though perhaps not imposs ble to conjecture. The historian of the war ascribes his abstinence to a religious motive, telling us that the auguries were not favorable for the Persians crossing the Tigris. But there is no other evidence that the Persians of this period were the slaves of any such superstition as that noted by Ammianus, nor any probability that a monarch of Sapor's force of character would have suffered his military policy to be affected by omens. We must therefore ascribe the conduct of the Persian king to some cause not recorded by the historian—same failure of health, or some peril from internal or external enemies which called him away from the scene of his recent exploits, just at the time when his continued presence there was most important. Once before in his lifetime, an invasion of his eastern provinces had required his immediate presence, and allowed his adversary to quit Mesopotamia and march against Magnentius. It is not improbable that a fresh attack of the same or some other barbarians now again happened opportunely for the Romans, calling Sapor away, and thus enabling Constantius to turn his hack upon the East, and set out for Europe in order to meet Julian.

The meeting, however, was not destined to take place. On his way from Antioch to Constantinople the unfortunate Constantius, anxious and perhaps over-fatigued, fell sick at Mopsucrene, in Cilicia, and died there, after a short illness, towards the close of A.D. 361. Julian the Apostate succeeded peacefully to the empire whereto he was about to assert his right by force of arms; and Sapor found that the war which he had provoked with Rome, in reliance upon his adversary's weakness and incapacity, had to be carried on with a prince of far greater natural powers and of much superior military training.

## CHAPTER X

*Julian becomes Emperor of Rome. His Resolution to invade Persia. His Views and Motives. His Proceedings. Proposals of Sapor rejected. Other Embassies. Relations of Julian with Armenia. Strength of his Army. His invasion of Mesopotamia. His Line of March. Siege of Perisabor; of Maogamalcha. Battle of the Tigris. Further Progress of Julian checked by his Inability to invest Ctesiphon. His Retreat. His Death. Retreat continued by Jovian. Sapor offers Terms of Peace. Peace made by Jovian. Its Conditions. Reflections on the Peace and on the Termination of the Second Period of Struggle between Rome and Persia.*

*"Julianus, redacta ad unum se orbis Romani curatione, glorise nimis cupidus, in Persas proficiscitur."—Aurel. Viet. Epit. §43.*

The prince on whom the government of the Roman empire, and consequently the direction of the Persian war, devolved by the death of Constantius, was in the flower of his age, proud, self-confident, and full of energy. He had been engaged for a period of four years in a struggle with the rude and warlike tribes of Germany, had freed the whole country west of the Rhine from the presence of those terrible warriors, and had even carried fire and sword far into the wild and savage districts on the right bank of the river, and compelled the Alemanni and other powerful German tribes to make their submission to the majesty of Rome. Personally brave, by temperament restless, and inspired with an ardent desire to rival or eclipse the glorious deeds of those heroes of former times who had made themselves a name in history, he viewed the disturbed condition of the East at the time of his accession not as a trouble, not as a drawback upon the delights of empire, but as a happy circumstance, a fortunate opportunity for distinguishing himself by some great achievement. Of all the Greeks, Alexander appeared to him the most illustrious; of all his predecessors on the imperial throne, Trajan and Marcus Aurelius were those whom he most wished to emulate. But all these princes had either led or sent expeditions into the far East, and had aimed at uniting in one the fairest provinces of Europe and Asia. Julian appears, from the first moment that he found himself peaceably established upon the throne, to have resolved on undertaking in person a great expedition against Sapor, with the object of avenging upon Persia the ravages and defeats of the last sixty years, or at any rate of obtaining such successes as might justify his assuming the title of "Persicus." Whether he really entertained any hope of rivalling Alexander, or supposed it possible that he should effect "the final conquest of Persia," may be doubted. Acquainted, as he must have been, with the entire course of Roman warfare in these parts from the attack of Crassus to the last defeat of his own immediate predecessor, he can scarcely have regarded the subjugation of Persia as an easy matter, or have expected to do much more than strike terror into the "barbarians" of the East, or perhaps obtain from them the cession of another province. The sensible officer, who, after accompanying him in his expedition, wrote the history of the campaign, regarded his actuating motives as the delight that he took in war, and the desire of a new title. Confident in his own military talent, in his training, and in his power to inspire enthusiasm in an army, he no doubt looked to reap laurels sufficient to justify him in making his attack; but the wild schemes ascribed to him, the conquest of the Sassanian kingdom, and the subjugation of Hyrcania and India, are figments (probably) of the imagination of his historians.

Julian entered Constantinople on the 11th of December, A.D. 361; he quitted it towards the end of May,12 A.D. 362, after residing there less than six months. During this period, notwithstanding the various important matters in which he was engaged, the purifying of the court, the depression of the Christians, the restoration and revivification of Paganism, he found time to form plans and make preparations for his intended eastern expedition, in which he was anxious to engage as soon as possible. Having designated for the war such troops as could be spared from the West, he committed them and their officers to the charge of two generals, carefully chosen, Victor, a Roman of distinction, and the Persian refugee, Prince Hormisdas, who conducted the legions without difficulty to Antioch. There Julian himself arrived in June or July 14 after having made a stately progress through Asia Minor; and it would seem that he would at once have marched against the enemy, had not his counsellors strongly urged the necessity of a short delay, during which the European troops might be rested, and adequate preparations made for the intended invasion. It was especially necessary to provide stores and ships, since the new emperor had resolved not to content himself with an ordinary campaign upon the frontier, but rather to imitate the examples of Trajan and Severus, who had carried the Roman eagles to the extreme south of Mesopotamia. Ships, accordingly, were collected, and probably built during the winter of A.D. 362-3; provisions were laid in; warlike stores, military engines, and the like accumulated; while the impatient monarch, galled by the wit and raillery of the gay Antiochenes, chafed at his compelled inaction, and longed to exchange the war of words in which he was engaged with his subjects for the ruder contests of arms wherewith use had made him more familiar.

It must have been during the emperor's stay at Antioch that he received an embassy from the court of Persia, commissioned to sound his inclinations with regard to the conclusion of a peace. Sapor had seen, with some disquiet, the sceptre of the Roman world assumed by an enterprising and courageous youth, inured to warfare and ambitious of military glory. He was probably very well informed as to the general condition of the Roman State and the personal character of its administrator; and the tidings which he received concerning the intentions and preparations, of the new prince were such as caused him some apprehension, if not actual alarm. Under these circumstance she sent an embassy with overtures, the exact nature of which is not known, but which, it is probable, took for their basis the existing territorial limits of the two countries. At least, we hear of no offer of surrender or submission on Sapor's part; and we can scarcely suppose that, had such offers been made, the Roman writers would have passed them over in silence. It is not surprising that Julian lent no favorable ear to the envoys, if these were their instructions; but it would have been better for his reputation had he replied to them with less of haughtiness and rudeness. According to one authority, he tore up before their faces the autograph letter of their master; while, according to another, he responded, with a contemptuous smile, that "there was no occasion for an exchange of thought between him and the Persian king by messengers, since he intended very shortly to treat with him in person." Having received this rebuff, the envoys of Sapor took their departure, and conveyed to their sovereign the intelligence that he must prepare himself to resist a serious invasion.

About the same time various offers of assistance reached the Roman emperor from the independent or semi-independent princes and chieftains of the regions adjacent to Mesopotamia. Such overtures were sure to be made by the heads of the plundering desert tribes to any powerful invader, since it would be hoped that a share in the booty might be obtained without much participation in the danger. We are told that Julian promptly rejected these offers, grandly saying that it was for Rome rather to give aid to her allies than to receive assistance from them. It appears, however, that at least two exceptions were made to the general principle thus magniloquently asserted. Julian had taken into his service, ere he quitted Europe, a strong body of Gothic auxiliaries; and, while at Antioch, he sent to the Saracens, reminding them of their promise to lend him troops, and calling upon them to fulfil it. If the advance on Persia was to be made by the line of the Euphrates, an alliance with these agile sons of the desert was of first-rate importance, since the assistance which they could render as friends was considerable, and the injury which they could inflict as enemies was almost beyond calculation. It is among the faults of Julian in this campaign that he did not set more store by the Saracen alliance, and make greater efforts to maintain it; we shall find that after a while he allowed the brave nomads to become disaffected, and to exchange their friendship with him for hostility. Had he taken more care to attach them cordially to the side of Rome, it is quite possible that his expedition might have had a prosperous issue.

There was another ally, whose services Julian regarded himself as entitled not to request, but to command. Arsaces, king of Armenia, though placed on his throne by Sapor, had (as we have seen) transferred his allegiance to Constantius, and voluntarily taken up the position of a Roman feudatory. Constantius had of late suspected his fidelity; but Arsaces had not as yet, by any overt act, justified these suspicions, and Julian seems to have regarded him as an assured friend and ally. Early in A.D. 363 he addressed a letter to the Armenian monarch, requiring him to levy a considerable force, and hold himself in readiness to execute such orders as he would receive within a short time. The style, address, and purport of this letter were equally distasteful to Arsaces, whose pride was outraged, and whose indolence was disturbed, by the call thus suddenly made upon him. His own desire was probably to remain neutral; he felt no interest in the standing quarrel between his two powerful neighbors; he was under obligations to both of them; and it was for his advantage that they should remain evenly balanced. We cannot ascribe to him any earnest religious feeling; but, as one who kept up the profession of Christianity, he could not but regard with aversion the Apostate, who had given no obscure intimation of his intention to use his power to the utmost in order to sweep the Christian religion from the face of the earth. The disinclination of their monarch to observe the designs of Julian was shared, or rather surpassed, by his people, the more educated portion of whom were strongly attached to the new faith and worship. If the great historian of Armenia is right in stating that Julian at this time offered an open insult to the Armenian religion, we must pronounce him strangely imprudent. The alliance of Armenia was always of the utmost importance to Rome in any attack upon the East. Julian seems to have gone out of his way to create offence in this quarter, where his interests required that he should exercise all his powers of conciliation.

The forces which the emperor regarded as at his disposal, and with which he expected to take the field, were the following. His own troops amounted to 83,000 or (according to another account) to 95,000 men. They consisted chiefly of Roman legionaries, horse and foot, but included a strong body of Gothic auxiliaries. Armenia was expected to furnish a considerable force, probably not less than 20,000 men; and the light horse of the Saracens would, it was thought, be tolerably numerous. Altogether, an army of above a hundred thousand men was about to be launched on the devoted Persia, which was believed unlikely to offer any effectual, if even any serious, resistance.

The impatience of Julian scarcely allowed him to await the conclusion of the winter. With the first breath of spring he put his forces in motion, and, quitting Antioch, marched with all speed to the Euphrates. Passing Litarbi, and then Hiapolis, he crossed the river by a bridge of boats in the vicinity that place, and proceeded by Batnee to the important city of Carrhae, once the home of Abraham. Here he halted for a few days and finally fixed his plans. It was by this time well known to the Romans that there were two, and two only, convenient roads whereby Southern Mesopotamia was to be reached, one along the line of the Mons Masius to the Tigris, and then along the banks of that stream, the other down the valley of the Euphrates to the great alluvial plain on the lower course of the rivers. Julian had, perhaps, hitherto doubted which line he should follow in person. The first had been preferred by Alexander and by Trajan, the second by the younger Cyrus, by Avidius Cassius, and by Severus. Both lines were fairly practicable; but that of the Tigris was circuitous, and its free employment was only possible under the condition of Armenia being certainly friendly. If Julian had cause to suspect, as it is probable that he had, the fidelity of the Armenians, he may have felt that there was one line only which he could with prudence pursue. He might send a subsidiary force by the doubtful route which could advance to his aid if matters went favorably, or remain on the defensive if they assumed a threatening aspect; but his own grand attack must be by the other. Accordingly he divided his forces. Committing a body of troops, which is variously estimated at from

18,000 to 30,000, into the hands of Procopius, a connection of his own, and Sebastian, Duke of Egypt, with orders that they should proceed by way of the Mons Masius to Armenia, and, uniting themselves with the forces of Arsaces, invade Northern Media, ravage it, and then join him before Ctesiphon by the line of the Tigris, he reserved for himself and for his main army the shorter and more open route down the valley of the Euphrates. Leaving Carrhae on the 26th of March, after about a week's stay, he marched southward, at the head of 65,000 men, by Davana and along the course of the Belik, to Callinicus or Nicophorium, near the junction of the Belik with the Euphrates. Here the Saracen chiefs came and made their submission, and were graciously received by the emperor, to whom they presented a crown of gold. At the same time the fleet made its appearance, numbering at least 1100 vessels, of which fifty were ships of war, fifty prepared to serve as pontoons, and the remaining thousand, transports laden with provisions, weapons, and military engines.

From Callinicus the emperor marched along the course of the Euphrates to Circusium, or Circesium, at the junction of the Khabour with the Euphrates, arriving at this place early in April. Thus far he had been marching through his own dominions, and had had no hostility to dread. Being now about to enter the enemy's country, he made arrangements for the march which seem to have been extremely judicious. The cavalry was placed under the command of Arinthseus and Prince Hormisdas, and was stationed at the extreme left, with orders to advance on a line parallel with the general course of the river. Some picked legions under the command of Nevitta formed the right wing, and, resting on the Euphrates, maintained communication with the fleet. Julian, with the main part of his troops, occupied the space intermediate between these two extremes, marching in a loose column which from front to rear covered a distance of above nine miles. A flying corps of fifteen hundred men acted as an avant-guard under Count Lucilianus, and explored the country in advance, feeling on all sides for the enemy. The rear was covered by a detachment under Secundinus, Duke of Osrhoene, Dagalaiphus, and Victor.

Having made his dispositions, and crossed the broad stream of the Khabour, on the 7th of April, by a bridge of boats, which he immediately broke up, Julian continued his advance along the course of the Euphrates, supported by his fleet, which was not allowed either to outstrip or to lag behind the army. The first halt was at Zaitha, famous as the scene of the murder of Gordian, whose tomb was in its vicinity. Here Julian encouraged his soldiers by an eloquent speech, in which he recounted the past successes of the Roman arms, and promised them an easy victory over their present adversary. He then, in a two days' march, reached Dura, a ruined city, destitute of inhabitants, on the banks of the river; from which a march of four days more brought him to Anathan, the modern Anah, a strong fortress on an island in the mid-stream, which was held by a Persian garrison. An attempt to surprise the place by a night attack having failed, Julian had recourse to persuasion, and by the representations of Prince Hormisdas induced its defenders to surrender the fort and place themselves at his mercy. It was, perhaps, to gall the Antiochenes with an indication of his victorious progress that he sent his prisoners under escort into Syria, and settled them in the territory of Chalcis, at no great distance from the city of his aversion. Unwilling further to weaken his army by detaching a garrison to hold his conquest, he committed Anathan to the flames before proceeding further down the river.

About eight miles below Anathan, another island and another fortress were held by the enemy. Thilutha is described as stronger than Anathan, and indeed as almost impregnable. Julian felt that he could not attack it with any hope of success, and therefore once more submitted to use persuasion. But the garrison, feeling themselves secure, rejected his overtures; they would wait, they said, and see which party was superior in the approaching conflict, and would then attach themselves to the victors. Meanwhile, if unmolested by the invader, they would not interfere with his advance, but would maintain a neutral attitude. Julian had to determine whether he would act in the spirit of an

Alexander, and, rejecting with disdain all compromise, compel by force of arms an entire submission, or whether he would take lower ground, accept the offer made to him, and be content to leave in his rear a certain number of unconquered fortresses. He decided that prudence required him to take the latter course, and left Thilutha unassailed. It is not surprising that, having admitted the assumption of a neutral position by one town, he was forced to extend the permission to others, and so to allow the Euphrates route to remain, practically, in the hands of the Persians.

A. five days' march from Thilutha brought the army to a point opposite Diacira, or Hit, a town of ancient repute, and one which happened to be well provided with stores and provisions. Though the place lay on the right bank of the river, it was still exposed to attack, as the fleet could convey any number of troops from one shore to the other. Being considered untenable, it was deserted by the male inhabitants, who, however, left some of their women behind them. We obtain an unpleasant idea of the state of discipline which the philosophic emperor allowed to prevail, when we find that his soldiers, "without remorse and without punishment, massacred these defenceless persons." The historian of the war records this act without any appearance of shame, as if it were a usual occurrence, and no more important than the burning of the plundered city which followed.

From Hit the army pursued its march, through Sitha and Megia, to Zaragardia or Ozogardana, where the memory of Trajan's expedition still lingered, a certain pedestal or pulpit of stone being known to the natives as "Trajan's tribunal." Up to this time nothing had been seen or heard of any Persian opposing army; one man only on the Roman side, so far as we hear, had been killed. No systematic method of checking the advance had been adopted; the corn was everywhere found standing; forage was plentiful; and there were magazines of grain in the towns. No difficulties had delayed the invaders but such as Nature had interposed to thwart them, as when a violent storm on one occasion shattered the tents, and on another a sudden swell of the Euphrates wrecked some of the corn transports, and interrupted the right wing's line of march. But this pleasant condition of things was not to continue. At Hit the rolling Assyrian plain had come to an end, and the invading army had entered upon the low alluvium of Babylonia, a region of great fertility, intersected by numerous canals, which in some places were carried the entire distance from the one river to the other. The change in the character of the country encouraged the Persians to make a change in their tactics. Hitherto they had been absolutely passive; now at last they showed themselves, and commenced the active system of perpetual harassing warfare in which they were adepts. A surena, or general of the first rank, appeared in the field, at the head of a strong body of Persian horse, and accompanied by a sheikh of the Saracenic Arabs, known as Malik (or "King") Rodoseces. Retreating as Julian advanced, but continually delaying his progress, hanging on the skirts of his army, cutting off his stragglers, and threatening every unsupported detachment, this active force changed all the conditions of the march, rendering it slow and painful, and sometimes stopping it altogether. We are told that on one occasion Prince Hormisdas narrowly escaped falling into the surena's hands. On another, the Persian force, having allowed the Roman vanguard to proceed unmolested, suddenly showed itself on the southern bank of one of the great canals connecting the Euphrates with the Tigris, and forbade the passage of Julian's main army. It was only after a day and a night's delay that the emperor, by detaching troops under Victor to make a long circuit, cross the canal far to the east, recall Lucilianus with the vanguard, and then attack the surena's troops in the rear, was able to overcome the resistance in his front, and carry his army across the cutting.

Having in this way effected the passage, Julian continued his march along the Euphrates, and in a short time came to the city of Perisabor (Mruz Shapur), the most important that he had yet reached, and reckoned not much inferior to Otesiphon. As the inhabitants steadily refused all accommodation, and insulted Hormisdas, who was sent to treat with them, by the reproach that he was a deserter and a traitor, the emperor determined to form the siege of the place and see if he could not compel it to a surrender. Situated between the Euphrates and one of the numerous canals derived from it, and further protected by a trench drawn across from the canal to the river, Perisabor occupied a sort of island, while at the same time it was completely surrounded with a double wall. The citadel, which lay towards the north, and overhung the Euphrates, was especially strong; and the garrison was brave, numerous, and full of confidence. The walls, however, composed in part of brick laid in bitumen, were not of much strength; and the Roman soldiers found little difficulty in shattering with the ram one of the corner towers, and so making an entrance into the place. But the real struggle now began. The brave defenders retreated into the citadel, which was of imposing height, and from this vantage-ground galled the Romans in the town with an incessant shower of arrows, darts, and stones. The ordinary catapults and balistae of the Romans were no match for such a storm descending from such a height; and it was plainly necessary, if the place was to be taken, to have recourse to some other device. Julian, therefore, who was never sparing of his own person, took the resolution, on the second day of the siege, of attempting to burst open one of the gates. Accompanied by a small band, who formed a roof over his head with their shields, and by a few sappers with their tools, he approached the gate-tower, and made his men commence their operations. The doors, however, were found to be protected with iron, and the fastenings to be so strong that no immediate impression could be made; while the alarmed garrison, concentrating its attention on the threatened spot, kept up a furious discharge of missiles on their daring assailants. Prudence counselled retreat from the dangerous position which had been taken up; and the emperor, though he felt acutely the shame of having failed, retired. But his mind, fertile in resource, soon formed a new plan. He remembered that Demetrius Poliorcetes had acquired his surname by the invention and use of the "Helepolis," a movable tower of vast height, which placed the assailants on a level with the defenders even of the loftiest ramparts. He at once ordered the construction of such a machine; and, the ability of his engineers being equal to the task, it rapidly grew before his eyes. The garrison saw its growth with feelings very opposite to those of their assailant; they felt that they could not resist the new creation, and anticipated its employment by a surrender, Julian agreed to spare their lives, and allowed them to withdraw and join their countrymen, each man taking with him a spare garment and a certain sum of money. The other stores contained within the walls fell to the conquerors, who found them to comprise a vast quantity of corn, arms, and other valuables. Julian distributed among his troops whatever was likely to be serviceable; the remainder, of which he could make no use, was either burned or thrown into the Euphrates.

The latitude of Ctesiphon was now nearly reached, but Julian still continued to descend the Euphrates, while the Persian cavalry made occasional dashes upon his extended line, and sometimes caused him a sensible loss. At length he came to the point where the Nahr-Malcha, or "Royal river," the chief of the canals connecting the Euphrates with the Tigris, branched off from the more western stream, and ran nearly due east to the vicinity of the capital. The canal was navigable by his ships, and he therefore at this point quitted the Euphrates, and directed his march eastward along the course of the cutting, following in the footsteps of Severus, and no doubt expecting, like him, to capture easily the great metropolitan city. But his advance across the neck of land which here separates the Tigris from the Euphrates was painful and difficult, since the enemy laid the country under water, and at every favorable point disputed his progress. Julian, however, still pressed forward, and advanced, though slowly. By felling the palms which grew abundantly in this region, and forming with them rafts supported by inflated skins, he was able to pass the inundated district, and to approach within about eleven miles of Ctesiphon. Here his further march was obstructed by a fortress, built (as it would seem) to defend the capital, and fortified with especial care. Ammianus calls this place Maoga-malcha, while Zosimus gives it the name of Besuchis; but both agree that it was a large town, commanded by a strong citadel, and held by a brave and numerous garrison. Julian might perhaps have left it unassailed, as he had left already several towns upon his line of march; but a daring attempt made against himself by a portion of the garrison caused him to feel his honor concerned in taking the place; and the result was that he once more arrested his steps, and, sitting down before the walls, commenced a formal siege. All the usual arts of attack and defence were employed on either side for several days, the chief novel feature in the warfare being the use by the besieged of blazing balls of bitumen, which they shot from their lofty towers against the besiegers' works and persons. Julian, however, met this novelty by a device on his side which was uncommon; he continued openly to assault the walls and gates with his battering rams, but he secretly gave orders that the chief efforts of his men should be directed to the formation of a mine, which should be carried under both the walls that defended the place, and enable him to introduce suddenly a body of troops into the very heart of the city. His orders were successfully executed; and while a general attack upon the defences occupied the attention of the besieged, three corps introduced through the mine suddenly showed themselves in the town itself, and rendered further resistance hopeless. Maogamalcha, which a little before had boasted of being impregnable, and had laughed to scorn the vain efforts of the emperor, suddenly found itself taken by assault and undergoing the extremities of sack and pillage. Julian made no efforts to prevent a general massacre, and the entire population, without distinction of age or sex, seems to have been put to the sword. The commandant of the fortress, though he was at first spared, suffered death shortly after on a frivolous charge. Even a miserable remnant, which had concealed itself in caves and cellars, was hunted out, smoke and fire being used to force the fugitives from their hiding-places, or else cause them to perish in the darksome dens by suffocation. Thus there was no extremity of savage warfare which was not used, the fourth century anticipating some of the horrors which have most disgraced the nineteenth.

Nothing now but the river Tigris intervened between Julian and the great city of Ctesiphon, which was plainly the special object of the expedition. Ctesiphon, indeed, was not to Persia what it had been to Parthia; but still it might fairly be looked upon as a prize of considerable importance. Of Parthia it had been the main, in later times perhaps the sole, capital; to Persia it was a secondary rather than a primary city, the ordinary residence of the court being Istakr, or Persepolis. Still the Persian kings seem occasionally to have resided at Ctesiphon; and among the secondary cities of the empire it undoubtedly held a high rank. In the neighborhood were various royal hunting-seats, surrounded by shady gardens, and adorned with paintings or bas-reliefs; while near them were parks or "paradises," containing the game kept for the prince's sport, which included lions, wild boars, and bears of remarkable fierceness. As Julian advanced, these pleasaunces fell, one after another, into his hands, and were delivered over to the rude soldiery, who trampled the flowers and shrubs under foot, destroyed the wild beasts, and burned the residences. No serious resistance was as yet made by any Persian force to the progress of the Romans, who pressed steadily forward, occasionally losing a few men or a few baggage animals, but drawing daily nearer to the great city, and on their way spreading ruin and desolation over a most fertile district, from which they drew abundant supplies as they passed through it, while they left it behind them blackened, wasted, and almost without inhabitant. The Persians seem to have had orders not to make, as yet, any firm stand. One of the sons of Sapor was now at their head, but no change of tactics occurred. As Julian drew near, this prince indeed quitted the shelter of Ctesiphon, and made a reconnaissance in force; but when he fell in with the Roman advanced guard under Victor, and saw its strength, he declined an engagement, and retired without coming to blows.

Julian had now reached the western suburb of Ctesiphon, which had lost its old name of Seleucia and was known as Coche. The capture of this place would, perhaps, not have been difficult; but, as the broad and deep stream of the Tigris flowed between it and the main town, little would have been gained by the occupation. Julian felt that, to attack Ctesiphon with success, he must, like Trajan and Severus, transport his army to the left bank of the Tigris, and deliver his assault upon the defences that lay beyond that river. For the safe transport of his army he trusted to his fleet, which he had therefore caused to enter the Nahr-Malcha, and to accompany his troops thus far. But at Coche he found that the Nahr-Malcha, instead of joining the Tigris, as he had expected, above Ctesiphon, ran into it at some distance below. To have pursued this line with both fleet and army would have carried him too far into the enemy's country, have endangered his communications, and especially have cut him off from the Armenian army under Procopius and Sebastian, with which he was at this time looking to effect a junction. To have sent the fleet into the Tigris below Coche, while the army occupied the right bank of the river above it, would, in the first place, have separated the two, and would further have been useless, unless the fleet could force its way against the strong current through the whole length of the hostile city. In this difficulty Julian's book-knowledge was found of service. He had studied with care the campaigns of his predecessors in these regions, and recollected that one of them at any rate had made a cutting from the Nahr-Malcha, by which he had brought his fleet into the Tigris above Ctesiphon. If this work could be discovered, it might, he thought, in all probability be restored. Some of the country people were therefore seized, and, inquiry being made of them, the line of the canal was pointed out, and the place shown at which it had been derived from the Nahr-Malcha. Here the Persians had erected a strong dam, with sluices, by means of which a portion of the water could occasionally be turned into the Roman cutting. Julian had the cutting cleared out, and the dam torn down; whereupon the main portion of the stream rushed at once into the old channel, which rapidly filled, and was found to be navigable by the Roman vessels. The fleet was thus brought into the Tigris above Coche; and the army advancing with it encamped upon the right bank of the river.

The Persians now for the first time appeared in force. As Julian drew near the great stream, he perceived that his passage of it would not be unopposed. Along the left bank, which was at this point naturally higher than the right, and which was further crowned by a wall built originally to fence in one of the royal parks, could be seen the dense masses of the enemy's-horse and foot, stretching away to right and left, the former encased in glittering armor, the latter protected by huge wattled shields. Behind these troops were discernible the vast forms of elephants, looking (says the historian) like moving mountains, and regarded by the legionaries with extreme dread. Julian felt that he could not ask his army to cross the stream openly in the face of a foe thus advantageously posted. He therefore waited the approach of night. When darkness had closed in, he made his dispositions; divided his fleet into portions; embarked a number of his troops; and, despite the dissuasions of his officers, gave the signal for the passage to commence. Five ships, each of them conveying eighty soldiers, led the way, and reached the opposite shore without accident. Here, however, the enemy received them with a sharp fire of burning darts, and the two foremost were soon in flames. At the ominous sight the rest of the fleet wavered, and might have refused to proceed further, had not Julian, with admirable presence of mind, exclaimed aloud—"Our men have crossed and are masters of the bank—that fire is the signal which I bade them make if they were victorious." Thus encouraged, the crews plied their oars with vigor, and impelled the remaining vessels rapidly across the stream. At the same time, some of the soldiers who had not been put on board, impatient to assist their comrades, plunged into the stream, and swam across supported by their shields. Though a stout resistance was offered by the Persians, it was found impossible to withstand the impetuosity of the Roman attack. Not only were the half-burned vessels saved, the flames extinguished, and the men on board rescued from their perilous position, but everywhere the Roman troops made good their landing, fought their way up the bank against a storm of missile weapons, and drew up in good order upon its summit. A pause probably now occurred, as the armies could not see each other in the darkness; but, at dawn of day, Julian, having made a fresh arrangement of his troops, led them against the dense array of the enemy, and engaged in a hand-to-hand combat, which lasted from morning to midday, when it was terminated by the flight of the Persians. Their leaders, Tigranes, Narseus, and the Surena, are said to have been the first to quit the field and take refuge within the defences of Ctesiphon. The example thus set was universally followed; and the entire Persian army, abandoning its camp and baggage, rushed in the wildest confusion across the plain to the nearest of the city gates, closely pursued by its active foe up to the very foot of the walls. The Roman writers assert that Ctesiphon might have been entered and taken, had not the general, Victor, who was wounded by a dart from a catapult, recalled his men as they were about to rush in through the open gateway. It is perhaps doubtful whether success would really have crowned such audacity. At any rate the opportunity passed—the runaways entered the town—the gate closed upon them; and Ctesiphon was safe unless it were reduced by the operations of a regular siege.

But the fruits of the victory were still considerable. The entire Persian army collected hitherto for the defence of Ctesiphon had been defeated by one-third of the Roman force under Julian. The vanquished had left 2,500 men dead upon the field, while the victors had lost no more than seventy-five. A rich spoil had fallen into the hands of the Romans, who found in the abandoned camp couches and tables of massive silver, and on the bodies of the slain, both men and horses, a profusion of gold and silver ornaments, besides trappings and apparel of great magnificence. A welcome supply of provisions was also furnished by the lands and houses in the neighborhood of Ctesiphon; and the troops passed from a state of privation to one of extreme abundance, so that it was feared lest they might suffer from excess.

Affairs had now reached a point when it was necessary to form a definite resolution as to what should be the further aim and course of the expedition. Hitherto all had indicated an intention on the part of Julian to occupy Ctesiphon, and thence dictate a peace. His long march, his toilsome canal-cutting, his orders to his second army, his crossing of the Tigris, his engagement with the Persians in the plain before Ctesiphon, were the natural steps conducting to such a result, and are explicable on one hypothesis and one hypothesis only. He must up to this time have designed to make himself master of the great city, which had been the goal of so many previous invasions, and had always fallen whenever Rome attacked it. But, having overcome all the obstacles in his path, and having it in his power at once to commence the siege, a sudden doubt appears to have assailed him as to the practicability of the undertaking. It can scarcely be supposed that the city was really stronger now than it had been under the Parthians; much less can it be argued that Julian's army was insufficient for the investment of such a place. It was probably the most powerful army with which the Romans had as yet invaded Southern Mesopotamia; and it was amply provided with all the appurtenances of war. If Julian did not venture to attempt what Trajan and Avidius Cassius and Septimius Severus had achieved without difficulty, it must have been because the circumstances under which he would have had to make the attack were different from those under which they had ventured and succeeded. And the difference—a most momentous one—was this. They besieged and captured the place after defeating the greatest force that Parthia could bring into the field against them. Julian found himself in front of Ctesiphon before he had crossed swords with the Persian king, or so much as set eyes on the grand army which Sapor was known to have collected. To have sat down before Ctesiphon under such circumstances would have been to expose himself to great peril; while he was intent upon the siege, he might at any time have been attacked by a relieving army under the Great King, have been placed between two fires, and compelled to engage at extreme disadvantage. It was a consideration of this danger that impelled the council of war, whereto he submitted the question, to pronounce the siege of Ctesiphon too hazardous an operation, and to dissuade the emperor from attempting it.

But, if the city were not to be besieged, what course could with any prudence be adopted? It would have been madness to leave Ctesiphon unassailed, and to press forward against Susa and Persepolis. It would have been futile to remain encamped before the walls without commencing a siege. The heats of summer had arrived, and the malaria of autumn was not far off. The stores brought by the fleet were exhausted; and there was a great risk in the army's depending wholly for its subsistence on the supplies that it might be able to obtain from the enemy's country. Julian and his advisers must have seen at a glance that if the Romans were not to attack Ctesiphon, they must retreat. And accordingly retreat seems to have been at once determined on. As a first step, the whole fleet, except some dozen vessels, was burned, since twelve was a sufficient number to serve as pontoons, and it was not worth the army's while to encumber itself with the remainder. They could only have been tracked up the strong stream of the Tigris by devoting to the work some 20,000 men; thus greatly weakening the strength of the armed force, and at the same time hampering its movements. Julian, in sacrificing his ships, suffered simply a pecuniary loss—they could not possibly have been of any further service to him in the campaign.

Retreat being resolved upon, it only remained to determine what route should be followed, and on what portion of the Roman territory the march should be directed. The soldiers clamored for a return by the way whereby they had come but many valid objections to this course presented themselves to their commanders. The country along the line of the Euphrates had been exhausted of its stores by the troops in their advance; the forage had been consumed, the towns and villages desolated. There would be neither food nor shelter for the men along this route; the season was also unsuitable for it, since the Euphrates was in full flood, and the moist atmosphere would be sure to breed swarms of flies and mosquitoes. Julian saw that by far the best line of retreat was along the Tigris, which had higher banks than the Euphrates, which was no longer in flood, and which ran through a tract that was highly productive and that had for many years not been visited by an enemy. The army, therefore, was ordered to commence its retreat through the country lying on the left bank of the Tigris, and to spread itself over the fertile region, in the hope of obtaining ample supplies. The march was understood to be directed on Cordyene (Kurdistan), a province now in the possession of Rome, a rich tract, and not more than about 250 miles distant from Ctesiphon.

Before, however, the retreat commenced, while Julian and his victorious army were still encamped in sight of Ctesiphon, the Persian king, according to some writers, sent an embassy proposing terms of peace. Julian's successes are represented as having driven Sapor to despair—"the pride of his royalty was humbled in the dust; he took his repasts on the ground; and the grief and anxiety of his mind were expressed by the disorder of his hair." He would, it is suggested, have been willing "to purchase, with one half of his kingdom, the safety of the remainder, and would have gladly subscribed himself, in a treaty of peace, the faithful and dependent ally of the Roman conqueror." Such are the pleasing fictions wherewith the rhetorician of Antioch, faithful to the memory of his friend and master, consoled himself and his readers after Julian's death. It is difficult to decide whether there underlies them any substratum of truth. Neither Ammianus nor Zosimus makes the slightest allusion to any negotiations at all at this period; and it is thus open to doubt whether the entire story told by Libanius is not the product of his imagination. But at any rate it is quite impossible that the Persian king can have made any abject offers of submission, or have been in a state of mind at all akin to despair. His great army, collected from all quarters, was intact; he had not yet condescended to take the field in person; he had lost no important town, and his adversary had tacitly confessed his inability to form the siege of a city which was far from being the greatest in the empire. If Sapor, therefore, really made at this time overtures of peace, it must have been either with the intention of amusing Julian, and increasing his difficulties by delaying his retreat, or because he thought that Julian's consciousness of his difficulties would induce him to offer terms which he might accept.

The retreat commenced on June 16. Scarcely were the troops set in motion, when an ominous cloud of dust appeared on the southern horizon, which grew larger as the day advanced; and, though some suggested that the appearance was produced by a herd of wild asses, and others ventured the conjecture that it was caused by the approach of a body of Julian's Saracenic allies, the emperor himself was not deceived, but, understanding that the Persians had set out in pursuit, he called in his stragglers, massed his troops, and pitched his camp in a strong position. Day-dawn showed that he had judged aright, for the earliest rays of the sun were reflected from the polished breastplates and cuirasses of the Persians, who had drawn up at no great distance during the night. A combat followed in which the Persian and Saracenic horse attacked the Romans vigorously, and especially threatened the baggage, but were repulsed by the firmness and valor of the Roman foot. Julian was able to continue his retreat after a while, but found himself surrounded by enemies, some of whom, keeping in advance of his troops, or hanging upon his flanks, destroyed the corn and forage that his men so much needed; while others, pressing upon his rear, retarded his march, and caused him from time to time no inconsiderable losses. The retreat under these circumstances was slow; the army had to be rested and recruited when it fell in with any accumulation of provisions; and the average progress made seems to have been not much more than ten miles a day. This tardy advance allowed the more slow-moving portion of the Persian army to close in upon the retiring Romans; and Julian soon found himself closely followed by dense masses of the enemy's troops, by the heavy cavalry clad in steel panoplies, and armed with long spears, by large bodies of archers, and even by a powerful corps of elephants. This grand army was under the command of a general whom the Roman writers call Meranes, and of two sons of Sapor. It pressed heavily upon the Roman rearguard; and Julian, after a little while, found it necessary to stop his march, confront his pursuers, and offer them battle. The offer was accepted, and an engagement took place in a tract called Maranga. The enemy advanced in two lines—the first composed of the mailed horsemen and the archers intermixed, the second of the elephants. Julian prepared his army to receive the attack by disposing it in the form of a crescent, with the centre drawn back considerably; but as the Persians advanced into the hollow space, he suddenly led his troops forward at speed, allowing the archers scarcely time to discharge their arrows before he engaged them and the horse in close combat. A long and bloody struggle followed; but the Persians were unaccustomed to hand-to-hand fighting and disliked it; they gradually gave ground, and at last broke up and fled, covering their retreat, however, with the clouds of arrows which they knew well how to discharge as they retired. The weight of their arms, and the fiery heat of the summer sun, prevented the Romans from carrying the pursuit very far. Julian recalled them quickly to the protection of the camp, and suspended his march for some days while the wounded had their hurts attended to.

The Persian troops, having suffered heavily in the battle, made no attempt to storm the Roman camp. They were content to spread themselves on all sides, to destroy or carry off all the forage and provisions, and to make the country, through which the Roman army must retire, a desert. Julian's forces were already suffering severely from scarcity of food, and the general want was but very slightly relieved by a distribution of the stores set apart for the officers and for the members of the imperial household. Under these circumstances it is not surprising that Julian's firmness deserted him, and that he began to give way to melancholy forebodings, and to see visions and omens which portended disaster and death. In the silence of his tent, as he studied a favorite philosopher during the dead of night, he thought he saw the Genius of the State, with veiled head and cornucopia, stealing away through the hangings slowly and sadly. Soon afterwards, when he had just gone forth into the open air to perform averting sacrifices, the fall of a shooting star seemed to him a direct threat from Mars, with whom he had recently quarrelled. The soothsayers were consulted, and counselled abstinence from all military movement; but the exigencies of the situation caused their advice to be for once contemned. It was only by change of place that there was any chance of obtaining supplies of food; and ultimate extrication from the perils that surrounded the army depended on a steady persistence in retreat.

At dawn of day, therefore, on the memorable 26th of June, A.D. 363, the tents were struck, and the Roman army continued its march across the wasted plain, having the Tigris at some little distance on its left, and some low hills upon its right. The enemy did not anywhere appear; and the troops advanced for a time without encountering opposition. But, as they drew near the skirts of the hills, not far from Samarah, suddenly an attack was made upon them. The rearguard found itself violently assailed; and when Julian hastened to its relief, news came that the van was also engaged with the enemy, and was already in difficulties. The active commander now hurried towards the front, and had accomplished half the distance, when the main Persian attack was delivered upon his right centre, and to his dismay he found himself entangled amid the masses of heavy horse and elephants, which had thrown his columns into confusion. The suddenness of the enemy's appearance had prevented him from donning his complete armor; and as he fought without a breastplate, and with the aid of his light-armed troops restored the day, falling on the foe from behind and striking the backs and houghs of the horses and elephants, the javelin of a horseman, after grazing the flesh of his arm, fixed itself in his right side, penetrating-through the ribs to the liver. Julian, grasping the head of the weapon, attempted to draw it forth, but in vain—the sharp steel cut his fingers, and the pain and loss of blood caused him to fall fainting from his steed. His guards, who had closed around him, carefully raised him up, and conveyed him to the camp, where the surgeons at once declared the wound mortal. The sad news spread rapidly among the soldiery, and nerved them to desperate efforts—if they must lose their general, he should, they determined, be avenged. Striking their shields with their spears, they everywhere rushed upon the enemy with incredible ardor, careless whether they lived or died, and only seeking to inflict the greatest possible loss on those opposed to them. But the Persians, who had regarded the day as theirs, resisted strenuously, and maintained the fight with obstinacy till evening closed in and darkness put a stop to the engagement. The losses were large on both sides; the Roman right wing had suffered greatly; its commander, Anatolius, master of the offices, was among the slain, and the prefect Sallust was with difficulty saved by an attendant. The Persians, too, lost their generals Meranes and Nohodares; and with them no fewer than fifty satraps and great nobles are said to have perished. The rank and file no doubt suffered in proportion; and the Romans were perhaps justified in claiming that the balance of advantage upon the day rested with them. But such advantage as they could reasonably assert was far more than counterbalanced by the loss of their commander, who died in his tent towards midnight on the day of the battle. Whatever we may think of the general character of Julian, or of the degree of his intellectual capacity, there can be no question as to his excellence as a soldier, or his ability as a commander in the field. If the expedition which he had led into Persia was to some extent rash—if his preparations for it had been insufficient, and his conduct of it not wholly faultless; if consequently he had brought the army of the East into a situation of great peril and difficulty—yet candor requires us to acknowledge that of all the men collected in the Roman camp he was the fittest to have extricated the army from its embarrassments, and have conducted it, without serious disaster or loss of honor, into a position of safety. No one, like Julian, possessed the confidence of the troops; no one so combined experience in command with the personal activity and vigor that was needed under the circumstances. When the leaders met to consult about the appointment of a successor to the dead prince, it was at once apparent how irreparable was their loss. The prefect Sallust, whose superior rank and length of service pointed him out for promotion to the vacant post, excused himself on account of his age and infirmities. The generals of the second grade—Arintheseus, Victor, Nevitta, Dagalaiphus—had each their party among the soldiers, but were unacceptable to the army generally. None could claim any superior merit which might clearly place him above the rest; and a discord that might have led to open strife seemed impending, when a casual voice pronounced the name of Jovian, and, some applause following the suggestion, the rival generals acquiesced in the choice; and this hitherto insignificant officer was suddenly invested with the purple and saluted as "Augustus" and "Emperor." Had there been any one really fit to take the command, such an appointment could not have been made; out, in the evident dearth of warlike genius, it was thought best that one whose rank was civil rather than military should be preferred, for the avoidance of jealousies and contentions. A deserter carried the news to Sapor, who was not now very far distant, and described the new emperor to him as effeminate and slothful. A fresh impulse was given to the pursuit by the intelligence thus conveyed; the army engaged in disputing the Roman retreat was reinforced by a strong body of cavalry; and Sapor himself pressed forward with all haste, resolved to hurl his main force on the rear of the retreating columns.

It was with reluctance that Jovian, on the day of his elevation to the supreme power (June 27, A.D. 363), quitted the protection of the camp, and proceeded to conduct his army over the open plain, where the Persians were now collected in great force, prepared to dispute the ground with him inch by inch. Their horse and elephants again fell upon the right wing of the Romans, where the Jovians and Herculians were now posted, and, throwing those renowned corps into disorder, pressed on, driving them across the plain in headlong flight and slaying vast numbers of them. The corps would probably have been annihilated, had they not in their flight reached a hill occupied by the baggage train, which gallantly came to their aid, and, attacking the horse and elephants from higher ground, gained a signal success. The elephants, wounded by the javelins hurled down upon them from above, and maddened with the pain, turned upon their own side, and, roaring frightfully, carried confusion among the ranks of the horse, which broke up and fled. Many of the frantic animals were killed by their own riders or by the Persians on whom they were trampling, while others succumbed to the blows dealt them by the enemy. There was a frightful carnage, ending in the repulse of the Persians and the resumption of the Roman march. Shortly before night fell, Jovian and his army reached Samarah, then a fort of no great size upon the Tigris, and, encamping in its vicinity, passed the hours of rest unmolested. The retreat now continued for four days along the left bank of the Tigris, the progress made each day being small, since the enemy incessantly obstructed the march, pressing on the columns as they retired, but when they stopped drawing off, and declining an engagement at close quarters. On one occasion they even attacked the Roman camp, and, after insulting the legions with their cries, forced their way through the preatorian gate, and had nearly penetrated to the royal tent, when they were met and defeated by the legionaries. The Saracenic Arabs were especially troublesome. Offended by the refusal of Julian to continue their subsidies, they had transferred their services wholly to the other side, and pursued the Romans with a hostility that was sharpened by indignation and resentment. It was with difficulty that the Roman army, at the close of the fourth day, reached Dura, a small place upon the Tigris, about eighteen miles north of Samarah. Here a new idea seized the soldiers. As the Persian forces were massed chiefly on the left bank of the Tigris, and might find it difficult to transfer themselves to the other side, it seemed to the legionaries that they would escape half their difficulties if they could themselves cross the river, and place it between them and their foes. They had also a notion that on the west side of the stream the Roman frontier was not far distant, but might be reached by forced marches in a few days. They therefore begged Jovian to allow them to swim the stream. It was in vain that he and his officers opposed the project; mutinous cries arose; and, to avoid worse evils, he was compelled to consent that five hundred Gauls and Sarmatians, known to be expert swimmers, should make the attempt. It succeeded beyond his hopes. The corps crossed at night, surprised the Persians who held the opposite bank, and established themselves in a safe position before the dawn of day. By this bold exploit the passage of the other troops, many of whom could not swim, was rendered feasible, and Jovian proceeded to collect timber, brushwood, and skins for the formation of large rafts on which he might transport the rest of his army.

These movements were seen with no small disquietude by the Persian king. The army which he had regarded as almost a certain prey seemed about to escape him. He knew that his troops could not pass the Tigris by swimming; he had, it is probable, brought with him no boats, and the country about Dura could not supply many; to follow the Romans, if they crossed the stream, he must construct a bridge, and the construction of a bridge was, to such unskilful engineers as the Persians, a work of time. Before it was finished the legions might be beyond his reach, and so the campaign would end, and he would have gained no advantage from it. Under these circumstances he determined to open negotiations with the Romans, and to see if he could not extract from their fears some important concessions. They were still in a position of great peril, since they could not expect to embark and cross the stream without suffering tremendous loss from the enemy before whom they would be flying. And it was uncertain what perils they might not encounter beyond the river in traversing the two hundred miles that still separated them from Roman territory. The Saracenic allies of Persia were in force on the further side of the stream; and a portion of Sapor's army might be conveyed across in time to hang on the rear of the legions and add largely to their difficulties. At any rate, it was worth while to make overtures and see what answer would be returned. If the idea of negotiating were entertained at all, something would be gained; for each additional day of suffering and privation diminished the Roman strength, and brought nearer the moment of absolute and complete exhaustion. Moreover, a bridge might be at once commenced at some little distance, and might be pushed forward, so that, if the negotiations failed, there should be no great delay in following the Romans across the river.

Such were probably the considerations which led Sapor to send as envoys to the Roman camp at Dura the Surena and another great noble, who announced that they came to offer terms of peace. The great king, they said, having respect to the mutability of human affairs, was desirous of dealing mercifully with the Romans, and would allow the escape of the remnant which was left of their army, if the Caesar and his advisers accepted the conditions that he required. These conditions would be explained to any envoys whom Jovian might empower to discuss them with the Persian plenipotentiaries. The Roman emperor and his council gladly caught at the offer; and two officers of high rank, the general Arintheus and the prefect Sallust, were at once appointed to confer with Sapor's envoys, and ascertain the terms on which peace would be granted. They proved to be such as Roman pride felt to be almost intolerable; and great efforts were made to induce Sapor to be content with less. The negotiations lasted for four days; but the Persian monarch was inexorable; each day diminished his adversary's strength and bettered his own position; there was no reason why he should make any concession at all; and he seems, in fact, to have yielded nothing of his original demands, except points of such exceedingly slight moment that to insist on them would have been folly.

The following were the terms of peace to which Jovian consented. First, the five provinces east of the Tigris, which had been ceded to Rome by Narses, the grandfather of Sapor, after his defeat by Galerius, were to be given back to Persia, with their fortifications, their inhabitants, and all that they contained of value. The Romans in the territory were, however, to be allowed to withdraw and join their countrymen. Secondly, three places in Eastern Mesopotamia, Nisibis, Singara, and a fort called "the Camp of the Moors," were to be surrendered, but with the condition that not only the Romans, but the inhabitants generally, might retire ere the Persians took possession, and carry with them such of their effects as were movable. The surrender of these places necessarily involved that of the country which they commanded, and can scarcely imply less than the withdrawal of Rome from any claim to dominion over the region between the Tigris and the Khabour. Thirdly, all connection between Armenia and Rome was to be broken off; Arsaces was to be left to his own resources; and in any quarrel between him and Persia Rome was precluded from lending him aid. On these conditions a peace was concluded for thirty years; oaths to observe it faithfully were interchanged; and hostages were given and received on either side, to be retained until the stipulations of the treaty were executed.

The Roman historian who exclaims that it would have been better to have fought ten battles than to have conceded a single one of these shameful terms, commands the sympathy of every reader, who cannot fail to recognize in his utterance the natural feeling of a patriot. And it is possible that Julian, had he lived, would have rejected so inglorious a peace, and have preferred to run all risks rather than sign it. But in that case there is every reason to believe that the army would have been absolutely destroyed, and a few stragglers only have returned to tell the tale of disaster. The alternative which Ammianus suggests—that Jovian, instead of negotiating, should have pushed on to Cordyene, which he might have reached in four days—is absurd; for Cordyeno was at least a hundred and fifty miles distant from Dura, and, at the rate of retreat which Jovian had found possible (four and a half miles a day), would have been reached in three days over a month! The judgment of Eutropius, who, like Ammianus, shared in the expedition, is probably correct—that the peace, though disgraceful, was necessary. Unless Jovian was prepared to risk not only his own life, but the lives of all his soldiers, it was essential that he should come to terms; and the best terms that he could obtain were those which he has been blamed for accepting.

It is creditable to both parties that the peace, once made, was faithfully observed, all its stipulations being honestly and speedily executed. The Romans were allowed to pass the river without molestation from Sapor's army, and, though they suffered somewhat from the Saracens when landing on the other side, were unpursued in their retreat, and were perhaps even, at first, supplied to some extent with provisions. Afterwards, no doubt, they endured for some days great privations; but a convoy with stores was allowed to advance from Roman Mesopotamia into Persian territory, which met the famished soldiers at a Persian military post, called Ur or Adur, and relieved their most pressing necessities. On the Roman side, the ceded provinces and towns were quietly surrendered; offers on the part of the inhabitants to hold their own against the Persians without Roman aid were refused; the Roman troops were withdrawn from the fortresses; and the Armenians were told that they must henceforth rely upon themselves, and not look to Rome for help or protection. Thus Jovian, though strongly urged to follow ancient precedent, and refuse to fulfil the engagements contracted under the pressure of imminent peril, stood firm, and honorably performed all the conditions of the treaty. The second period of struggle between Rome and Persia had thus a termination exactly the reverse of the first. Rome ended the first period by a great victory and a great diplomatic success. At the close of the second she had to relinquish all her gains, and to draw back even behind the line which she occupied when hostilities first broke out. Nisibis, the great stronghold of Eastern Mesopotamia, had been in her possession ever since the time of Verus. Repeatedly attacked by Parthia and Persia, it had never fallen; but once, after which it had been soon recovered; and now for many years it had come to be regarded as the bulwark of the Roman power in the East, and as carrying with it the dominion of Western Asia.102 A fatal blow was dealt to Roman prestige when a city held for near two hundred years, and one honored with the name of "colony," was wrested from the empire and occupied by the most powerful of its adversaries. Not only Amida and Carrhae, but Antioch itself, trembled at a loss which was felt to lay open the whole eastern frontier to attack, and which seemed ominous of further retrogression. Although the fear generally felt proved to be groundless, and the Roman possessions in the East were not, for 200 years, further curtailed by the Persians, yet Roman influence in Western Asia from this time steadily declined, and Persia came to be regarded as the first power in these regions. Much credit is due to Sapor II. for his entire conduct of the war with Constantius, Julian, and Jovian. He knew when to attack and when to remain upon the defensive, when to press on the enemy and when to hold himself in reserve and let the enemy follow his own devices. He rightly conceived from the first the importance of Nisibis, and resolutely persisted in his determination to acquire possession of it, until at last he succeeded. When, in A.D. 337, he challenged Rome to a trial of strength, he might have seemed rash and presumptuous. But the event justified him. In a war which lasted twenty-seven years, he fought numerous pitched battles with the Romans, and was never once defeated. He proved himself greatly superior as a general to Constantius and Jovian, and not unequal to Julian. By a combination of courage, perseverance, and promptness, he brought the entire contest to a favorable issue, and restored Persia, in A.D. 363, to a higher position than that from which she had descended two generations earlier. If he had done nothing more than has already come under our notice, he would still have amply deserved that epithet of "Great" which, by the general consent of historians, has been assigned to him. He was undoubtedly among the greatest of the Sassanian monarchs, and may properly be placed above all his predecessors, and above all but one of those who succeeded him.

CHAPTER XI

*Attitude of Armenia during the War between Sapor and Julian. Sapor's Treachery towards Arsaces. Sapor conquers Armenia. He attacks Iberia, deposes Sauromaces, and sets up a new King. Resistance and Capture of Artogerassa. Difficulties of Sapor. Division of Iberia between the Roman and Persian Pretenders. Renewal of Hostilities between Rome and Persia. Peace made with Valens. Death of Sapor. His Coins.*

"*Rex Persidis, longaevus ille Sapor, post imperatoris Juliani excessum et pudendse pacis icta foedera . . . irqectabat Armeniae manum.*"—*Amm. Marc, xxvii. 18.*

The successful issue of Sapor's war with Julian and Jovian resulted in no small degree from the attitude which was assumed by Armenia soon after Julian commenced his invasion. We have seen that the emperor, when he set out upon his expedition, regarded Armenia as an ally, and in forming his plans placed considerable dependence on the contingent which he expected from Arsaces, the Armenian monarch. It was his intention to attack Ctesiphon with two separate armies, acting upon two converging lines. While he himself advanced with his main force by way of the Euphrates valley and the Nahr-Malcha, he had arranged that his two generals, Procopius and Sebastian, should unite their troops with those of the Armenian king, and, after ravaging a fertile district of Media, make their way towards the great city, through Assyria and Adiabene, along the left bank of the Tigris. It was a bitter disappointment to him when, on nearing Ctesiphon, he could see no signs and hear no tidings of the northern army, from which he had looked for effectual aid at this crisis of the campaign. We have now to consider how this failure came about, what circumstances induced that hesitation and delay on the part of Sebastian and Procopius which had at any rate a large share in frustrating Julian's plans and causing the ill-success of his expedition.

It appears that the Roman generals, in pursuance of the orders given them, marched across Northern Mesopotamia to the Armenian borders, and were there joined by an Armenian contingent which Arsaces sent to their assistance. The allies marched together into Media, and carried fire and sword through the fruitful district known as Chiliacomus, or "the district of the Thousand Villages." They might easily have advanced further; but the Armenians suddenly and without warning drew off and fell back towards their own country. According to Moses of Chorene, their general, Zurseus, was actuated by a religious motive; it seemed to him monstrous that Armenia, a Christian country, should embrace the cause of an apostate, and he was prepared to risk offending his own sovereign rather than lend help to one whom he regarded as the enemy of his faith. The Roman generals, thus deserted by their allies, differed as to the proper course to pursue. While one was still desirous of descending the course of the Tigris, and making at least an attempt to effect a junction with Julian, the other forbade his soldiers to join in the march, and insisted on falling back and re-entering Mesopotamia. As usual in such cases, the difference of opinion resulted in a policy of inaction. The attempt to join Julian was given up; and the second army, from which he had hoped so much, played no further part in the campaign of A.D. 363.

We are told that Julian heard of the defection of the Armenians while he was still on his way to Ctesiphon, and immediately sent a letter to Arsaces, complaining of his general's conduct, and threatening to exact a heavy retribution on his return from the Persian war, if the offence of Zurseus were not visited at once with condign punishment. Arsaces was greatly alarmed at the message; and, though he made no effort to supply the shortcomings of his officer by leading or sending fresh troops to Julian's assistance, yet he hastened to acquit himself of complicity in the misconduct of Zurseus by executing him, together with his whole family. Having thus, as he supposed, secured himself against Julian's anger, he took no further steps, but indulged his love of ease and his distaste for the Roman alliance by remaining wholly passive during the rest of the year.

But though the attitude taken by Armenia was thus, on the whole, favorable to the Persians, and undoubtedly contributed to Sapor's success, he was himself so far from satisfied with the conduct of Arsaces that he resolved at once to invade his country and endeavor to strip him of his crown. As Rome had by the recent treaty relinquished her protectorate over Armenia, and bound herself not to interfere in any quarrel between the Armenians and the Persians, an opportunity was afforded for bringing Armenia into subjection which an ambitious monarch like Sapor was not likely to let slip. He had only to consider whether he would employ art or violence, or whether he would rather prefer a judicious admixture of the two. Adopting the last-named course as the most prudent, he proceeded to intrigue with a portion of the Armenian satraps, while he made armed incursions on the territories of others, and so harassed the country that after a while the satraps generally went over to his side, and represented to Arsaces that no course was open to him but to make his submission. Having brought matters to this point, Sapor had only further to persuade Arsaces to surrender himself, in order to obtain the province which he coveted, almost without striking a blow. He therefore addressed Arsaces a letter which, according to the only writer who professes to give its terms, was expressed as follows:

"Sapor, the offspring of Ormazd, comrade of the sun, king of kings, sends greeting to his dear brother, Arsaces, king of Armenia, whom he holds in affectionate remembrance. It has come to our knowledge that thou hast approved thyself our faithful friend, since not only didst thou decline to invade Persia with Caesar, but when he took a contingent from thee thou didst send messengers and withdraw it. Moreover, we have not forgotten how thou actedst at the first, when thou didst prevent him from passing through thy territories, as he wished. Our soldiers, indeed, who quitted their post, sought to cast on thee the blame due to their own cowardice. But we have not listened to them: their leader we punished with death, and to thy realm, I swear by Mithra, we have done no hurt. Arrange matters then so that thou mayest come to us with all speed, and consult with us concerning our common advantage. Then thou canst return home."

Arsaces, on receiving this missive, whatever suspicions he may have felt, saw no course open to him but to accept the invitation. He accordingly quitted Armenia and made his way to the court of Sapor, where he was immediately seized and blinded. He was then fettered with chains of silver, according to a common practice of the Persians with prisoners of distinction, and was placed in strict confinement in a place called "the Castle of Oblivion."

But the removal of their head did not at once produce the submission of the people. A national party declared itself under, Pharandzem, the wife, and Bab (or Para), the son of Arsaces, who threw themselves into the strong fortress of Artogerassa (Ardakers), and there offered to Sapor a determined resistance. Sapor committed the siege of this place to two renegade Armenians, Cylaces and Artabannes, while at the same time he proceeded to extend his influence beyond the limits of Armenia into the neighboring country of Iberia, which was closely connected with Armenia, and for the most part followed its fortunes.

Iberia was at this time under the government of a king bearing the name of Sauromaces, who had received his investiture from Rome, and was consequently likely to uphold Roman interests. Sapor invaded Iberia, drove Sauromaces from his kingdom, and set up a new monarch in the person of a certain Aspacures, on whose brow he placed the coveted diadem. He then withdrew to his own country, leaving the complete subjection of Armenia to be accomplished by his officers, Cylaces and Artabannes, or, as the Armenian historians call them, Zig and Garen.

Cylaces and Artabannes commenced the siege of Artogerassa, and for a time pressed it with vigor, while they strongly urged the garrison to make their submission. But, having entered within the walls to negotiate, they were won over by the opposite side, and joined in planning a treacherous attack on the besieging force, which was surprised at night and compelled to retire. Para took advantage of their retreat to quit the town and throw himself on the protection of Valens, the Roman emperor, who permitted him to reside in regal state at Neocaesarea. Shortly afterwards, however, by the advice of Cylaces and Artabannes, he returned into Armenia, and was accepted by the patriotic party as their king, Rome secretly countenancing his proceedings. Under these circumstances the Persian monarch once more took the field, and, entering Armenia at the head of a large army, drove Para, with his counsellors Cylaces and Artabannes, to the mountains, renewed the siege of Artogerassa, and forced it to submit, captured the queen Pharandzem, together with the treasure of Arsaces, and finally induced Para to come to terms, and to send him the heads of the two arch-traitors. The resistance of Armenia would probably now have ceased, had Rome been content to see her old enemy so aggrandized, or felt her hands absolutely tied by the terms of the treaty of Dura.

But the success of Sapor thus far only brought him into greater difficulties. The Armenians and Iberians, who desired above all things liberty and independence, were always especially hostile to the power from which they felt that they had for the time being most to fear. As Christian nations, they had also at this period an additional ground of sympathy with Rome, and of aversion from the Persians, who were at once heathens and intolerant. The patriotic party in both countries was thus violently opposed to the establishment of Sapor's authority over them, and cared little for the artifices by which he sought to make it appear that they still enjoyed freedom and autonomy. Above all, Rome, being ruled by monarchs who had had no hand in making the disgraceful peace of A.D. 363, and who had no strong feeling of horror or religious obligation in the matter of treaties with barbarians, was preparing herself to fly in the face of her engagements, and, regarding her own interest as her highest law, to interfere effectually in order to check the progress of Persia in North-Western Asia.

Rome's first open interference was in Iberia. Iberia had perhaps not been expressly named in the treaty, and support might consequently be given to the expelled Sauromaces without any clear infraction of its conditions. The duke Terentius was ordered, therefore, towards the close of A.D. 370, to enter Iberia with twelve legions and replace upon his throne the old Roman feudatory. Accordingly he invaded the country from Lazica, which bordered it upon the north, and found no difficulty in conquering it as far as the river Cyrus. On the Cyrus, however, he was met by Aspacures, the king of Sapor's choice, who made proposals for an accommodation. Representing himself as really well-inclined to Rome, and only prevented from declaring himself by the fact that Sapor held his son as a hostage, he asked Terentius' consent to a division of Iberia between himself and his rival, the tract north of the Cyrus being assigned to the Roman claimant, and that south of the river remaining under his own government. Terentius, to escape further trouble, consented to the arrangement; and the double kingdom was established. The northern and western portions of Iberia were made over to Sauromaces; the southern and eastern continued to be ruled by Aspacures.

When the Persian king received intelligence of these transactions he was greatly excited. To him it appeared clear that by the spirit, if not by the letter, of the treaty of Dura, Rome had relinquished Iberia equally with Armenia; and he complained bitterly of the division which had been made of the Iberian territory, not only without his consent, but without his knowledge. He was no doubt aware that Rome had not really confined her interference to the region with which she had some excuse for intermeddling, but had already secretly intervened in Armenia, and was intending further intervention. The count Arintheus had been sent with an army to the Armenian frontier about the same time that Terentius had invaded Iberia, and had received positive instructions to help the Armenians if Sapor molested them. It was in vain that the Persian monarch appealed to the terms of the treaty of Dura—Rome dismissed his ambassadors with contempt, and made no change in her line of procedure. Upon this Sapor saw that war was unavoidable; and accordingly he wasted no more time in embassies, but employed himself during the winter, which had now begun, in collecting as large a force as he could, in part from his allies, in part from his own subjects, resolving to take the field in the spring, and to do his best to punish Rome for her faithlessness.

Rome on her part made ready to resist the invasion which she knew to be impending. A powerful army was sent to guard the East under count Trajan, and Vadomair, ex-king of the Alemanni; but so much regard for the terms of the recent treaty was still felt, or pretended, that the generals received orders to be careful not to commence hostilities, but to wait till an attack was made on them. They were not kept long in expectation. As soon as winter was over, Sapor crossed the frontier (A.D. 371) with a large force of native cavalry and archers, supported by numerous auxiliaries, and attacked the Romans near a place called Vagabanta. The Roman commander gave his troops the order to retire; and accordingly they fell back under a shower of Persian arrows, until, several having been wounded, they felt that they could with a good face declare that the rupture of the peace was the act of the Persians. The retreat was then exchanged for an advance, and after a brief engagement the Romans were victorious, and inflicted a severe loss upon their adversaries. But the success was not followed by results of any importance. Neither side seems to have been anxious for another general encounter; and the season for hostilities was occupied by a sort of guerilla warfare, in which the advantage rested alternately with the Persians and the Romans. At length, when the summer was ended, the commanders on either side entered into negotiations; and a truce was made which allowed Sapor to retire to Ctesiphon, and the Roman emperor, who was now personally directing the war, to go into winter quarters at Antioch.

After this the war languished for two or three years. Valens was wholly deficient in military genius, and was quite content if he could maintain a certain amount of Roman influence in Armenia and Iberia, while at the same time he protected the Roman frontier against Persian invasion. Sapor was advanced in years, and might naturally desire repose, having been almost constantly engaged in military expeditions since he reached the age of sixteen. Negotiations seem to have alternated with hostilities during the interval between A.D. 371 and 376; but they resulted in nothing, until, in this last-named year, a peace was made, which gave tranquillity to the East during the remainder of the reign of Sapor.

The terms upon which this peace was concluded are obscure. It is perhaps most probable that the two contracting powers agreed to abstain from further interference with Iberia and Armenia, and to leave those countries to follow their own inclinations. Armenia seems by the native accounts to have gravitated towards Rome under these circumstances, and Iberia is likely to have followed her example. The tie of Christianity attached these countries to the great power of the West; and, except under compulsion, they were not likely at this time to tolerate the yoke of Persia for a day. When Jovian withdrew the Roman protection from them, they were forced for a while to submit to the power which they disliked; but no sooner did his successors reverse his policy, and show themselves ready to uphold the Armenians and Iberians against Persia, than they naturally reverted to the Roman side, and formed an important support to the empire against its Eastern rival.

The death of Sapor followed the peace of A.D. 376 within a few years. He died A.D. 379 or 380, after having reigned seventy years. It is curious that, although possessing the crown for so long a term, and enjoying a more brilliant reign than any preceding monarch, he neither left behind him any inscriptions, nor any sculptured memorials. The only material evidences that we possess of his reign are his coins, which are exceedingly numerous. According to Mordtmann, they may be divided into three classes, corresponding to three periods in his life. The earliest have on the reverse the fire-altar, with two priests, or guards, looking towards the altar, and with the flame rising from the altar in the usual way. The head on the obverse is archaic in type, and very much resembles that of Sapor I. The crown has attached to it, in many cases, that "cheek-piece" which is otherwise confined to the first three monarchs of the line. These coins are the best from an artistic point of view; they greatly resemble those of the first Sapor, but are distinguishable from them, first, by the guards looking towards the altar instead of away from it; and, secondly, by a greater profusion of pearls about the king's person. The coins of the second period lack the "cheek-piece," and have on the reverse the fire-altar without supporters; they are inferior as works of art to those of the first period, but much superior to those of the third. These last, which exhibit a marked degeneracy, are especially distinguished by having a human head in the middle of the flames that rise from the altar. Otherwise they much resemble in their emblems the early coins, only differing from them in being artistically inferior. The ordinary legends upon the coins are in no respect remarkable; but occasionally we find the monarch taking the new and expressive epithet of Toham, "the Strong." [PLATE XIX., Fig. 1.]

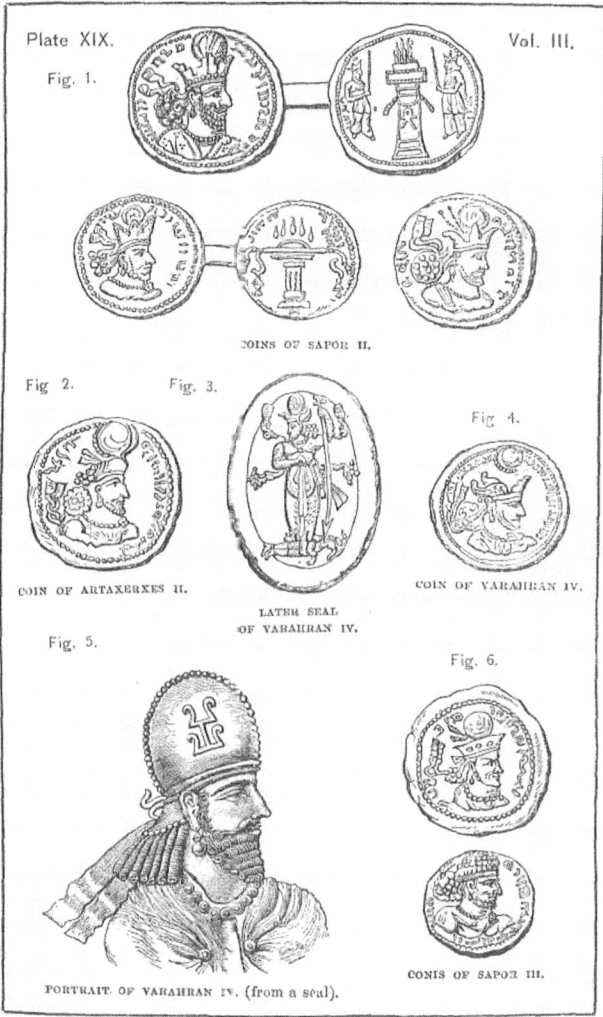

Plate XIX.

Fig. 1.

Vol. III.

COINS OF SAPOR II.

Fig 2.

Fig. 3.

Fig 4.

COIN OF ARTAXERXES II.

LATER SEAL OF VARAHRAN IV.

COIN OF VARAHRAN IV.

Fig. 5.

Fig. 6.

PORTRAIT OF VARAHRAN IV. (from a seal).

COINS OF SAPOR III.

PLATE XIX

CHAPTER XII

*Short Reigns of Artaxerxes II. and Sapor III. Obscurity of their History. Their Relations with Armenia. Monument of Sapor III. at Tdkht-i-Bostan. Coins of Artaxerxes II. and Sapor III. Reign of Varahran IV. His Signets. His Dealings with Armenia. His Death.*

The glorious reign of Sapor II., which carried the New Persian Empire to the highest point whereto it had yet attained, is followed by a time which offers to that remarkable reign a most complete contrast. Sapor had occupied the Persian throne for a space approaching nearly to three-quarters of a century; the reigns of his next three successors amounted to no more than twenty years in the aggregate. Sapor had been engaged in perpetual wars, had spread the terror of the Persian arms on all sides, and ruled more gloriously than any of his predecessors. The kings who followed him were pacific and unenterprising; they were almost unknown to their neighbors, and are among the least distinguished of the Sassanian monarchs. More especially does this character attach to the two immediate successors of Sapor II., viz. Artaxerxes II. and Sapor III. They reigned respectively four and five years; and their annals during this period are almost a blank. Artaxerxes II., who is called by some the brother of Sapor II., was more probably his son. He succeeded his father in A.D. 379, and died at Ctesiphon in A.D. 383. He left a character for kindness and amiability behind him, and is known to the Persians as Nihoukar, or "the Beneficent," and to the Arabs as Al Djemil, "the Virtuous." According to the "Modjmel-al-Tewarikh," he took no taxes from his subjects during the four years of his reign, and thereby secured to himself their affection and gratitude. He seems to have received overtures from the Armenians soon after his accession, and for a time to have been acknowledged by the turbulent mountaineers as their sovereign. After the murder of Bab, or Para, the Romans had set up, as king over Armenia, a certain Varaztad (Pharasdates), a member of the Arsacid family, but no near relation of the recent monarchs, assigning at the same time the real direction of affairs to an Armenian noble named Moushegh, who belonged to the illustrious family of the Mamigonians. Moushegh ruled Armenia with vigor, but was suspected of maintaining over-friendly relations with the Roman emperor, Valens, and of designing to undermine and supplant his master. Varaztad, after a while, having been worked on by his counsellors, grew suspicious of him, and caused him to be executed at a banquet. This treachery roused the indignation of Moushegh's brother Manuel, who raised a rebellion against Varaztad, defeated him in open fight, and drove him from his kingdom. Manuel then brought forward the princess Zermandueht, widow of the late king Para, together with her two young sons, Arsaces and Valarsaces, and, surrounding all three with royal pomp, gave to the two princes the name of king, while he took care to retain in his own hands the real government of the country. Under these circumstances he naturally dreaded the hostility of the Roman emperor, who was not likely to see with patience a monarch, whom he had set upon the throne, deprived of his kingdom by a subject. To maintain the position which he had assumed, it was necessary that he should contract some important alliance; and the alliance always open to Armenia when she had quarrelled with Rome was with the Persians. It seems to have been soon after Artaxerxes II. succeeded his father, that Manuel sent an embassy to him, with letters and rich gifts, offering, in return for his protection, to acknowledge him as lord-paramount of Armenia, and promising him unshakable fidelity. The offer was, of course, received with extreme satisfaction; and terms were speedily arranged. Armenia was to pay a fixed tribute, to receive a garrison of ten thousand Persians and to provide adequately for their support, to allow a Persian satrap to divide with Manuel the actual government of the country, and to furnish him with all that was necessary for his court and table. On the other hand, Arsacos and Valarsaces, together (apparently) with their mother, Zermandueht, were to be allowed the royal title and,honors; Armenia was to be protected in case of invasion; and Manuel was to be maintained in his office of Sparapet or generalissimo of the Armenian forces. We cannot say with certainty how long this arrangement remained undisturbed; most probably, however, it did not continue in force more than a few years. It was most likely while Artaxerxes still ruled Persia, that the rupture described by Faustus occurred. A certain Meroujan, an Armenian noble, jealous of the power and prosperity of Manuel, persuaded him that the Persian commandant in Armenia was about to seize his person, and either to send him a prisoner to Artaxerxes, or else to put him to death. Manuel, who was so credulous as to believe the information, thought it necessary for his own safety to anticipate the designs of his enemies, and, falling upon the ten thousand Persians with the whole of the Armenian army, succeeded in putting them all to the sword, except their commander, whom he allowed to escape. War followed between Persia and Armenia with varied success, but on the whole Manuel had the advantage; he repulsed several Persian invasions, and maintained the independence and integrity of Armenia till his death, without calling in the aid of Rome. When, however, Manuel died, about A.D. 383, Armenian affairs fell into confusion; the Romans were summoned to give help to one party, the Persians to render assistance to the other; Armenia became once more the battle-ground between the two great powers, and it seemed as if the old contest, fraught with so many calamities, was to be at once renewed. But the circumstances of the time were such that neither Rome nor Persia now desired to reopen the contest. Persia was in the hands of weak and unwarlike sovereigns, and was perhaps already threatened by Scythic hordes upon the east. Rome was in the agonies of a struggle with the ever-increasing power of the Goths; and though, in the course of the years A.D. 379-382, the Great Theodosius had established peace in the tract under his rule, and delivered the central provinces of Macedonia and Thrace from the intolerable ravages of the barbaric invaders, yet the deliverance had been effected at the cost of introducing large bodies of Goths into the heart of the empire, while still along the northern frontier lay a threatening cloud, from which devastation and ruin might at any time burst forth and overspread the provinces upon the Lower Danube. Thus both the Roman emperor and the Persian king were well disposed towards peace. An arrangement was consequently made, and in A.D. 384, five years after he had ascended the throne, Theodosius gave audience in Constantinople to envoys from the court of Persepolis, and concluded with them a treaty whereby matters in Armenia were placed on a footing which fairly satisfied both sides, and the tranquillity of the East was assured. The high contracting powers agreed that Armenia should be partitioned between them. After detaching from the kingdom various outlying districts, which could be conveniently absorbed into their own territories, they divided the rest of the country into two unequal portions. The smaller of these, which comprised the more western districts, was placed under the protection of Rome, and was committed by Theodosius to the Arsaces who had been made king by Manuel, the son of the unfortunate Bab, or Para, and the grandson of the Arsaces contemporary with Julian. The larger portion, which consisted of the regions lying towards the east, passed under the suzerainty of Persia, and was confided by Sapor III., who had succeeded Artaxerxes II., to an Arsacid, named Chosroes, a Christian, who was given the title of king, and received in marriage at the same time one of Sapor's sisters. Such were the terms on which Rome and Persia brought their contention respecting Armenia to a conclusion. Friendly relations were in this way established between the two crowns, which continued undisturbed for the long space of thirty-six years (A.D. 384-420).

Sapor III. appears to have succeeded his brother Artaxerxes in A.D. 383, the year before the conclusion of the treaty. It is uncertain whether Artaxerxes vacated the throne by death, or was deposed in consequence of cruelties whereof he was guilty towards the priests and nobles. Tabari and Macoudi, who relate his deposition, are authors on whom much reliance cannot be placed; and the cruelties reported accord but ill with the epithets of "the Beneficent" and "the Virtuous," assigned to this monarch by others. Perhaps it is most probable that he held the throne till his death, according to the statements of Agathias and Eutychius. Of Sapor III., his brother and successor, two facts only are recorded—his conclusion of the treaty with the Romans in A.D. 384, and his war with the Arabs of the tribe of Yad, which must have followed shortly afterwards. It must have been in consequence of his contest with the latter, whom he attacked in their own country, that he received from his countrymen the appellation of "the Warlike," an appellation better deserved by either of the other monarchs who had borne the same name.

Sapor III. left behind him a sculptured memorial, which is still to be seen in the vicinity of Kermanshah. [PLATE XX.] It consists of two very similar figures, looking towards each other, and standing in an arched frame. On either side of the figures are inscriptions in the Old Pehlevi character, whereby we are enabled to identify the individuals represented with the second and the third Sapor. The inscriptions run thus:—"Pathkell zani mazdisn shahia Shahpuhri, malkan malJca Allan ve Anilan, minuchitli min yazdan, bari mazdisn shahia Auhr-mazdi, malkan malka Allan ve Anilan, minuchitli min yazdan, napi shahia Narshehi malkan malka;" and "Pathkeli mazdisn shahia Shahpuhri, malkan mallca Allan ve Anilan, minuchitli min yazdan, bari mazdisn shahia Shahpuhri, malkan malka Allan ve Anilan, minuchitli min yazdan, napi shahia Auhrmazdi, malkan malka." They are, it will be seen, identical in form, with the exception that the names in the right-hand inscription are "Sapor, Hormisdas, Narses," while those in the left-hand one are "Sapor, Sapor, Hormisdas." It has been supposed that the right-hand figure was erected by Sapor II., and the other afterwards added by Sapor III.; but the unity of the whole sculpture, and its inclusion under a single arch, seem to indicate that it was set up by a single sovereign, and was the fruit of a single conception. If this be so, we must necessarily ascribe it to the later of the two monarchs commemorated, i.e. to Sapor III., who must be supposed to have possessed more than usual filial piety, since the commemoration of their predecessors upon the throne is very rare among the Sassanians.

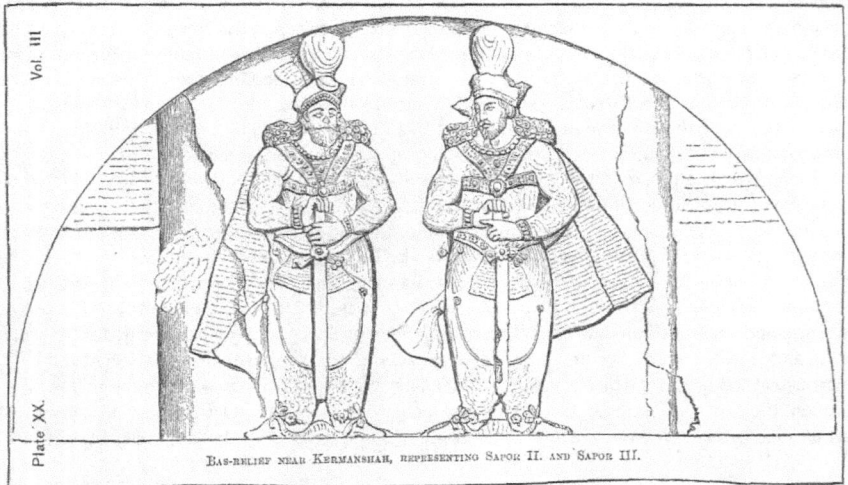

BAS-RELIEF NEAR KERMANSHAH, REPRESENTING SAPOR II. AND SAPOR III.

PLATE XX

The taste of the monument is questionable. An elaborate finish of all the details of the costume compensates but ill for a clumsiness of contour and a want of contrast and variety, which indicate a low condition of art, and compare unfavorably with the earlier performances of the Neo-Persian sculptors. It may be doubted whether, among all the reliefs of the Sassanians, there is one which is so entirely devoid of artistic merit as this coarse and dull production.

The coins of Sapor III. and his predecessor, Artaxerxes II., have little about them that is remarkable. Those of Artaxerxes bear a head which is surmounted with the usual inflated ball, and has the diadem, but is without a crown—a deficiency in which some see an indication that the prince thus represented was regent rather than monarch of Persia. [PLATE XIX. Fig. 2.] The legends upon the coins are, however, in the usual style of royal epigraphs, running commonly—"Mazdisn bag Artah-shetri malkan malka Air an ve Aniran," or "the Ormazd-worshipping divine Artaxerxes, king of the kings of Iran and Turan." They are easily distinguishable from those of Artaxerxes I., both by the profile, which is far less marked, and by the fire-altar on the reverse, which has always two supporters, looking towards the altar. The coins of Sapor III. present some unusual types. [PLATE XIX. Fig. 6.] On some of them the king has his hair bound with a simple diadem, without crown or cap of any kind. On others he wears a cap of a very peculiar character, which has been compared to a biretta, but is really altogether sui generis. The cap is surmounted by the ordinary inflated ball, is ornamented with jewels, and is bound round at bottom with the usual diadem. The legend upon the obverse of Sapor's coins is of the customary character; but the reverse bears usually, besides the name of the king, the word atur, which has been supposed to stand for Aturia or Assyria; this explanation, however, is very doubtful.

The coins of both kings exhibit marks of decline, especially on the reverse, where the drawing of the figures that support the altar is very inferior to that which we observe on the coins of the kings from Sapor I. to Sapor II. The characters on both obverse and reverse are also carelessly rendered, and can only with much difficulty be deciphered.

Sapor III. died A.D. 388, after reigning a little more than five years. He was a man of simple tastes, and is said to have been fond of exchanging the magnificence and dreary etiquette of the court for the freedom and ease of a life under tents. On an occasion when he was thus enjoying himself, it happened that one of those violent hurricanes, to which Persia is subject, arose, and, falling in full force on the royal encampment, blew down the tent wherein he was sitting. It happened unfortunately that the main tent-pole struck him, as it fell, in a vital part, and Sapor died from the blow. Such at least was the account given by those who had accompanied him, and generally believed by his subjects. There were not, however, wanting persons to whisper that the story was untrue—that the real cause of the catastrophe which had overtaken the unhappy monarch was a conspiracy of his nobles, or his guards, who had overthrown his tent purposely, and murdered him ere he could escape from them.

The successor of Sapor III. was Varahran IV., whom some authorities call his brother and others his son. This prince is known to the oriental writers as "Varahran Kerm-an-sh-ah," or "Varahran, king of Carmania." Agathias tells us that during the lifetime of his father he was established as governor over Kerman or Carmania, and thus obtained the appellation which pertinaciously adhered to him. A curious relic of antiquity, fortunately preserved to modern times amid so much that has been lost, confirms this statement. It is the seal of Varahran before he ascended the Persian throne, and contains, besides his portrait, beautifully cut an inscription, which is read as follows:—"Varahran Kerman malka, bari mazdisn bag Shahpuh-ri malkan malka Axran ve Aniran, minuchitri min yazclan," or "Varahran, king of Kerman, son of the Ormazd-worshipping divine Sapor, king of the kings of Iran and Turan, heaven-descended of the race of the gods." [PLATE XIX. Fig. 5.] Another seal, belonging to him probably after he had become monarch of Persia, contains his full-length portrait, and exhibits him as trampling under foot a prostrate figure, supposed to represent a Roman, by which it would appear that he claimed to have gained victories or advantages over Rome. [PLATE XIX. Figs. 3 and 4.] It is not altogether easy to understand how this could have been. Not only do the Roman writers mention no war between the Romans and Persians at this time, but they expressly declare that the East remained in profound repose during the entire reign of Varahran, and that Rome and Persia continued to be friends. The difficulty may, however, be perhaps explained by a consideration of the condition of affairs in Armenia at this time; for in Armenia Rome and Persia had still conflicting interests, and, without having recourse to arms, triumphs might be obtained in this quarter by the one over the other.

On the division of Armenia between Arsaces and Chosroes, a really good understanding had been established, which had lasted for about six years. Arsaces had died two years after he became a Roman feudatory; and, at his death, Rome had absorbed his territories into her empire, and placed the new province under the government of a count. No objection to the arrangement had been made by Persia, and the whole of Armenia had remained for four years tranquil and without disturbance. But, about A.D. 390, Chosroes became dissatisfied with his position, and entered into relations with Rome which greatly displeased the Armenian monarch. Chosroes obtained from Theodosius his own appointment to the Armenian countship, and thus succeeded in uniting both Roman and Persian Armenia under his government. Elated with this success, he proceeded further to venture on administrative acts which trenched, according to Persian views, on the rights of the lord paramount. Finally, when Varahran addressed to him a remonstrance, he replied in insulting terms, and, renouncing his authority, placed the whole Armenian kingdom under the suzerainty and protection of Rome. War between the two great powers must now have seemed imminent, and could indeed only have been avoided by great moderation and self-restraint on the one side or the other. Under these circumstances it was Rome that drew back. Theodosius declined to receive the submission which Chosroes tendered, and refused to lift a finger in his defence. The unfortunate prince was forced to give himself up to Varahan, who consigned him to the Castle of Oblivion, and placed his brother, Varabran-Sapor, upon the Armenian throne. These events seem to have fallen into the year A.D. 391, the third year of Varahran, who may well have felt proud of them, and have thought that they formed a triumph over Rome which deserved to be commemorated.

The character of Varahran IV. is represented variously by the native authorities. According to some of them, his temper was mild, and his conduct irreproachable. Others say that he was a hard man, and so neglected the duties of his station that he would not even read the petitions or complaints which were addressed to him. It would seem that there must have been some ground for these latter representations, since it is generally agreed that the cause of his death was a revolt of his troops, who surrounded him and shot at him with arrows. One shaft, better directed than the rest, struck him in a vital part, and he fell and instantly expired. Thus perished, in A.D. 399, the third son of the Great Sapor, after a reign of eleven years.

## CHAPTER XIII

*Accession of Isdigerd I. Peaceful Character of his Reign. His Alleged Guardianship of Theodosius II. His leaning towards Christianity, and consequent Unpopularity with his Subjects. His Change of view and Persecution of the Christians. His relations with Armenia. II. Coins. His Personal Character. His Death.*

Varahran IV. was succeeded (A.D. 399) by his son, Izdikerti or Isdigerd I. whom the soldiers, though they had murdered his father, permitted to ascend the throne without difficulty. He is said, at his accession, to have borne a good character for prudence and moderation, a character which he sought to confirm by the utterance on various occasions of high-sounding moral sentiments. The general tenor of his reign was peaceful; and we may conclude therefore that he was of an unwarlike temper, since the circumstances of the time were such as would naturally have induced a prince of any military capacity to resume hostilities against the Romans. After the arrangement made with Rome by Sapor III. in A.D. 384, a terrible series of calamities had befallen the empire. Invasions of

Ostrogoths and Franks signalized the years A.D. 386 and 388; in A.D. 387 the revolt of Maximus seriously endangered the western moiety of the Roman state; in the same year occurred an outburst of sedition at Antioch, which was followed shortly by the more dangerous sedition, and the terrible massacre of Thessalonica; Argobastes and Eugenius headed a rebellion in A.D. 393; Gildo the Moor detached Africa from the empire in A.D. 386, and maintained a separate dominion on the southern shores of the Mediterranean for twelve years, from A.D. 386 to 398; in A.D. 395 the Gothic warriors within and without the Roman frontier took arms, and under the redoubtable Alaric threatened at once the East and the West, ravaged Greece, captured Corinth, Argos, and Sparta, and from the coasts of the Adriatic already marked for their prey the smiling fields of Italy. The rulers of the East and West, Arcadius and Honorius, were alike weak and unenterprising; and further, they were not even on good terms, nor was either likely to trouble himself very greatly about attacks upon the territories of the other. Isdigerd might have crossed the Euphrates, and overrun or conquered the Asiatic provinces of the Eastern Empire, without causing Honorious a pang, or inducing him to stir from Milan. It is true that Western Rome possessed at this time the rare treasure of a capable general; but Stilicho was looked upon with fear and aversion by the emperor of the East, and was moreover fully occupied with the defence of his own master's territories. Had Isdigerd, on ascending the throne in A.D. 399, unsheathed the sword and resumed the bold designs of his grandfather, Sapor II., he could scarcely have met with any serious or prolonged resistance. He would have found the East governed practically by the eunuch Eutropius, a plunderer and oppressor, universally hated and feared; he would have had opposed to him nothing but distracted counsels and disorganized forces; Asia Minor was in possession of the Ostrogoths, who, under the leadership of Tribigild, were ravaging and destroying far and wide; the armies of the State were commanded by Gainas, the Goth, and Leo, the wool-comber, of whom the one was incompetent, and the other unfaithful; there was nothing, apparently, that could have prevented him from overrunning Roman Armenia, Mesopotamia, and Syria, or even from extending his ravages, or his dominion, to the shores of the AEgean. But the opportunity was either not seen, or was not regarded as having any attractions. Isdigerd remained tranquil and at rest within the walls of his capital. Assuming as his special title the characteristic epithet of "Ramashtras," "the most quiet," or "the most firm," he justified his assumption of it by a complete abstinence from all military expeditions.

When Isdigerd had reigned peaceably for the space of nine years, he is said to have received a compliment of an unusual character. Arcadius, the emperor of the East, finding his end approaching, and anxious to secure a protector for his son Theodosius, a boy of tender age, instead of committing him to the charge of his uncle Honorius, or selecting a guardian for him from among his own subjects, by a formal testamentary act, we are told, placed his child under the protection of the Persian monarch. He accompanied the appointment by a solemn appeal to the magnanimity of Isdigerd, whom he exhorted at some length to defend with all his force, and guide with his best wisdom, the young king and his kingdom. According to one writer, he further appended to this trust a valuable legacy—no less than a thousand pounds weight of pure gold, which he begged his Persian brother to accept as a token of his goodwill. When Arcadius died, and the testament was opened, information of its contents was sent to Isdigerd, who at once accepted the charge assigned to him, and addressed a letter to the Senate of Constantinople, in which he declared his determination to punish any attempt against his ward with the extremest severity. Unable to watch over his charge in person, he selected for his guide and instructor a learned eunuch of his court, by name Antiochus, and sent him to Constantinople, where for several years he was the young prince's constant companion. Even after his death or expulsion, which took place in consequence of the intrigues of Pulcheria, Theodosius's elder sister, the Persian monarch continued faithful to his engagements. During the whole of his reign he not only remained at peace with the Romans, but avoided every act that they could have regarded as in the least degree unfriendly.

Such is the narrative which has come down to us on the authority of historians, the earliest of whom wrote a century and a half after Arcadius's death. Modern criticism has, in general, rejected the entire story, on this account, regarding the silence of the earlier writers as outweighing the positive statements of the later ones. It should, however, be borne in mind, first that the earlier writers are few in number, and that their histories are very meagre and scanty; secondly, that the fact, if fact it were, was one not very palatable to Christians; and thirdly, that, as the results, so far as Rome was concerned, were negative, the event might not have seemed to be one of much importance, or that required notice. The character of Procopius, with whom the story originates, should also be taken into consideration, and the special credit allowed him by Agathias for careful and diligent research. It may be added, that one of the main points of the narrative—the position of Antiochus at Constantinople during the early years of Theodosius—is corroborated by the testimony of a contemporary, the bishop Synesius, who speaks of a man of this name, recently in the service of a Persian, as all-powerful with the Eastern emperor. It has been supposed by one writer that the whole story grew out of this fact; but the basis scarcely seems to be sufficient; and it is perhaps most probable that Arcadius did really by his will commend his son to the kind consideration of the Persian monarch, and that that monarch in consequence sent him an adviser, though the formal character of the testamentary act, and the power and position of Antiochus at the court of Constantinople, may have been overstated. Theodosius no doubt owed his quiet possession of the throne rather to the good disposition towards him of his own subjects than to the protection of a foreigner; and Isdigerd refrained from all attack on the territories of the young prince, rather by reason of his own pacific temper than in consequence of the will of Arcadius.

The friendly relations established, under whatever circumstances, between Isdigerd and the Roman empire of the East seemed to have inclined the Persian monarch, during a portion of his reign, to take the Christians into his favor, and even to have induced him to contemplate seeking admission into the Church by the door of baptism. Antiochus, his representative at the Court of Arcadius, openly wrote in favor of the persecuted sect; and the encouragement received from this high quarter rapidly increased the number of professing Christians in the Persian territories. The sectaries, though oppressed, had long been allowed to have their bishops; and Isdigerd is said to have listened with approval to the teaching of two of them, Marutha, bishop of Mesopotamia, and Abdaas, bishop of Ctesiphon. Convinced of the truth of Christianity, but unhappily an alien from its spirit, he commenced a persecution of the Magians and their most powerful adherents, which caused him to be held in detestation by his subjects, and has helped to attach to his name the epithets of "Al-Khasha," "the Harsh," and "Al-Athim," "the Wicked." But the' persecution did not continue long. The excessive zeal of Abdaas after a while provoked a reaction; and Isdigerd, deserting the cause which he had for a time espoused, threw himself (with all the zeal of one who, after nearly embracing truth, relapses into error) into the arms of the opposite party. Abdaas had ventured to burn down the great Fire-Temple of Ctesiphon, and had then refused to rebuild it. Isdigerd authorized the Magian hierarchy to retaliate by a general destruction of the Christian churches throughout the Persian dominions, and by the arrest and punishment of all those who acknowledged themselves to believe the Gospel. A fearful slaughter of the Christians in Pergia followed during five years; some, eager for the earthly glory and the heavenly rewards of martyrdom, were forward to proclaim themselves members of the obnoxious sect; others, less courageous or less inclined to self-assertion, sought rather to conceal their creed; but these latter were carefully sought out, both in the towns and in the country districts, and when convicted were relentlessly put to death. Nor was mere death regarded as enough. The victims were subjected, besides, to cruel sufferings of various kinds, and the greater number of them expired under torture. Thus Isdigerd alternately oppressed the two religious professions, to one or other of which belonged the great mass of his subjects; and, having in this way given both parties reason to hate him, earned and acquired a unanimity of execration which has but seldom been the lot of persecuting monarchs.

At the same time that Isdigerd allowed this violent persecution of the Christians in his own kingdom of Persia, he also sanctioned an attempt to extirpate Christianity in the dependent country of Armenia. Varahran-Sapor, the successor of Chosroes, had ruled the territory quietly and peaceably for twenty-one years. He died A.D. 413, leaving behind him a single son, Artases, who was at his father's death aged no more than ten years. Under these circumstances, Isaac, the Metropolitan of Armenia, proceeded to the court of Ctesiphon, and petitioned Isdigerd to replace on the Armenian throne the prince who had been deposed twenty-one years earlier, and who was still a prisoner on parole in the "Castle of Oblivion"—viz. Chosroes. Isdigerd acceded to the request; and Chosroes was released from confinement and restored to the throne from which he had been expelled by Varahran IV. in A.D. 391. He, however, survived his elevation only a year. Upon his decease, A.D. 413, Isdigerd selected for the viceroyship, not an Arsacid, not even an Armenian, but his own son, Sapor, whom he forced upon the reluctant provincials, compelling them to acknowledge him as monarch (A.D. 413-414). Sapor was instructed to ingratiate himself with the Armenian nobles, by inviting them to visit him, by feasting them, making them presents, holding friendly converse with them, hunting with them; and was bidden to use such influence as he might obtain to convert the chiefs from Christianity to Zoroastrianism. The young prince appears to have done his best; but the Armenians were obstinate, resisted his blandishments, and remained Christians in spite of all his efforts. He reigned from A.D. 414 to 418, at the end of which time, learning that his father had fallen into ill health, he quitted Armenia and returned to the Persian court, in order to press his claims to the succession. Isdigerd died soon afterwards (A.D. 419 or 420); and Sapor made an attempt to seize the throne; but there was another pretender whose partisans had more strength, and the viceroy of Armenia was treacherously assassinated in the palace of his father. Armenia remained for three years in a state of anarchy; and it was not till Varahran V. had been for some time established upon the Persian throne that Artases was made viceroy, under the name of Artasiris or Artaxerxes.

The coins of Isdigerd I. are not remarkable as works of art; but they possess some features of interest. They are numerous, and appear to have been issued from various mints, but all bear a head of the same type. [PLATE XXI., Fig. 1.] It is that of a middle-aged man, with a short beard and hair gathered behind the head in a cluster of curls. The distinguishing mark is the headdress, which has the usual inflated ball above a fragment of the old mural crown, and further bears a crescent in front. The reverse has the usual fire-altar with supporters, and is for the most part very rudely executed. The ordinary legend is, on the obverse, "Mazdisn bag ramashtras Izdikerti, malkan malka Airan," or "the Ormazd-worshipping divine most peaceful Isdigerd, king of the kings of Iran;" and on the reverse, Ramashtras Izdikerti, "the most peaceful Isdigerd." In some cases, there is a second name, associated with that of the monarch, on the reverse, a name which reads either "Ardashatri" (Artaxerxes) or, "Varahran." It has been conjectured that, where the name of "Artaxerxes" occurs, the reference is to the founder of the empire; while it is admitted that the "Varahran" intended is almost certainly Isdigerd's son and successor, Varahran V., the "Bahram-Grur" of the modern Persians. Perhaps a more reasonable account of the matter would be that Isdigerd had originally a son Artaxerxes, whom he intended to make his successor, but that this son died or offended him, and that then he gave his place to Varahran.

Fig. 1.

COIN OF ISDIGERD I.

Fig. 2.

COIN OF VARAHRAN V.

Fig. 3.

COIN OF ISDIGERD II.

Fig. 4.

COIN OF BALAS.

Fig. 5.

COIN OF HORMISDAS III.
(doubtful).

Fig. 6.

COIN OF PEROZES.

PLATE XXI

The character of Isdigerd is variously represented. According to the Oriental writers, he had by nature an excellent disposition, and at the time of his accession was generally regarded as eminently sage, prudent, and virtuous; but his conduct after he became king disappointed all the hopes that had been entertained of him. He was violent, cruel, and pleasure-seeking; he broke all laws human and divine; he plundered the rich, ill-used the poor, despised learning, left those who did him a service unrewarded, suspected everybody. He wandered continually about his vast empire, not to benefit his subjects, but to make them all suffer equally. In curious contrast with these accounts is the picture drawn of him by the Western authors, who celebrate his magnanimity and his virtue, his peaceful temper, his faithful guardianship of Theodosius, and even his exemplary piety. A modern writer has suggested that he was in fact a wise and tolerant prince, whose very mildness and indulgence offended the bigots of his own country, and caused them to represent his character in the most odious light, and do their utmost to blacken his memory. But this can scarcely be accepted as the true explanation of the discrepancy. It appears from the ecclesiastical historians that, whatever other good qualities Isdigerd may have possessed, tolerance at any rate was not among his virtues. Induced at one time by Christian bishops almost to embrace Christianity, he violently persecuted the professors of the old Persian religion. Alarmed at a later period by the excessive zeal of his Christian preceptors, and probably fearful of provoking rebellion among his Zoroastrian subjects, he turned around upon his late friends, and treated them with a cruelty even exceeding that previously exhibited towards their adversaries. It was probably this twofold persecution that, offending both professions, attached to Isdigerd in his own country the character of a harsh and bad monarch. Foreigners, who did not suffer from his caprices or his violence, might deem him magnanimous and a model of virtue. His own subjects with reason detested his rule, and branded his memory with the well-deserved epithet of Al-Athim, "the Wicked."

A curious tale is told as to the death of Isdigerd. He was still in the full vigor of manhood when one day a horse of rare beauty, without bridle or caparison, came of its own accord and stopped before the gate of his palace. The news was told to the king, who gave orders that the strange steed should be saddled and bridled, and prepared to mount it. But the animal reared and kicked, and would not allow any one to come near, till the king himself approached, when the creature totally changed its mood, appeared gentle and docile, stood perfectly still, and allowed both saddle and bridle to be put on. The crupper, however, needed some arrangement, and Isdigerd in full confidence proceeded to complete his task, when suddenly the horse lashed out with one of his hind legs, and dealt the unfortunate prince a blow which killed him on the spot. The animal then set off at speed, disembarrassed itself of its accoutrements, and galloping away was never seen any more. The modern historian of Persia compresses the tale into a single phrase, and tells us that "Isdigerd died from the kick of a horse:" but the Persians of the time regarded the occurrence as an answer to their prayers, and saw in the wild steed an angel sent by God.


CHAPTER XIV

*Internal Troubles on the Death of Isdigerd I. Accession of Varahran V. His Persecution of the Christians. His War with Rome. His Relations with Armenia from A.D. 422 to A.D. 428. His Wars with the Scythic Tribes on his Eastern Frontier. His Strange Death. His Coins. His Character.*

It would seem that at the death of Isdigerd there was some difficulty as to the succession. Varahran, whom he had designated as his heir, appears to have been absent from the capital at the time; while another son, Sapor, who had held the Armenian throne from A.D. 414 to 418, was present at the seat of government, and bent on pushing his claims. Varahran, if we may believe the Oriental writers, who are here unanimous, had been educated among the Arab tribes dependent on Persia, who now occupied the greater portion of Mesopotamia. His training had made him an Arab rather than a Persian; and he was believed to have inherited the violence, the price, and the cruelty of his father. His countrymen were therefore resolved that they would not allow him to be king. Neither were they inclined to admit the claims of Sapor, whose government of Armenia had not been particularly successful, and whose recent desertion of his proper post for the advancement of his own private interests was a crime against his country which deserved punishment rather than reward. Armenia had actually revolted as soon as he quitted it, had driven out the Persian garrison, and was a prey to rapine and disorder. We cannot be surprised that, under these circumstances,

Sapor's machinations and hopes were abruptly terminated, soon after his father's demise, by his own murder. The nobles and chief Magi took affairs into their own hands. Instead of sending for Varahran, or awaiting his arrival, they selected for king a descendant of Artaxerxes I. only remotely related to Isdigerd—a prince of the name of Chosroes—and formally placed him upon the throne. But Varahran was not willing to cede his rights. Having persuaded the Arabs to embrace his cause, he marched upon Ctesiphon at the head of a large force, and by some means or other, most probably by the terror of his arms, prevailed upon Chosroes, the nobles, and the Magi, to submit to him. The people readily acquiesced in the change of masters; Chosroes descended into a private station, and Varahran, son of Isdigerd, became king.

Varahran seems to have ascended the throne in A.D. 420. He at once threw himself into the hands of the priestly party, and, resuming the persecution of the Christians which his father had carried on during his later years, showed himself, to one moiety of his subjects at any rate, as bloody and cruel as the late monarch. Tortures of various descriptions were employed; and so grievous was the pressure put upon the followers of Christ that in a short time large numbers of the persecuted sect quitted the country, and placed themselves under the protection of the Romans. Varahran had to consider whether he would quietly allow the escape of these criminals, or would seek to enforce his will upon them at the risk of a rupture with Rome. He preferred the bolder line of conduct. His ambassadors were instructed to require the surrender of the refugees at the court of Constantinople; and when Theodosius, to his honor, indignantly rejected the demand, they had orders to protest against the emperor's decision, and to threaten him with their master's vengeance.

It happened that at the time there were some other outstanding disputes, which caused the relations of the two empires to be less amicable than was to be desired. The Persians had recently begun to work their gold mines, and had hired experienced persons from the Romans, whose services they found so valuable that when the period of the hiring was expired they would not suffer the miners to quit Persia and return to their homes. They are also said to have ill-used the Roman merchants who traded in the Persian territories, and to have actually robbed them of their merchandise.

These causes of complaint were not, however, it would seem, brought forward by the Romans, who contented themselves with simply refusing the demand for the extradition of the Christian fugitives, and refrained from making any counter-claims. But their moderation was not appreciated; and the Persian monarch, on learning that Rome would not restore the refugees, declared the peace to be at an end, and immediately made preparations for war. The Romans had, however, anticipated his decision, and took the field in force before the Persians were ready. The command was entrusted to a general bearing the strange name of Ardaburius, who marched his troops through Armenia into the fertile province of Arzanene, and there defeated Narses, the leader whom Varahran had sent against him. Proceeding to plunder Arzanene, Ardaburius suddenly heard that his adversary was about to enter the Roman province of Mesopotamia, which was denuded of troops, and seemed to invite attack. Hastily concluding his raid, he passed from Arzanene into the threatened district, and was in time to prevent the invasion intended by Narses, who, when he found his designs forestalled, threw himself into the fortress of Nisibis, and there stood on the defensive. Ardaburius did not feel himself strong enough to invest the town; and for some time the two adversaries remained inactive, each watching the other. It was during this interval that (if we may credit Socrates) the Persian general sent a challenge to the Roman, inviting him to fix time and place for a trial of strength between the two armies. Ardaburius prudently declined the overture, remarking that the Romans were not accustomed to fight battles when their enemies wished, but when it suited themselves. Soon afterwards he found himself able to illustrate his meaning by his actions. Having carefully abstained from attacking Nisibis while his strength seemed to him insufficient, he suddenly, upon receiving large reinforcements from Theodosius, changed his tactics, and, invading Persian Mesopotamia, marched upon the stronghold held by Narses, and formally commenced its siege.

Hitherto Varahran, confident in his troops or his good fortune, had left the entire conduct of the military operations to his general; but the danger of Nisibis—that dearly won and highly prized possession—seriously alarmed him, and made him resolve to take the field in person with all his forces. Enlisting on his side the services of his friends the Arabs, under their great sheikh, Al-Amundarus (Moundsir), and collecting together a strong body of elephants, he advanced to the relief of the beleaguered town. Ardaburius drew off on his approach, burned his siege artillery, and retired from before the place. Nisibis was preserved; but soon afterwards a disaster is said to have befallen the Arabs, who, believing themselves about to be attacked by the Roman force, were seized with a sudden panic, and, rushing in headlong flight to the Euphrates (!) threw themselves into its waters, encumbered with their clothes and arms, and there perished to the number of a hundred thousand.

The remaining circumstances of the war are not related by our authorities in chronological sequence. But as it is certain that the war lasted only two years, and as the events above narrated certainly belong to the earlier portion of it, and seem sufficient for one campaign, we may perhaps be justified in assigning to the second year, A.D. 421, the other details recorded—viz., the siege of Theodosiopolis, the combat between Areobindus and Ardazanes, the second victory of Ardaburius, and the destruction of the remnant of the Arabs by Vitianus.

Theodosiopolis was a city built by the reigning emperor, Theodosius II., in the Roman portion of Armenia, near the sources of the Euphrates. It was defended by strong walls, lofty towers, and a deep ditch. Hidden channels conducted an unfailing supply of water into the heart of the place, and the public granaries were large and generally well stocked with provisions. This town, recently built for the defence of the Roman Armenia, was (it would seem) attacked in A.D. 421 by Varahran in person. He besieged it for above thirty days. and employed against it all the means of capture which were known to the military art of the period. But the defence was ably conducted by the bishop of the city, a certain Eunomius, who was resolved that, if he could prevent it, an infidel and persecuting monarch should never lord it over his see. Eunomius not merely animated the defenders, but took part personally in the defence, and even on one occasion discharged a stone from a balista with his own hand, and killed a prince who had not confined himself to his military duties, but had insulted the faith of the besieged. The death of this officer is said to have induced Varahran to retire, and not further molest Theodosiopolis.

While the fortified towns on either side thus maintained themselves against the attacks made on them, Theodosius, we are told, gave an independent command to the patrician Procopius, and sent him at the head of a body of troops to oppose Varahran. The armies met, and were on the point of engaging when the Persian monarch made a proposition to decide the war, not by a general battle, but by a single combat. Procopius assented; and a warrior was selected on either side, the Persians choosing for their champion a certain Ardazanes, and the Romans "Areobindus the Goth," count of the "Foederati." In the conflict which followed the Persian charged his adversary with his spear, but the nimble Goth avoided the thrust by leaning to one side, after which he entangled Ardazanes in a net, and then despatched him with his sword. The result was accepted by Varahran as decisive of the war, and he desisted, from any further hostilities. Areobindus received the thanks of the emperor for his victory, and twelve years later was rewarded with the consulship.

But meanwhile, in other portions of the wide field over which the war was raging, Rome had obtained additional successes. Ardaburius, who probably still commanded in Mesopotamia, had drawn the Persian force opposed to him into an ambuscade, and had destroyed it, together with its seven generals. Vitianus, an officer of whom nothing more is known, had exterminated the remnant of the Arabs not drowned in the Euphrates. The war had gone everywhere against the Persians; and it is not improbable that Varahran, before the close of A.D. 421, proposed terms of peace.

Peace, however, was not exactly made till the next year. Early in A.D. 422, a Roman envoy, by name Maximus, appeared in the camp of Varahran, and, when taken into the presence of the great king, stated that he was empowered by the Roman generals to enter into negotiations, but had had no communication with the Roman emperor, who dwelt so far off that he had not heard of the war, and was so powerful that, if he knew of it, he would regard it as a matter of small account. It is not likely that Varahran was much impressed by these falsehoods; but he was tired of the war; he had found that Rome could hold her own, and that he was not likely to gain anything by prolonging it; and he was in difficulties as to provisions, whereof his supply had run short. He was therefore well inclined to entertain Maximus's proposals favorably. The corps of the "Immortals," however, which was in his camp, took a different view, and entreated to be allowed an opportunity of attacking the Romans unawares, while they believed negotiations to be going on, considering that under such circumstances they would be certain of victory. Varahran, according to the Roman writer who is here our sole authority, consented. The Immortals made their attack, and the Romans were at first in some danger; but the unexpected arrival of a reinforcement saved them, and the Immortals were defeated and cut off to a man. After this, Varahran made peace with Rome through the instrumentality of Maximus, consenting, it would seem, not merely that Rome should harbor the Persian Christians, if she pleased, but also that all persecution of Christians should henceforth cease throughout his own empire.

The formal conclusion of peace was accompanied, and perhaps helped forward, by the well-judging charity of an admirable prelate. Acacius, bishop of Amida, pitying the condition of the Persian prisoners whom the Romans had captured during their raid into Arzanene, and were dragging off into slavery, interposed to save them; and, employing for the purpose all the gold and silver plate that he could find in the churches of his diocese, ransomed as many as seven thousand captives, supplied their immediate wants with the utmost tenderness, and sent them to Varahran, who can scarcely have failed to be impressed by an act so unusual in ancient times. Our sceptical historian remarks, with more apparent sincerity than usual, that this act was calculated "to inform, the Persian king of the true spirit of the religion which he persecuted," and that the name of the doer might well "have dignified the saintly calendar." These remarks are just; and it is certainly to be regretted that, among the many unknown or doubtful names of canonized Christians to which the Church has given her sanction, there is no mention made of Acacius of Amida.

Varahran was perhaps the more disposed to conclude his war with Rome from the troubled condition of his own portion of Armenia, which imperatively required his attention. Since the withdrawal from that region of his brother Sapor in A.D. 418 or 419, the country had had no king. It had fallen into a state of complete anarchy and wretchedness; no taxes were collected; the roads were not safe; the strong robbed and oppressed the weak at their pleasure. Isaac, the Armenian patriarch, and the other bishops, had quitted their sees and taken refuge in Roman Armenia, where they were received favorably by the prefect of the East, Anatolius, who no doubt hoped by their aid to win over to his master the Persian division of the country. Varahran's attack on Theodosiopolis had been a counter movement, and had been designed to make the Romans tremble for their own possessions, and throw them back on the defensive. But the attack had failed; and on its failure the complete loss of Armenia probably seemed imminent. Varahran therefore hastened to make peace with Rome, and, having so done, proceeded to give his attention to Armenia, with the view of placing matters there on a satisfactory footing. Convinced that he could not retain Armenia unless with the good-will of the nobles, and believing them to be deeply attached to the royal stock of the Arsacids, he brought forward a prince of that noble house, named Artases, a son of Varahran-Sapor, and, investing him with the ensigns of royalty, made him take the illustrious name of Artaxerxes, and delivered into his hands the entire government of the country. These proceedings are assigned to the year A.D. 422, the year of the peace with Rome, and must have followed very shortly after the signature of the treaty.

It might have been expected that this arrangement would have satisfied the nobles of Armenia, and have given that unhappy country a prolonged period of repose. But the personal character of Artaxerxes was, unfortunately, bad; the Armenian nobles were, perhaps, capricious; and after a trial of six years it was resolved that the rule of the Arsacid monarch could not be endured, and that Varahran should be requested to make Armenia a province of his empire, and to place it under the government of a Persian satrap. The movement was resisted with all his force by Isaac, the patriarch, who admitted the profligacy of Artaxerxes and deplored it, but held that the role of a Christian, however lax he might be, was to be preferred to that of a heathen, however virtuous. The nobles, however, were determined; and the opposition of Isaac had no other result than to involve him in the fall of his sovereign. Appeal was made to the Persian king and Varahran, in solemn state, heard the charges made against Artaxerxes by his subjects, and listened to his reply to them. At the end he gave his decision. Artaxerxes was pronounced to have forfeited his crown, and was deposed; his property was confiscated, and his person committed to safe custody. The monarchy was declared to be at an end; and Persarmenia was delivered into the hands of a Persian governor. The patriarch Isaac was at the same time degraded from his office and detained in Persia as a prisoner. It was not till some years later that he was released, allowed to return into Armenia, and to resume, under certain restrictions, his episcopal functions.

The remaining circumstances of the reign of Varahran V. come to us wholly through the Oriental writers, amid whose exaggerations and fables it is very difficult to discern the truth. There can, however, be little doubt that it was during the reign of this prince that those terrible struggles commenced between the Persians and their neighbors upon the north-east which continued, from the early part of the fifth till the middle of the sixth century, to endanger the very existence of the empire. Various names are given to the people with whom Persia waged her wars during this period. They are called Turks, Huns, sometimes even Chinese, but these terms seem, to be used in a vague way, as "Scythian" was by the ancients; and the special ethnic designation of the people appears to be quite a different name from any of them It is a name the Persian form of which is Haithal or Haiathleh, the Armenian Hephthagh, and the Greek "Ephthalites," or sometimes "Nephthalites." Different conjectures have been formed as to its origin: but none of them can be regarded as more than an ingenious theory. All that we know of the Ephthalites is, that they were established in force, during the fifth and sixth centuries of our era, in the regions east of the Caspian, especially in those beyond the Oxus river, and that they were generally regarded as belonging to the Scythic or Finno-Turkic population, which, at any rate from B.C. 200, had become powerful in that region. They were called "White Huns" by some of the Greeks; but it is admitted that they were quite distinct from the Huns who invaded Europe under Attila; and it may be doubted whether the term "Hun" is more appropriate to them than that of Turk or even of Chinese. The description of their physical character and habits left us by Procopius, who wrote when they were at the height of their power, is decidedly adverse to the view that they were really Huns. They were a light-complexioned race, whereas the Huns were decidedly swart; they were not il -looking, whereas the Huns were hideous; they were an agricultural people, while the Huns were nomads; they had good laws, and were tolerably well civilized, but the Huns were savages. It is probable that they belonged to the Thibetic or Turkish stock, which has always been in advance of the Finnic, and has shown a greater aptitude for political organization and social progress.

We are told that the war of Varahran V. with this people commenced with an invasion of his kingdom by their Khacan, or Kahn, who crossed the Oxus with an army of 35,000 (or, according to others, of 250,000) men, and carried fire and sword into some of the most fertile provinces of Persia. The rich oasis, known as Meru or Merv, the ancient Margiana, is especially mentioned as overrun by his troops, which are said by some to have crossed the Elburz range into Khorassan and to have proceeded westward as far as Kei, or Rhages. When news of the invasion reached the Persian court, the alarm felt was great; Varahran was pressed to assemble his forces at once and encounter the unknown enemy; he, however, professed complete indifference, said that the Almighty would preserve the empire, and that, for his own part, he was going to hunt in Azerbijan, or Media Atropatene. During his absence the government could be conducted by Narses, his brother. All Persia was now thrown into consternation; Varahran was believed to have lost his senses; and it was thought that the only prudent course was to despatch an embassy to the Khacan, and make an arrangement with him by which Persia should acknowledge his suzerainty and consent to pay him a tribute. Ambassadors accordingly were sent; and the invaders, satisfied with the offer of submission, remained in the position which they had taken up, waiting for the tribute, and keeping slack guard, since they considered that they had nothing to fear. Varahran, however, was all the while preparing to fall upon them unawares. He had started for Azerbijan with a small body of picked warriors; he had drawn some further strength from Armenia; he proceeded along the mountain line through Taberistan, Hyrcania, and Nissa (Nishapur), marching only by night, and carefully masking his movements. In this way he reached the neighborhood of Merv unobserved. He then planned and executed a night attack on the invading army which was completely successful. Attacking his adversaries suddenly and in the dark—alarming them, moreover, with strange noises, and at the same time assaulting them with the utmost vigor—he put to flight the entire Tatar army. The Khan himself was killed; and the flying host was pursued to the banks of the Oxus. The whole of the camp equipage fell into the hands of the victors; and Khatoun, the wife of the great Khan, was taken. The plunder was of enormous value, and comprised the royal crown with its rich setting of pearls. After this success, Varahran, to complete his victory, sent one of his generals across the Oxus at the head of a large force, and falling upon the Tatars in their own country defeated them a second time with great slaughter. The enemy then prayed for peace, which was granted them by the victorious Varahran, who at the same time erected a column to mark the boundary of his empire in this quarter, and, appointing his brother Narses governor of Khorassan, ordered him to fix his residence at Balkh, and to prevent the Tatars from making incursions across the Oxus. It appears that these precautions were successful, for we hear nothing of any further hostilities in this quarter during the remainder of Varahran's reign.

The adventures of Varahran in India, and the enlargement of his dominions in that direction by the act of the Indian king, who is said so have voluntarily ceded to him Mekran and Scinde in return for his services against the Emperor of China, cannot be regarded as historical. Scarcely more so is the story that Persia had no musicians in his day, for which reason he applied to the Indian monarch, and obtained from him twelve thousand performers, who became the ancestors of the Lurs. After a reign which is variously estimated at nineteen, twenty, twenty-one, and twenty-three years, Varahran died by a death which would have been thought incredible, had not a repetition of the disaster, on the traditional site, been witnessed by an English traveller in comparatively recent times. The Persian writers state that Varahran was engaged in the hunt of the wild ass, when his horse came suddenly upon a deep pool, or spring of water, and either plunged into it or threw his rider into it, with the result that Varahran sank and never reappeared. The supposed scene of the incident is a valley between Ispahan and Shiraz. Here, in 1810, an English soldier lost his life through bathing in the spring traditionally declared to be that which proved fatal to Varahran. The coincidence has caused the general acceptance of a tale which would probably have been otherwise regarded as altogether romantic and mythical.

The coins of Varahran V. are chiefly remarkable for their rude and coarse workmanship and for the number of the mints from which they were issued. The mint-marks include Ctesiphon, Ecbatana,

Isaphan, Arbela, Ledan, Nehavend, Assyria, Chuzistan, Media, and Kerman, or Carmania. The ordinary legend is, upon the obverse, Mazdisn bag Varahran malha, or Mazdisn bag Varahran rasti malha, and on the reverse, "Yavahran," together with a mint-mark. The head-dress has the mural crown in front and behind, but interposes between these two detached fragments a crescent and a circle, emblems, no doubt, of the sun and moon gods. The reverse shows the usual fire-altar, with guards, or attendants, watching it. The king's head appears in the flame upon the altar. (PLATE XXI. Fig. 2).

According to the Oriental writers, Varahran V. was one of the best of the Sassanian princes. He carefully administered justice among his numerous subjects, remitted arrears of taxation, gave pensions to men of science and letters, encouraged agriculture, and was extremely liberal in the relief of poverty and distress. His faults were, that he was over-generous and over-fond of amusements, especially of the chase. The nickname of "Bahram-Gur," by which he is known to the Orientals, marks this last-named predilection, transferring to him, as it does, the name of the animal which was the especial object of his pursuit. But he was almost equally fond of dancing and of games. Still it does not appear that his inclination for amusements rendered him neglectful of public affairs, or at all interfered with his administration of the State. Persia is said to have been in a most flourishing condition during his reign. He may not have gained all the successes that are ascribed to him; but he was undoubtedly an active prince, brave, energetic, and clear-sighted. He judiciously brought the Roman war to a close when a new and formidable enemy appeared on his north-eastern frontier; he wisely got rid of the Armenian difficulty, which had been a stumbling block in the way of his predecessors for two hundred years; he inflicted a check on the aggressive Tatars, which indisposed them to renew hostilities with Persia for a quarter of a century. It would seem that he did not much appreciate art but he encouraged learning, and did his best to advance science.

## CHAPTER XV

### Reign of Isdigerd II. His War with Rome. His Nine Years' War with the Ephthalites. His Policy towards Armenia. His Second Ephthalite War. His Character. His Coins.

The successor of Varahan V. was his son, Isdigerd the Second, who ascended the Persian throne without opposition in the year A.D. 440. His first act was to declare war against Rome. The Roman forces were, it would seem, concentrated in the vicinity of Nisibis; and Isdigerd may have feared that they would make an attack upon the place. He therefore anticipated them, and invaded the empire with an army composed in part of his own subjects, but in part also of troops from the surrounding nations. Saracens, Tzani, Isaurians, and Huns (Ephthalites?) served under his standard; and a sudden incursion was made into the Roman territory, for which the imperial officers were wholly unprepared. A considerable impression would probably have been produced, had not the weather proved exceedingly unpropitious. Storms of rain and hail hindered the advance of the Persian troops, and allowed the Roman generals a breathing space, during which they collected an army. But the Emperor Theodosius was anxious that the flames of war should not be relighted in this quarter; and his instructions to the prefect of the East, the Count Anatolius, were such as speedily led to the conclusion, first of a truce for a year, and then of a lasting treaty. Anatolius repaired as ambassador to the Persian camp, on foot and alone, so as to place himself completely in Isdigerd's power—an act which so impressed the latter that (we are told) he at once agreed to make peace on the terms which Anatolius suggested. The exact nature of these terms is not recorded; but they contained at least one unusual condition. The Romans and Persians agreed that neither party should construct any new fortified post in the vicinity of the other's territory—a loose phrase which was likely to be variously interpreted, and might easily lead to serious complications.

It is difficult to understand this sudden conclusion of peace by a young prince, evidently anxious to reap laurels, who in the first year of his reign had, at the head of a large army, invaded the dominions of a neighbor. The Roman account, that he invaded, that he was practically unopposed, and that then, out of politeness towards the prefect of the East, he voluntarily retired within his own frontier, "having done nothing disagreeable," is as improbable a narrative as we often meet with, even in the pages of the Byzantine historians. Something has evidently been kept back. If Isdigerd returned, as Procopius declares, without effecting anything, he must have been recalled by the occurrence of troubles in some other part of his empire. But it is, perhaps, as likely that he retired, simply because he had effected the object with which he engaged in the war. It was a constant practice of the Romans to advance their frontier by building strong towns on or near a debatable border, which attracted to them the submission of the neighboring district. The recent building of Theodosiopolis in the eastern part of Roman Armenia had been an instance of this practice. It was perhaps being pursued elsewhere along the Persian border, and the invasion of Isdigerd may have been intended to check it. If so, the proviso of the treaty recorded by Procopius would have afforded him the security which he required, and have rendered it unnecessary for him to continue the war any longer.

His arms shortly afterwards found employment in another quarter. The Tatars of the Transoxianian regions were once more troublesome; and in order to check or prevent the incursions which they were always ready to make, if they were unmolested, Isdigerd undertook a long war on his northeastern frontier, which he conducted with a resolution and perseverance not very common in the East. Leaving his vizier, Mihr-Narses, to represent him at the seat of government, he transferred his own residence to Nishapm, in the mountain region between the Persian and Kharesmian deserts, and from that convenient post of observation directed the military operations against his active enemies, making a campaign against them regularly every year from A.D. 443 to 451. In the year last mentioned he crossed the Oxus, and, attacking the Ephthalites in their own territory, obtained a complete success, driving the monarch from the cultivated portion of the country, and forcing him to take refuge in the desert. So complete was his victory that he seems to have been satisfied with the result, and, regarding the war as terminated, to have thought the time was come for taking in hand an arduous task, long contemplated, but not hitherto actually attempted.

This was no less a matter than the forcible conversion of Armenia to the faith of Zoroaster. It has been already noted that the religious differences which—from the time when the Armenians, anticipating Constantine, adopted as the religion of their state and nation the Christian faith (ab. A.D. 300)—separated the Armenians from the Persians, were a cause of weakness to the latter, more especially in their contests with Rome. Armenia was always, naturally, upon the Roman side, since a religious sympathy united it with the the court of Constantinople, and an exactly opposite feeling tended to detach it from the court of Ctesiphon. The alienation would have been, comparatively speaking, unimportant, after the division of Armenia between the two powers, had that division been regarded by either party as final, or as precluding the formation of designs upon the territory which each had agreed should be held by the other. But there never yet had been a time when such designs had ceased to be entertained; and in the war which Isdigerd had waged with Theodosius at the beginning of his reign, Roman intrigues in Persarmenia had forced him to send an army into that country. The Persians felt, and felt with reason, that so long as Armenia remained Christian and Persia held to the faith of Zoroaster, the relations of the two countries could never be really friendly; Persia would always have a traitor in her own camp; and in any time of difficulty—especially in any difficulty with Rome—might look to see this portion of her territory go over to the enemy. We cannot be surprised if Persian statesmen were anxious to terminate so unsatisfactory a state of things, and cast about for a means whereby Armenia might be won over, and made a real friend instead of a concealed enemy.

The means which suggested itself to Isdigerd as the simplest and most natural was, as above observed, the conversion of the Armenians to the Zoroastrian religion. In the early part of his reign he entertained a hope of effecting his purpose by persuasion, and sent his vizier, Mihr-Narses, into the country, with orders to use all possible peaceful means—gifts, blandishments, promises, threats, removal of malignant chiefs—to induce Armenia to consent to a change of religion. Mihr-Narses did his best, but failed signally. He carried off the chiefs of the Christian party, not only from Armenia, but from Iberia and Albania, telling them that Isdigerd required their services against the Tatars, and forced them with their followers to take part in the Eastern war. He committed Armenia to the care of the Margrave, Vasag, a native prince who was well inclined to the Persian cause, and gave him instructions to bring about the change of religion by a policy of conciliation. But the Armenians were obstinate. Neither threats, nor promises, nor persuasions had any effect. It was in vain that a manifesto was issued, painting the religion of Zoroaster in the brightest colors, and requiring all persons to conform to it. It was to no purpose that arrests were made, and punishments threatened. The Armenians declined to yield either to argument or to menace; and no progress at all was made in the direction of the desired conversion.

In the year A.D. 450, the patriarch Joseph, by the general desire of the Armenians, held a great assembly, at which it was carried by acclamation that the Armenians were Christians, and would continue such, whatever it might cost them. If it was hoped by this to induce Isdigerd to lay aside his proselytizing schemes, the hope was a delusion. Isdigerd retaliated by summoning to his presence the principal chiefs, viz., Vasag, the Margrave; the Sparapet, or commander-in-chief, Vartan, the Mamigonian; Vazten, prince of Iberia; Vatche, king of Albania, etc.; and having got them into his power, threatened them with immediate death, unless they at once renounced Christianity and made profession of Zoroastrianism. The chiefs, not having the spirit of martyrs, unhappily yielded, and declared themselves converts; whereupon Isdigerd sent them back to their respective countries, with orders to force everywhere on their fellow-countrymen a similar change of religion.

Upon this, the Armenians and Iberians broke out in open revolt. Vartan, the Mamigonian, repenting of his weakness, abjured his new creed, resumed the profession of Christianity, and made his peace with Joseph, the patriarch. He then called the people to arms, and in a short time collected a force of a hundred thousand men. Three armies were formed, to act separately under different generals. One watched Azerbijan, or Media Atropatene whence it was expected that their main attack would be made by the Persians; another, under Vartan, proceeded to the relief of Albania, where proceedings were going on similar to those which had driven Armenia into rebellion; the third, under Vasag, occupied a central position in Armenia, and was intended to move wherever danger should threaten. An attempt was at the same time made to induce the Roman emperor, Marcian, to espouse the cause of the rebels, and send troops to their assistance; but this attempt was unsuccessful. Marcian had but recently ascended the throne, and was, perhaps, scarcely fixed in his seat. He was advanced in years, and naturally unenterprising. Moreover, the position of affairs in Western Europe was such that Marcian might expect at any moment to be attacked by an overwhelming force of northern barbarians, cruel, warlike, and unsparing. Attila was in A.D. 451 at the height of his power; he had not yet been worsted at Chalons; and the terrible Huns, whom he led, might in a few months destroy the Western, and be ready to fall upon the Eastern empire. Armenia, consequently, was left to her own resources, and had to combat the Persians single-handed. Even so, she might probably have succeeded, have maintained her Christianity, or even recovered her independence, had her people been of one mind, and had no defection from the national cause manifested itself. But Vasag, the Marzpan, had always been half-hearted in the quarrel; and, now that the crisis was come, he determined on going wholly over to the Persians. He was able to carry with him the army which he commanded; and thus Armenia was divided against itself; and the chance of victory was well-nigh lost before the struggle had begun. When the Persians took the field they found half Armenia ranged upon their side; and, though a long and bloody contest followed, the end was certain from the beginning. After much desultory warfare, a great battle was fought in the sixteenth year of Isdigerd (A.D. 455 or 456) between the Christian Armenians on the one side, and the Persians, with their Armenian abettors, on the other. The Persians were victorious; Vartan, and his brother, Hemaiiag, were among the slain; and the patriotic party found that no further resistance was possible. The patriarch, Joseph, and the other bishops, were seized, carried off to Persia, and martyred. Zoroastrianism was enforced upon the Armenian nation. All accepted it, except a few, who either took refuge in the dominions of Rome, or fled to the mountain fastnesses of Kurdistan.

The resistance of Armenia was scarcely overborne, when war once more broke out in the East, and Isdigerd was forced to turn his attention to the defence of his frontier against the aggressive Ephthalites, who, after remaining quiet for three or four years, had again flown to arms, had crossed the Oxus, and invaded Khorassan in force. On his first advance the Persian monarch was so far successful that the invading hordes seems to have retired, and left Persia to itself; but when Isdigerd, having resolved to retaliate, led his own forces into the Ephthalite country, they took heart, resisted him, and, having tempted him into an ambuscade, succeeded in inflicting upon him a severe defeat. Isdigerd was forced to retire hastily within his own borders, and to leave the honors of victory to his assailants, whose triumph must have encouraged them to continue year after year their destructive inroads into the north-eastern provinces of the empire.

It was not long after the defeat which he suffered in this quarter that Isdigerd's reign came to an end. He died A.D. 457, after having held the throne for seventeen or (according to some) for nineteen years. He was a prince of considerable ability, determination, and courage. That his subjects called him "the Clement" is at first sight surprising, since clemency is certainly not the virtue that any modern writer would think of associating with his name. But we may assume from the application of the term that, where religious considerations did not come into play, he was fair and equitable, mild-tempered, and disinclined to harsh punishments. Unfortunately, experience tells us that natural mildness is no security against the acceptance of a bigot's creed; and, when a policy of persecution has once been adopted, a Trajan or a Valerian will be as unsparing as a Maximin or a Galerius. Isdigerd was a bitter and successful persecutor of Christianity, which he—for a time at any rate—stamped out, both from his own proper dominions, and from the newly-acquired province of Armenia. He would have preferred less violent means; but, when they failed, he felt no scruples in employing the extremest and severest coercion. He was determined on uniformity; and uniformity he secured, but at the cost of crushing a people, and so alienating them as to make it certain that they would, on the first convenient occasion, throw off the Persian yoke altogether.

The coins of Isdigerd II. nearly resemble those of his father, Varahran V., differing only in the legend, and in the fact that the mural crown of Isdigerd is complete. The legend is remarkably short, being either Masdisn kadi Tezdikerti, or merely Kadi Yezdikerti—i.e. "the Ormazd-worshipping great Isdigerd;" or "Isdigord the Great." The coins are not very numerous, and have three mint-marks only, which are interpreted to mean "Khuzistan," "Ctesiphon," and "Nehavend." [PLATE XXI., Fig. 3.]

CHAPTER XVI

*Right of Succession disputed between the two Sons of Isdigerd II., Perozes (or Firuz) and Hormisdas. Civil War for two years. Success of Perozes, through aid given him by the Ephthalites. Great Famine. Perozes declares War against the Ephthalites, and makes an Expedition into their Country. His ill success. Conditions of Peace granted him. Armenian Revolt and War. Perozes, after*

On the death of Isdigerd II. (A.D. 457) the throne was seized by his younger son Hormisdas, who appears to have owed his elevation, in a great measure, to the partiality of his father. That monarch, preferring his younger son above his elder, had made the latter governor of the distant Seistan, and had thus removed him far from the court, while he retained Hormisdas about his own person. The advantage thus secured to Hormisdas enabled him when his father died to make himself king; and Perozes was forced, we are told, to fly the country, and place himself under the protection of the Ephthalite monarch, who ruled in the valley of the Oxus, over Bactria, Tokaristan, Badakshan, and other neighboring districts. This king, who bore the name of Khush-newaz, received him favorably, and though at first, out of fear for the power of Persia, he declined to lend him troops, was induced after a while to adopt a bolder policy. Hormisdas, despite his epithet of Ferzan, "the Wise," was soon at variance with his subjects, many of whom gathered about Perozes at the court which he was allowed to maintain in Taleqan, one of the Ephthalite cities. Supported by this body of refugees, and by an Ephthalite contingent, Perozes ventured to advance against his brother. His army, which was commanded by a certain Raham, or Ram, a noble of the Mihran family, attacked the forces of Hormisdas, defeated them, and made Hormisdas himself a prisoner. The troops of the defeated monarch, convinced by the logic of success. deserted their late leader's cause, and went over in a body to the conqueror. Perozes, after somewhat more than two years of exile, was acknowledged as king by the whole Persian people, and, quitting Taleqan, established himself at Ctesiphon, or Al Modain, which had now become the main seat of government. It is uncertain what became of Hormisdas. According to the Armenian writers, Raham, after defeating him, caused him to be put to death; but the native historian, Mirkhond, declares that, on the contrary, Perozes forgave him for having disputed the succession, and amiably spared his life.

The civil war between the two brothers, short as it was, had lasted long enough to cost Persia a province. Vatche, king of Aghouank (Albania) took advantage of the time of disturbance to throw off his allegiance, and succeeded in making himself independent. It was the first object of Perozes, after establishing himself upon the throne, to recover this valuable territory. He therefore made war upon Vatche, thought that prince was the son of his sister, and with the help of his Ephthalite allies, and of a body of Alans whom he took into his service, defeated the rebellious Albanians and completely subjugated the revolted country.

A time of prosperity now ensued. Perozes ruled with moderation and justice. He dismissed his Ephthalite allies with presents that amply contented them, and lived for five years in great peace and honor. But in the seventh year, from the death of his father, the prosperity of Persia was suddenly and grievously interrupted by a terrible drought, a calamity whereto Asia has in all ages been subject, and which often produces the most frightful consequences. The crops fail; the earth becomes parched and burnt up; smiling districts are change into wildernesses; fountains and brooks cease to flow; then the wells have no water: finally even the great rivers are reduced to threads, and contain only the scantiest supply of the life-giving fluid in their channels. Famine under these circumstances of necessity sets in; the poor die by hundreds; even the rich have a difficulty in sustaining life by means of food imported from a distance. We are told that the drought in the reign of Perozes was such that at last there was not a drop of water either in the Tigris or the Oxus; all the sources and fountains, all the streams and brooks failed; vegetation altogether ceased; the beasts of the field and the fowls of the air perished; nowhere through the whole empire was a bird to be seen; the wild animals, even the reptiles, disappeared altogether. The dreadful calamity lasted for seven years, and under ordinary circumstances the bulk of the population would have been swept off; but such were the "wisdom and the beneficence of the Persian monarch," that during the entire duration of the scourge not a single person, or, according to another account, but one person, perished of hunger. Perozes began by issuing general orders that the rich should come to the relief of their poorer brethren; he required the governors of towns, and the head-men of villages, to see that food was supplied to those in need, and threatened that for each poor man in a town or village who died of want he would put a rich man to death. At the end of two years, finding that the drought continued, he declined to take any revenue from his subjects, remitting taxes of all kinds, whether they were money imposts or contributions in kind. In the fourth year, not content with these measures, he went further: opened the treasury doors and made distributions of money from his own stores to those in need. At the same time he imported corn from Greece, from India, from the valley of the Oxus, and from Abyssinia, obtaining by these means such ample supplies that he was able to furnish an adequate sustenance to all his subjects. The result was that not only did the famine cause no mortality among the poorer classes, but no one was even driven to quit the country in order to escape the pressure of the calamity.

Such is the account which is given by the Oriental authors of the terrible famine which they ascribe to the early part of the reign of Perozes. It is difficult, however, to suppose that the matter has not been very much exaggerated, since we find that, as early as A.D. 464-5, when the famine should have been at its height, Perozes had entered upon a great war and was hotly engaged in it, his ambassadors at the same time being sent to the Greek court, not to ask supplies of food, but to request a subsidy on account of his military operations. The enemy which had provoked his hostility was the powerful nation of the Ephthalites, by whose aid he had so recently obtained the Persian crown. According to a contemporary Greek authority, more worthy of trust than most writers of his age and nation, the origin of the war was a refusal on the part of the Ephthalites to make certain customary payments which the Persians viewed in the light of a tribute. Perozes determined to enforce his just rights, and marched his troops against the defaulters with this object. But in his first operations he was unsuccessful, and after a time he thought it best to conclude the war, and content himself with taking a secret revenge upon his enemy, by means of an occult insult. He proposed to Khush-newaz to conclude a treaty of peace, and to strengthen the compact by adding to it a matrimonial alliance. Khush-newaz should take to wife one of his daughters, and thus unite the interests of the two reigning families. The proposal was accepted by the Ephthalite monarch; and he readily espoused the young lady who was sent to his court apparelled as became a daughter of Persia. In a little time, however, he found that he had been tricked: Perozes had not sent him his daughter, but one of his female slaves; and the royal race of the Ephthalite kings had been disgraced by a matrimonial union with a person of servile condition. Khush-newaz was justly indignant; but dissembled his feelings, and resolved to repay guile with guile. He wrote to Perozes that it was his intention to make war upon a neighboring tribe, and that he wanted officers of experience to conduct the military operations. The Persian monarch, suspecting nothing, complied with the request, and sent three hundred of his chief officers to Khush-newaz, who immediately seized them, put some to death, and, mutilating the remainder, commanded them to return to their sovereign, and inform him that the king of the Ephthalites now felt that he had sufficiently avenged the trick of which he had been the victim. On receiving this message Perozes renewed the war, advanced towards the Ephthalite country, and fixed his head-quarters in Hyrcania, at the city of Gurgan, He was accompanied by a Greek of the name of Eusebius, an ambassador from the Emperor Zeno, who took back to Constantinople the following account of the campaign.

When Perozes, having invaded the Ephthalite territory, fell in with the army of the enemy, the latter pretended to be seized with a panic, and at once took to flight. The retreat was directed upon a portion of the mountain region, where a broad and good road led into a spacious plain, surrounded on all sides by wooded hills, steep and in places precipitous. Here the mass of the Ephthalite troops was cunningly concealed amid the foliage of the woods, while a small number, remaining visible, led the Persians into the cul-de-sac, the whole army unsuspectingly entering, and only learning their danger when they saw the road whereby they had entered blocked up by the troops from the hills.

The officers then apprehended the true state of the case, and perceived that they had been cleverly entrapped; but none of them, it would seem, dared to inform the monarch that he had been deceived by a stratagem. Application was made to Eusebius, whose ambassadorial character would protect him from an outbreak, and he was requested to let Perozes know how he was situated, and exhort him to endeavor to extricate himself by counsel rather than by a desperate act. Eusebius upon this employed the Oriental method of apologue, relating to Perozes how a lion in pursuit of a goat got himself into difficulties, from which all his strength could not enable him to make his escape. Perozes apprehended his meaning, understood the situation, and, desisting from the pursuit, prepared to give battle where he stood. But the Ephthalite monarch had no wish to push matters to extremities. Instead of falling on the Persians from every side, he sent an embassy to Perozes and offered to release him from his perilous situation, and allow him to return with all his troops to Persia, if he would swear a perpetual peace with the Ephthalites and do homage to himself as his lord and master, by prostration. Perozes felt that he had no choice but to accept these terms, hard as he might think them. Instructed by the Magi, he made the required prostration at the moment of sunrise, with his face turned to the east, and thought thus to escape the humiliation of abasing himself before a mortal by the mental reservation that the intention of his act was to adore the great Persian divinity. He then swore to the peace, and was allowed to return with his army intact into Persia.

It seems to have been soon after the conclusion of his disgraceful treaty that serious troubles once more broke out in Armenia. Perozes, following out the policy of his father, Isdigerd, incessantly persecuted the Christians of his northern provinces, especially those of Armenia, Georgia, and Albania. So severe were his measures that vast numbers of the Armenians quitted their country, and, placing themselves under the protection of the Greek Emperor, became his subjects, and entered into his service. Armenia was governed by Persian officials, and by apostate natives who treated their Christian fellow-countrymen with extreme rudeness, insolence, and injustice. Their efforts were especially directed against the few noble families who still clung to the faith of Christ, and had not chosen to expatriate themselves. Among these the most important was that of the Mamigonians, long celebrated in Armenian history, and at this time reckoned chief among the nobility. The renegades sought to discredit this family with the Persians; and Vahan, son of Hemaiiag, its head, found himself compelled to visit, once and again, the court of Persia, in order to meet the charges of his enemies and counteract the effect of their calumnies. Successful in vindicating himself, and received into high favor by Perozes, he allowed the sunshine of prosperity to extort from him what he had guarded firmly against all the blasts of persecution—to please his sovereign, he formally abjured the Christian faith, and professed himself a disciple of Zoroaster. The triumph of the anti-Christian party seemed now secured; but exactly at this point a reaction set in. Vahan became a prey to remorse, returned secretly to his old creed and longed for an opportunity of wiping out the shame of his apostasy by perilling his life for the Christian cause. The opportunity was not long in presenting itself. In A.D. 481 Perozes suffered a defeat at the hand of the barbarous Koushans, who held at this time the low Caspian tract extending from Asterabad to Derbend. Iberia at once revolted, slew its Zoroastrian king, Vazken, and placed a Christian, Vakhtang, upon the throne. The Persian governor of Armenia, having received orders to quell the Iberian rebellion, marched with all the troops that he could muster into the northern province, and left the Armenians free to follow their own devices. A rising immediately took place. Vahan at first endeavored to check the movement, being doubtful of the power of Armenia to cope with Persia, and feeling sure that the aid of the Greek emperor could not be counted on. But the the popular enthusiasm overleaped all resistance; everywhere the Christian party rushed to arms, and swore to free itself; the Persians with their adherents fled the country; Artaxata, the capital, was besieged and taken; the Christians were completely victorious, and, having made themselves masters of all Persarmenia, proceeded to establish a national government, placing at their head as king, Sahag, the Bagratide, and appointing Vahan, the Mamigonian, to be Sparapet, or "Commander-in-Chief."

Intelligence of these events recalled the Persian governor, Ader-Veshnasp, from Iberia. Returning into his province at the head of an army of no great size, composed of Atropatenians, Medes, and Cadusians, he was encountered by Vasag, a brother of Vahan, on the river Araxes, with a small force, and was completely defeated and slain.

Thus ended the campaign of A.D. 481. In A.D. 482 the Persians made a vigorous attempt to recover their lost ground by sending two armies, one under Ader-Nerseh against Armenia, and the other under Mihran into Iberia. Vahan met the army of Ader-Nerseh in the plain of Ardaz, engaged it, and defeated it after a sharp struggle, in which the king, Sahag, particularly distinguished himself. Mihran was opposed by Vakhtang, the Iberian king, who, however, soon found himself overmatched, and was forced to apply to Armenia for assistance. The Armenians came to his aid in full force; but their generosity was ill rewarded. Vakhtang plotted to make his peace with Persia by treacherously betraying his allies into their enemies' hands; and the Armenians, forced to fight at tremendous disadvantage, suffered a severe defeat. Sahag, the king, and Vasag, one of the brothers of Vahan, were slain; Vahan himself escaped, but at the head of only a few followers, with whom he fled to the highland district of Daik, on the borders of Home and Iberia. Here he was "hunted upon the mountains" by Mihran, and would probably have been forced to succumb before the year was out, had not the Persian general suddenly received a summons from his sovereign, who needed his aid against the Roushans of the low Caspian region. Mihran, compelled to obey this call, had to evacuate Armenia, and Vahan in a few weeks recovered possession of the whole country.

The year A.D. 483 now arrived, and another desperate attempt was made to crush the Armenian revolt. Early in the spring a Persian army invaded Armenia, under a general called Hazaravougd. Vahan allowed himself to be surprised, to be shut up in the city of Dovin, and to be there besieged. After a while he made his escape, and renewed the guerilla warfare in which he was an adept; but the Persians recovered most of the country, and he was himself, on more than one occasion, driven across the border and obliged to seek refuge in Roman Armenia, whither his adversary had no right to follow him. Even here, however, he was not safe. Hazaravougd, at the risk of a rupture with Rome, pursued his flying foe across the frontier; and Vahan was for some time in the greatest danger. But the Persian system of constantly changing the commands of their chief officers saved him. Hazaravougd received orders from the court to deliver up Armenia to a newly appointed governor, named Sapor, and to direct his own efforts to the recovery of Iberia, which was still in insurrection. In this latter enterprise he was successful; Iberia submitted to him; and Vakhtang fled to Colchis. But in Armenia the substitution of Sapor for Hazaravougd led to disaster. After a vain attempt to procure the assassination of Vahan by two of his officers, whose wives were Roman prisoners, Sapor moved against him with a strong body of troops; but the brave Mamigonian, falling upon his assailant unawares, defeated him with great loss, and dispersed his army. A second battle was fought with a similar result; and the Persian force, being demoralized, had to retreat; while Vajian, taking the offensive, established himself in Dovin, and once more rallied to his side the great mass of the nation. Affairs were in this state, when suddenly there arrived from the east intelligence of the most supreme importance, which produced a pause in the Armenian conflict and led to the placing of Armenian affairs on a new footing.

Perozes had, from the conclusion of his treaty with the Ephthalite monarch (ab. A.D. 470), been tormented with the feeling that he had suffered degradation and disgrace. He had, perhaps, plunged into the Armenian and other wars in the hope of drowning the recollection of his shame, in his own mind as well as in the minds of others. But fortune had not greatly smiled on him in these struggles; and any credit that he obtained from them was quite insufficient to produce forgetfulness of his great disaster. Hence, as time went on, he became more and more anxious to wipe out the memory of the past by a great and signal victory over his conquerors. He therefore after some years determined to renew the war. It was in vain that the chief Mobed opposed himself to this intention; it was in vain that his other counsellors sought to dissuade him, that his general, Bahram, declared against the infraction of the treaty, and that the soldiers showed themselves reluctant to fight. Perozes had resolved, and was not to be turned from his resolution. He collected from all parts of the empire a veteran force, amounting, it is said, 50 to 100,000 men, and 500 elephants, placed the direction of affairs at the court in the hands of Balas (Palash), his son or brother, and then marched upon the north-eastern frontier, with the determination to attack and defeat the Ephthalites or perish in the attempt. According to some Oriental writers he endeavored to escape the charge of having falsified his engagements by a curious subterfuge. The exact terms of his oath to Khush-newaz, the Ephthalite king, had been that he would never march his forces past a certain pillar which that monarch had erected to mark the boundary line between the Persian and Ephthalite dominions. Perozes persuaded himself that he would sufficiently observe his engagement if he kept its letter; and accordingly he lowered the pillar, and placed it upon a number of cars, which were attached together and drawn by a train of fifty elephants, in front of his army. Thus, however deeply he invaded the Ephthalite country, he never "passed beyond" the pillar which he had sworn not to pass. In his own judgment he kept his vow, but not in that of his natural advisers. It is satisfactory to find that the Zoroastrian priesthood, speaking by the mouth of the chief Mobed, disclaimed and exposed the fallacy of this wretched casuistry.

The Ephthalite monarch, on learning the intention of Perozes, prepared to meet his attack by stratagem. He had taken up his position in the plain near Balkh, and had there established his camp, resolved to await the coming of the enemy. During the interval he proceeded to dig a deep and broad trench in front of his whole position, leaving only a space of some twenty or thirty yards, midway in the work, untouched. Having excavated the trench, he caused it to be filled with water, and covered carefully with boughs of trees, reeds, and earth, so as to be undistinguishable from the general surface of the plain on which he was encamped. On the arrival of the Persians in his front, he first of all held a parley with Perozes, in which, after reproaching him with his ingratitude and breach of faith, he concluded by offering to renew the peace. Perozes scornfully refused; whereupon the Ephthalite prince hung on the point of a lance the broken treaty, and, parading it in front of the Persian troops, exhorted them to avoid the vengeance which was sure to fall on the perjured by deserting their doomed monarch. Upon this, half the army, we are told, retired; and Khush-newaz proceeded to effect the destruction of the remainder by means of the plan which he had so carefully prepared beforehand. He sent a portion of his troops across the ditch, with orders to challenge the Persians to an engagement, and, when the fight began, to fly hastily, and, returning within the ditch by the sound passage, unite themselves with the main army. The entire Persian host, as he expected, pursued the fugitives, and coming unawares upon the concealed trench plunged into it, was inextricably entangled, and easily destroyed. Perozes himself, several of his sons, and most of his army perished. Mruz-docht, his daughter, the chief Mobed, and great numbers of the rank and file were made prisoners. A vast booty was taken. Khush-newaz did not tarnish the glory of his victory by any cruelties; he treated the captives tenderly, and caused search to be made for the body of Perozes, which was found and honorably interred.

Thus perished Perozes, after a reign of (probably) twenty-six years. He was undoubtedly a brave prince, and entitled to the epithet of Al Merdaneh, "the Courageous," which he received from his subjects. But his bravery, unfortunately, verged upon rashness, and was unaccompanied (so far as appears) by any other military quality. Perozes had neither the sagacity to form a good plan of campaign, nor the ability to conduct a battle. In all the wars wherein he was personally engaged he was unsuccessful, and the only triumphs which gilded his arms were gained by his generals. In his civil administration, on the contrary, he obtained a character for humanity and justice; and, if the Oriental accounts of his proceedings during the great famine are to be regarded as trustworthy, we must admit that his wisdom and benevolence were such as are not commonly found in those who bear rule in the East. His conduct towards Khush-newaz has generally been regarded as the great blot upon his good fame; and it is certainly impossible to justify the paltry casuistry by which he endeavored to reconcile his actions with his words at the time of his second invasion. But his persistent hostility towards the Ephthalites is far from inexcusable, and its motive may have been patriotic rather than personal. He probably felt that the Ephthalite power was among those from which Persia had most to fear, and that it would have been weak in him to allow gratitude for a favor conferred upon himself to tie his hands in a matter where the interests of his country were vitally concerned. The Ephthalites continued for nearly a century more to be among the most dangerous of her neighbors to Persia; and it was only by frequent attacks upon them in their own homes that Persia could reasonably hope to ward off their ravages from her territory.

It is doubtful whether we possess any coins of Hormisdas III., the brother and predecessor of Perozes. Those which are assigned to him by Mordtmann bear a name which has no resemblance to his; and those bearing the name of Ram, which Mr. Taylor considers to be coins of Hormisdas, cannot have been issued under his authority, since Ram was the guardian and general, not of Hormisdas, but of his brother. Perhaps the remarkable specimen figured by M. Longperier in his valuable work, which shows a bull's head in place of the usual inflated ball, may really belong to this prince. The legend upon it is read without any doubt as Auhrimazd, or "Hormisdas;" and in general character it is certainly Sassanian, and of about this period. [PLATE XXI., Fig. 5.]

The coins of Perozes are undoubted, and are very numerous. They are distinguished generally by the addition to the ordinary crown of two wings, one in front of the crown, and the other behind it, and bear the legend, Kadi Piruzi, or Mazdisn Kadi Piruzi, i.e., "King Perozes," or "the Ormazd-worshipping king Perozes." The earring of the monarch is a triple pendant. On the reverse, besides the usual fire-altar and supporters, we see on either side of the altar-flame a star and a crescent. The legend here is M—probably for malka, "king"—or else Kadi, together with a mint-mark. The mints named are numerous, comprising (according to Mordtmann) Persepolis, Ispahan, Rhages, Nehavend, Darabgherd, Zadracarta, Nissa, Behistun, Chuzistan, Media, Kerman, and Azerbijan; or (according to Mr. Thomas) Persepolis, Rasht, Nehavend, Darabgherd, Baiza, Modai'n, Merv, Shiz, Iran, Kerman, Yezd, and fifteen others. The general character of the coinage is rude and coarse, the reverse of the coins showing especial signs of degradation. [PLATE XXI., Fig. 6.]

Besides his coins, one other memorial of the reign of Perozes has escaped the ravages of time. This is a cup or vase, of antique and elegant form, engraved with a hunting-scene, which has been thus described by a recent writer: "This cup, which comes from Russia, has a diameter of thirty-one centimetres, and is shaped like a ewer without handles. At the bottom there stands out in relief the figure of a monarch on horseback, pursuing at full speed various wild animals; before him fly a wild boar and wild sow, together with their young, an ibex, an antelope, and a buffalo. Two other boars, an ibex, a buffalo, and an antelope are strewn on the ground, pierced with arrows. The king has an aquiline nose, an eye which is very wide open, a short beard, horizontal moustaches of considerable length, the hair gathered behind the head in quite a small knot, and the ear ornamented with a double pendant, pear-shaped; the head of the monarch supports a crown, which is mural at the side and back, while it bears a crescent in front; two wings surmounting a globe within a crescent form the upper part of the head-dress. On his right the king carries a short dagger and a quiver full of arrows, on his left a sword. Firuz, who has the finger-guard of an archer on his right hand, is represented in the act of bending a large bow made of horn." There would seem to be no doubt that the work thus described is rightly assigned to Perozes.

CHAPTER XVII

*Accession of Balas or Palash. His Relationship to Perozes. Peace made with the Ephthalites.*
*Pacification of Armenia and General Edict of Toleration. Revolt of Zareh, Son of Perozes, and*
*Suppression of the Revolt with the help of the Armenians. Flight of Kobad to the Ephthalites.*
*Further Changes in Armenia. Vahan made Governor. Death of Balas; his Character. Coins ascribed*
*to him.*

Perozes was succeeded by a prince whom the Greeks call Balas, the Arabs and later Persians Palash,
but whose real name appears to have been Valakhesh or Volagases. Different accounts are given of
his relationship to his predecessor, the native writers unanimously representing him as the son of
Perozes and brother of Kobad, while the Greeks and the contemporary Armenians declare with one
voice that he was Kobad's uncle and Perozes's brother. It seems on the who e most probable that
the Greeks and Armenians are right and we may suppose that Perozes, having no son whom he
could trust to take his place when he quitted his capital in order to take the management of the
Ephthalite war, put the regency and the guardianship of his children into the hands of his brother,
Valakhesh, who thus, not unnaturally, became king when it was found that Perozes had fallen.

The first efforts of the new monarch were of necessity directed towards an arrangement with the
Ephthalites, whose signal victory over Perozes had laid the north-eastern frontier of Persia open to
their attack. Balas, we are told, employed on this service the arms and arts of an officer named
Sukhra or Sufraii, who was at the time governor of Seistan. Sukhra collected an imposing force, and
conducted it to the Ephthalite border, where he alarmed Khush-newaz by a display of his own skill
with the bow. He then entered into negotiations and obtained the release of Firuz-docht, of the
Grand Mobed, and of the other important prisoners, together with the restoration of a large portion
of the captured booty, but was probably compelled to accept on the part of his sovereign some
humiliating conditions. Procopius informs us that, in consequence of the defeat of Perozes, Persia
became subject to the Ephthalites and paid them tribute for two years; and this is so probable a
result, and one so likely to have been concealed by the native writers, that his authority must be
regarded as outweighing the silence of Mirkhond and Tabari. Balas, we must suppose, consented to
become an Ephthalite tributary, rather than renew the war which had proved fatal to his brother. If
he accepted this position, we can well understand that Khush-newaz would grant him the small
concessions of which the Persian writers boast; while otherwise the restoration of the booty and the
prisoners without a battle is quite inconceivable.

Secure, so long as he fulfilled his engagements, from any molestation in this quarter, Balas was able
to turn his attention to the north-western portion of his dominions, and address himself to the
difficult task of pacifying Armenia, and bringing to an end the troubles which had now for several
years afflicted that unhappy province. His first step was to nominate as Marzpan, or governor, of
Armenia, a Persian who bore the name of Nikhor, a man eminent for justice and moderation. Nikhor,
instead of attacking Vahan, who held almost the whole of the country, since the Persian troops had
been withdrawn on the news of the death of Perozes, proposed to the Armenian prince that they
should discuss amicably the terms upon which his nation would be content to end the war and
resume its old position of dependence upon Persia. Vahan expressed his willingness to terminate the
struggle by an arrangement, and suggested the following as the terms on which he and his
adherents would be willing to lay down their arms:

(1) The existing fire-altars should be destroyed, and no others should be erected in Armenia.

(2) The Armenians should be allowed the full and free exercise of the Christian religion, and no
Armenians should be in future tempted or bribed to declare themselves disciples of Zoroaster.

(3) If converts were nevertheless made from Christianity to Zoroastrianism, places should not be given to them.

(4) The Persian king should in person, and not by deputy, administer the affairs of Armenia. Nikhor expressed himself favorable to the acceptance of these terms; and, after an exchange of hostages, Vahan visited his camp and made arrangements with him for the solemn ratification of peace on the aforesaid conditions. An edict of toleration was issued, and it was formally declared that "every one should be at liberty to adhere to his own religion, and that no one should be driven to apostatize." Upon these terms peace was concluded between Vahan and Nikhor, and it was only necessary that the Persian monarch should ratify the terms for them to become formally binding.

While matters were in this state, and the consent of Balas to the terms agreed upon had not yet been positively signified, an important revolution took place at the court of Persia. Zareh, a son of Perozes, preferred a claim to the crown, and was supported in his attempt by a considerable section of the people. A civil war followed; and among the officers employed to suppress it was Nikhor, the governor of Armenia. On his appointment he suggested to Vahan that it would lend great force to the Armenian claims if under the existing circumstances the Armenians would furnish effective aid to Balas, and so enable him to suppress the rebellion. Vahan saw the importance of the conjuncture, and immediately sent to Nikhor's aid a powerful body of cavalry under the command of his own nephew, Gregory. Zareh was defeated, mainly in consequence of the great valor and excellent conduct of the Armenian contingent. He fled to the mountains, but was pursued, and was very shortly afterwards made prisoner and slain.

Soon after this, Kobad, son of Perozes, regarding the crown as rightfully his, put forward a claim to it, but, meeting with no success, was compelled to quit Persia and throw himself upon the kind protection of the Ephthalites, who were always glad to count among their refugees a Persian pretender. The Ephthalites, however, made no immediate stir—it would seem, that so long as Balas paid his tribute they were content, and felt no inclination to disturb what seemed to them a satisfactory arrangement.

The death of Zareh and the flight of Kobad left Balas at liberty to resume the work which their rebellions had interrupted—the complete pacification of Armenia. Knowing how much depended upon Vahan, he summoned him to his court, received him with the highest honors, listened attentively to his representations, and finally agreed to the terms which Vahan had formulated. At the same time he replaced Nikhor by a governor named Antegan, a worthy successor, "mild, prudent, and equitable;" and, to show his confidence in the Mamigonian prince, appointed him to the high office of Commander-in-Chief, or "Sparapet." This arrangement did not, however, last long. Antegan, after ruling Armenia for a few months, represented to his royal master that it would be the wisest course to entrust Vahan with the government, that the same head which had conceived the terms of the pacification might watch over and ensure their execution. Antegan's recommendation approved itself to the Persian monarch, who proceeded to recall his self-denying councillor, and to install Vahan in the vacant office. The post of Sparapet was assigned to Vart, Vahan's brother. Christianity was then formally reestablished as the State religion of Armenia; the fire-altars were destroyed; the churches reclaimed and purified; the hierarchy restored to its former position and powers. A reconversion of almost the whole nation to the Christian faith was the immediate result; the apostate Armenians recanted their errors, and abjured Zoroastrianism; Armenia, and with it Iberia, were pacified; and the two provinces which had been so long a cause of weakness to Persia grew rapidly into main sources of her strength and prosperity.

The new arrangement had not been long completed when Balas died (A.D. 487). It is agreed on all hands that he held the throne for no more than four years, and generally allowed that he died peaceably by a natural death. He was a wise and just prince, mild in his temper, averse to military enterprises, and inclined to expect better results from pacific arrangements than from wars and expeditions. His internal administration of the empire gave general satisfaction to his subjects; he protected and relieved the poor, extended cultivation, and punished governors who allowed any men in their province to fall into indigence. His prudence and moderation are especially conspicuous in his arrangement of the Armenian difficulty, whereby he healed a chronic sore that had long drained, the resources of his country. His submission to pay tribute to the Ephthalites may be thought to indicate a want of courage or of patriotism; but there are times when the purchase of a peace is a necessity; and it is not clear that Balas was minded to bear the obligation imposed on him a moment longer than was necessary. The writers who record the fact that Persia submitted for a time to pay a tribute limit the interval during which the obligation held to a couple of years. It would seem, therefore, that Balas, who reigned four years, must, a year at least before his demise, have shaken off the Ephthalite yoke and ceased to make any acknowledgment of dependence. Probably it was owing to the new attitude assumed by him that the Ephthalites, after refusing to give Kobad any material support for the space of three years, adopted a new policy in the year of Balas's death (A.D. 487), and lent the pretender a force with which he was about to attack his uncle when news reached him that attack was needless, since Balas was dead and his own claim to the succession undisputed. Balas nominated no successor upon his death-bed, thus giving in his last moments an additional proof of that moderation and love of peace which had characterized his reign.

Coins, which possess several points of interest, are assigned to Balas by the best authorities. They bear on the obverse the head of the king with the usual mural crown surmounted by a crescent and inflated ball. The beard is short and curled. The hair falls behind the head, also in curls. The earring, wherewith the ear is ornamented, has a double pendent. Flames issue from the left shoulder, an exceptional peculiarity in the Sassanian series, but one which is found also among the Indo-Scythian kings with whom Balas was so closely connected. The full legend upon the coins appears to be Hur Kadi Valdk-dshi, "Volagases, the Fire King." The reverse exhibits the usual fire-altar, but with the king's head in the flames, and with the star and crescent on either side, as introduced by Pe-rozes. It bears commonly the legend, ValaJcdshi, with a mint-mark. The mints employed are those of Iran, Kerman, Ispahan, Nisa, Ledan, Shiz, Zadracarta, and one or two others. [PLATE XXI., Fig. 4].

CHAPTER XVIII

*First reign of Kobad. His Favorites, Sufral and Sapor. His Khazar War. Rise, Teaching, and influence of Mazdak. His Claim to Miraculous Powers. Kobad adopts the new Religion, and attempts to impose it on the Armenians. Revolt of Armenia under Vahan, successful. Kobad yields. General Rebellion in Persia, and Deposition of Kobad. Escape of Mazdak. Short Reign of Zamasp. His Coins.*

Πέρσας οἶδα νόμοισι τοῖσδε χρεωμένους.—Herod. i. 131.

When Kobad fled to the Ephthalites on the failure of his attempt to seize the crown, he was received, we are told, with open arms; but no material aid was given to him for the space of three years. However, in the fourth year of his exile, a change came over the Ephthalite policy, and he returned to his capital at the head of an army, with which Khush-newaz had furnished him. The change is reasonably connected with the withholding of his tribute by Balas; and it is difficult to suppose that Kobad, when he accepted Ephthalite aid, did not pledge himself to resume the subordinate position which his uncle had been content to hold for two years. It seems certain that he was accompanied to his capital by an Ephthalite contingent, which he richly rewarded before dismissing it. Owing his throne to the aid thus afforded him, he can scarcely have refused to make the expected acknowledgment. Distinct evidence on the point is wanting; but there can be little doubt that for some years Kobad held the Persian throne on the condition of paying tribute to Khush-newaz, and recognizing him as his lord paramount.

During the early portion of his first reign, which extended from A.D. 487 to 498, we are told that he entrusted the entire administration of affairs to Suklira, or Sufrai, who had been the chief minister of his uncle. Sufrai's son, Zer-Mihr, had faithfully adhered to him throughout the whole period of his exile, and Kobad did not regard it as a crime that the father had opposed his ambition, and thrown the weight of his authority into the scale against him. He recognized fidelity as a quality that deserved reward, and was sufficiently magnanimous to forgive an opposition that had sprung from a virtuous motive, and, moreover, had not succeeded. Sufrai accordingly governed Persia for some years; the army obeyed him, and the civil administration was completely in his hands. Under these circumstances it is not surprising that Kobad after a while grew jealous of his subordinate, and was anxious to strip him of the quasi-regal authority which he exercised and assert his own right to direct affairs. But, alone, he felt unequal to such a task. He therefore called in the assistance of an officer who bore the name of Sapor, and had a command in the district of Rhages. Sapor undertook to rid his sovereign of the incubus whereof he complained, and, with the tacit sanction of the monarch, he contrived to fasten a quarrel on Sufrai which he pushed to such an extremity that, at the end of it, he dragged the minister from the royal apartment to a prison, had him heavily ironed, and in a few days caused him to be put to death. Sapor, upon this, took the place previously occupied by Sufrai; he was recognized at once as Prime Minister, and Sipehbed, or commander-in-chief of the troops. Kobad, content to have vindicated his royal power by the removal of Sufrai, conceded to the second favorite as much as he had allowed to the first, and once more suffered the management of affairs to pass wholly into the hands of a subject.

The only war in which Persia seems to have been engaged during the first reign of Kobad was one with the Khazars. This important people, now heard of for the first time in Persian history, appears to have occupied, in the reign of Kobad, the steppe country between the Wolga and the Don, whence they made raids through the passes of the Caucasus into the fertile provinces of Iberia, Albania, and Armenia. Whether they were Turks, as is generally believed, or Circassians, as has been ingeniously argued by a living writer, is doubtful; but we cannot be mistaken in regarding them as at this time a race of fierce and terrible barbarians, nomadic in their habits, ruthless in their wars, cruel and uncivilized in their customs, a fearful curse to the regions which they overrun and desolated. We shall meet with them again, more than once, in the later history, and shall have to trace to their hostility some of the worst disasters that befel the Persian arms. On this occasion it is remarkable that they were repulsed with apparent ease. Kobad marched against their Khan in person, at the head of a hundred thousand men, defeated him in a battle, destroyed the greater portion of his army, and returned to his capital with an enormous booty. To check their incursions, he is said to have built on the Armenian frontier a town called Amid, by which we are probably to understand, not the ancient Amida (or Diarbekr), but a second city of the name, further to the east and also further to the north, on the border line which separated Armenia from Iberia.

The triumphant return of Kobad from his Khazar war might have seemed likely to secure him a long and prosperous reign; but at the moment when fortune appeared most to smile upon him, an insidious evil, which had been gradually but secretly sapping the vitals of his empire, made itself apparent, and, drawing the monarch within the sphere of its influence, involved him speedily in difficulties which led to the loss of his crown. Mazdak, a native of Persepolis, or, according to others, of Nishapur, in Khorassan, and an Archimagus, or High Priest of the Zoroastrian religion, announced himself, early in the reign of Kobad, as a reformer of Zoroastrianism, and began to make proselytes to the new doctrines which he declared himself commissioned to unfold. All men, he said, were, by God's providence, born equal—none brought into the world any property, or any natural right to possess more than another. Property and marriage were mere human inventions, contrary to the will of God, which required an equal division of the good things of this world among all, and forbade the appropriation of particular women by individual men. In communities based upon property and marriage, men might lawfully vindicate their natural rights by taking their fair share of the good things wrongfully appropriated by their fellows Adultery, incest, theft, were not really crimes, but necessary steps towards re-establishing the laws of nature in such societies. To these communistic views, which seem to have been the original speculations of his own mind, the Magian reformer added tenets borrowed from the Brahmins or from some other Oriental ascetics, such as the sacredness of animal life, the necessity of abstaining from animal food, other than milk, cheese, or eggs, the propriety of simplicity in apparel, and the need of abstemiousness and devotion. He thus presented the spectacle of an enthusiast who preached a doctrine of laxity and self-indulgence, not from any base or selfish motive, but simply from a conviction of its truth. We learn without surprise that the doctrines of the new teacher were embraced with ardor by large classes among the Persians, by the young of all ranks, by the lovers of pleasure, by the great bulk of the lower orders. But it naturally moves our wonder that among the proselytes to the new religion was the king. Kobad, who had nothing to gain from embracing a creed which levelled him with his subjects, and was scarcely compatible with the continuance of monarchical rule, must have been sincere in his profession; and we inquire with interest, what were the circumstances which enabled Mazdak to attach to his cause so important and so unlikely a convert.

The explanation wherewith we are furnished by our authorities is, that Mazdak claimed to authenticate his mission by the possession and exhibition of miraculous powers. In order to impose on the weak mind of Kobad he arranged and carried into act an elaborate and clever imposture. He excavated a cave below the fire-altar, on which he was in the habit of offering, and contrived to pass a tube from the cavern to the upper surface of the altar, where the sacred flame was maintained perpetually. Having then placed a confederate in the cavern, he invited the attendance of Kobad, and in his presence appeared to hold converse with the fire itself, which the Persians viewed as the symbol and embodiment of divinity. The king accepted the miracle as an absolute proof of the divine authority of the new teacher, and became thenceforth his zealous adherent and follower.

It may be readily imagined that the conversion of the monarch to such a creed was, under a despotic government, the prelude to disorders, which soon became intolerable. Not content with establishing community of property and of women among themselves, the sectaries claimed the right to plunder the rich at their pleasure, and to carry off for the gratification of their own passions the inmates of the most illustrious harems. In vain did the Mobeds declare that the new religion was false, was monstrous, ought not to be tolerated for an hour. The followers of Mazdak had the support of the monarch, and this protection secured them complete impunity. Each day they grew bolder and more numerous. Persia became too narrow a field for their ambition, and they insisted on spreading their doctrines into the neighboring countries. We find traces of the acceptance of their views in the distant West; and the historians of Armenia relate that in that unhappy country they so pressed their religion upon the people that an insurrection broke out, and Persia was in danger of losing, by intolerance, one of her most valued dependencies.

Vatian, the Mamigonian, who had been superseded in his office by a fresh Marzpan, bent on forcing the Armenians to adopt the new creed, once more put himself forward as his country's champion, took arms in defence of the Christian faith, and endeavored to induce the Greek emperor, Anastasius, to accept the sovereignty of Persarmenia, together with the duty of protecting it against its late masters. Fear of the consequences, if he provoked the hostility of Persia, caused Anastasius to hesitate; and things might have gone hardly with the unfortunate Armenians, had not affairs in Persia itself come about this time to a crisis

The Mobeds and the principal nobles had in vain protested against the spread of the new religion and the patronage lent it by the Court. At length appeal was made to the chief Mobed, and he was requested to devise a remedy for the existing evils, which were generally felt to have passed the limits of endurance. The chief Mobed decided that, under the circumstances of the time, no remedy could be effectual but the deposition of the head of the State, through whose culpable connivance the disorders had attained their height. His decision was received with general acquiescence. The Persian nobles agreed with absolute unanimity to depose Kobad, and to place upon the throne another member of the royal house. Their choice fell upon Zamasp, a brother of Kobad, who was noted for his love of justice and for the mildness of his disposition. The necessary arrangements having been made, they broke out into universal insurrection, arrested Kobad, and committed him to safe custody in the "Castle of Oblivion," proclaimed Zamasp, and crowned him king with all the usual formalities. An attempt was then made to deal the new religion a fatal blow by the seizure and execution of the heresiarch, Mazdak. But here the counter-revolution failed. Mazdak was seized indeed and imprisoned; but his followers rose at once, broke open his prison doors, and set him at liberty. The government felt itself too weak to insist on its intended policy of coercion. Mazdak was allowed to live in retirement unmolested, and to increase the number of his disciples.

The reign of Zamasp appears to have lasted from A.D. 498 to A.D. 501, or between two and three years. He was urged by the army to put Kobad to death, but hesitated to adopt so extreme a course, and preferred retaining his rival as a prisoner. The "Castle of Oblivion" was regarded as a place of safe custody; but the ex-king contrived in a short time to put a cheat on his guards and effect his escape from confinement. Like other claimants of the Persian throne, he at once took refuge with the Ephthalites, and sought to persuade the Great Khan to embrace his cause and place an army at his disposal. The Khan showed himself more than ordinarily complaisant. He can scarcely have sympathized with the religious leanings of his suppliant; but he remembered that he had placed him upon the throne, and had found him a faithful feudatory and a quiet neighbor. He therefore received him with every mark of honor, betrothed him to one of his own daughters, and lent him an army of 30,000 men. With this force Kobad returned to Persia, and offered battle to Zamasp. Zamasp declined the conflict. He had not succeeded in making himself popular with his subjects, and knew that a large party desired the return of his brother. It is probable that he did not greatly desire a throne. At any rate, when his brother reached the neighborhood of the capital, at the head of the 30,000 Ephthalites and of a strong body of Persian adherents, Zamasp determined upon submission. He vacated the throne in favor of Kobad, without risking the chance of a battle, and descended voluntarily into a private station. Different stories are told of his treatment by the restored monarch. According to Procopius, he was blinded after a cruel method long established among the Persians; but Mirkhond declares that he was pardoned, and even received from his brother marked signs of affection and favor.

The coins of Zamasp have the usual inflated ball and mural crown, but with a crescent in place of the front limb of the crown. The ends of the diadem appear over the two shoulders. On either side of the head there is a star, and over either shoulder a crescent. Outside the encircling ring, or "pearl border," we see, almost for the first time, three stars with crescents. The reverse bears the usual fire-altar, with a star and crescent on either side of the flame. The legend is extremely brief, being either Zamasp or Bag Zamasp, i.e. "Zamaspes," or "the divine Zamaspes." [PLATE XXII., Fig. 1.]

Plate XXII.

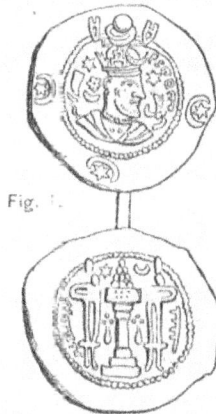

Fig. 1.

COIN OF ZAMASP.

Fig 2.

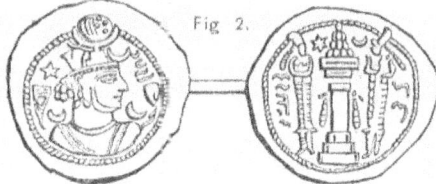

COIN OF KOBAD.

Fig. 3.

COIN OF CHOSROES I.

Fig. 4.

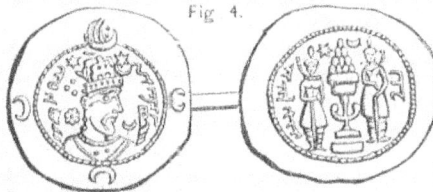

COIN OF CHOSROES I.

PLATE XXII

CHAPTER XIX

*Second Reign of Kobad. His Change of Attitude towards the Followers of Mazdak. His Cause of Quarrel with Rome. First Roman War of Kobad. Peace made A.D. 505. Rome fortifies Daras and Theodosiopolis. Complaint made by Persia. Negotiations of Kobad with Justin: Proposed Adoption of Chosroes by the Latter. Internal Troubles in Persia. Second Roman War of Kobad, A.D. 524-531. Death of Kobad. His Character. His coins.*

The second reign of Kobad covered a period of thirty years, extending from A.D. 501 to A.D. 531. He was contemporary, during this space, with the Roman emperors Anastasius, Justin, and Justinian, with Theodoric, king of Italy, with Cassiodorus, Symmachus, Boethius, Procopius, and Belisarius. The Oriental writers tell us but little of this portion of his history. Their silence, however, is fortunately compensated by the unusual copiousness of the Byzantines, who deliver, at considerable length, the entire series of transactions in which Kobad was engaged with the Constantinopolitan emperors, and furnish some interesting notices of other matters which occupied him. Procopius especially, the eminent rhetorician and secretary of Belisarius, who was born about the time of Kobad's restoration to the Persian thrones and became secretary to the great general four years before Kobad's death, is ample in his details of the chief occurrences, and deserves a confidence which the Byzantines can rarely claim, from being at once a contemporary and a man of remarkable intelligence. "His facts," as Gibbon well observes, "are collected from the personal experience and free conversation of a soldier, a statesman, and a traveller; his style continually aspires, and often attains, to the merit of strength and elegance; his, reflections, more especially in the speeches, which he too frequently inserts, contain a rich fund of political knowledge; and the historian, excited by the generous ambition of pleasing and instructing posterity, appears to disdain the prejudices of the people and the flattery of courts."

The first question which Kobad had to decide, when, by the voluntary cession of his brother, Zamasp, he remounted his throne, was the attitude which he should assume towards Mazdak and his followers. By openly favoring the new religion and encouraging the disorders of its votaries, he had so disgusted the more powerful classes of his subjects that he had lost his crown and been forced to become a fugitive in a foreign country. He was not prepared to affront this danger a second time. Still, his attachment to the new doctrine was not shaken; he held the views propounded to be true, and was not ashamed to confess himself an unwavering adherent of the communistic prophet. He contrived, however, to reconcile his belief with his interests by separating the individual from the king. As a man, he held the views of Mazdak; but, as a king, he let it be known that he did not intend to maintain or support the sectaries in any extreme or violent measures. The result was that the new doctrine languished; Mazdak escaped persecution and continued to propagate his views; but, practically, the progress of the new opinions was checked; they had ceased to command royal advocacy, and had consequently ceased to endanger the State; they still fermented among the masses, and might cause trouble in the future; but for the present they were the harmless speculations of a certain number of enthusiasts who did not venture any more to carry their theories into practice.

Kobad had not enjoyed the throne for more than a year before his relations with the great empire on his western frontier became troubled, and, after some futile negotiations, hostilities once more broke out. It appears that among the terms of the peace concluded in A.D. 442 between Isdigerd II. and the younger Theodosius, the Romans had undertaken to pay annually a certain sum of money as a contribution towards the expenses of a fortified post which the two powers undertook to maintain in the pass of Derbend, between the last spurs of the Caucasus and the Caspian. This fortress, known as Juroi-pach or Biraparach, commanded the usual passage by which the hordes of the north were accustomed to issue from their vast arid steppes upon the rich and populous regions of the south for the purpose of plundering raids, if not of actual conquests. Their incursions threatened almost equally Roman and Persian territory, and it was felt that the two nations were alike interested in preventing them. The original agreement was that both parties should contribute equally, alike to the building and to the maintaining of the fortress; but the Romans were so occupied in other wars that the entire burden actually fell upon the Persians. These latter, as was natural, made from time to time demands upon the Romans for the payment of their share of the expenses; but it seems that these efforts were ineffectual, and the debt accumulated. It was under these circumstances that Kobad. finding himself in want of money to reward adequately his Ephthalite allies, sent an embassy to Anastasius, the Roman emperor, with a peremptory demand for a remittance. The reply of Anastasius was a refusal. According to one authority he declined absolutely to make any payment; according to another, he expressed his willingness to lend his Persian brother a sum of money on receiving the customary acknowledgment, but refused an advance on any other terms. Such a response was a simple repudiation of obligations voluntarily contracted, and could scarcely fail to rouse the indignation of the Persian monarch. If he learned further that the real cause of the refusal was a desire to embroil Persia with the Ephthalites, and to advance the interests of Rome by leading her enemies to waste each other's strength in an internecine conflict, he may have admired the cunning of his rival, but can scarcely have felt the more amicably disposed towards him.

The natural result followed. Kobad at once declared war. The two empires had now been uninterruptedly at peace for sixty, and, with the exception of a single campaign (that of A.D. 441), for eighty years. They had ceased to feel that respect for each other's arms and valor which experience gives, and which is the best preservative against wanton hostilities. Kobad was confident in his strength, since he was able to bring into the field, besides the entire force of Persia, a largo Ephthalite contingent, and also a number of Arabs. Anastasius, perhaps, scarcely thought that Persia would go to war on account of a pecuniary claim which she had allowed to be disregarded for above half a century. The resolve of Kobad evidently took him by surprise; but he had gone too far to recede. The Roman pride would not allow him to yield to a display of force what he had refused when demanded peacefully; and he was thus compelled to maintain by arms the position which he had assumed without anticipating its consequences.

The war began by a sudden inroad of the host of Persia into Roman Armenia. where Theodosiopolis was still the chief stronghold and the main support of the Roman power. Unprepared for resistance, this city was surrendered after a short siege by its commandant, Constantine, after which the greater part of Armenia was overrun and ravaged. From Armenia Kobad conducted his army into Northern Mesopotamia, and formed the siege of Amida about the commencement of the winter. The great strength of Amida has been already noticed in this volume. Kobad found it ungarrisoned, and only protected by a small force, cantoned in its neighborhood, under the philosopher, Alypius. But the resolution of the townsmen, and particularly of the monks, was great; and a most strenuous resistance met all his efforts to take the place. At first his hope was to effect a breach in the defences by means of the ram; but the besieged employed the customary means of destroying his engines, and, where these failed, the strength and thickness of the walls was found to be such that no serious impression could be made on them by the Persian battering train. It was necessary to have recourse to some other device; and Kobad proceeded to erect a mound in the immediate neighborhood of the wall, with a view of dominating the town, driving the defenders from the battlements, and then taking the place by escalade. He raised an immense work; but it was undermined by the enemy, and at last fell in with a terrible crash, involving hundreds in its ruin. It is said that after this failure Kobad despaired of success, and determined to draw off his army; but the taunts and insults of the besieged, or confidence in the prophecies of the Magi, who saw an omen of victory in the grossest of all the insults, caused him to change his intention and still continue the siege. His perseverance was soon afterwards rewarded. A soldier discovered in the wall the outlet of a drain or sewer imperfectly blocked up with rubble, and, removing this during the night, found himself able to pass through the wall into the town. He communicated his discovery to Kobad, who took his measures accordingly. Sending, the next night, a few picked men through the drain, to seize the nearest tower, which happened to be slackly guarded by some sleepy monks, who the day before had been keeping festival, he brought the bulk of his troops with scaling ladders to the adjoining portion of the wall, and by his presence, exhortations, and threats, compelled them to force their way into the place. The inhabitants resisted strenuously, but were overpowered by numbers, and the carnage in the streets was great. At last an aged priest, shocked at the indiscriminate massacre, made bold to address the monarch himself and tell him that it was no kingly act to slaughter captives. "Why, then, did you elect to fight?" said the angry prince. "It was God's doing," replied the priest, astutely; "He willed that thou shouldest owe thy conquest of Amida, not to our weakness, but to thy own valor." The flattery pleased Kobad, and induced him to stop the effusion of blood; but the sack was allowed to continue; the whole town was pillaged; and the bulk of the inhabitants were carried off as slaves.

The siege of Amida lasted eighty days, and the year A.D. 503 had commenced before it was over. Anastasius, on learning the danger of his frontier town, immediately despatched to its aid a considerable force, which he placed under four commanders—Areobindus, the grandson of the Gothic officer of the same name who distinguished himself in the Persian war of Theodosius; Celer, captain of the imperial guard; Patricius, the Phrygian; and Hypatius, one of his own nephews. The army, collectively, is said to have been more numerous than any that Rome had ever brought into the field against the Persians but it was weakened by the divided command, and it was moreover broken up into detachments which acted independently of each other. Its advent also was tardy. Not only did it arrive too late to save Amida, but it in no way interfered with the after-movements of Kobad, who, leaving a small garrison to maintain his new conquest, carried off the whole of his rich booty to his city of Nisibis, and placed the bulk of his troops in a good position upon his own frontier. When Areobindus, at the head of the first division, reached Amida and heard that the Persians had fallen back, he declined the comparatively inglorious work of a siege, and pressed forward, anxious to carry the war into Persian territory. He seems actually to have crossed the border and invaded the district of Arzanene, when news reached him that Kobad was marching upon him with all his troops, whereupon he instantly fled, and threw himself into Constantia, leaving his camp and stores to be taken by the enemy. Meanwhile another division of the Roman army, under Patrilcius and Hypatius, had followed in the steps of Areobindus, and meeting with the advance-guard of Kobad, which consisted of eight hundred Ephthalites, had destroyed it almost to a man.

Ignorant, however, of the near presence of the main Persian army, this body of troops allowed itself soon afterwards to be surprised on the banks of a stream, while some of the men were bathing and others were taking their breakfast, and was completely cut to pieces by Kobad, scarcely any but the generals escaping.

Thus far success had been wholly on the side of the Persians; and if circumstances had permitted Kobad to remain at the seat of war and continue to direct the operations of his troops in person, there is every to reason to believe that he would have gained still greater advantages. The Roman generals were incompetent; they were at variance among themselves; and they were unable to control the troops under their command. The soldiers were insubordinate, without confidence in their officers, and inclined to grumble at such an unwonted hardship as a campaign prolonged into the winter. Thus all the conditions of the war were in favor of Persia. But unfortunately for Kobad, it happened that, at the moment when his prospects were the fairest, a danger in another quarter demanded his presence, and required him to leave the conduct of the Roman war to others. An Ephthalite invasion called him to the defence of his north-eastern frontier before the year A.D. 503 was over, and from this time the operations in Mesopotamia were directed, not by the king in person, but by his generals. A change is at once apparent. In A.D. 504 Celer invaded Arzanene, destroyed a number of forts, and ravaged the whole province with fire and sword. Thence marching southward, he threated Nisibis, which is said, to have been within a little of yielding itself. Towards winter Patricius and Hypatius took heart, and, collecting an army, commenced the siege of Amida, which they attempted to storm on several occasions, but without success. After a while they turned the siege into a blockade, entrapped the commander of the, Persian garrison, Glones, by a stratagem, and reduced the defenders of the place to such distress that it would have been impossible to hold put much longer. It seems to have been when matters were at this point that an ambassador of high rank arrived from Kobac, empowered to conclude a peace, and instructed to declare his master's willingness to surrender all his conquests, including Amida, on the payment of a considerable sum of money. The Roman generals, regarding Amida as impregnable, and not aware of the exhaustion of its stores, gladly consented. They handed over to the Persians a thousand pounds' weight of gold, and received in exchange the captured city and territory. A treaty was signed by which the contracting powers undertook to remain at peace and respect each other's dominions for the space of seven years. No definite arrangement seems to have been made with respect to the yearly payment on account of the fortress, Birapa-rach, the demand for which had occasioned the war. This claim remained in abeyance, to be pressed or neglected, as Persia might consider her interests to require.

The Ephthalite war, which compelled Kobad to make peace with Anastasius, appears to have occupied him uninterruptedly for ten years. During its continuance Rome took advantage of her rival's difficulties to continue the system (introduced under the younger Theodosius) of augmenting her own power, and crippling that of Persia, by establishing strongly fortified posts upon her border in the immediate vicinity of Persian territory. Not content with restoring Theodosiopolis and greatly strengthening it defences, Anastasius erected an entirely new fortress at Daras, on the southern skirts of the Mons Masius, within twelve miles of Nisibis, at the edge of the great Mesopotamian plain. This place was not a mere fort, but a city; it contained churches, baths, porticoes, large granaries, and extensive cisterns. It constituted a standing menace to Persia; and its erection was in direct violation of the treaty made by Theodosius with Isdigerd II., which was regarded as still in force by both nations.

We cannot be surprised that Kobad, when his Ephthalite war was over, made formal complaint at Constantinople (ab. A.D. 517); of the infraction of the treaty. Anastasius was unable to deny the charge. He endeavored at first to meet it by a mixture of bluster with professions of friendship; but when this method did not appear effectua he had recourse to an argument whereof the Persians on most occasions acknowledged the force. By the expenditure of a large sum of money he either corrupted the ambassadors of Kobad, or made them honestly doubt whether the sum paid would not satisfy their master.

In A.D. 518 Anastasius died, and the imperial authority was assumed by the Captain of the Guard, the "Dacian peasant," Justin. With him Kobad very shortly entered jinto negotiations. He had not, it is clear, accepted the pecuniary sacrifice of Anastasius as a complete satisfaction. He felt that he had many grounds of quarrel with the Romans There was the old matter of the annual payment due on account of the fortress of Biraparach; there was the recent strengthening of Theodosiopolis, and building of Daras; there was moreover an interference of Rome at this time in the region about the Caucasus which was very galling to Persia and was naturally resented by her monarch. One of the first proceedings of Justin after he ascended the throne was to send an embassy with rich gifts to the court of a certain Hunnic chief of these parts, called Ziligdes or Zilgibis, and to conclude a treaty with him by which the Hun bound himself to assist the Romans against the Persians. Soon afterwards a Lazic prince, named Tzath, whose country was a Persian dependency, instead of seeking inauguration from Kobad, proceeded on the death of his father to the court of Constantinople, and expressed his wish to become a Christian, and to hold his crown as one of Rome's vassal monarchs. Justin gave this person a warm welcome, had him baptized, married him to a Roman lady of rank, and sent him back to Lazica adorned with a diadem and robes that sufficiently indicated his dependent position. The friendly relations established between Rome and Persia by the treaty of A.D. 505 were, under these circumstances, greatly disturbed, and on both sides it would seem that war was expected to break out. But neither Justin nor Kobad was desirous of a rupture. Both were advanced in years, and both had domestic troubles to occupy them. Kobad was at this time especially anxious about the succession. He had four sons, Kaoses, Zames, Phthasuarsas, and Chosroes, of whom Kaoses was the eldest. This prince, however, did not please him. His affections were fixed on his fourth son, Chosroes, and he had no object more at heart than to secure the crown for this favorite child. The Roman writers tell us that instead of resenting the proceedings of Justin in the years A.D. 520-522, Kobad made the strange proposal to him about this time that he should adopt Chosroes, in order that that prince might have the aid of the Romans against his countrymen, if his right of succession should be disputed. It is, no doubt, difficult to believe that such a proposition should have been made; but the circumstantial manner in which Procopius, writing not forty years after, relates the matter, renders it almost impossible for us to reject the story as a pure fabrication. There must have been some foundation for it. In the negotiations between Justin and Kobad during the early years of the former, the idea of Rome pledging herself to acknowledge Chosroes as his father's successor must have been brought forward. The proposal, whatever its exact terms, led however to no result. Rome declined to do as Kobad desired; and thus another ground of estrangement was added to those which had previously made the renewal of the Roman war a mere question of time.

It is probable that the rupture would have occurred earlier than it did had not Persia about the year A.D. 523 become once more the scene of religious discord and conspiracy. The followers of Mazdak had been hitherto protected by Kobad, and had lived in peace and multiplied throughout all the provinces of the empire. Content with the toleration which they enjoyed, they had for above twenty years created no disturbance, and their name had almost disappeared from the records of history. But as time went on they began to feel that their position was insecure. Their happiness, their very safety, depended upon a single life; and as Kobad advanced in years they grew to dread more and more the prospect which his death would open. Among his sons there was but one who had embraced their doctrine; and this prince, Phthasuarsas, had but little chance of being chosen to be his father's successor. Kaoses enjoyed the claim of natural right; Chosroes was his father's favorite; Zames had the respect and good wishes of the great mass of the people; Phthasuarsas was disliked by the Magi, and, if the choice lay with them, was certain to be passed over. The sectaries therefore determined not to wait the natural course of events, but to shape them to their own purposes. They promised Phthasuarsas to obtain by their prayers his father's abdication and his own appointment to succeed him, and asked him to pledge himself to establish their religion as that of the State when he became king. The prince consented; and the Mazdakites proceeded to arrange their plans, when, unfortunately for them, Kobad discovered, or suspected, that a scheme was on foot to deprive him of his crown. Whether the designs of the sectaries were really treasonable or not is uncertain; but whatever they were, an Oriental monarch was not likely to view them with favor. In the East it is an offence even to speculate on the death of the king; and Kobad saw in the intrigue which had been set on foot a criminal and dangerous conspiracy. He determined at once to crush the movement. Inviting the Mazdakites to a solemn assembly, at which he was to confer the royal dignity on Phthasuarsas, he caused his army to surround the unarmed multitude and massacre the entire number.

Relieved from this peril, Kobad would at once have declared war against Justin, and have marched an army into Roman territory, had not troubles broken out in Iberia, which made it necessary for him to stand on the defensive. Adopting the intolerant policy so frequently pursued, and generally with such ill results, by the Persian kings, Kobad had commanded Gurgenes, the Iberian monarch, to renounce Christianity and profess the Zoroastrian religion. Especially he had required that the

Iberian custom of burying the dead should be relinquished, and that the Persian practice of exposing corpses to be devoured by dogs and birds of prey should supersede the Christian rite of sepulture. Gurgenes was too deeply attached to his faith to entertain these propositions for a moment. He at once shook off the Persian yoke, and, declaring himself a vassal of Rome, obtained a promise from Justin that he would never desert the Iberian cause. Rome, however, was not prepared to send her own armies into this distant and inhospitable region; her hope was to obtain aid from the Tatars of the Crimea, and to play off these barbarians against the forces wherewith Kobad might be expected shortly to vindicate his authority. An attempt to engage the Crimeans generally in this service was made, but it was not successful. A small force was enrolled and sent to the assistance of Gurgenes. But now the Persians took the field in strength. A large army was sent into Iberia by Kobad, under a general named Boes. Gurgenes saw resistance to be impossible. He therefore fled the country, and threw himself into Lazica, where the difficult nature of the ground, the favor of the natives, and the assistance of the Romans enabled him to maintain himself. Iberia, however, was lost, and passed once more under the Persians, who even penetrated into Lazic territory and occupied some forts which commanded the passes between Lazica and Iberia.

Rome, on her part, endeavored to retaliate (A.D. 526) by invading Persarmenia and Mesopotamia. The campaign is remarkable as that in which the greatest general of the age, the renowned and unfortunate Belisarius, first held a command and thus commenced the work of learning by experience the duties of a military leader. Hitherto a mere guardsman, and still quite a youth, trammelled moreover by association with a colleague, he did not on this occasion reap any laurels. A Persian force under two generals, Narses and Aratius, defended Persarmenia, and, engaging the Romans under Sittas and Belisarius, succeeded in defeating them. At the same time, Licelarius, a Thracian in the Roman service, made an incursion into the tract about Nisibis, grew alarmed without cause and beat a speedy retreat. Hereupon Justin recalled him as incompetent, and the further conduct of the war in Mesopotamia was entrusted to Belisarius, who took up his headquarters at Daras.

The year A.D. 527 seems to have been one in which nothing of importance was attempted on either side. At Constantinople the Emperor Justin had fallen into ill health, and, after associating his nephew Justinian on the 1st of April, had departed this life on the 1st of August. About the same time Kobad found his strength insufficient for active warfare, and put the command of his armies into the hands of his sons. The struggle continued in Lazica, but with no decisive result. At Daras, Belisarius, apparently, stood on the defensive. It was not till A.D. 528 had set in that he resumed operations in the open field, and prepared once more to measure his strength against that of Persia.

Belisarius was stirred from his repose by an order from court. Desirous of carrying further the policy of gaining ground by means of fortified posts, Justinian, who had recently restored and strengthened the frontier city of Martyropolis, on the Nymphius, sent instructions to Belisarius, early in A.D. 528, to the effect that he was to build a new fort at a place called Mindon, on the Persian border a little to the left of Nisibis. The work was commenced, but the Persians would not allow it to proceed. An army which numbered 30,000 men, commanded by Xerxes, son of Kobad, and Perozes, the Mihran, attacked the Roman workmen; and when Belisarius, reinforced by fresh troops from Syria and Phoenicia, ventured an engagement, he was completely defeated and forced to seek safety in flight. The attempted fortification was, upon this, razed to the ground; and the Mihran returned, with numerous prisoners of importance, into Persia.

It is creditable to Justinian that he did not allow the ill-success of his lieutenant to lead to his recall or disgrace. On the contrary, he chose exactly the time of his greatest depression to give him the title of "General of the East." Belisarius upon this assembled at Daras an imposing force, composed of Romans and allies, the latter being chiefly Massagetse. The entire number amounted to 25,000 men;

and with this army he would probably have assumed the offensive, had not the Persian general of the last campaign, Perozes the Mihran, again appeared in the field, at the head of 40,000 Persians and declared his intention of besieging and taking Daras. With the insolence of an Oriental he sent a message to Belisarius, requiring him to have his bath prepared for the morrow, as after taking the town he would need that kind of refreshment. Belisarius contented himself, in reply, with drawing out his troops in front of Daras in a position carefully prepared beforehand, where both his centre and his flanks would be protected by a deep ditch, outside of which there would be room to act for his cavalry. Perozes, having reconnoitred the position, hesitated to attack it without a greater advantage of numbers, and sent hastily to Nisibis for 10,000 more soldiers, while he allowed the day to pass without anything more serious than a demonstration of his calvary against the Roman left, and some insignificant single combats.

The next morning his reinforcement arrived; and after some exchange of messages with Belisarius, which led to no result, he commenced active operations. Placing his infantry in the centre, and his horse upon either wing, as the Romans had likewise done, and arranging his infantry so that one half should from time to time relieve the other, he assaulted the Roman line with a storm of darts and arrows. The Romans replied with their missile weapons; but the Persians had the advantage of numbers; they were protected by huge wattled shields; and they were more accustomed to this style of warfare than their adversaries. Still the Romans held out; but it was a relief to them when the missile weapons were exhausted on both sides, and a closer fight began along the whole line with swords and spears. After a while the Roman left was in difficulties. Here the Cadiseni (Cadusians?) under Pituazes routed their opponents, and were pursuing them hastily when the Massagetic horse, commanded by Sunicas and Aigan, and three hundred Heruli under a chief called Pharas, charged them on their right flank, and at once threw them into disorder. Three thousand fell, and the rest were driven back upon their main body, which, still continued to fight bravely. The Romans did not push their advantage, but were satisfied to reoccupy the ground from which they had been driven.

Scarcely was the battle re-established in this quarter when the Romans found themselves in still greater difficulties upon their right. Here Perozes had determined to deliver his main attack. The corps of Immortals, which he had kept in reserve, and such troops as he could spare from his centre, were secretly massed upon his own left, and charged the Roman right with such fury that it was broken and began a hasty retreat. The Persians pursued in a long column, and were carrying all before them, when once more an impetuous flank charge of the barbarian cavalry, which now formed an important element in the Roman armies, changed the face of affairs, and indeed decided the fortune of the day. The Persian column was actually cut in two by the Massagetic horse; those who had advanced the furthest were completely separated from their friends, and were at once surrounded and slain. Among them was the standard-bearer of Baresmanes, who commanded the Persian left. The fall of this man increased the general confusion. In vain did the Persian column, checked in its advance, attempt an orderly retreat. The Romans assaulted it in front and on both flanks, and a terrible carnage ensued. The crowning disaster was the death of Baresmanes, who was slain by Sunicas, the Massa-Goth; whereupon the whole Persian army broke and fled without offering any further resistance. Here fell 5000, including numbers of the "Immortals." The slaughter would have been still greater, had not Belisarius and his lieutenant, Termogenes, with wise caution restrained the Roman troops and recalled them quickly from the pursuit of the enemy, content with the success which they had achieved. It was so long since a Roman army had defeated a Persian one in the open field that the victory had an extraordinary value, and it would have been foolish to risk a reverse in the attempt to give it greater completeness.

While these events took place in Mesopotamia, the Persian arms were also unsuccessful in the Armenian highlands, whither Kobad had sent a second army to act offensively against Rome, under the conduct of a certain Mermeroes. The Roman commanders in this region were Sittas, the former colleague of Belisarius, and Dorotheas, a general of experience. Their troops did not amount to more than half the number of the enemy, yet they contrived to inflict on the Persians two defeats, one in their own territory, the other in Roman Armenia. The superiority thus exhibited by the Romans encouraged desertions to their side; and in some instances the deserters were able to carry over with them to their new friends small portions of Persian territory.

In the year A.D. 531, after a vain attempt at negotiating terms of peace with Rome, the Persians made an effort to recover their laurels by carrying the war into a new quarter and effecting a new combination. Alamandarus, sheikh of the Saracenic Arabs, had long been a bitter enemy of the Romans, and from his safe retreat in the desert had been accustomed for fifty years to ravage, almost at his will, the eastern provinces of the empire. Two years previously he had carried fire and sword through the regions of upper Syria, had burned the suburbs of Chalcis, and threatened the Roman capital of the East, the rich and luxurious Antioch. He owed, it would seem, some sort of allegiance to Persia, although practically he was independent, and made his expeditions when and where he pleased. However, in A.D. 531, he put himself at the disposal of Persia, proposed a joint expedition, and suggested a new plan of campaign. "Mesopotamia and Osrhoene," he said, "on which the Persians were accustomed to make their attacks, could better resist them than almost any other part of the Roman territory, In these provinces were the strongest of the Roman cities, fortified according to the latest rules of art, and plentifully supplied with every appliance of defensive warfare. There, too, were the best and bravest of the Roman troops, and an army more numerous than Rome had ever employed against Persia before. It would be most perilous to risk an encounter on this ground. Let Persia, however, invade the country beyond the Euphrates, and she would find but few obstacles. In that region there were no strong fortresses, nor was there any army worth mention. Antioch itself, the richest and most populous city of the Roman East, was without a garrison, and, if it were suddenly assaulted. could probably be taken. The incursion might be made, Antioch sacked, and the booty carried off into Persian territory before the Romans in Mesopotamia received intelligence of what was happening." Kobad listened with approval, and determined to adopt the bold course suggested to him. He levied a force of 15,000 cavalry, and, placing it under the command of a general named Azarethes, desired him to take Alamandarus for his guide and make a joint expedition with him across the Euphrates. It was understood that the great object of the expedition was the capture of Antioch.

The allied army crossed the Euphrates below Circesium, and ascended the right bank of the river till they neared the latitude of Antioch, when they struck westward and reached Gabbula (the modern Jabul), on the north shore of the salt lake now known as the Sabakhah. Here they learned to their surprise that the movement, which they had intended to be wholly unknown to the Romans, had come to the ears of Belisarius, who had at once quitted Daras, and proceeded by forced marches to the defence of Syria, into which he had thrown himself with an army of 20,000 men, Romans, Isaurians, Lycaonians, and Arabs. His troops were already interposed between the Persians and their longed-for prey, Belisarius having fixed his headquarters at Chalcis, half a degree to the west of Gabbula, and twenty-five miles nearer to Antioch. Thus balked of their purpose, and despairing of any greater success than they had already achieved, the allies became anxious to return to Persia with the plunder of the Syrian towns and villages which they had sacked on their advance. Belisarius was quite content that they should carry off their spoil, and would have considered it a sufficient victory to have frustrated the expedition without striking a blow. But his army was otherwise minded; they were eager for battle, and hoped doubtless to strip the flying foe of his rich booty. Belisarius was at last forced, against his better judgment, to indulge their desires and allow an engagement, which was fought on the banks of the Euphrates, nearly opposite Callinicus. Here the conduct of the Roman troops in action corresponded but ill to the anxiety for a conflict. The infantry indeed stood firm, notwithstanding that they fought fasting; but the Saracenic Arabs, of whom a portion were on the Roman side, and the Isaurian and Lycaonian horse, who had been among the most eager for the fray, offered scarcely any resistance; and, the right wing of the Romans being left exposed by their flight, Belisarius was compelled to make his troops turn their faces to the enemy and their backs to the Euphrates, and in this position, where defeat would have been ruin, to meet and resist all the assaults of the foe until the shades of evening fell, and he was able to transport his troops in boats across the river. The honors of victory rested with the Persians, but they had gained no substantial advantage; and when Azarethes returned to his master he was not unjustly reproached with having sacrificed many lives for no appreciable result. The raid into Syria had failed of its chief object; and Belisarius, though defeated, had returned, with the main strength of his army intact, into Mesopotamia. The battle of Callinicus was fought on Easter Eve, April 19.

Azarethes probably reached Ctesiphon and made his report to Kobad towards the end of the month. Dissatisfied with what Azarethes had achieved, and feeling that the season was not too far advanced for a second campaign, Kobad despatched an army under three chiefs, into Mesopotamia, where Sittas was now the principal commander on the Roman side, as Belisarius had been hastily summoned to Byzantium in order to be employed against the "Vandals" in Africa. This force found no one to resist in the open field, and was therefore able to invade Sophene and lay siege to the Roman fortress of Martyropolis. Martyropolis was ill provisioned, and its walls were out of repair. The Persians must soon have taken it, had not Sittas contrived to spread reports of a diversion which the Huns were about to make as Roman allies. Fear of being caught between two fires paralyzed the Persian commanders; and before events undeceived them, news arrived in the camp that Kobad was dead, and that a new prince sat upon the throne. Under these circumstances, Chanaranges, the chief of the Persian commanders, yielded to representations made by Sittas, that peace would now probably be made between the contending powers, and withdrew his army into Persian territory.

Kobad had, in fact, been seized with paralysis on the 8th of September, and after an illness which lasted only five days, had expired. Before dying, he had communicated to his chief minister, Mebodes, his earnest desire that Chosroes should succeed him upon the throne, and, acting under the advice of Mebodes, had formally left the crown to him by a will duly executed. He is said by a contemporary to have been eighty-two years old at his death, an age very seldom attained by an Oriental monarch. His long life was more than usually eventful, and he cannot be denied the praise of activity, perseverance, fertility of resource, and general military capacity. But he was cruel and fickle; he disgraced his ministers and his generals on insufficient grounds; he allowed himself, from considerations of policy, to smother his religious convictions; and he risked subjecting Persia to the horrors of a civil war, in order to gratify a favoritism which, however justified by the event, seems to have rested on no worthy motive. Chosroes was preferred on account of his beauty, and because he was the son of Kobad's best-loved wife, rather than for any good qualities; and inherited the kingdom, not so much because he had shown any capacity to govern as because he was his father's darling.

The coins of Kobad are, as might be expected from the length of his reign, very numerous. In their general appearance they resemble those of Zamasp, but do not exhibit quite so many stars and crescents. The legend on the obverse is either "Kavdt" or "Kavdt" afzui, i.e. "Kobad," or "May Kobad be increased." The reverse shows the regnal year, which ranges from eleven to forty-three, together with a mint-mark. The mint-marks, which are nearly forty in number, comprise almost all those of Perozes, together with about thirteen others. [PLATE XXII. Fig. 2.]

CHAPTER XX

*Accession of Chosroes I. (Anushirwari). Conspiracy to dethrone him crushed. General Severity of his Government. He concludes Peace with Rome, A.D. 533. Terms of the Peace. Causes Which led to its Rupture. First Roman War of Chosroes, A.D. 540-544. Second Roman War, A.D. 549-557. Eastern Wars. Conquest of Arabia Felix. Supposed Campaign in India. War with the Turks. Revolt of Persarmenia. Third Roman War, A.D. 572-579. Death of Chosroes.*

The accession of Chosroes was not altogether undisputed, Kaoses, the eldest of the sons of Kobad, regarding himself as entitled to the crown by right of birth, assumed the insignia of royalty on the death of his father, and claimed to be acknowledged as monarch. But Mebodes, the Grand Vizier, interposed with the assertion of a constitutional axiom, that no one had the right of taking the Persian crown until it was assigned to him by the assembly of the nobles. Kaoses, who thought he might count on the goodwill of the nobles, acquiesced; and the assembly being convened, his claims were submitted to it. Hereupon Mebodes brought forward the formal testament of Kobad, which he had hitherto concealed, and, submitting it to the nobles, exhorted them to accept as king the brave prince designated by a brave and successful father. His eloquence and authority prevailed; the claims of Kaoses and of at least one other son of Kobad were set aside; and, in accordance with his father's will, Chosroes was proclaimed lawful monarch of Persia.

But a party among the nobles were dissatisfied with the decision to which the majority had come. They dreaded the restlessness, and probably feared the cruelty, of Chosroes. It might have been expected that they would have espoused the cause of the disappointed Kaoses, which had a solid basis of legality to rest upon; but, apparently, the personal character of Kaoses was unsatisfactory, or at any rate, there was another prince whose qualities conciliated more regard and aroused more enthusiasm. Zanies, the second son of Kobad, had distinguished himself repeatedly in the field, and was the idol of a considerable section of the nation, who had long desired that he should govern them. Unfortunately, however, he possessed a disqualification fatal in the eyes of Orientals; he had, by disease or mischance, lost one of his eyes, and this physical blemish made it impossible that he should occupy the Persian throne. Under these circumstances an ingenious plan was hit upon. In order to combine respect for law and usage with the practical advantage of being governed by the man of their choice, the discontented nobles conceived the idea of conferring the crown on a son of Zames, a boy named after his grandfather Kobad, on whose behalf Zames would naturally be regent. Zames readily came into the plot; several of his brothers, and, what is most strange, Chosroes' maternal uncle, the Aspebed, supported him; the conspiracy seemed nearly sure of success, when by some accident it was discovered, and the occupant of the throne took prompt and effectual measures to crush it. Zames, Kaoses, and all the other sons of Kobad were seized by order of Chosroes, and, together with their entire male offspring, were condemned to death. The Aspebed, and the other nobles found to have been accessory to the conspiracy, were, at the same time, executed. One prince alone, the intended puppet-king, Kobad, escaped, through the compassion of the Persian who had charge of him, and, after passing many years in concealment, became a refugee at the Court of Constantinople, where he was kindly treated by Justinian.

When Chosroes had by these means secured himself against the claims of pretenders, he proceeded to employ equal severity in repressing the disorders, punishing the crimes, and compelling the abject submission of his subjects. The heresiarch Mazdak, who had escaped the persecution instituted in his later years by Kobad, and the sect of the Mazdakites, which, despite that persecution, was still strong and vigorous, were the first to experience the oppressive weight of his resentment; and the corpses of a hundred thousand martyrs blackening upon gibbets proved the determination of the new monarch to make his will law, whatever the consequences. In a similar spirit the hesitation of Mebodes to obey instantaneously an order sent him by the king was punished capitally, and with circumstances of peculiar harshness, by the stern prince, who did not allow gratitude for old benefits to affect the judgments which he passed on recent offences. Nor did signal services in the field avail to save Chanaranges, the nobleman who preserved the young Kobad, from his master's vengeance. The conqueror of twelve nations, betrayed by an unworthy son, was treacherously entrapped and put to death on account of a single humane act which had in no way harmed or endangered the jealous monarch.

The fame of Chosroes rests especially on his military exploits and successes. On first ascending the throne he seems, however, to have distrusted his capacity for war; and it was with much readiness that he accepted the overtures for peace made by Justinian, who was anxious to bring the Eastern war to a close, in order that he might employ the talents of Belisarius in the reduction of Africa and Italy. A truce was made between Persia and Rome early in A.D. 532; and the truce was followed after a short interval by a treaty—known as "the endless peace"—whereby Rome and Persia made up their differences and arranged to be friends on the following conditions: (1) Rome was to pay over to Persia the sum of eleven thousand pounds of gold, or about half a million of our money, as her contribution towards the maintenance of the Caucasian defences, the actual defence being undertaken by Persia; (2) Daras was to remain a fortified post, but was not to be made the Roman head-quarters in Mesopotamia, which were to be fixed at Constantia; (3) the district of Pharangium and the castle of Bolon, which Rome had recently taken from Persia, were to be restored, and Persia on her part was to surrender the forts which she had captured in Lazica; (4) Rome and Persia were to be eternal friends and allies, and were to aid each other whenever required with supplies of men and money. Thus was terminated the thirty years' war, which, commencing in A.D. 502 by the attack of Kobad on Annastasius, was brought to a close in A.D. 532, and ratified by Justinian in the year following.

When Chosroes consented to substitute close relations of amity with Rome for the hereditary enmity which had been the normal policy of his house, he probably expected that no very striking or remarkable results would follow. He supposed that the barbarian neighbors of the empire on the north and on the west would give her arms sufficient employment, and that the balance of power in Eastern Europe and Western Asia would remain much as before. But in these expectations he was disappointed. Justinian no sooner found his eastern frontier secure than he directed the whole force of the empire upon his enemies in the regions of the west, and in the course of half a dozen years (A.D. 533-539), by the aid of his great general, Belisarius, he destroyed the kingdom of the Vandals in the region about Carthage and Tunis, subdued the Moors, and brought to its last gasp the power of the Ostrogoths in Italy. The territorial extent of his kingdom was nearly doubled by these victories; his resources were vastly increased; the prestige of his arms was enormously raised; veteran armies had been formed which despised danger, and only desired to be led against fresh enemies; and officers had been trained capable of conducting operations of every kind, and confident, under all circumstances, of success. It must have been with feelings of dissatisfaction and alarm not easily to be dissembled that the Great King heard of his brother's long series of victories and conquests, each step in which constituted a fresh danger to Persia by aggrandizing the power whom she had chiefly to fear. At first his annoyance found a vent in insolent demands for a share of the Roman spoils, which Justinian thought it prudent to humor but, as time went on, and the tide of victory flowed more and more strongly in one direction, he became less and less able to contain himself, and more and more determined to renounce his treaty with Rome and renew the old struggle for supremacy. His own inclination, a sufficiently strong motive in itself, was seconded and intensified by applications made to him from without on the part of those who had especial reasons for dreading the advance of Rome, and for expecting to be among her next victims. Witiges, the Ostrogoth king of Italy, and Bassaces, an Armenian chief, were the most important of these applicants. Embassies from these opposite quarters reached Chosroes in the same year, A.D. 539, and urged him for his own security to declare war against Justinian before it was too late. "Justinian," the ambassadors said, "aimed at universal empire. His aspirations had for a while been kept in check by Persia, and by Persia alone, the sole power in the world that he feared. Since the 'endless peace' was made, he had felt himself free to give full vent to his ambitious greed, had commenced a course of aggression upon all the other conterminous nations, and had spread war and confusion on all sides. He had destroyed the kingdom of the Vandals in Africa, conquered the Moors, deceived the Goths of Italy by professions of friendship, and then fallen upon them with all his forces, violated the rights of Armenia and driven it to rebellion, enslaved the Tzani and the Lazi, seized the Greek city of Bosporus, and the 'Isle of Palms' on the shores of the Red Sea, solicited the alliance of barbarous Huns and Ethiopians, striven to sow discord between the Persian monarch and his vassals, and in every part of the world shown himself equally grasping and restless. What would be the consequence if Persia continued to hold aloof? Simply that all the other nations would in turn be destroyed, and she would find herself face to face with their destroyer, and would enjoy the poor satisfaction of being devoured last. But did she fear to be reproached with breaking the treaty and forfeiting her pledged word? Rome had already broken it by her intrigues with the Huns, the Ethiopians, and the Saracens; and Persia would therefore be free from reproach if she treated the peace as no longer existing. The treaty-breaker is not he who first draws the sword, but he who sets the example of seeking the other's hurt. Or did Persia fear the result of declaring war? Such fear was unreasonable, for Rome had neither troops, nor generals to oppose to a sudden Persian attack. Sittas was dead; Belisarius and the best of the Roman forces were in Italy. If Justinian recalled Belisarius, it was not certain that he would obey; and, in the worst case, it would be in favor of Persia that the Goths of Italy, and the Armenians who for centuries had been subjects of Rome, were now ready to make common cause with her." Thus urged, the Persian king determined on openly declaring war and making an attack in force on the eastern provinces of the empire.

The scene of contest in the wars between Rome and Persia had been usually either Mesopotamia or Armenia. On rare occasions only had the traditional policy been departed from, and attempts made to penetrate into the richer parts of the Roman East, and to inflict serious injury on the empire by carrying fire and sword into peaceful and settled provinces. Kobad, however, had in his later years ventured to introduce a new system, and had sent troops across the Euphrates into Syria in the hope of ravaging that fertile region and capturing its wealthy metropolis, Antioch. This example Chosroes now determined to follow. Crossing the great stream in the lower portion of its course, he led his troops up its right bank, past Circesium, Zenobia, and Callinicus, to Suron, a Roman town on the west side of the river. As this small place ventured to resist him, Chosroes, bent upon terrifying the other towns into submission, resolved to take a s gnal revenge. Though the garrison, after losing their commandant, made overtures for a surrender, he insisted on entering forcibly at one of the gates, and then, upon the strength of this violent entrance, proceeded to treat the city as one taken by storm, pillaged the houses, massacred a large portion of the inhabitants, enslaved the others, and in conclusion set the place on fire and burned it to the ground. It was perhaps in a fit of remorse, though possibly only under the influence of greed, that shortly afterwards he allowed the neighboring bishop of Sergiopolis to ransom these unfortunate captives, twelve thousand, in number, for the modest sum of two hundred pounds of gold.

From Suron the invading army advanced to Hierapolis, without encountering the enemy, who did not dare to make any resistance in the open field, but sought the protection of walls and strongholds. The defences of Hierapolis were in tolerable order; its garrison was fairly strong; and the Great King therefore prudently resolved to allow the citizens to ransom themselves and their city at a moderate price. Two thousand pounds of silver was the amount fixed upon; and this sum was paid without any complaint by the Hierapolites. Plunder, not conquest, was already distinctly set before the invader's mind as his aim; and it is said that he even offered at this period to evacuate the Roman territory altogether upon receiving a thousand pounds of gold. But the Romans were not yet brought so low as to purchase a peace; it was thought that Antioch and the other important towns might successfully defy the Persian arms, and hoped that Justinian would soon send into the field an army strong enough to cope with that of his adversary. The terms, therefore, which Chosroes offered by the mouth of Megas, bishop of Berhcea, were rejected; the Antiochenes were exhorted to remain firm; Ephraim, the bishop, was denounced to the authorities for counselling submission; and it was determined to make no pacific arrangement, but to allow Chosroes to do his worst. The Persian, on his side, was not slack or remiss. No sooner had he received the ransom of Hierapolis than he advanced upon Berhoea (now Aleppo), which he reached in four days. Observing that the defences were weak, he here demanded twice the ransom that he had accepted from the Hierapolites, and was only induced to forego the claim by the tears and entreaties of the good bishop, who convinced him at length that the Berhoeans could not pay so large a sum, and induced him to accept the half of it. A few more days' march brought him from Aleppo to the outskirts of Antioch; and after an interval of nearly three centuries the "Queen of the East," the richest and most magnificent of Oriental cities, was once more invested by Persian troops and threatened by a Sassanian monarch.

A great calamity had fallen upon Antioch only fourteen years previously. The entire town had been ruined by a succession of terrible earthquakes, which commenced in October, A.D. 525, and terminated in August of the ensuing year. All for a time was havoc and disorder. A landslip had covered a portion of the city, and in the remainder almost every house was overthrown. But the liberality of Justinian, the spirit of the inhabitants, and the efforts of the governor, had effaced these disasters; and the city, when the Persians appeared before it, was in most respects grander and more magnificent than ever. The defences were, however, it would seem, imperfect. The citadel especially, which was on the high ground south of the city, had been constructed with small attention to the rules of engineering art, and was dominated by a height at a little distance, which ought to have been included within the walls. Nor was this deficiency compensated by any strength in the garrison, or any weight of authority or talent among those with whom rested the command. Justinian had originally sent his nephew, Germanus, to conduct the defence of the Syrian capital, while Buzes, an officer who had gained some repute in the Armenian war, was entrusted with the general protection of the East until Belisarius should arrive from Italy; but Germanus, after a brief stay, withdrew from Antioch into Cilicia, and Buzes disappeared without any one knowing whither he had betaken himself. Antioch was left almost without a garrison; and had not Theoctistus and Molatzes, two officers who commanded in the Lebanon, come to the rescue and brought with them a body of six thousand disciplined troops, it is scarcely possible that any resistance should have been made. As it was, the resistance was brief and ineffectual. Chosroes at once discerned the weak point in the defences, and, having given a general order to the less trusty of his troops to make attacks upon the lower town in various places, himself with the flower of the army undertook the assault upon the citadel. Here the commanding position so unaccountably left outside the walls enabled the Persians to engage the defenders almost on a level, and their superior skill in the use of missile weapons soon brought the garrison into difficulties. The assailants, however, might perhaps still have been repulsed, had not an unlucky accident supervened, which, creating a panic, put it in the power of the Persians by a bold movement to enter the place. The Romans, cramped for room upon the walls, had extemporized some wooden stages between the towers, which they hung outside by means of ropes. It happened that, in the crush and tumult, one of these stages gave way; the ropes broke, and the beams fell with a crash to the earth, carrying with them a number of the defenders. The noise made by the fall was great, and produced a general impression that the wall itself had been broken down; the towers and battlements were at once deserted; the Roman soldiers rushed to the gates and began to quit the town; while the Persians took advantage of the panic to advance their scaling ladders, to mount the walls, and to make themselves masters of the citadel. Thus Antioch was taken. The prudence of Chosroes was shown in his quietly allowing the armed force to withdraw; his resolve to trample down all resistance appeared in his slaughter of the Antiochone youth, who with a noble recklessness continued the conflict after the soldiers had fled; his wish to inspire terror far and wide made him deliver the entire city, with few exceptions, to the flames; while his avarice caused him to plunder the churches, and to claim as his own the works of art, the marbles, bronzes, tablets, and pictures, with which the Queen of the Roman East was at this time abundantly provided. But, while thus gratifying his most powerful passions, he did not lose sight of the opportunity to conclude an advantageous peace. Justinian's ambassadors had long been pressing him to come to terms with their master. He now consented to declare the conditions on which he was ready to make peace and withdraw his army. Rome must pay him, as an indemnity for the cost of the war, the sum of five thousand pounds of gold, and must also contract to make a further payment of five hundred pounds of gold annually, not as a tribute, but as a fair contribution towards the expense of maintaining the Caspian Gates and keeping out the Huns. If hostages were given him, he would consent to abstain from further acts of hostility while Justinian was consulted on these proposals, and would even begin at once to withdraw his army. The ambassadors readily agreed to these terms, and it was understood that a truce would be observed until Justinian's answer should be delivered to Chosroes.

But the Great King, in thus formulating the terms on which he would be content to make peace, did not intend to tie his own hands, or to allow the Syrian cities before which he had not yet appeared to be quit of him without the payment of ransom. After visiting Seleucia, the port of Antioch at the mouth of the Orontes, bathing in the blue waters of the Mediterranean, and offering sacrifice to the (setting?) sun upon the shore, he announced his intention of proceeding to Apameia, a city on the middle Orontes, which was celebrated for its wealth, and particularly for its possession of a fragment of the "true cross," enshrined in a case which the pious zeal of the faithful had enriched with gold and jewels of extraordinary value. Received peacefully into the city by the submissive inhabitants, instead of fixing their ransom at a definite sum, he demanded and obtained all the valuables of the sacred treasury, including the precious relic which the Apamaeans regarded as the most important of their possessions. As, however, it was the case, and not its contents, that he coveted, while he carried off the former, he readily restored the latter to the prayers of the bishop and inhabitants.

From Apameia Chosroes returned to Antioch, and after witnessing the games of the amphitheatre and securing victory to the green champion because Justinian preferred the blue, he set out at last on his return to Persia, taking care to visit, upon his way to the Euphrates, the city of Chalcis, the only important place in Northern Syria that had hitherto escaped him. The Chalcidians were required not only to ransom themselves by a sum of money, but to give up to Chosroes the Roman soldiers who garrisoned their town. By a perjury that may well be forgiven them, they avoided the more important concession, but they had to satisfy the avarice of the conqueror by the payment of two hundred pounds of gold. The Persian host then continued its march, and reaching the Euphrates at Obbane, in the neighborhood of Barbalissus crossed by a bridge of boats in three days. The object of Chosroes in thus changing his return line of march was to continue in Roman Mesopotamia the course which he had adopted in Syria since the conclusion of the truce—i.e. to increase his spoil by making each important city ransom itself. Edessa, Constantina, and Daras were successively visited, and purchased their safety by a contribution. According to Procopius, the proceedings before Daras were exceptional. Although Chosroes, before he quitted Edossa, had received a communication from Justinian accepting the terms arranged with the Roman envoys at Antioch, yet, when he reached Daras, he at once resolved upon its siege. The city was defended by two walls, an outer one of moderate strength, and an inner one sixty feet high, with towers at intervals, whose height was a hundred feet. Chosroes, having invested the place, endeavored to penetrate within the defences by means of a mine; but, his design having been betrayed, the Romans met him with a countermine, and completely foiled his enterprise. Unwilling to spend any more time on the siege, the Persian monarch upon this desisted from his attempt, and accepted the contribution of a thousand pounds of silver as a sufficient redemption for the great fortress.

Such is the account of the matter given to us by Procopius, who is our only extant authority for the details of this war. But the account is violently improbable. It represents Chosroes as openly flying in the face of a treaty the moment that he had concluded it, and as departing in a single instance from the general tenor of his proceedings in all other cases. In view of the great improbability of such a course of action, it is perhaps allowable to suppose that Procopius has been for once carried away by partisanship, and that the real difference between the case of Daras and the other towns consisted in this, that Daras alone refused to pay its ransom, and Chosroes had, in consequence, to resort to hostilities in order to enforce it.

Still, no doubt, the whole conduct of Chosroes in enforcing ransoms from the towns after the conclusion of the truce was open to serious question, and Justinian was quite justified in treating his proceedings as a violation of his recent engagements. It is not unlikely that, even without any such excuse, he would shortly have renewed the struggle, since the return of Belisarius in triumph from the Italian war had placed at his service for employment in the East a general from whose abilities much was naturally expected. As it was, Justinian was able, on receiving intelligence of the fines levied on Apameia, Chalcis, Edessa, Constantina, and Daras, and of the hostile acts committed against the last-named place, with great show of reason and justice, to renounce the recently concluded peace, and to throw on the ill faith of Chosroes the blame of the rupture.

The Persian prince seems to have paid but little heed to the denunciation. He passed the winter in building and beautifying a Persian Antioch in the neighborhood of Ctesiphon, assigning it as a residence to his Syrian captives, for whose use he constructed public baths and a spacious hippodrome, where the entertainments familiar to them from their youth were reproduced by Syrian artists. The new city was exempt from the jurisdiction of Persian satraps, and was made directly dependent upon the king, who supplied it with corn gratuitously, and allowed it to become an inviolable asylum for all such Greek slaves as should take shelter in it, and be acknowledged as their kinsmen by any of the inhabitants. A model of Greek civilization was thus brought into close contact with the Persian court, which could amuse itself with the contrasts, if it did not learn much from the comparison, of European and Asiatic manners and modes of thought.

The campaign of A.D. 540 was followed by one of a very different character in A.D. 541. An unexpected offer suddenly made to the Persian king drew him from his capital, together with the bulk of his troops, to one of the remotest portions of the Persian territory, and allowed the Romans, instead of standing on their defence, to assume an aggressive in Mesopotamia, and even to retaliate the invasion which the year before Chosroes had conducted into the heart of their empire. The hostile operations of A.D. 541 had thus two distinct and far-distant scenes; in the one set the Persians, in the other the Romans, took the offensive; the two wars, for such they in reality were, scarcely affected one another; and it will therefore be convenient to keep the accounts of them distinct and separate. To commence with.

I. The LAZIO WAR.—Lazica had been a dependency of Rome from the time when Tzath, upon his conversion to Christianity, professed himself the vassal of Justin, and received the insignia of royalty from his new patron (A.D. 522). The terms of the connection had been at the first honorable to the weaker nation, which paid no tribute, admitted no Roman garrison, and was troubled by no Roman governor. As time went on, however, the Romans gradually encroached upon the rights of their dependants; they seized and fortified a strong post, called Petra, upon the coast, appointed a commandant who claimed an authority as great as that of the Lazic king, and established a commercial monopoly which pressed with great severity upon the poorer classes of the Lazi. Under these circumstances the nation determined on revolt; and in the winter of A.D. 540-1 Lazic ambassadors visited the court of Persia, exposed the grievances of their countrymen, and besought Chosroes to accept their submission, and extend to them the protection of his government. The province was distant, and possessed few attractions; whatever the tales told of its ancient wealth, or glories, or trade, in the time of Chosroes it was poor and unproductive, dependent on its neighbors for some of the necessaries and all the conveniences of life, and capable of exporting nothing but timber, slaves, and skins. It might have been expected, under such circumstances, that the burden of the protectorate would have been refused; out there was an advantage, apparent or real, in the position of the country, discovered by the sagacity of Chosroes or suggested to him by the interested zeal of the envoys, which made its possession seem to the Persian king a matter of the highest importance, and induced him to accept the offer made him without a moment's delay. Lazica, the ancient Colchis and the modern Mingrelia and Imeritia, bordered upon the Black Sea, which the Persian dominions did not as yet touch. Once in possesion of this tract, Chosroes conceived that he might launch a fleet upon the Euxine, command its commerce, threaten or ravage its shores, and even sail against Constantinople and besiege the Roman emperor in his capital. The Persian king therefore acceded to the request of the envoys, and, pretending to be called into Iberia by a threatened invasion of the Huns, led a large army to the Lazic border, was conducted into the heart of the country by the envoys, received the submission of Gubazes, the king, and then, pressing on to the coast, formed the siege of Petra, where the Roman forces were collected. Petra offered a stout resistance, and repulsed more than one Persian assault; but it was impossible for the small garrison to cope with the numbers, the engineering skill, and the ardor of the assailants. After the loss of their commandant, Johannes, and the fall of one of the principal towers, the soldiers capitulated; Petra was made over to the Persians, who restored and strengthened its defences, and Lazica became for the time a Persian province.

II. The War in Mesopotamia.—Belisarius, on reaching the eastern frontier, fixed his head-quarters at Daras, and, finding that the Persians had no intention of invading Syria or Roman Mesopotamia, resolved to lead his troops into the enemy's territory. As his forces were weak in numbers, ill-armed, and ill-supplied, he could scarcely hope to accomplish any great enterprise; but it was important to recover the Roman prestige after the occurrences of the preceding year, and to show that Rome was willing to encounter in the open field any force that the Persians could bring against her. He therefore crossed the frontier and advanced in the direction of Nisibis, less with the intention of attacking the town than of distinctly offering battle to the troops collected within it. His scheme succeeded; a small force, which he threw out in advance, drew the enemy from the walls; and their pursuit of this detachment brought them into contact with the main army of Belisarius, which repulsed them and sent them flying into the town. Having thus established his superiority in the field, the Roman general, though he could not attack Nisibis with any prospect of success, was able to adopt other offensive measures. He advanced in person a day's march beyond Nisibis, and captured the fort of Sisauranon. Eight hundred Persian cavalry of the first class were made prisoners, and sent by Belisarius to Byzantium, where they were despatched by Justinian to Italy, where they served against the Goths. Arethas, the chief of the Saracens who fought on the side of Rome, was sent still further in advance. The orders given him were to cross the Tigris into Assyria, and begin to ravage it, but to return within a short time to the camp, and bring a report of the strength of the Persians beyond the river. If the report was favorable, Belisarius intended to quit Mesopotamia, and take the whole Roman force with him into Assyria. His plans, however, were frustrated by the selfish Arab, who, wishing to obtain the whole Assyrian spoil for himself, dismissed his Roman troops, proceeded to plunder the rich province on his own account, and sent Belisarius no intelligence of what he was so doing. After waiting at Sisauranon till the heats of summer had decimated his army, the Roman general was compelled to retreat by the discontent of the soldiery and the representations of his principal officers. He withdrew his forces within the Roman frontier without molestation from the enemy, and was shortly afterwards summoned to Constantinople to confer on the state of affairs with, the emperor.

The military operations of the next year (A.D. 542) were comparatively unimportant. Chosroes collected a large army, and, repeating the movement of A.D. 540, made his appearance in Commagene early in the year, intending to press forward through Syria into Palestine, and hoping to make himself master of the sacred treasures which he knew to be accumulated in the Holy City of Jerusalem. He found the provincial commanders, Buzes and Justus, despondent and unenterprising, declined to meet him in the field, and content to remain shut up within the walls of Hierapolis. Had these been his only opponents the campaign would probably have proved a success; but, at the first news of his invasion, Justinian despatched Belisarius to the East, for the second time, and this able general, by his arts or by his reputation, succeeded in arresting the steps of Chosroes and frustrating his expedition. Belisarius took up his head-quarters at Europus, on the Euphrates, a little to the south of Zeugma, and, spreading his troops on both banks of the river, appeared both to protect the Roman province and to threaten the return of the enemy. Chosroes having sent an emissary to the Roman camp under the pretence of negotiating, but really to act the part of a spy, was so impressed (if we may believe Procopius) by the accounts which he received of the ability of the general and the warlike qualities of his soldiers, that he gave up the idea of advancing further, and was content to retire through Roman Mesopotamia into his own territories. He is said even to have made a convention that he would commit no hostile act as he passed through the Roman province; but if so, he did not keep the engagement. The city of Callinicus lay in his way; its defences were undergoing repairs, and there was actually a gap in one place where the old wall had been pulled down and the new one had not yet been built. The Persian king could not resist the temptation of seizing this easy prey; he entered the undefended town, enslaved all whom he found in it, and then razed the place to the ground. Such is the account which the Byzantine historian gives of the third campaign of Chosroes against the Romans, and of the motive and manner of his retreat. Without taxing him with falsehood, we may suspect that, for the glorification of his favorite hero, he has kept back a portion of the truth. The retreat of Chosroes may be ascribed with much probability to the advance of another danger, more formidable than Belisarius, which exactly at this time made its appearance in the country whereto he was hastening. It was in the summer of A.D. 542 that the plague broke out at Pelusium, and spread from that centre rapidly into the rest of Egypt and also into Palestine. Chosroes may well have hesitated to confront this terrible foe. He did not ultimately escape it; but he might hope to do so, and it would clearly have been the height of imprudence to have carried out his intention of invading Palestine when the plague was known to be raging there.

The fourth year of the Roman war (A.D. 543) opened with a movement of the Persian troops toward the Armenian frontier, consequent upon the desertion of the Persian cause by the Roman Armenians in the course of the winter. Chosroes in person once more led the attack, and proceeded as far as Azerbijan; but, the pestilence breaking out in his army, he hastily retreated, after some futile attempts at negotiation with the Roman officers opposed to him. Belisarius had this year been sent to Italy, and the Roman army of the East, amounting to thirty thousand men, was commanded by as many as fifteen generals, almost of equal rank, among whom there was little concert or agreement. Induced to take the offensive by the retirement of the Persian king, these incapable officers invaded Persarmenia with all their troops, and proceeded to plunder its rich plains and fertile valleys. Encountering suddenly and unexpectedly the Persian general Nabedes, who, with a small force, was strongly posted at a village called Anglon, they were compelled to engage at disadvantage; their troops, entangled in difficult ground, found themselves attacked in their rear by an ambush; Narses, the bravest of them, fell; and, a general panic seizing the entire multitude, they fled in the extremest disorder, casting away their arms, and pressing their horses till they sank and expired. The Persians pursued, but with caution, and the carnage was not so great as might have been expected; but vast numbers of the disarmed fugitives were overtaken and made prisoners by the enemy; and the arms, animals, and camp equipment which fell into the hands of the Persians amply compensated all previous losses, and left Persarmenia the richer for the inroad.

The ravages of the pestilence having ceased, Chosroes, in the following year (A.D. 544), again marched westward in person, and laid siege to the city of Edessa. It would seem that he had now resolved not to be content with plundering raids, but to attempt at any rate the permanent conquest of some portion of the Roman territory. Edessa and Daras were the two towns on which the Roman possession of Western Mesopotamia at this time mainly depended. As the passing of Nisibis, in A.D. 363, from Roman into Persian hands, had given to Persia a secure hold on the eastern portion of the country between the rivers, so the occupation of Edessa and Daras could it have been effected, would have carried with it dominion over the more western regions. The Roman frontier would in this way have been thrown back to the Euphrates. Chosroes must be understood as aiming at this grand result in the siege which he so pertinaciously pressed, and which Edessa so gallantly resisted, during the summer of A.D. 544. The elaborate account which Procopius gives of the siege may be due to a sense of its importance. Chosroes tried, not force only, but every art known to the engineering science of the period; he repeated his assaults day after day; he allowed the defenders no repose; yet he was compelled at last to own himself baffled by the valor of the small Roman garrison and the spirit of the native inhabitants, to burn his works, and to return home. The five hundred pounds of gold which he extorted at last from Martinus, the commandant of the place, may have been a salve to his wounded pride; but it was a poor set-off against the loss of men, of stores, and of prestige, which he had incurred by his enterprise.

It was, perhaps, his repulse from the walls of Edessa that induced Chosroes, in A.D. 545, seriously to entertain the proposals for an arrangement which were made to him by the ambassadors of Justinian. Throughout the war their had been continual negotiations; but hitherto the Persian king had trifled with his antagonist, and had amused himself with discussing terms of accommodation without any serious purpose. Now at last, after five years of incessant hostilities, in which he had gained much glory but little profit, he seems to have desired a breathing-space. Justinian's envoys visited him at Ctesiphon, and set forth their master's desire to conclude a regular peace. Chosroes professed to think that the way for a final arrangement would be best prepared by the conclusion, in the first instance, of a truce. He proposed, n lieu of a peace, a cessation of hostilities for five years, during the course of which the causes of quarrel between the two nations might be considered, and a good understanding established. It shows the weakness of the Empire, that Justinian not only accepted this proposal, but was content to pay for the boon granted him. Chosroes received as the price of the five years truce the services of a Greek physician and two thousand pounds of gold.

The five years' truce seems to have been observed with better faith by the Persian than by the Roman monarch. Alamundarus indeed, though a Persian vassal, regarded himself as entitled, despite the truce, to pursue his quarrel with his natural enemy, Arethas, who acknowledged the suzerainty of Rome; but Chosroes is not even accused of instigating his proceedings; and the war between the vassals was carried on without dragging either of the two lords-paramount into its vortex. Thus far, then, neither side had any cause of complaint against the other. If we were bound to accept the Roman story of a project formed by Chosroes for the surprise and seizure of Daras, we should have to admit that circumstances rather than his own will saved the Persian monarch from the guilt of being the first to break the agreement. But the tale told by Procopius is improbable; and the Roman belief of it can have rested at best only upon suspicion. Chosroes, it is allowed, committed no hostile act; and it may well be doubted whether he really entertained the design ascribed to him. At any rate, the design was not executed, nor even attempted; and the peace was thus not broken on his part. It was reserved for Rome in the fourth year of the truce (A.D. 549) expressly, to break its provisions by accepting the Lazi into alliance and sending them a body of eight thousand men to help them against the Persians.

Very soon after their submission to Persia the Lazi had repented of their rash and hasty action. They found that they had gained nothing, while in some respects they had lost, by their change of masters. The general system of the Persian administration was as arbitrary and oppressive as the Roman. If the commercial monopoly, whereof they so bitterly complained, had been swept away, commerce itself had gone with it, and they could neither find a market for their own products, nor obtain the commodities which they required. The Persian manners and customs introduced into their country, if not imposed upon themselves, were detestable to the Lazi, who were zealous and devout Christians, and possessed by the spirit of intolerance. Chosroes, after holding the territory for a few years, became convinced that Persia could not retain it unless the disaffected population were removed and replaced by faithful subjects. He designed therefore, we are told, to deport the entire Lazic nation, and to plant the territory with colonies of Persians and others, on whose fidelity he could place full reliance. As a preliminary step, he suggested to his lieutenant in Lazica that he should contrive the assassination of Gubazes, the Lazic king, in whom he saw an obstacle to his project. Phabrizus, however, failed in his attempt to execute this commission; and his failure naturally produced the immediate revolt of the province, which threw itself once more into the arms of Rome, and, despite the existing treaty with the Persians, was taken by Justinian under his protection.

The Lazic war, which commenced in consequence of this act of Justinian's, continued almost without intermission for nine years—from A.D. 549 to 557. Its details are related at great length by Procopius and Agathias, who view the struggle as one which vitally concerned the interests of their country. According to them, Chosroes was bent upon holding Lazica in order to construct at the mouth of the Phasis a great naval station and arsenal, from which his fleets might issue to command the commerce or ravage the shores of the Black Sea. There is no doubt that the country was eminently fitted for such a purpose. The soil is for the most part richly fertile; the hills are everywhere covered with forests of noble trees; the Rion (Phasis) is deep and broad towards its mouth; and there are other streams also which are navigable. If Chosroes entertained the intentions ascribed to him, and had even begun the collection of timber for ship-building at Petra on the Euxine as early as A.D. 549, we cannot be surprised at the attitude assumed by Rome, or at her persistent efforts to recover possession of the Lazic territory.

The war was opened by an attack upon the great centre of the Persian power, Petra. This place, which was strongly situated on a craggy rock projecting into the sea, had been carefully fortified by Justinian before Lazica passed into the possession of Chosroes, and had since received important additions to its defences at the hands of the Persians. It was sufficiently provisioned, and was defended by a body of fifteen hundred men. Dagisthseus, the Roman commander, besieged it with his entire force of eight thousand men, and succeeded by his constant attacks in reducing the garrison to little more than a fourth of its original number. Baffled in one attempt to effect a breach by means of a mine, he had contrived to construct another, and might have withdrawn his props, destroyed the wall, and entered the place, had he not conceived the idea of bargaining with the emperor for a specific reward in case he effected the capture. Whilst he waited for his messenger to bring a reply, the Persian general, Memeroes, forced the passes from Iberia into Lazica, and descended the valley of the Phasis with an army of 30,000 men. Dagisthalus in alarm withdrew, and Petra was relieved and revictualled. The walls were repaired hastily with sandbags, and the further defence was entrusted to a fresh garrison of 3000 picked soldiers. Mermeroes then, finding it difficult to obtain supplies for his large army, retired into Persarmenia, leaving only five thousand Persians in the country besides the garrison of Petra. This small force was soon afterwards surprised by the combined Romans and Lazi, who completely defeated it, destroying or making prisoners almost the entire number.

In the ensuing year, A.D. 550, the Persians took the field under a fresh general, Chorianes, who brought with him a considerable army, composed of Persians and Alans. The allied Romans and Lazi, under Dagisthseus and Gubazes, gave battle to this new foe on the banks of the Hippis (the Tschenikal?); and though the Lazi, who had insisted on taking the lead and fighting separately, were at the first encounter routed by the Persian horse, yet in the end Roman discipline and stubbornness triumphed. Their solid line of footmen, bristling with spears, offered an impervious barrier to the cavalry of the enemy, which did not dare to charge, but had recourse to volleys of missiles. The Romans responded with the same; and the battle raged for a while on something like even terms, the superior rapidity of the Asiatics being counterbalanced by the better protection which their shields gave to the Europeans, until at last, by a stroke of fortune, Rome obtained the victory. A chance arrow killed Chorianes, and his army instantly fled. There was a short struggle at the Persian camp; but the Romans and Lazi captured it. Most of the Persians were here put to the sword; the few who escaped quitted Lazica and returned to their own country.

Soon afterwards Dagisthseus was superseded by Bessas, and the siege of Petra was recommenced. The strength of the place had been considerably increased since the former attack upon it. A new wall of great height and solidity had been built upon a framework of wood in the place which Dagisthaeus had so nearly breached; the Roman mines had been filled up with gravel; arms, offensive and defensive, had been collected in extraordinary abundance; a stock of flour and of salted meat had been laid in sufficient to support the garrison of 3000 men for five years; and a store of vinegar, and of the pulse from which it was made, had likewise been accumulated. The Roman general began by attempting to repeat the device of his predecessor, attacking the defences in the same place and by the same means; but, just as his mine was completed, the new wall with its framework of wood sank quietly into the excavation, without suffering any disturbance of its parts, while enough of it still remained above the surface to offer an effectual bar to the assailants. It seemed hopeless to recommence the mine in this place, and elsewhere the nature of the ground made mining impossible; some other mode of attack had therefore to be adopted, or the siege must have been abandoned. Rome generally took towns by the battering-ram; but the engines in use were of such heavy construction that they could not be dragged up an ascent like that upon which Petra stood. Bessas was in extreme perplexity, when some Hunnic allies, who happened to be in his camp, suggested a mode of constructing a ram, as effective as the ordinary one, which should nevertheless be so light that it could be carried on the shoulders of forty men. Three such machines were quickly made; and under their blows the wall would soon have given way, had not the defenders employed against them the terrible agency of fire, showering upon them from the walls lighted casks of sulphur, bitumen, and naphtha, which last was known to the Greeks of Colchis as "Medea's oil." Uncertain of succeeding in this attack, the Roman general gallantly led a scaling party to another portion of the walls, and, mounting at the head of his men, attempted to make good his footing on the battlements. Thrown headlong to the ground, but undeterred by his fall, he was about to repeat his attempt, when he found it needless. Almost simultaneously his troops had in two other places penetrated into the town. One band had obtained an entrance by scaling the rocks in a place supposed to be inaccessible; a second owed its success to a combination of accidents. First, it had happened that a gap had shown itself in the piece of the wall which sank into the Roman mine, and a violent struggle had ensued between the assailants and defenders at this place.

Then, while this fight was going on, the fire which the Persians were using against the Roman battering-rams had been by a shift of wind blown back upon themselves, and the wooden structure from which they fought had been ignited, and in a short time entirely consumed, together with its inmates. At sight of the conflagration, the Persians who stood in the gap had lost heart, and had allowed the Roman troops to force their way through it into Petra. Thus fell the great Lazic fortress, after a resistance which is among the most memorable in history. Of the three thousand defenders, seven hundred had been killed in the siege; one thousand and seventy were destroyed in the last assault. Only seven hundred and thirty were made prisoners; and of these no fewer than seven hundred and twelve were found to be wounded. The remaining five hundred threw themselves into the citadel, and there resisted to the last extremity, refusing all terms of capitulation, and maintaining themselves against an overwhelming force, until at last by sword and fire they perished to a man.

The siege of Petra was prolonged far into the winter, and the year A.D. 551 had begun ere the resistance ceased. Could the gallant defenders have maintained themselves for a few more weeks, they might not improbably have triumphed. Mermeroes, the Persian commander of two years previously, took the field with the commencement of spring, and, at the head of a large body of cavalry, supported by eight elephants, began his march to the coast, hoping to relieve the beleaguered garrison. Unfortunately he was too late. On his march he heard of the capture of Petra, and of its complete destruction by Bessas, who feared lest the Persians should again occupy the dangerous post. Mermeroes had no difficulty in establishing Persian rule through almost the whole of Lazica. The Romans did not dare to meet him in the field. Archssopolis, indeed, repulsed his attack; but no other important place in the entire country remained subject to the Empire. Qubazes and his followers had to hide themselves in the recesses of the mountains. Quartering his troops chiefly on the upper Phasis, about Kutais and its neighborhood, Mermeroes strengthened his hold on the country by building forts or receiving their submission, and even extended the Persian dominion beyond Lazica into Scymnia and Suania. Still Rome, with her usual tenacity, maintained a hold upon certain tracts; and Gubazes, faithful to his allies even in the extremity of their depression, maintained a guerilla war, and hoped that some day fortune would cease to frown on him.

Meanwhile, at Byzantium, fresh negotiations were in progress, and hopes were entertained of an arrangement by which all the differences between the two great powers would be satisfactorily adjusted. Isdigunas again represented his master at the Byzantine court, and conducted the diplomatic contest with skill and ability. Taxing Justinian with more than one infraction of the truce concluded in A.D. 545, he demanded the payment of a lump sum of two thousand six hundred pounds of gold, and expressed the willingness of Chosroes to conclude on these terms a fresh truce for five years, to take effect from the delivery of the money. With regard to the extent of country whereto the truce should apply, he agreed to an express limitation of its range—the settled provinces of both empires should be protected by it, but Lazica and the country of the Saracens should be excluded from its operation. Justinian consented to these terms, despite the opposition of many of his subjects, who thought that Rome degraded herself by her repeated payments of money to Persia, and accepted a position little better than that of a Persian tributary.

Thus the peace of A.D. 551 did nothing towards ending the Lazic war, which, after languishing through the whole of A.D. burst out again with renewed vigor in the spring of A.D. 553. Mermeroes in that year advanced from Kutais against Telephis, a strong fort in the possession of Rome, expelled the commandant, Martinus, by a stratagem, pressed forward against the combined Roman forces, which fled before him from Ollaria, and finally drove them to the coast and cooped them up in "the Island," a small tract near the mouth of the Phasis between that stream and the Doconus. On his return he was able to reinforce a garrison which he had established at Onoguris in the immediate neighborhood of Archseopolis, as a means of annoying and weakening that important station. He may naturally have hoped in one or two more campaigns to have driven the last Roman out of the country and to have attached Lazica permanently to the empire of the great king.

Unluckily, however, for Persia, the fatigues which the gallant veteran had undergone in the campaign of A.D. 553 proved more than his aged frame could endure, and he had scarcely reached Kutais when he was seized with a fatal malady, to which he succumbed in the course of the winter. Chosroes appointed as his successor a certain Nachoragan, who is said to have been a general of repute, but who proved himself quite unequal to the position which he was called upon to fill, and in the course of two years ruined the Persian cause in Lazica. The failure was the more signal from the fact that exactly at the time of his appointment circumstances occurred which seriously shook the Roman influence over the Lazi, and opened a prospect to Persia transcending aught that she could reasonably have hoped. This was nothing less than a most serious quarrel between Gubazes, the Lazic king, and some of the principal Roman commanders—a quarrel which involved consequences fatal to both parties. Gubazes, disgusted with the negligence or incapacity of the Roman chiefs, had made complaint of them to Justinian; they had retaliated by accusing him of meditating desertion, and had obtained the emperor's consent to his arrest, and to the use of violence if he offered resistance. Armed with this mandate, they contrived in a little time to fasten a quarrel upon him; and, when he declined to do as they required, they drew their swords upon him and slew him. The Lazic nation was, naturally enough, alienated by this outrage, and manifested an inclination to throw itself absolutely into the arms of Persia. The Romans, dispirited at the attitude of their allies, and at variance among themselves, could for some months after Gubazes' death have offered but little resistance to an enterprising enemy. So demoralized were they that an army of 50,000 is said to have fled in dismay when attacked by a force of Persians less than a twelfth of their number, and to have allowed their camp to be captured and plundered. During this critical time Nachoragan remained inactive in Iberia, and contented himself with sending messengers into Lazica to announce his near approach and to animate and encourage his party. The result was such as might have been expected. The Lazi, finding that Persia made no effort to take advantage of their abstention, and that Rome despite of it maintained possession of the greater portion of their country, came to the conclusion that it would be unwise to desert their natural allies on account of a single outrage, however monstrous, and agreed to renew their close alliance with Rome on condition that the murderers of Gubazes should be punished, and his brother, Tzathes, appointed king in his place. Justinian readily gave his consent; and the year A.D. 555 saw the quarrel ended, and the Lazi once more heartily in accord with, their Roman protectors.

It was when affairs were in this state, and he had exactly missed his opportunity, that Nachoragan took the field, and, advancing from Iberia into the region about Kutai's with an army amounting to 60,000 men,1 made preparations for carrying on the war with vigor. He was opposed by Martinus, Justin, and Babas, the two former of whom with the bulk of the Roman forces occupied the region on the lower Phasis, known as "the Island," while Babas held the more central position of Archseopolis. Nachoragan, after losing about 2,000 of his best troops in the vicinity of this last-named place, resolved to challenge the Romans to a decisive encounter by attacking the important post of Phasis at the mouth of the river. With some skill he succeeded in passing the Roman camp on the island, and in establishing himself in the plain directly south of Phasis before the Roman generals guessed his purpose. They, however, were able by a quick movement to throw themselves into the town, and the struggle became one between fairly balanced forces, and was conducted with great obstinacy. The town was defended on the south by an outer palisade, a broad ditch protected by sharp stakes and full of water, and an inner bulwark of considerable height but constructed wholly of wood. The Phasis guarded it on the north; and here a Roman fleet was stationed which lent its aid to the defenders at the two extremities of their line. The yards of the ships were manned with soldiers, and boats were hung from them containing slingers, archers, and even workers of catapults, who delivered their weapons from an elevation exceeding that of the towers. But Nachoragan had the advantage of numbers; his men soon succeeded in filling up part of the ditch; and the wooden bulwark could scarcely have long resisted his attacks, if the contest had continued to be wholly one of brute strength. But the Roman commander, Martinus, finding himself inferior in force, brought finesse and stratagem to his aid. Pretending to receive intelligence of the sudden arrival of a fresh Roman army from Byzantium, he contrived that the report should reach Nachoragan and thereby cause him to divide his troops, and send half of them to meet the supposed reinforcements. Then, when the Persian general nevertheless renewed his assault, Martinus sent secretly 5,000 men under Justin to a short distance from Phasis; and this detachment, appearing suddenly when the contest was going on at the wall, was naturally taken for the newly arrived army, and caused a general panic. The Persians, one and all, took to flight; a general sally was made by the Romans in Phasis; a rout and a carnage followed, which completely disheartened the Persian leader, and led him to give up his enterprise. Having lost nearly one-fourth of his army, Nachoragan drew off to Kutai's, and shortly afterwards, leaving the command of the Persians in Lazica to Vaphrizes, retired to winter quarters in Iberia.

The failure of Nachoragan, following closely upon the decision of the Lazi to maintain their alliance with Rome in spite of the murder of Gubazes, seems to have convinced the Persian monarch that, in endeavoring to annex Lazica, he had engaged in a hopeless enterprise, and that it would be the most prudent and judicious course to yield to the inevitable, and gradually withdraw from a position which was untenable. Having meted out to Nachoragan the punishment usually assigned to unsuccessful commanders in Persia, he sent an ambassador to Byzantium in the spring of A.D. 556, and commenced negotiations which he intended to be serious. Diplomacy seems to have been as averse in the days of Chosroes as in our own to an undignified rapidity of proceeding. Hence, though there could be little to debate where both parties were substantially at one, the negotiations begun in May A.D. 556 were not concluded till after the commencement of the following year. A complete suspension of hostilities was then agreed upon, to extend to Lazica no less than to the other dominions of the two monarchs. In Lazica each party was to keep what it possessed, territory, cities, and castles. As this joint occupation was scarcely suitable for a permanent arrangement, it was provided that the two belligerents should, during the continuance of the truce, proceed to settle the terms on which a lasting peace might be established.

An interval of five years elapsed before the happy result, for which both parties had expressed themselves anxious, was accomplished. It is uncertain how Chosroes was occupied during this period; but there are some grounds for believing that he was engaged in the series of Oriental wars whereof we shall have to speak presently. Success appears to have crowned his arms wherever he directed them; but he remained undazzled by his victories, and still retained the spirit of moderation which had led him in A.D. 557 to conclude the general truce. He was even prepared, after five years of consideration, to go further in the line of pacific policy on which he had then entered, and, in order to secure the continuance of his good relations with Rome, was willing to relinquish all claim to the sovereignty of Lazica. Under these circumstances, ambassadors of the highest rank, representing the two powers, met on the frontier between Daras and Nisibis, proclaimed the power and explained the motives of their respective sovereigns, and after a lengthy conference formulated a treaty of peace. The terms, which are given at length by a writer of the succeeding generation, may be briefly expressed as follows: (1) the Persians were to withdraw from Lazica, to give up all claim to it, and to hand over its possession to the Romans; (2) they were in return to receive from Rome an annual sum of 30,000 pieces of gold, the amount due for the first seven years being paid in advance; (3) the Christians in Persia were guaranteed the full and free exercise of their religion, but were forbidden to make converts from the disciples of Zoroaster; (4) commercial intercourse was to be allowed between the two empires, but the merchants were restricted to the use of certain roads and certain emporia; (5) diplomatic intercourse was to be wholly free, and the goods of ambassadors were to be exempt from duty; (6) Daras was to continue a fortified town, but no new fortresses were to be built upon the frontier by either nation, and Daras itself was not to be made the headquarters of the Prefect of the East, or to be held by an unnecessarily large garrison; (7) all disputes arising between the two nations were to be determined by courts of arbitration; (8) the allies of the two nations were to be included in the treaty, and to participate in its benefits and obligations; (9) Persia was to undertake the sole charge of maintaining the Caspian Gates against the Huns and Alans; (10) the peace was made for a period of fifty years. It has been held that by this treaty Justinian consented to become a tributary of the Persian Empire; and undoubtedly it was possible for Oriental vanity to represent the arrangement made in this light. But the million and a half, which Rome undertook to pay in the course of the next fifty years, might well be viewed by the Romans as an outlay for which they received an ample return in the cession to them of the Persian part of Lazica, and in the termination of their obligation to contribute towards the maintenance of the Caspian Gates. If there was any real danger of those results following from the Persian occupation of Lazica which both nations anticipated, the sum must be considered to have been one of the best investments ever made by a State. Even if we believe the dangers apprehended to have been visionary, yet it cannot be viewed as an exorbitant price to have paid for a considerable tract of fertile country, a number of strong fortresses, and the redemption of an obligation which could not with honor be disowned.

To Chosroes the advantage secured by the treaty was similar to that which Rome had obtained by the peace of A.D. 532. Being no longer under any necessity of employing his forces against the Romans in the north-west, he found himself free to act with greatly increased effect against his enemies in the east and in the south. Already, in the interval between the conclusion of the general truce and of the fifty years' peace, he had, as it seems, invaded the territories of the Ephthalites, and, with the help of the Great Khan of the Turks, inflicted upon this people, so long one of Persia's most formidable enemies, a severe defeat. According to Tabari, he actually slew the Ephthalite monarch, ravaged his territory, and pillaged his treasures. About the same time he had also had a war with the Khazars, had overrun their country, wasted it with fire and sword, and massacred thousands of the inhabitants. He now entertained designs against Arabia and perhaps India, countries on which he could not hope to make an impression without earnest and concentrated effort. It was doubtless with the view of extending his influence into these quarters that the Persian monarch evacuated Lazica, and bound his country to maintain peace with Rome for the next half-century.

The position of affairs in Arabia was at the time abnormal and interesting. For the most part that vast but sterile region has been the home of almost countless tribes, living independently of one another, each under its own sheikh or chief, in wild and unrestrained freedom. Native princes have seldom obtained any widely extended dominion over the scattered population; and foreign powers have still more rarely exercised authority for any considerable period over the freedom-loving descendants of Ishmael. But towards the beginning of the sixth century of our era the Abyssinians of Axum, a Christian people, "raised" far "above the ordinary level of African barbarism" by their religion and by their constant intercourse with Rome, succeeded in attaching to their empire a large portion of the Happy Arabia, and ruled it at first from their African capital, but afterwards by means of a viceroy, whose dependence on the Negus of Abyssinia was little more than nominal. Abraha, an Abyssinian of high rank, being deputed by the Negus to re-establish the authority of Abyssinia over the Yemen when it was shaken by a great revolt, made himself master of the country, assumed the crown, established Abyssinians in all the chief cities, built numerous churches, especially one of great beauty at Sana, and at his death left the kingdom to his eldest son, Yaksoum. An important Christian state was thus established in the Great Peninsula; and it was natural that Justinian should see with satisfaction, and Chosroes with some alarm, the growth of a power in this quarter which was sure to side with Rome and against Persia, if their rivalry should extend into these parts. Justinian had hailed with pleasure the original Abyssinian conquest, and had entered into amicable relations with both the Axumites and their colonists in the Yemen. Chosroes now resolved upon a counter movement. He would employ the quiet secured to him by the peace of A.D. 562 in a great attack upon the Abyssinian power in Arabia. He would drive the audacious Africans from the soil of Asia, and would earn the eternal gratitude of the numerous tribes of the desert. He would extend Persian influence to the shores of the Arabian Gulf, and so confront the Romans along the whole line of their eastern boundary. He would destroy the point d'appui which Rome had acquired in South-western Asia, and so at once diminish her power and augment the strength and glory of Persia.

The interference of Chosroes in the affairs of a country so distant as Western Arabia involved considerable difficulties; but his expedition was facilitated by an application which he received from a native of the district in question. Saif, the son of Dsu-Yezm, descended from the race of the old Homerite kings whom the Abyssinians had conquered, grew up at the court of Abraha in the belief that that prince, who had married his mother, was not his step-father, but his father. Undeceived by an insult which Masrouq, the true son of Abraha and successor of Yaksoum, offered him, Saif became a refugee at the court of Chosroes, and importuned the Great King to embrace his quarrel and reinstate him on the throne of his fathers. He represented the Homerite population of Yemen as groaning under the yoke of their oppressors and only waiting for an opportunity to rise in revolt and shake it off. A few thousand Persian troops, enough to form the nucleus of an army, would suffice; they might be sent by sea to the port of Aden, near the mouth of the Arabian Gulf, where the Homerites would join them in large numbers; the combined forces might then engage in combat with the Abyssinians, and destroy them or drive them from the land. Chosroes took the advice tendered him, so far at any rate as to make his expedition by sea. His ships were assembled in the Persian Gulf; a certain number of Persian troops were embarked on board them; and the flotilla proceeded, under the conduct of Saif, first to the mouth of the Gulf, and then along the southern coast of Arabia to Aden. Encouraged by their presence, the Plomerites rose against their foreign oppressors; a war followed, of which the particulars have been disfigured by romance; but the result is undoubted—the Abyssinian strangers were driven from the soil of Arabia; the native race recovered its supremacy; and Saif, the descendant of the old Homerite kings, was established, as the vassal or viceroy of Chosroes, on the throne of his ancestors. This arrangement, however, was not lasting. Saif, after a short reign, was murdered by his body-guard; and Chosroes then conferred the government of Yemen upon a Persian officer, who seems to have borne the usual title of Marzpan, and to have been in no way distinguished above other rulers of provinces. Thus the Homerites in the end gained nothing by their revolt but a change of masters. They may, however, have regarded the change as one worth making, since it gave them the mild sway of a tolerant heathen in lieu of the persecuting rule of Christian bigots.

According to some writers, Chosroes also, in his later years, sent an expedition by sea against some portion of Hindustan, and received a cession of territory from an Indian monarch. But the country of the monarch is too remote for belief, and the ceded provinces seem to have belonged to Persia previously. It is therefore, perhaps, most probable that friendly intercourse has been exaggerated into conquest, and the reception of presents from an Indian potentate metamorphosed into the gain of territory. Some authorities do not assign to Chosroes any Indian dominion; and it is at least doubtful whether he made any expedition in this direction.

A war, however, appears certainly to have occupied Chosroes about this period on his north-eastern frontier. The Turks had recently been advancing in strength and drawing nearer to the confines of Persia. They had extended their dominion over the great Ephthalite kingdom, partly by force of arms, partly through the treachery of Katulphus, an Ephthalite chieftain; they had received the submission of the Sogdians, and probably of other tribes of the Transoxianian region, previously held in subjection by the Ephthalites; and they aspired to be acknowledged as a great power, the second, if not the first, in this part of Asia. It was perhaps rather with the view of picking a quarrel than in the hope of any valuable pacific result, that, about the close of A.D. 567, Diza-bul, the Turkish Khan, sent ambassadors to Chosroes with proposals for the establishment of free commercial intercourse between the Turks and Persians, and even for the conclusion of a treaty of friendship and alliance between the two nations. Chosroes suspected the motive for the overture, but was afraid openly to reject it. He desired to discourage intercourse between his own nation and the Turks, but could devise no better mode of effecting his purpose than by burning the Turkish merchandise offered to him after he had bought it, and by poisoning the ambassadors and giving out that they had fallen victims to the climate. His conduct exasperated the Turkish Khan, and created a deep and bitter hostility between the Turks and Persians. It was at once resolved to send an embassy to Constantinople and offer to the Greek emperor the friendship which Chosroes had scorned. The embassy reached the Byzantine court early in A.D. 568, and was graciously received by Justin, the nephew of Justinian, who had succeeded his uncle on the imperial throne between three and four years previously. A treaty of alliance was made between the two nations; and a Roman embassy, empowered to ratify it, visited the Turkish court in the Altai mountains during the course of the next year (A.D. 569), and drew closer the bonds of friendship between the high contracting powers. But meanwhile Dizabul, confident in his own strength, had determined on an expedition into Persia. The Roman ambassador, Zemarchus, accompanied him on a portion of his march, and witnessed his insulting treatment of a Persian envoy, sent by Chosroes to meet him and deprecate his attack. Beyond this point exact information fails us; but we may suspect that this is the expedition commemorated by Mirk-hond, wherein the Great Khan, having invaded the Persian territory in force, made himself master of Shash, Ferghana, Samarkand, Bokhara, Kesh, and Nesf, but, hearing that Hornisdas, son of Chosroes, was advancing against him at the head of a numerous army, suddenly fled, evacuating all the country that he had occupied, and retiring to the most distant portion of Turkestan. At any rate the expedition cannot have had any great success; for shortly afterwards (A.D. 571) we find Turkish ambassadors once more visiting the Byzantine court, and entreating Justin to renounce the fifty years' peace and unite with them in a grand attack upon the common enemy, which, if assaulted simultaneously on either side, might (they argued) be almost certainly crushed. Justin gave the ambassadors no definite reply, but renewed the alliance with Dizabul, and took seriously into consideration the question whether he should not yield to the representations made to him, and renew the war which Justinian had terminated nine years previously.

There were many circumstances which urged him towards a rupture. The payments to be made under the fifty years' peace had in his eyes the appearance of a tribute rendered by Rome to Persia, which was, he thought, an intolerable disgrace. A subsidy, not very dissimilar, which Justinian had allowed the Saracenic Arabs under Persian rule, he had already discontinued; and hostilities had, in consequence, already commenced between the Persian and the Roman Saracens. The successes of Chosroes in Western Arabia had at once provoked his jealousy, and secured to Rome, in that quarter, an important ally in the great Christian kingdom of Abyssinia. The Turks of Central Asia had sought his friendship and offered to combine their attacks with his, if he would consent to go to war. Moreover, there was once more discontent and even rebellion in Armenia, where the proselytizing zeal of the Persian governors had again driven the natives to take up arms and raise the standard of independence. Above all, the Great King, who had warred with such success for twenty years against his uncle, was now in advanced age, and seemed to have given signs of feebleness, inasmuch as in his recent expeditions he had individually taken no part, but had entrusted the command of his troops to others. Under these circumstances, Justin, in the year A.D. 572, determined to renounce the peace made ten years earlier with the Persians, and to recommence the old struggle. Accordingly he at once dismissed the Persian envoy, Sebocthes, with contempt, refused wholly to make the stipulated payment, proclaimed his intention of receiving the Armenian insurgents under his protection, and bade Chosroes lay a finger on them at his peril. He then appointed Marcian to the prefecture of the East, and gave him the conduct of the war which was now inevitable.

No sooner did the Persian monarch find his kingdom seriously menaced than, despite his advanced age, he immediately took the field in person. Giving the command of a flying column of 6000 men to Adarman, a skilful general, he marched himself against the Romans, who under Marcian had defeated a Persian force, and were besieging Nisibis, forced them to raise the siege, and, pressing forward as they retired, compelled them to seek shelter within the walls of Daras, which he proceeded to invest with his main army. Meanwhile Adarman, at the head of the troops entrusted to him, crossed the Euphrates near Circesium, and, having entered Syria, carried fire and sword far and wide over that fertile province. Repulsed from Antioch, where, however, he burnt the suburbs of the town, he invaded Coelesyria, took and destroyed Apamea, and then, recrossing the great river, rejoined Chosroes before Daras. The renowned fortress made a brave defence. For about five months it resisted, without obtaining any relief, the entire force of Chosroes, who is said to have besieged it with 40,000 horse and 100,000 foot. At last, on the approach of winter, it could no longer hold out; enclosed within lines of circumvallation, and deprived of water by the diversion of its streams into new channels, it found itself reduced to extremity, and forced to submit towards the close of A.D. 573. Thus the great Roman fortress in these parts was lost in the first year of the renewed war; and Justin, alarmed at his own temerity, and recognizing his weakness, felt it necessary to retire from the conduct of affairs, and deliver the reins of empire to stronger hands. He chose as his coadjutor and successor the Count Tiberius, a Thracian by birth, who had long stood high in his confidence; and this prince, in conjunction with the Empress Sophia, now took the direction of the war.

The first need was to obtain a breathing-space. The Persian king having given an opening for negotiations, advantage was taken of it by the joint rulers to send an envoy, furnished with an autograph letter from the empress, and well provided with the best persuasives of peace, who was to suggest an armistice for a year, during which a satisfactory arrangement of the whole quarrel might be agreed upon. Tiberius thought that within this space he might collect an army sufficiently powerful to re-establish the superiority of the Roman arms in the east; Chosroes believed himself strong enough to defeat any force that Rome could now bring into the field. A truce for a year was therefore concluded, at the cost to Rome of 45,000 aurei; and immense efforts were at once made by Tiberius to levy troops from his more distant, provinces, or hire them from the lands beyond his borders. An army of 150,000 men was, it is said, collected from the banks of the Danube and the Rhine, from Scythia, Pannonia, Moesia, Illyricum, and Isauria; a general of repute, Justinian, the son of Germanus, was selected to command them; and the whole force was concentrated upon the eastern frontier but, after all these preparations, the Caesar's heart failed him, and, instead of offering battle to the enemy, Tiberius sent a second embassy to the Persian head-quarters, early in A.D. 575, and besought an extension of the truce. The Romans desired a short term of peace only, but wished for a general suspension of hostilities between the nations; the Persians advocated a longer interval, but insisted that the truce should not extend to Armenia. The dispute continued till the armistice for a year had run out; and the Persians had resumed hostilities and threatened Constantina before the Romans would give way. At length it was agreed that there should be peace for three years, but that Armenia should be exempt from its operation. Rome was to pay to Persia, during the continuance of the truce, the sum of 30,000 aurei annually.

No sooner was the peace concluded than Chosroes put himself at the head of his army, and, entering Armenia Proper, proceeded to crush the revolt, and to re-establish the Persian authority throughout the entire region. No resistance was offered to him; and he was able, before the close of the year, to carry his arms into the Roman territory of Armenia Minor, and even to threaten Cappadocia. Here Justinian opposed his progress; and in a partial engagement, Kurs (or Cursus), a leader of Scythians in the Roman service, obtained an advantage over the Persian rear-guard, captured the camp and the baggage, but did not succeed in doing any serious damage. Chosroes soon afterwards revenged himself by surprising and destroying a Roman camp during the night; he then took and burnt the city of Melitene (Malatiyeh); after which, as winter was approaching, he retired across the Euphrates, and returned into his own country. Hereupon Justinian seems to have invaded Persian Armenia, and to have enriched his troops with its plunder; according to some writers, he even penetrated as far as the Caspian Sea, and embarked upon its waters; he continued on Persian soil during the whole of the winter, and it was not till the spring came that he re-entered Roman territory (A.D. 576).

The campaign of A.D. 576 is somewhat obscure. The Romans seem to have gained certain advantages in Northern Armenia and Iberia, while Chosroes on his part carried the war once more into Armenia Minor, and laid siege to Theodosiopolis, which, however, he was unable to take. Negotiations were upon this resumed, and had progressed favorably to a certain, point, when news arrived of a great disaster to the Roman arms in Armenia, which changed the face of affairs and caused the Persian negotiators to break up the conference. Tam-chosro, a Persian general, had completely defeated the Roman army under Justinian. Armenia had returned to its allegiance. There seemed every reason to believe that more was to be gained by arms than by diplomacy, and that, when the three years peace had run out, the Great King might renew the general war with a prospect of obtaining important successes.

There are no military events which can be referred to the year A.D. 577. The Romans and Persians amused each other with alternate embassies during its course, and with negotiations that were not intended to have any result. The two monarchs made vast preparations; and with the spring of A.D. 578 hostilities recommenced. Chosroes is accused of having anticipated the expiration of the truce by a period of forty days; but it is more probable that he and the Romans estimated the date of its expiration differently. However this was, it is certain that his generals, Mebodes and Sapoes, took the field in early spring with 20,000 horse, and entering the Roman Armenia laid waste the country, at the same time threatening Constantina and Theodosiopolis. Simultaneously Tamchosro, quitting Persarmenia, marched westward and plundered the country about Amida (Diarbekr). The Roman commander Maurice, who had succeeded Justinian, possessed considerable military ability. On this occasion, instead of following the ordinary plan of simply standing on the defensive and endeavoring to repulse the invaders, he took the bolder course of making a counter movement. Entering Persarmenia, which he found denuded of troops, he carried all before him, destroying the forts, and plundering the country. Though the summer heats brought on him an attack of fever, he continued without pause his destructive march; invaded and occupied Arzanene, with its stronghold, Aphumon, carried off the population to the number of 10,090, and, pressing forwards from Arzanene into Eastern Mesopotamia, took Singara, and carried fire and sword over the entire region as far as the Tigris. He even ventured to throw a body of skirmishers across the river into Cordyene (Kurdistan); and these ravagers, who were commanded by Kurs, the Scythian, spread devastation over a district where no Roman soldier had set foot since its cession by Jovian. Agathias tells us that Chosroes was at the time enjoying his summer villeggiatura in the Kurdish hills, and saw from his residence the smoke of the hamlets which the Roman troops had fired. He hastily fled from the danger, and shut himself up within the walls of Ctesiphon, where he was soon afterwards seized with the illness which brought his life to a close.

Meanwhile Kurs, unconscious probably of the prize that had been so near his grasp, recrossed the Tigris with his booty and rejoined Maurice, who on the approach of winter withdrew into Roman territory, evacuating all his conquests excepting Arzanene. The dull time of winter was, as usual, spent in negotiations; and it was thought that a peace might have been concluded had Chosroes lived. Tiberius was anxious to recover Daras, and was willing to withdraw the Roman forces wholly from Persarmenia and Iberia, and to surrender Arzanene and Aphumon, if Daras were restored to him. He would probably have been content even to pay in addition a sum of money. Chosroes might perhaps have accepted these terms; but while the envoys empowered to propose them were on their way to his court, early in the year A.D. 579, the aged monarch died in his palace at Ctesiphon after a reign of forty-eight years.

CHAPTER XXI

*Administration of Persia under Chosroes I. Fourfold Division of the Empire. Careful Surveillance of those entrusted with Power. Severe Punishment of Abuse of Trust. New System of Taxation introduced. Correction of Abuse connected with the Military Service. Encouragement of Agriculture and Marriage. Belief of Poverty. Care for Travellers. Encouragement of Learning. Practice of*

*Toleration within certain Limits. Domestic Life of Chosroes. His Wives. Revolt and Death of his Son, Nushizad. Coins of Chosroes. Estimate of his Character.*

A general consensus of the Oriental writers marks the reign of the first Chosroes as a period not only of great military activity, but also of improved domestic administration. Chosroes found the empire in a disordered and ill-regulated condition, taxation arranged on a bad system, the people oppressed by unjust and tyrannical governors, the military service a prey to the most scandalous abuses, religious fanaticism rampant, class at variance with class, extortion and wrong winked at, crime unpunished, agriculture languishing, and the masses throughout almost the whole of the country sullen and discontented. It was his resolve from the first to carry out a series of reforms—to secure the administration of even-handed justice, to put the finances on a better footing, to encourage agriculture, to relieve the poor and the distressed, to root out the abuses that destroyed the efficiency of the army, and to excise the gangrene of fanaticism which was eating into the heart of the nation. How he effected the last named object by his wholesale destruction of the followers of Mazdak has been already related; but it appeared unadvisable to interrupt, the military history of the reign by combining with it any account of the numerous other reforms which he accomplished. It remains therefore to consider them in this place, since they are certainly not the least remarkable among the many achievements of this great monarch.

Persia, until the time of Anushirwan, had been divided into a multitude of provinces, the satraps or governors of which held their office directly under the crown. It was difficult for the monarch to exercise a sufficient superintendence over so large a number of rulers, many of them remote from the court, and all united by a common interest. Chosroes conceived the plan of forming four great governments, and entrusting them to four persons in whom he had confidence, whose duty it should be to watch the conduct of the provincial satraps to control them, direct them, or report their misconduct to the crown. The four great governments were those of the east, the north, the south, and the west. The east comprised Khorassan, Seistan, and Kirman; the north, Armenia, Azer-bijan, Ghilan, Koum, and Isfahan; the south, Fars and Ahwaz; the west, Irak, or Babylonia, Assyria, and Mesopotamia.

It was not the intention of the monarch, however, to put a blind trust in his instruments. He made personal progresses through his empire from, time to time, visiting each province in turn and inquiring into the condition of the inhabitants. He employed continually an army of inspectors and spies, who reported to him from all quarters the sufferings or complaints of the oppressed, and the neglects or misdoings of those in authority. On the occurrence of any specially suspicious circumstance, he appointed extraordinary commissions of inquiry, which, armed with all the power of the crown, proceeded to the suspected quarter, took evidence, and made a careful report of whatever wrongs or malpractices they discovered.

When guilt was brought home to incriminated persons or parties, the punishment with which they were visited was swift and signal. We have seen how harsh were the sentences passed by Chosroes upon those whose offences attacked his own person or dignity. An equal severity appears in his judgments, where there was no question of his own wrongs, but only of the interests of his subjects. On one occasion he is said to have executed no fewer than eighty collectors of taxes on the report of a commission charging them with extortion. Among the principal reforms which Chosroes is said to have introduced was his fresh arrangement of the taxation. Hitherto all lands had paid to the State a certain proportion of their produce, a proportion which varied, according to the estimated richness of the soil, from a tenth to one-half. The effect was to discourage all improved cultivation, since it was quite possible that the whole profit of any increased outlay might be absorbed by the State, and also to cramp and check the liberty of the cultivators in various ways, since the produce could not be touched until the revenue official made his appearance and carried off the share of the crop which he had a right to take. Chosroes resolved to substitute a land-tax for the proportionate payments in kind, and thus at once to set the cultivator at liberty with respect to harvesting his crops and to allow him the entire advantage of any augmented production which might be secured by better methods of farming his land. His tax consisted in part of a money payment, in part of a payment in kind; but both payments were fixed and invariable, each measure of ground being rated in the king's books at one dirhem and one measure of the produce. Uncultivated land, and land lying fallow at the time, were exempt; and thus the scheme involved, not one survey alone, but a recurring (annual) survey, and an annual registration of all cultivators, with the quantity of land under cultivation held by each, and the nature of the crop or crops to be grown by them. The system was one of much complication, and may have pressed somewhat hardly upon the poorer and less productive soils; but it was an immense improvement upon the previously existing practice, which had all the disadvantages of the modern tithe system, aggravated by the high rates exacted and by the certainty that, in any disputed case, the subject would have had a poor chance of establishing his right against the crown. It is not surprising that the caliphs, when they conquered Persia, maintained unaltered the land system of Chosroes which they found established, regarding it as, if not perfect, at any rate not readily admitting of much improvement.

Besides the tax upon arable lands, of which we have hitherto spoken, Chosroes introduced into into Persia various other imposts. The fruit trees were everywhere counted, and a small payment required for each. The personality of the citizens was valued, and a graduated property-tax established, which, however, in the case of the most opulent, did not exceed the moderate sum of forty-eight dirhems (about twenty-seven shillings). A poll-tax was required of Jews and Christians, whereof we do not know the amount. From all these burdens liberal exemptions were made on account of age and sex; no female paid anything; and males above fifty years of age or under twenty were also free of charge. Due notice was given to each individual of the sum for which he was liable, by the publication in each province, town, and village, of a tax table, in which each citizen or alien could see against his name the amount about to be claimed of him, with the ground upon which it was regarded as due. Payment had to made by instalments, three times each year, at the end of every four months.

In order to prevent the unfair extortion, which in the ancient world was always, with reason or without, charged upon collectors of revenue, Chosroes, by the advice of the Grand Mobed, authorized the Magian priests everywhere to exercise a supervision over the receivers of taxes, and to hinder them from exacting more than their due. The priests were only too happy to discharge this popular function; and extortion must have become rare under a system which comprised so efficient a safeguard.

Another change ascribed to Chosroes is a reform of the administration of the army. Under the system previously existing, Chosroes found that the resources of the state were lavishly wasted, and the result was a military force inefficient and badly accoutred. No security was taken that the soldiers possessed their proper equipments or could discharge the duties appropriate to their several grades. Persons came before the paymaster, claiming the wages of a cavalry soldier, who possessed no horse, and had never learned to ride. Some, who called themselves soldiers, had no knowledge of the use of any weapon at all; others claimed for higher grades of the service than those whereto they really belonged; those who drew the pay of cuirassiers were destitute of a coat of mail; those who professed themselves archers were utterly incompetent to draw the bow. The established rates of pay varied between a hundred dirhems a year and four thousand, and persons entitled to the lowest rate often received an amount not much short of the highest. The evil was not only that the treasury was robbed by unfair claims and unfounded pretences, but that artifice and false seeming were encouraged, while at the same time the army was brought into such a condition that no dependence could be placed upon it. If the number who actually served corresponded to that upon the rolls, which is uncertain, at any rate all the superior arms of the service fell below their nominal strength, and the lower grades were crowded with men who were only soldiers in name.

As a remedy against these evils, Chosroes appointed a single paymaster-general, and insisted on his carefully inspecting and reviewing each body of troops before he allowed it to draw its pay. Each man was to appear before him fully equipped and to show his proficiency with his weapon or weapons; horse soldiers were to bring their horses, and to exhibit their mastery over the animals by putting them through their paces, mounting and dismounting, and performing the other usual exercises. If any clumsiness were noted, or any deficiency in the equipment, the pay was to be withheld until the defect observed had been made good. Special care was to be taken that no one drew the pay of a class superior to that whereto he really belonged—of an archer, for instance, when he was in truth a common soldier, or of a trooper when he served not in the horse, but in the foot.

A curious anecdote is related in connection with these military reforms. When Babek, the new paymaster, was about to hold his first review, he issued an order that all persons belonging to the army then present in the capital should appear before him on a certain day. The troops came; but Babek dismissed them on the ground that a certain person whose presence was indispensable had not made his appearance. Another day was appointed, with the same result, except that Babek on this occasion plainly intimated that it was the king whom he expected to attend. Upon this Chosroes, when a third summons was issued, took care to be present, and came fully equipped, as he thought, for battle. But the critical eye of the reviewing officer detected an omission, which he refused to overlook—the king had neglected to bring with him two extra bow-strings. Chosroes was required to go back to his palace and remedy the defect, after which he was allowed to pass muster, and then summoned to receive his pay. Babek affected to consider seriously what the pay of the commander-in-chief ought to be, and decided that it ought to exceed that of any other person in the army. He then, in the sight of all, presented the king with four thousand and one dirhems, which Chosroes received and carried home. Thus two important principles were thought to be established—that no defect of equipment whatsoever should be overlooked in any officer, however high his rank, and that none should draw from the treasury a larger amount of pay than 4,000 dirhems (L112. of our money).

The encouragement of agriculture was an essential element in the system of Zoroaster; and Chosroes, in devoting his attention to it, was at once performing a religious duty and increasing the resources of the state. It was his earnest desire to bring into cultivation all the soil which was capable of it; and with this object he not only issued edicts commanding the reclamation of waste lands, but advanced from the treasury the price of the necessary seed-corn, implements, and beasts to all poor persons willing to carry out his orders. Other poor persons, especially the infirm and those disabled by bodily defect, were relieved from his privy purse; mendicancy was forbidden, and idleness made an offence. The lands forfeited by the followers of Mazdak were distributed to necessitous cultivators. The water system was carefully attended to; river and torrent courses were cleared of obstructions and straightened; the superfluous water of the rainy season was stored, and meted out with a wise economy to those who tilled the soil, in the spring and summer.

The prosperity of a country depends in part upon the laborious industry of the inhabitants, in part upon their numbers. Chosroes regarded Persia as insufficiently peopled, and made efforts to increase the population by encouraging and indeed compelling marriage. All marriageable females were required to provide themselves with husbands; if they neglected this duty, the government interfered, and united them to unmarried men of their own class. The pill was gilt to these latter by the advance of a sufficient dowry from the public treasury, and by the prospect that, if children resulted from the union, their education and establishment in life would be undertaken by the state.

Another method of increasing the population, adopted by Chosroes to a certain extent, was the settlement within his own territories of the captives whom he carried off from foreign countries in the course of his military expeditions. The most notorious instance of this policy was the Greek settlement, known as Rumia (Rome), established by Chosroes after his capture of Antioch (A.D. 540), in the near vicinity of Ctesiphon.

Oriental monarchs, in many respects civilized and enlightened, have often shown a narrow and unworthy jealousy of foreigners. Chosroes had a mind which soared above this petty prejudice. He encouraged the visits of all foreigners, excepting only the barbarous Turks, readily received them at his court, and carefully provided for their safety. Not only were the roads and bridges kept in the most perfect order throughout his territories, so as to facilitate locomotion, but on the frontiers and along the chief lines of route guard-houses were built and garrisons maintained for the express purpose of securing the safety of travellers. The result was that the court of Chosroes was visited by numbers of Europeans, who were hospitably treated, and invited, or even pressed, to prolong their visits.

To the proofs of wisdom and enlightenment here enumerated Chosroes added another, which is more surprising than any of them. He studied philosophy, and was a patron of science and learning. Very early in his reign he gave a refuge at his court to a body of seven Greek sages whom a persecuting edict, issued by Justinian, had induced to quit their country and take up their abode on Persian soil. Among the refugees was the erudite Damascius, whose work De Principiis is well known, and has recently been found to exhibit an intimate acquaintance with some of the most obscure of the Oriental religions. Another of the exiles was the eclectic philosopher Simplicius, "the most acute and judicious of the interpreters of Aristotle." Chosroes gave the band of philosophers a hospitable reception, entertained them at his table, and was unwilling that they should leave his court. They found him acquainted with the writings of Aristotle and Plato, whose works he had caused to be translated into the Persian tongue. If he was not able to enter very deeply into the dialectical and metaphysical subtleties which characterize alike the Platonic Dialogues and the Aristotelian treatises, at any rate he was ready to discuss with them such questions as the origin of the world, its destructibility or indestructibility, and the derivation of all things from one First Cause or from more. Later in his reign, another Greek, a sophist named Uranius, acquired his especial favor, became his instructor in the learning of his country, and was presented by him with a large sum of money. Further, Chosroes maintained at his court, for the space of a year, the Greek physician, Tribunus, and offered him any reward that he pleased at his departure. He also instituted at Gondi-Sapor, in the vicinity of Susa, a sort of medical school, which became by degrees a university, wherein philosophy, rhetoric, and poetry were also studied. Nor was it Greek learning alone which attracted his notice and his patronage. Under his fostering care the history and jurisprudence of his native Persia were made special objects of study; the laws and maxims of the first Artaxerxes, the founder of the monarchy, were called forth from the obscurity which had rested on them for ages, were republished and declared to be authoritative; while at the same time the annals of the monarchy were collected and arranged, and a "Shah-nameh," or "Book of the Kings," composed, which it is probable formed the basis of the great work of Firdausi. Even the distant land of Hindustan was explored in the search after varied knowledge, and contributed to the learning and civilization of the time the fables of Bidpai and the game of chess.

Though a fierce persecutor of the deluded followers of Mazdak, Chosroes admitted and practised, to some extent, the principles of toleration. On becoming king, he laid it down as a rule of his government that the actions of men alone, and not their thoughts, were subject to his authority. He was therefore bound not to persecute opinion; and we may suppose that in his proceedings against the Mazdakites he intended to punish their crimes rather than their tenets. Towards the Christians, who abounded in his empire, he certainly showed himself, upon the whole, mild and moderate. He married a Christian wife, and allowed her to retain her religion. When one of his sons became a Christian, the only punishment which he inflicted on him was to confine him to the palace. He augumented the number of the Christians in his dominions by the colonies which he brought in from abroad. He allowed to his Christian subjects the free exercise of their religion, permitted them to build churches, elect bishops, and conduct services at their pleasure, and even suffered them to bury their dead, though such pollution of the earth was accounted sacrilegious by the Zoroastrians. No unworthy compliances with the established cult were required of them. Proselytism, however, was not allowed; and all Christian sects were perhaps not viewed with equal favor. Chosroes, at any rate, is accused of persecuting the Catholics and the Monophysites, and compelling them to join the Nestorians, who formed the predominant sect in his dominions. Conformity, however, in things outward, is compatible with a wide diversity of opinion; and Chosroes, while he disliked differences of practice, seems certainly to have encouraged, at least in his earlier years, a freedom of discussion in religious matters which must have tended to shake the hereditary faith of his subjects. He also gave on one occasion a very remarkable indication of liberal and tolerant views. When he made his first peace with Rome, the article on which he insisted the most was one whereby the free profession of their known opinions and tenets in their own country was secured to the seven Grecian sages who had found at his court, in their hour of need, a refuge from persecution.

In his domestic relations Chosroes was unfortunate. With his chief wife, indeed, the daughter of the great Khan of the Turks, he seems to have lived always on excellent terms; and it was his love for her which induced him to select the son whom she had borne him for his successor on the throne. But the wife who stood next in his favor displeased him by her persistent refusal to renounce the religion of Christ and adopt that of her husband in its stead; and the quarrel between them must have been aggravated by the conduct of their child, Nushizad, who, when he came to years of discretion, deliberately preferred the faith of his mother to that of his father and of the nation. With this choice Chosroes was naturally offended; but he restrained his anger within moderate limits, and was content to punish the young prince by forbidding him to quit the precincts of the palace. Unhappy results followed. Nushizad in his confinement heard a rumor that his father, who had started for the Syrian war, was struck with sickness, was not likely to recover, was dead. It seemed to him a golden opportunity, of which he would be foolish not to make the most. He accordingly quitted his prison, spread the report of his father's death, seized the state treasure, and scattered it with a liberal hand among the troops left in the capital, summoned the Christians throughout the empire to his aid, assumed the title and state of king, was acknowledged by the whole of the southern province, and thought himself strong enough to take the offensive and attempt the subjugation of Irak. Here, however, he was met by Phabrizus (Firuz?), one of his father's generals, who completely defeated his army in a pitched battle. According to one account, Nushizad fell in the thick of the fight, mortally wounded by a chance arrow. According to another, he was made prisoner, and carried to Chosroes, who, instead of punishing him with death, destroyed his hopes of reigning by inflicting on him a cruel disfigurement.

The coins of Chosroes are very numerous, and offer one or two novel and curious types. The most remarkable have on the obverse the head of the king, presenting the full face, and surmounted by a mural crown with a low cap. The beard is close, and the hair arranged in masses on either side. There are two stars above the crown, and two crescents, one over either shoulder, with a star and crescent on the dress in front of each shoulder. The kings wears a necklace, from which hang three pendants. On the reverse these coins have a full-length figure of the king, standing to the front, with his two hands resting on the hilt of his straight sword, and its point placed between his feet. The crown worn resembles that on the obverse; and there is a star and crescent on either side of the head. The legend on the obverse is Khusludi afzum, "May Chosroes increase;" the reverse has, on the left Khusludi, with the regnal year; on the right, a longer legend which has not yet been satisfactorily interpreted. [PLATE XXII., Fig. 3.]

The more ordinary type on the coins of Chosroes I. is one differing but little from those of his father, Kobad, and his son, Hormazd IV. The obverse has the king's head in profile, and the reverse the usual fire-altar and supporters. The distinguishing mark of these coins is, in addition to the legend, that they have three simple crescents in the margin of the obverse, instead of three crescents with stars. [PLATE XXII., Fig. 4.]

A relic of Chosroes has come down to us, which is of great beauty. This is a cup composed of a number of small disks of colored glass, united by a gold setting, and having at the bottom a crystal, engraved with a figure of the monarch. As late as 1638 it was believed that the disks of glass were jacynths, garnets, and emeralds, while the stone which forms the base was thought to be a white sapphire. The original owner of so rare a drinking-vessel could (it was supposed) only be Solomon; and the figure at the bottom was accordingly supposed to represent the Jewish king. Archaeologists are now agreed that the engraving on the gem, which exactly resembles the figure upon the peculiar coins above described, represents Chosroes Anushirwan, and is of his age. There is no sufficient reason to doubt but that the cup itself is one out of which he was accustomed to drink.

It is the great glory of Anushirwan that the title which his subjects gave him was "the Just." According to European, and especially to modern ideas, this praise would seem to have undeserved; and thus the great historian of the Byzantine period has not scrupled to declare that in his external policy Chosroes was actuated by mere ambition, and that "in his domestic administration he deserved the appellation of a tyrant." Undoubtedly the punishments which he inflicted were for the most part severe; but they were not capricious, nor uniform, nor without reference to the character of the offence. Plotting against his crown or his person, when the conspirators were of full age, treasonable correspondence with the enemy, violation of the sanctity of the harem, and the proselytism which was strictly forbidden by the laws, he punished with death. But, when the rebel was a mere youth, he was content to inflict a disfigurement; whence the offence was less, he could imprison, or confine to a particular spot, or simply banish the culprit from his presence. Instances on record of his clemency to offenders, and others which show that, when his own interests were at stake, he steadily refused to make use of his unlimited power for the oppression of individuals. It is unlikely that Anushirwan was distinguished as "the Just" without a reason; and we may safely conclude from his acknowledged title that his subjects found his rule more fair and equitable than that of any previous monarch.

That the administration of Chosroes was wise, and that Persia prospered under his government, is generally admitted. His vigilance, his activity his care for the poor, his efforts to prevent or check oppression, are notorious, and cannot be gainsaid. Nor can it be doubted that he was brave, hardy, temperate, prudent, and liberal. Whether he possessed the softer virtues, compassion, kindliness, a tender and loving heart, is perhaps open to question. He seems, however, to have been a good husband and a good father, not easily offenced, and not over-severe whence offence was given him. His early severities against his brothers and their followers may be regarded as caused by the advice of others, and perhaps as justified by state policy. In his later life, when he was his own master, he was content to chastise rebellion more mildly.

Intellectually, there is no reason to believe that Chosroes rose very high above the ordinary Oriental level. The Persians, and even many Greeks, in his own day, exalted him above measure, as capable of apprehending the most subtle arguments and the deepest problems of philosophy; but the estimate of Agathias is probably more just, and this reduces him to a standard about which there is nothing surprising. It is to his credit that although engaged in almost perpetual wars, and burdened moreover with the administration of a mighty empire, he had a mind large enough to entertain the consideration also of intellectual problems, and to enjoy and take part in their discussion; but it could scarcely be expected that, with his numerous other employments, he should really sound to their utmost depths the profundities of Greek thought, or understand the speculative difficulties which separated the various schools one from another. No doubt his knowledge was superficial, and there may have been ostentation in the parade which he made of it; but we must not deny him the praise of a quick, active intellect, and a width of view rarely found in an Oriental.

It was not, however, in the field of speculative thought, but in that of practical effort, that Chosroes chiefly distinguished himself and gained his choicest laurels. The excellence of his domestic administration has been already noticed. But, great as he was in peace, he was greater in war. Engaged for nearly fifty years in almost uninterrupted contests, he triumphed in every quarter, and scarcely experienced a reverse. Victorious over the Romans, the Abyssinians, the Ephthalites, and the Turks, he extended the limits of his empire on all sides, pacified the discontented Armenia, crushed internal revolt, frustrated the most threatening combinations, and established Persia in a position which she had scarcely occupied since the days of Darius Hystaspis. Personally engaged in above a score of fights, by the admission of his enemies he was never defeated but once; and there are circumstances which make it probable that this single check was of slight importance. The one real failure that can be laid to his charge was in another quarter, and involved no military, but only a political blunder. In recoiling from the difficulties of the Lazic war, Chosroes had not to deplore any disgrace to his arms, but simply to acknowledge that he had misunderstood the temper of the Lazic people. In depreciation of his military talents it may be said that he was never opposed to any great general. With Belisarius it would certainly seem that he never actually crossed swords; but Justinian and Maurice (afterwards emperor), to whom he was opposed in his later years, were no contemptible antagonists. It may further be remarked that the collapse of Persia in her struggle with Rome as soon as Chosroes was in his grave is a tolerably decisive indication that she owed her long career of victory under his guidance to his possession of uncommon military ability.

CHAPTER XXII

*Accession of Hormisdas IV. His good Government in the Earlier Portion of his Reign. Invasion of Persia by the Romans under Maurice. Defeats of Adarman and Tamchosro. Campaign of Johannes. Campaigns of Philippicus and Heraclius. Tyranny of Hormisdas. He is attacked by the Arabs, Khazars, and Turks. Bahram defeats the Turks. His Attack on Lazica. He suffers a Defeat. Disgrace of Bahram. Dethronement of Hormisdas IV. and Elevation of Chosroes II. Character of Hormisdas. Coins of Hormisdas.*

At the death of Chosroes the crown was assumed without dispute or difficulty by his son, Hormazd, who is known to the Greek and Latin writers as Hormisdas IV. Hormazd was the eldest, or perhaps the only, son borne to Chosroes by the Turkish princess, Fakim, who, from the time of her marriage, had held the place of sultana, or principal wife. His illustrious descent on both sides, added to the express appointment of his father, caused him to be universally accepted as king; and we do not hear that even his half-brothers, several of whom were older than himself, put forward any claims in opposition to his, or caused him any anxiety or trouble. He commenced his reign amid the universal plaudits and acclamations of his subjects, whom he delighted by declaring that he would follow in all things the steps of his father, whose wisdom so much exceeded his own, would pursue his policy, maintain his officers in power, and endeavor in all respects to govern as he had governed. When the mobeds attempted to persuade him to confine his favor to Zoroastrians and persecute such of his subjects as were Jews or Christians he rejected their advice with the remark that, as in an extensive territory there were sure to be varieties of soil, so it was fitting that a great empire should embrace men of various opinions and manners. In his progresses from one part of his empire to another he allowed of no injury being done to the lands or gardens along the route, and punished severely all who infringed his orders. According to some, his good dispositions lasted only during the time that he enjoyed the counsel and support of Abu-zurd-mihir, one of the best advisers of his father; but when this venerated sage was compelled by the infirmities of age to quit his court he fell under other influences, and soon degenerated into the cruel tyrant which, according to all the authorities, he showed himself in his later years.

Meanwhile, however, he was engaged in important wars, particularly with the Roman emperors Tiberius and Maurice, who, now that the great Chosroes was dead, pressed upon Persia with augmented force, in the confident hope of recovering their lost laurels. On the first intelligence of the great king's death, Tiberius had endeavored to negotiate a peace with his successor, and had offered to relinquish all claim on Armenia, and to exchange Arzanene with its strong fortress, Aphumon, for Daras; but Hormisdas had absolutely rejected his proposals, declared that he would surrender nothing, and declined to make peace on any other terms than the resumption by Rome of her old system of paying an annual subsidy. The war consequently continued; and Maurice, who still held the command, proceeded, in the summer of A.D. 579, to take the offensive and invade the Persian territory. He sent a force across the Tigris under Romanus, Theodoric, and Martin, which ravaged Kurdistan, and perhaps penetrated into Media, nowhere encountering any large body of the enemy, but carrying all before them and destroying the harvest at their pleasure. In the next year, A.D. 580, he formed a more ambitious project. Having gained over, as he thought, Alamundarus, the leader of the Saracens dependent on Persia, and collected a fleet to carry his stores, he marched from Gircesium down the course of the Euphrates, intending to carry the war into Southern Mesopotamia, and perhaps hoping to capture Ctesiphon. He expected to take the Persians unawares, and may not unnaturally have looked to gain an important success; but, unhappily for his plans, Alamundarus proved treacherous. The Persian king was informed of his enemy's march, and steps were at once taken to render it abortive. Adarman was sent, at the head of a large army, into Roman Mesopotamia, where he threatened the important city of Callinicus in Maurice's rear. That general dared advance no further. On the contrary, he felt constrained to fall back, to give up his scheme, burn his fleet, and return hastily within the Roman frontier. On his arrival, he engaged Adarman near the city which he was attacking, defeated him, and drove him back into Persia.

In the ensuing spring, after another vain attempt at negotiation, the offensive was taken by the Persians, who, early in A.D. 581, crossed the frontier under Tam-chosro, and attacked the Roman city of Constantia, or Constantina. Maurice hastened to its relief; and a great battle was fought in the immediate vicinity of the city, wherein the Persians were completely defeated, and their commander lost his life. Further advantages might have been gained; but the prospect of the succession drew Maurice to Constantinople, where Tiberius, stricken with a mortal disease, received him with open arms, gave his daughter and the state into his care, and, dying soon after, left him the legacy of the empire, which he administered with success for above twenty years.

On quitting the East, Maurice devolved his command upon an officer who bore the very common name of Johannes, but was distinguished further by the epithet of Mustacon, on account of his abundant moustache. This seems to have been a bad appointment. Mustacon was unequal to the position. He gave the Persians battle at the conjunction of the Nymphius with the Tigris, but was defeated with considerable loss, partly through the misconduct of one of his captains. He then laid siege to Arbas, a strong fort on the Persian side of the Nymphius, while the main body of the Persians were attacking Aphumon in the neighboring district of Arzanene. The garrison of Arbas made signals of distress, which speedily brought the Persian army to their aid; a second battle was fought at Arbas, and Mustacon was again defeated, and forced to retire across the Nymphius into Roman territory. His incapacity was now rendered so clearly evident that Maurice recalled him, and gave the command of the army of the East to a new general, Philippicus, his brother-in-law.

The first and second campaigns of Philippicus, in the years A.D. 584 and 585, were of the most commonplace character. He avoided any general engagement, and contended himself with plundering inroads into the Persian territory on either side of the Upper Tigris, occasionally suffering considerably from want of water and provisions. The Persians on their part undertook no operations of importance until late in A.D. 585, when Philippicus had fallen sick. They then made attempts upon Monocartum and Martyropolis, which were unsuccessful, resulting only in the burning of a church and a monastery near the latter town. Neither side seemed capable of making any serious impression upon the other; and early the next year negotiations were resumed, which, however, resulted in nothing.

In his third campaign Philippicus adopted a bolder line of proceeding. Commencing by an invasion of Eastern Mesopotamia, he met and defeated the Persians in a great battle near Solachon, having first roused the enthusiasm of his troops by carrying along their ranks a miraculous picture of our Lord, which no human hand had painted. Hanging on the rear of the fugitives, he pursued them to Daras, which declined to receive within its walls an army that had so disgraced itself. The Persian commander withdrew his troops further inland; and Philippicus, believing that he had now no enemy to fear, proceeded to invade Arzanene, to besiege the stronghold of Chlomaron, and at the same time to throw forward troops into the more eastern parts of the country. He expected them to be unopposed; but the Persian general, having rallied his force and augmented it by fresh recruits, had returned towards the frontier, and, hearing of the danger of Arzanene, had flown to its defence. Philippicus was taken by surprise, compelled to raise the siege of Chlomaron, and to fall back in disorder. The Persians pressed on his retreat, crossed the Nymphius after him, and did not desist from the pursuit until the imperial general threw himself with his shattered army into the strong fortress of Amida. Disgusted and discredited by his ill-success, Philippicus gave over the active prosecution of the war to Heraclius, and, remaining at head-quarters, contented himself with a general supervision.

Heraclius, on receiving his appointment, is said to have at once assumed the offensive, and to have led an army, consisting chiefly or entirely of infantry, into Persian territory, which devastated the country on both sides of the Tigris, and rejoined Philippicus, without having suffered any disaster, before the winter. Philippicus was encouraged by the success of his lieutenant to continue him in command for another year; but, through prudence or jealousy, he was induced to intrust a portion only of the troops to his care, while he assigned to others the supreme authority over no less than one third of the Roman army. The result was, as might have been expected, inglorious for Rome. During A.D. 587 the two divisions acted separately in different quarters; and, at the end of the year, neither could boast of any greater success than the reduction, in each case, of a single fortress. Philippicus, however, seems to have been satisfied; and at the approach of winter he withdrew from the East altogether, leaving Heraclius as his representative, and returned to Constantinople.

During the earlier portion of the year A.D. 588 the mutinous temper of the Roman army rendered it impossible that any military operations should be undertaken. Encouraged by the disorganization of their enemies, the Persians crossed the frontier, and threatened Constantina, which was however saved by Germanus. Later in the year, the mutinous spirit having been quelled, a counter-expedition was made by the Romans into Arzanene. Here the Persian general, Maruzas, met them, and drove them from the province; but, following up his success too ardently, he received a complete defeat near Martyropolis, and lost his life in the battle. His head was cut off by the civilized conquerors, and sent as a trophy to Maurice.

The campaign of A.D. 589 was opened by a brilliant stroke on the part of the Persians, who, through the treachery of a certain Sittas, a petty officer in the Roman army, made themselves masters of

Martyropolis. It was in vain that Philippicus twice besieged the place; he was unable to make any impression upon it, and after a time desisted from the attempt. On the second occasion the garrison was strongly reinforced by the Persians under Mebodos and Aphraates, who, after defeating Philippicus in a pitched battle, threw a large body of troops into the town. Philippicus was upon this deprived of his office, and replaced by Comentiolus, with Heraclius as second in command. The new leaders, instead of engaging in the tedious work of a siege, determined on re-establishing the Roman prestige by a bold counter-attack. They invaded the Persian territory in force, ravaged the country about Nisibis, and brought Aphraates to a pitched battle at Sisarbanon, near that city. Victory seemed at first to incline to the Persians; Comentiolus was defeated and fled; but Horaclius restored the battle, and ended by defeating the whole Persian army, and driving it from the field, with the loss of its commander, who was slain in the thick of the fight. The next day the Persian camp was taken, and a rich booty fell into the hands of the conquerors, besides a number of standards. The remnant of the defeated army found a refuge within the walls of Nisibis. Later in the year Comentiolus recovered to some extent his tarnished laurels by the siege and capture of Arbas, whose strong situation in the immediate vicinity of Martyropolis rendered the position of the Persian garrison in that city insecure, if not absolutely untenable.

Such was the condition of affairs in the western provinces of the Persian Empire, when a sudden danger arose in the east, which had strange and most important consequences. According to the Oriental writers, Hormisdas had from a just monarch gradually become a tyrant; under the plea of protecting the poor had grievously oppressed the rich; through jealousy or fear had put to death no fewer than thirteen thousand of the upper classes, and had thus completely alienated all the more powerful part of the nation. Aware of his unpopularity, the surrounding tribes and peoples commenced a series of aggressions, plundered the frontier provinces, defeated the detachments sent against them under commanders who were disaffected, and everywhere brought the empire into the greatest danger. The Arabs crossed the Euphrates and spread themselves over Mesopotamia; the Khazars invaded Armenia and Azerbijan; rumor said that the Greek emperor had taken the field and was advancing on the side of Syria, at the head of 80,000 men; above all, it was quite certain that the Great Khan of the Turks had put his hordes in motion, had passed the Oxus with a countless host, occupied Balkh and Herat, and was threatening to penetrate into the very heart of Persia. The perilous character of the crisis is perhaps exaggerated; but there can be little doubt that the advance of the Turks constituted a real danger. Hormisdas, however, did not even now quit the capital, or adventure his own person. He selected from among his generals a certain Varahran or Bahram, a leader of great courage and experience, who had distinguished himself in the wars of Anushirwan, and, placing all the resources of the empire at his disposal, assigned to him the entire conduct of the Turkish struggle. Bahram is said to have contented himself with a small force of picked men, veterans between forty and fifty years of age, to have marched with them upon Balkh, contended with the Great Khan in several partial engagements, and at last entirely defeated him in a great battle, wherein the Khan lost his life. This victory was soon followed by another over the Khan's son, who was made prisoner and sent to Hormisdas. An enormous booty was at the same time despatched to the court; and Bahram himself was about to return, when he received his master's orders to carry his arms into another quarter.

It is supposed, by some that, while the Turkish hordes were menacing Persia upon the north-east, a Roman army, intended to act in concert with them, was sent by Maurice into Albania, which proceeded to threaten the common enemy in the north-west. But the Byzantine writers know of no alliance at this time between the Romans and Turks; nor do they tell of any offensive movement undertaken by Rome in aid of the Turkish invasion, or even simultaneously with it. According to them, the war in this quarter, which certainly broke out in A.D. 589, was provoked by Hormisdas himself, who, immediately after his Turkish victories, sent Bahram with an army to invade Colchis and Suania, or in other words to resume the Lazic war, from which Anushirwan had desisted twenty-seven years previously. Bahram found the province unguarded, and was able to ravage it at his will; but a Roman force soon gathered to its defence, and after some manoeuvres a pitched battle was fought on the Araxes, in which the Persian general suffered a defeat. The military results of the check were insignificant; but it led to an internal revolution. Hormisdas had grown jealous of his too successful lieutenant, and was glad of an opportunity to insult him. No sooner did he hear of Bahram's defeat than he sent off a messenger to the camp upon the Araxes, who deprived the general of his command, and presented to him, on the part of his master, a distaff, some cotton, and a complete set of women's garments. Stung to madness by the undeserved insult, Bahram retorted with a letter, wherein he addressed Hormisdas, not as the son, but as the daughter of Chosroes. Shortly afterwards, upon the arrival of a second messenger from the court, with orders to bring the recalcitrant commander home in chains, Bahram openly revolted, caused the envoy to be trampled upon by an elephant, and either by simply putting before the soldiers his services and his wrongs, or by misrepresenting to them the intentions of Hormisdas towards themselves, induced his whole army with one accord to embrace his cause.

The news of the great general's revolt was received with acclamations by the provinces. The army of Mesopotamia, collected at Nisibis, made common cause with that of Albania; and the united force, advancing on the capital by way of Assyria, took up a position upon the Upper Zab river. Hormisdas sent a general, Pherochanes, to meet and engage the rebels; but the emissaries of Bahram seduced his troops from their allegiance; Pherochanes was murdered; and the insurgent army, augmented by the force sent to oppose it, drew daily nearer to Ctesiphon. Meanwhile Hormisdas, distracted between hate and fear, suspecting every one, trusting no one, confined himself within the walls of the capital, where he continued to exercise the severities which had lost him the affections of his subjects. According to some, he suspected his son, Chosroes, of collusion with the enemy, and drove him into banishment, imprisoning at the same time his own brothers in-law, Bindoes and Bostam, who would be likely, he thought, to give their support to their nephew. These violent measures precipitated the evils which he feared; a general revolt broke out in the palace; Bostam and Bindoes, released from prison, put themselves at the head of the malcontents, and, rushing into the presence-chamber, dragged the tyrant from his throne, stripped him of the diadem, and committed him to the dungeon from which they had themselves escaped. The Byzantine historians believed that, after this, Hormisdas was permitted to plead his cause before an assembly of Persian nobles, to glorify his own reign, vituperate his eldest son, Chosroes, and express his willingness to abdicate in favor of another son, who had never offended him. They supposed that this ill-judged oration had sealed the fate of the youth recommended and of his mother, who were cut to pieces before the fallen monarch's eyes, while at the same time the rage of the assembly was vented in part upon Hormisdas himself, who was blinded, to make his restoration impossible. But a judicious critic will doubt the likelihood of rebels, committed as were Bindoes and Bostam, consenting to allow such an appeal as is described by Theophylact; and a perusal of the speeches assigned to the occasion will certainly not diminish his scepticism. The probability would seem to be that Hormisdas was blinded as soon as committed to prison, and that shortly afterwards he suffered the general fate of deposed sovereigns, being assassinated in his place of confinement.

The deposition of Hormisdas was followed almost immediately by the proclamation of his eldest son, Chosroes, the prince known in history as "Eberwiz" or "Parviz," the last great Persian monarch. The rebels at Ctesiphon had perhaps acted from first to last with his cognizance: at any rate, they calculated on his pardoning proceedings which had given him actual possession of a throne whereto, without their aid, he might never have succeeded. They accordingly declared him king of Persia without binding him by conditions, and without negotiating with Bahram, who was still in arms and at no great distance.

Before passing to the consideration of the eventful reign with which we shall now have to occupy ourselves, a glance at the personal character of the deceased monarch will perhaps be expected by the reader. Hormuzd is pronounced by the concurrent voice of the Greeks and the Orientals one of the worst princes that ever ruled over Persia. The fair promise of his early years was quickly clouded over; and during the greater portion of his reign he was a jealous and capricious tyrant, influenced by unworthy favorites, and stimulated to ever-increasing severities by his fears. Eminence of whatsoever kind roused his suspicions; and among his victims were included, besides the noble and the great, a large number of philosophers and men of science. His treatment of Bahram was at once a folly and a crime—an act of black ingratitude, and a rash step, whereof he had not counted the consequences. To his other vices he added those of indolence and effeminacy. From the time that he became king nothing could drag him from the soft life of the palace; in no single instance did he take the field, either against his country's enemies or his own. Miserable as was his end, we can scarcely deem him worthy of our pity, since there never lived a man whose misfortunes were more truly brought on him by his own conduct.

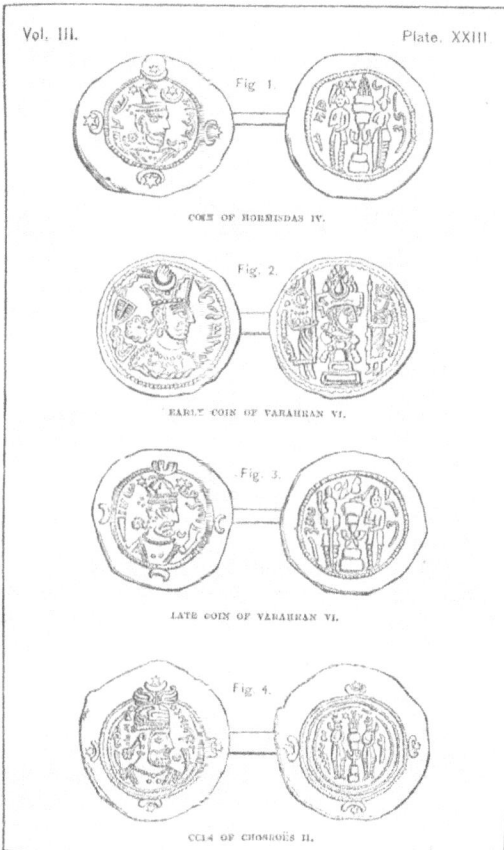

Vol. III.  Plate. XXIII

Fig. 1.

COIN OF HORMISDAS IV.

Fig. 2.

EARLY COIN OF VARAHRAN VI.

Fig. 3.

LATE COIN OF VARAHRAN VI.

Fig. 4.

COIN OF CHOSROËS II.

PLATE XXIII

The coins of Hormisdas IV. are in no respect remarkable. The head seems modelled on that of Chosroes, his father, but is younger. The field of the coin within the border is somewhat unduly crowded with stars and crescents. Stars and crescents also occur outside the border, replacing the simple crescents of Chosroes, and reproducing the combined stars and crescents of Zamasp. The legend on the obverse is Auhramazdi afzud, or sometimes Auhramazi afzun; on the reverse are commonly found, besides the usual fire-altar and supporters, a regnal year and a mint-mark. The regnal years range from one to thirteen; the number of the mint-marks is about thirty. [PLATE XXIII., Fig. 1.]

## CHAPTER XXIII

*Accession of Chosroes II. (Eberwiz). Bahram rejects his Terms. Contest between Chosroes and Bahram. Flight of Chosroes. Short Reign of Bahram (Varahran VI). Campaign of A.D. 591. Recovery of the Throne by Chosroes. Coins of Bahram.*

The position of Chosroes II. on his accession was one of great difficulty. Whether actually guilty of parricide or not, he was at any rate suspected by the greater part of his subjects of complicity in his father's murder. A rebel, who was the greatest Persian general of the time, at the head of a veteran army, stood arrayed against his authority. He had no established character to fall back upon, no merits to plead, nothing in fact to urge on his behalf but that he was the eldest son of his father, the legitimate representative of the ancient line of the Sassanidae. A revolution had placed him on the throne in a hasty and irregular manner; nor is it clear that he had ventured on the usual formality of asking the consent of the general assembly of the nobles to his coronation. Thus perils surrounded him on every side; but the most pressing danger of all, that which required to be immediately met and confronted, was the threatening attitude of Bahram, who had advanced from Adiabene to Holwan, and occupied a strong position not a hundred and fifty miles from the capital. Unless Bahram could be conciliated or defeated, the young king could not hope to maintain himself in power, or feel that he had any firm grasp of the sceptre.

Under these circumstances he took the resolution to try first the method of conciliation. There seemed to be a fair opening for such a course. It was not he, but his father, who had given the offence which drove Bahram into rebellion, and almost forced him to vindicate his manhood by challenging his detractor to a trial of strength. Bahram could have no personal ground of quarrel with him. Indeed that general had at the first, if we may believe the Oriental writers, proclaimed Chosroes as king, and given out that he took up arms in order to place him upon the throne. It was thought, moreover, that the rebel might feel himself sufficiently avenged by the death of his enemy, and might be favorably disposed towards those who had first blinded Hormisdas and then despatched him by the bowstring. Chosroes therefore composed a letter in which he invited Bahram to his court, and offered him the second place in the kingdom, if he would come in and make his submission. The message was accompanied by rich presents, and by an offer that if the terms proposed wera accepted they should be confirmed by oath.

The reply of Bahram was as follows: "Bahram, friend of the gods, conqueror, illustrious, enemy of tyrants, satrap of satraps, general of the Persian host, wise, apt for command, god-fearing, without reproach, noble, fortunate, successful, venerable, thrifty, provident, gentle, humane, to Chosroes the son of Hormisdas (sends greeting). I have received the letter which you wrote with such little wisdom, but have rejected the presents which you sent with such excessive boldness. It had been better that you should have abstained from sending either, more especially considering the irregularity of your appointment, and the fact that the noble and respectable took no part in the vote, which was carried by the disorderly and low-born. If then it is your wish to escape your father's fate, strip off the diadem which you have assumed and deposit it in some holy place, quit the palace, and restore to their prisons the criminals whom you have set at liberty, and whom you had no right to release until they had undergone trial for their crimes. When you have done all this, come hither, and I will give you the government of a province. Be well advised, and so farewell. Else, be sure you will perish like your father." So insolent a missive might well have provoked the young prince to some hasty act or some unworthy show of temper. It is to the credit of Chosroes that he restrained himself, and even made another attempt to terminate the quarrel by a reconciliation. While striving to outdo Bahram in the grandeur of his titles, he still addressed him as his friend. He complimented him on his courage, and felicitated him on his excellent health. "There were certain expressions," he said, "in the letter that he had received, which he was sure did not speak his friend's real feelings. The amanuensis had evidently drunk more wine than he ought, and, being half asleep when he wrote, had put down things that were foolish and indeed monstrous. But he was not disturbed by them. He must decline, however, to send back to their prisons those whom he had released, since favors granted by royalty could not with propriety be withdrawn; and he must protest that in the ceremony of his coronation all due formalities had been observed. As for stripping himself of his diadem, he was so far from contemplating it that he looked forward rather to extending his dominion over new worlds. As Bahram had invited him, he would certainly pay him a visit; but he would be obliged to come as a king, and if his persuasions did not produce submission he would have to compel it by force of arms. He hoped that Bahram would be wise in time, and would consent to be his friend and helper."

This second overture produced no reply; and it became tolerably evident that the quarrel could only be decided by the arbitrament of battle. Chosroes accordingly put himself at the head of such troops as he could collect, and marched against his antagonist, whom he found encamped on the Holwan River. The place was favorable for an engagement; but Chosroes had no confidence in his soldiers. He sought a personal interview with Bahram, and renewed his offers of pardon and favor; but the conference only led to mutual recriminations, and at its close both sides appealed to arms. During six days the two armies merely skirmished, since Chosroes bent all his efforts towards avoiding a general engagement; but on the seventh day Bahram surprised him by an attack after night had fallen,a threw his troops into confusion, and then, by a skilful appeal to their feelings, induced them to desert their leader and come over to his side. Chosroes was forced to fly. He fell back on Ctesiphon; but despairing of making a successful defence, with the few troops that remained faithful to him, against the overwhelming force which Bahram had at his disposal, he resolved to evacuate the capital, to quit Persia, and to throw himself on the generosity of some one of his neighbors. It is said that his choice was long undetermined between the Turks, the Arabs, the Khazars of the Caucasian region, and the Romans. According to some writers, after leaving Ctesiphon, with his wives and children, his two uncles, and an escort of thirty men, he laid his reins on his horse's neck, and left it to the instinct of the animal to determine in what direction he should flee. The sagacious beast took the way to the Euphrates; and Chosroes, finding himself on its banks, crossed the river, and, following up its course, reached with much difficulty the well-known Roman station of Circesium. He was not unmolested in his retreat. Bahram no sooner heard of his flight than he sent off a body of 4000 horse, with orders to pursue and capture the fugitive. They would have succeeded, had not Bindoes devoted himself on behalf of his nephew, and, by tricking the officer in command, enabled Chosroes to place such a distance between himself and his pursuers that the chase had to be given up, and the detachment to return, with no more valuable capture than Bindoes, to Ctesiphon.

Chosroes was received with all honor by Probus, the governor of Circesium, who the next day communicated intelligence of what had happened to Comentiolus, Prefect of the East, then resident at Hierapolis. At the same time he sent to Comentiolus a letter which Chosroes had addressed to

Maurice, imploring his aid against his enemies. Comentiolus approved what had been done, despatched a courier to bear the royal missive to Constantinople, and shortly afterwards, by the direction of the court, invited the illustrious refugee to remove to Hierapolis, and there take up his abode, till his cause should be determined by the emperor. Meanwhile, at Constantinople, after the letter of Chosroes had been read, a serious debate arose as to what was fittest to be done. While some urged with much show of reason that it was for the interest of the empire that the civil war should be prolonged, that Persia should be allowed to waste her strength and exhaust her resources in the contest, at the end of which it would be easy to conquer her, there were others whose views were less selfish or more far-sighted. The prospect of uniting the East and West into a single monarchy, which had been brought to the test of experiment by Alexander and had failed, did not present itself in a very tempting light to these minds. They doubted the ability of the declining empire to sway at once the sceptre of Europe and of Asia. They feared that if the appeal of Chosroes were rejected, the East would simply fall into anarchy, and the way would perhaps be prepared for some new power to rise up, more formidable than the kingdom of the Sassanidae. The inclination of Maurice, who liked to think himself magnanimous, coincided with the views of these persons: their counsels were accepted; and the reply was made to Chosroes that the Roman emperor accepted him as his guest and son, undertook his quarrel, and would aid him with all the forces of the empire to recover his throne. At the same time Maurice sent him some magnificent presents, and releasing the Persian prisoners in confinement at Constantinople, bade them accompany the envoys of Chosroes and resume the service of their master. Soon afterwards more substantial tokens of the Imperial friendship made their appearance. An army of 70,000 men arrived under Narses; and a subsidy was advanced by the Imperial treasury, amounting (according to one writer) to about two millions sterling.

But this valuable support to his cause was no free gift of a generous friend; on the contrary, it had to be purchased by great sacrifices. Chosroes had perhaps at first hoped that aid would be given him gratuitously, and had even regarded the cession of a single city as one that he might avoid making. But he learnt by degrees that nothing was to be got from Rome without paying for it; and it was only by ceding Persarmenia and Eastern Mesopotamia, with its strong towns of Martyropolis and Daras, that he obtained the men and money that were requisite.

Meanwhile Bahram, having occupied Ctesiphon, had proclaimed himself king, and sent out messengers on all sides to acquaint the provinces with the change of rulers. The news was received without enthusiasm, but with a general acquiescence; and, had Maurice rejected the application of Chosroes, it is probable that the usurper might have enjoyed a long and quiet reign. As soon, however, as it came to be known that the Greek emperor had espoused, the cause of his rival, Bahram found himself in difficulties: conspiracy arose in his own court, and had to be suppressed by executions; murmurs were heard in some of the more distant provinces; Armenia openly revolted and declared for Chosroes; and it soon appeared that in places the fidelity of the Persian troops was doubtful. This was especially the case in Mesopotamia, which would have to bear the brunt of the attack when the Romans advanced. Bahram therefore thought it necessary, though it was now the depth of winter, to strengthen his hold on the wavering province, and sent out two detachments, under commanders upon whom he could rely, to occupy respectively Anatho and Nisibis, the two strongholds of greatest importance in the suspected region. Miraduris succeeded in entering and occupying Anatho. Zadesprates was less fortunate; before he reached the neighborhood of Nisibis, the garrison which held that place had deserted the cause of the usurper and given in its adhesion to Chosroes; and, when he approached to reconnoitre, he was made the victim of a stratagem and killed by an officer named Rosas. Miraduris did not long survive him; the troops which he had introduced into Anatho caught the contagion of revolt, rose up against him, slew him, and sent his head to Chosroes.

The spring was now approaching, and the time for military operations on a grand scale drew near. Chosroes, besides his supporters in Mesopotamia, Roman and Persian, had a second army in Azerbijan, raised by his uncles Bindoes and Bostam, which was strengthened by an Armenian contingent. The plan of campaign involved the co-operation of these two forces. With this object Chosroes proceeded early in the spring, from Hierapolis to Constantina, from Constantina to Daras, and thence by way of Ammodicn to the Tigris, across which he sent a detachment, probably in the neighborhood of Mosul. This force fell in with Bryzacius, who commanded in these parts for Bahram, and surprising him in the first watch of the night, defeated his army and took Bryzacius himself prisoner. The sequel, which Theophylact appears to relate from the information of an eye-witness, furnishes a remarkable evidence of the barbarity of the times. Those who captured Bryzacius cut off his nose and his ears, and in this condition sent him to Chosroes. The Persian prince was overjoyed at the success, which no doubt he accepted as a good omen; he at once led his whole army across the river, and having encamped for the night at a place called Dinabadon, entertained the chief Persian and Roman nobles at a banquet. When the festivity was at its height, the unfortunate prisoner was brought in loaded with fetters, and was made sport of by the guests for a time, after which, at a signal from the king the guards plunged their swords into his body, and despatched him in the sight of the feasters. Having amused his guests with this delectable interlude, the amiable monarch concluded the whole by anointing them with perfumed ointment, crowning them with flowers, and bidding them drink to the success of the war. "The guests," says Theophylact, "returned, to their tents, delighted with the completeness of their entertainment, and told their friends how handsomely they had been treated, but the crown of all (they said) was the episode of Bryzacius."

Chosroes next day advanced across the Greater Zab, and, after marching four days, reached Alexandrian a position probably not far from Arbela, after which, in two days more, he arrived at Chnaethas, which was a district upon the Zab Asfal, or Lesser Zab River. Here he found himself in the immediate vicinity of Bahram, who had taken up his position on the Lesser Zab, with the intention probably of blocking the route up its valley, by which he expected that the Armenian army would endeavor to effect a junction with the army of Chosroes. Here the two forces watched each other for some days, and various manoeuvres were executed, which it is impossible to follow, since Theophylact, our only authority, is not a good military historian. The result, however, is certain. Bahram was out-manoeuvred by Chosroes and his Roman allies; the fords of the Zab were seized; and after five days of marching and counter-marching, the longed-for junction took place. Chosroes had the satisfaction of embracing his uncles Bindoes and Bostam, and of securing such a reinforcement as gave him a great superiority in numbers over his antagonist.

About the same time he received intelligence of another most important success. Before quitting Daras, he had despatched Mebodes, at the head of a small body of Romans, to create a diversion on the Mesopotomian side of the Tigris by a demonstration from Singara against Seleucia and Ctesiphon. He can hardly have expected to do more than distract his enemy and perhaps make him divide his forces. Bahram, however, was either indifferent as to the fate of the capital, or determined not to weaken the small army which was all that he could muster, and on which his whole dependence was placed. He left Seleucia and Ctesiphon to their fate. Mebodes and his small force marched southward without meeting an enemy, obtained possession of Seleucia without a blow after the withdrawal of the garrison, received the unconditional surrender of Ctesiphon, made themselves masters of the royal palace and treasures, proclaimed Chosroes king, and sent to him in his camp the most precious emblems of the Persian sovereignty. Thus, before engaging with his antagonist, Chosroes recovered his capital and found his authority once more recognized in the seat of government.

The great contest had, however, to be decided, not by the loss and gain of cities, nor by the fickle mood of a populace, but by trial of arms in the open field. Bahram was not of a temper to surrender his sovereignty unless compelled by defeat. He was one of the greatest generals of the age, and, though compelled to fight under every disadvantage, greatly outnumbered by the enemy, and with troops that were to a large extent disaffected, he was bent on resisting to the utmost, and doing his best to maintain his own rights. He seems to have fought two pitched battles with the combined Romans and Persians, and not to have succumbed until treachery and desertion disheartened him and ruined his cause. The first battle was in the plain country of Adiabene, at the foot of the Zagros range. Here the opposing armies were drawn out in the open field, each divided into a centre and two wings. In the army of Chosroes the Romans were in the middle, on the right the Persians, and the Armenians on the left. Narses, together with Chosroes, held the central position: Bahram was directly opposed to them. When the conflict began the Romans charged with such fierceness that Bahram's centre at once gave way; he was obliged to retreat to the foot of the hills, and take up a position on their slope. Here the Romans refused to attack him; and Chosroes very imprudently ordered the Persians who fought on his side to advance up the ascent. They were repulsed, and thrown into complete confusion; and the battle would infallibly have been lost, had not Narses come to their aid, and with his steady and solid battalions protected their retreat and restored the fight. Yet the day terminated with a feeling on both sides that Bahram had on the whole had the advantage in the engagement; the king de facto congratulated himself; the king de jure had to bear the insulting pity of his allies, and the reproaches of his own countrymen for occasioning them such a disaster.

But though Bahram might feel that the glory of the day was his, he was not elated by his success, nor rendered blind to the difficulties of his position. Fighting with his back to the mountains, he was liable, if he suffered defeat, to be entangled in their defiles and lose his entire force. Moreover, now that Ctesiphon was no longer his, he had neither resources nor point d'appui in the low country, and by falling back he would at once be approaching nearer to the main source of his own supplies, which was the country about Rei, south of the Caspian, and drawing his enemies to a greater distance from the sources of theirs. He may even have thought there was a chance of his being unpursued if he retired, since the Romans might not like to venture into the mountain region, and Chosroes might be impatient to make a triumphal entry into his capital. Accordingly, the use which Bahram made of his victory was quietly to evacuate his camp, to leave the low plain region, rapidly pass the mountains, and take up his quarters in the fertile upland beyond them, the district where the Lesser Zab rises, south of Lake Urumiyeh.

If he had hoped that his enemies would not pursue him, Bahram was disappointed. Chosroes himself, and the whole of the mixed army which supported his cause, soon followed on his footsteps, and pressing forward to Canzaca, or Shiz, near which he had pitched his camp, offered him battle for the second time. Bahram declined the offer, and retreated to a position on the Balarathus, where, however, after a short time, he was forced to come to an engagement. He had received, it would seem, a reinforcement of elephants from the provinces bordering on India, and hoped for some advantage from the employment of this new arm. He had perhaps augmented his forces, though it must be doubted whether he really on this occasion outnumbered his antagonist. At any rate, the time seemed to have come when he must abide the issue of his appeal to arms, and secure or lose his crown by a supreme effort. Once more the armies were drawn up in three distinct bodies; and once more the leaders held the established central position. The engagement began along the whole line, and continued for a while without marked result. Bahram then strengthened his left, and, transferring himself to this part of the field, made an impression on the Roman right. But Narses brought up supports to their aid, and checked the retreat, which had already begun, and which might soon have become general. Hereupon Bahram suddenly fell upon the Roman centre and endeavored to break it and drive it from the field; but Narses was again a match for him, and met his assault without flinching, after which, charging in his turn, he threw the Persian centre into confusion. Seeing this, the wings also broke, and a general flight began, whereupon 6000 of Bahram's troops deserted, and, drawing aside, allowed themselves to be captured. The retreat then became a rout. Bahram himself fled with 4,000 men. His camp, with all its rich furniture, and his wives and children, were taken. The elephant corps still held out and fought valiantly; but it was surrounded and forced to surrender. The battle was utterly lost; and the unfortunate chief, feeling that all hope was gone, gave the reins to his horse and fled for his life. Chosroes sent ten thousand men in pursuit, under Bostam, his uncle; and this detachment overtook the fugitives, but was repulsed and returned. Bahram continued his flight, and passing through Rei and Damaghan, reached the Oxus and placed himself under the protection of the Turks. Chosroes, having dismissed his Roman allies, re-entered Ctesiphon after a year's absence, and for the second time took his place upon the throne of his ancestors.

The coins of Bahram possess a peculiar interest. While there is no numismatic evidence which confirms the statement that he struck money in the name of the younger Chosroes, there are extant three types of his coins, two of which appear to belong to the time before he seated himself upon the throne, while one—the last—belongs to the period of his actual sovereignty. In his preregnal coins, he copied the devices of the last sovereign of his name who had ruled over Persia. He adopted the mural crown in a decided form, omitted the stars and crescents, and placed his own head amid the flames of the fire-altar. His legends were either Varahran Chub, "Bahram of the mace," or Varahran, maljcan malka, mazdisn, bagi, ramashtri, "Bahram, king of kings, Ormazd-worshipping, divine, peaceful." [PLATE XXIII, Fig. 2.]

The later coins follow closely the type of his predecessor, Hormisdas IV., differing only in the legend, which is, on the obverse, Varahran afzun, or "Varahran (may he be) greater;" and on the reverse the regnal year, with a mint-mark. The regnal year is uniformly "one;" the mint-marks are Zadracarta, Iran, and Nihach, an unknown locality. [PLATE XXIII., Fig 3.]

CHAPTER XXIV

*Second Reign of Chosroes II. (Eberwiz). His Rule at first Unpopular, His Treatment of his Uncles, Bindoes and Bostam. His vindictive Proceedings against Bahram. His supposed Leaning towards Christianity. His Wives, Shirin and Kurdiyeh. His early Wars. His Relations with the Emperor Maurice. His Attitude towards Phocas. Great War of Chosroes with Phocas, A.D. 603-610. War continued with Heraclius. Immense Successes of Chosroes, A.D. 611-620. Aggressive taken by Heraclius A.D. 622. His Campaigns in Persian Territory A.D. 622-628. Murder of Chosroes. His Character. His Coins.*

The second reign of Chosroes II., who is commonly known as Chosroes Eberwiz or Parwiz, lasted little short of thirty-seven years—from the summer of A.D. 591 to the February of A.D. 628. Externally considered, it is the most remarkable reign in the entire Sassanian series, embracing as it does the extremes of elevation and depression. Never at any other time did the Neo-Persian kingdom extend itself so far, or so distinguish itself by military achievements, as in the twenty years intervening between A.D. 602 and A.D. 622. Seldom was it brought so low as in the years immediately anterior and immediately subsequent to this space, in the earlier and in the later portions of the reign whose central period was so glorious.

Victorious by the help of Rome, Chosroes began his second reign amid the scarcely disguised hostility of his subjects. So greatly did he mistrust their sentiments towards him that he begged and obtained of Maurice the support of a Roman bodyguard, to whom he committed the custody of his person. To the odium always attaching in the minds of a spirited people to the ruler whose yoke is imposed upon them by a foreign power, he added further the stain of a crime which is happily rare at all times, and of which (according to the general belief of his subjects) no Persian monarch had ever previously been guilty. It was in vain that he protested his innocence: the popular belief held him an accomplice in his father's murder, and branded the young prince with the horrible name of "parricide."

It was no doubt mainly in the hope of purging himself from this imputation that, after putting to death the subordinate instruments by whom his father's life had been actually taken, he went on to institute proceedings against the chief contrivers of the outrage—the two uncles who had ordered, and probably witnessed, the execution. So long as the success of his arms was doubtful, he had been happy to avail himself of their support, and to employ their talents in the struggle against his enemies. At one moment in his flight he had owed his life to the self-devotion of Bindoes; and both the brothers had merited well of him by the efforts which they had made to bring Armenia over to his cause, and to levy a powerful army for him in that region. But to clear his own character it was necessary that he should forget the ties both of blood and gratitude, that he should sink the kinsman in the sovereign, and the debtor in the stern avenger of blood. Accordingly, he seized Bindoes, who resided at the court, and had him drowned in the Tigris. To Bostam, whom he had appointed governor of Rei and Khorassan, he sent an order of recall, and would undoubtedly have executed him, had he obeyed; but Bostam, suspecting his intentions, deemed it the wisest course to revolt, and proclaim himself independent monarch of the north country. Here he established himself in authority for some time, and is even said to have enlarged his territory at the expense of some of the border chieftains; but the vengeance of his nephew pursued him unrelentingly, and ere long accomplished his destruction. According to the best authority, the instrument employed was Bostam's wife, the sister of Bahram, whom Chosroes induced to murder her husband by a promise to make her the partner of his bed.

Intrigues not very dissimilar in their character had been previously employed to remove Bahram, whom the Persian monarch had not ceased to fear, notwithstanding that he was a fugitive and an exile. The Khan of the Turks had received him with honor on the occasion of his flight, and, according to some authors, had given him his daughter in marriage. Chosroes lived in dread of the day when the great general might reappear in Persia, at the head of the Turkish hordes, and challenge him to renew the lately-terminated contest.

He therefore sent an envoy into Turkestan, well supplied with rich gifts, whose instructions were to procure by some means or other the death of Bahram. Having sounded the Khan upon the business and met with a rebuff, the envoy addressed himself to the Khatun, the Khan's wife, and by liberal presents induced her to come into his views. A slave was easily found who undertook to carry out his mistress's wishes, and Bahram was despatched the same day by means of a poisoned dagger. It is painful to find that one thus ungrateful to his friends and relentless to his enemies made, to a certain extent, profession of Christianity. Little as his heart can have been penetrated by its spirit, Chosroes seems certainly, in the earlier part of his reign, to have given occasion for the suspicion, which his subjects are said to have entertained, that he designed to change his religion, and confess himself a convert to the creed of the Greeks. During the period of his exile, he was, it would seem, impressed by what he saw and heard, of the Christian worship and faith; he learnt to feel or profess a high veneration for the Virgin; and he adopted the practice, common at the time, of addressing his prayers and vows to the saints and martyrs, who were practically the principal objects of the Oriental Christians' devotions. Sergius, a martyr, hold in high repute by the Christians of Osrhoene and Mesopotamia, was adopted by the superstitious prince as a sort of patron saint; and it became his habit, in circumstances of difficulty, to vow some gift or other to the shrine of St. Sergius at

Sergiopolis, in case of the event corresponding to his wishes. Two occasions are recorded where, on sending his gift, he accompanied it with a letter explaining the circumstances of his vow and its fulfilment; and even the letters themselves have come down to us, but in a Greek version. In one, Chosroes ascribes the success of his arms on a particular occasion to the influence of his self-chosen patron; in the other, he credits him with having procured by his prayers the pregnancy of Sira (Shirin), the most beautiful and best beloved of his wives. It appears that Sira was a Christian, and that in marrying her Chosroes had contravened the laws of his country, which forbade the king to have a Christian wife. Her influence over him was considerable, and she is said to have been allowed to build numerous churches and monasteries in and about Ctesiphon. When she died, Chosroes called in the aid of sculpture to perpetuate her image, and sent her statue to the Roman Emperor, to the Turkish Khan, and to various other potentates.

Chosroes is said to have maintained an enormous seraglio; but of these secondary wives, none is known to us even by name, except Kurdiyeh, the sister of Bahram and widow of Bostam, whom she murdered at Chosroes's suggestion.

During the earlier portion of his reign Chosroes seems to have been engaged in but few wars, and those of no great importance. According to the Armenian writers, he formed a design of depopulating that part of Armenia which he had not ceded to the Romans, by making a general levy of all the males, and marching them off to the East, to fight against the Ephthalites; but the design did not prosper, since the Armenians carried all before them, and under their native leader, Smbat, the Bagratunian, conquered Hyrcania and Tabaristan, defeated repeatedly the Koushans and the Ephthalites, and even engaged with success the Great Khan of the Turks, who came to the support of his vassals at the head of an army consisting of 300.000 men. By the valor and conduct of Smbat, the Persian dominion was re-established in the north-eastern mountain region, from Mount Demavend to the Hindu Kush; the Koushans, Turks, and Ephthalitos were held in check; and the tide of barbarism, which had threatened to submerge the empire on this side, was effectually resisted and rolled back.

With Rome Chosroes maintained for eleven years the most friendly and cordial relations. Whatever humiliation he may have felt when he accepted the terms on which alone Maurice was willing to render him aid, having once agreed to them, he stifled all regrets, made no attempt to evade his obligations, abstained from every endeavor to undo by intrigue what he had done, unwillingly indeed, but yet with his eyes open. Once only during the eleven years did a momentary cloud arise between him and his benefactor. In the year A.D. 600 some of the Saracenic tribes dependent on Rome made an incursion across the Euphrates into Persian territory, ravaged it far and wide, and returned with their booty into the desert. Chosroes was justly offended, and might fairly have considered that a casus belli had arisen; but he allowed himself to be pacified by the representations of Maurice's envoy, George, and consented not to break the peace on account of so small a matter. George claimed the concession as a tribute to his own amiable qualities; but it is probable that the Persian monarch acted rather on the grounds of general policy than from any personal predilection.

Two years later the virtuous but perhaps over-rigid Maurice was deposed and murdered by the centurion, Phocas, who, on the strength of his popularity with the army, boldly usurped the throne. Chosroes heard with indignation of the execution of his ally and friend, of the insults offered to his remains, and of the assassination of his numerous sons, and of his brother. One son, he heard, had been sent off by Maurice to implore aid from the Persians; he had been overtaken and put to death by the emissaries of the usurper; but rumor, always busy where royal personages are concerned, asserted that he lived, that he had escaped his pursuers, and had reached Ctesiphon. Chosroes was too much interested in the acceptance of the rumor to deny it; he gave out that Theodosius was at his court, and notified that it was his intention to assert his right to the succession. When, five months after his coronation, Phocas sent an envoy to announce his occupation of the throne, and selected the actual murderer of Maurice to fill the post, Chosroes determined on an open rupture. He seized Lilius, the envoy, threw him into prison, announced his intention of avenging his deceased benefactor, and openly declared war against Rome.

The war burst out the next year (A.D. 603). On the Roman side there was disagreement, and even civil war; for Narses, who had held high command in the East ever since he restored Chosroes to the throne of his ancestors, on hearing of the death of Maurice, took up arms against Phocas, and, throwing himself into Edessa, defied the forces of the usurper. Germanus, who commanded at Daras, was a general of small capacity, and found himself quite unable to make head, either against Narses in Edessa, or against Chosroes, who led his troops in person into Mesopotamia. Defeated by Chosroes in a battle near Daras, in which he received a mortal wound, Germanus withdrew to Constantia, where he died eleven days afterwards. A certain Leontius, a eunuch, took his place, but was equally unsuccessful. Chosroes defeated him at Arxamus, and took a great portion of his army prisoners; whereupon he was recalled by Phocas, and a third leader, Domentziolus, a nephew of the emperor, was appointed to the command. Against him the Persian monarch thought it enough to employ generals. The war now languished for a short space; but in A.D. 605 Chosroes came up in person against Daras, the great Roman stronghold in these parts, and besieged it for the space of nine months, at the end of which time it surrendered. The loss was a severe blow to the Roman prestige, and was followed in the next year by a long series of calamities. Chosroes took Tur-abdin, Hesen-Cephas, Mardin, Capher-tuta, and Amida. Two years afterwards, A.D. 607, he captured Harran (Carrhse), Ras-el-ain (Resaina), and Edessa, the capital of Osrhoene, after which he pressed forward to the Euphrates, crossed with his army into Syria, and fell with fury on the Roman cities west of the river. Mabog or Hierapolis, Kenneserin, and Berhoea (now Aleppo), were invested and taken in the course of one or at most two campaigns; while at the same time (A.D. 609) a second Persian army, under a general whose name is unknown, after operating in Armenia, and taking Satala and Theodosiopolis, invaded Cappadocia and threatened the great city of Caesarea Mazaca, which was the chief Roman stronghold in these parts. Bands of marauders wasted the open country, carrying terror through the fertile districts of Phyrgia and Galatia, which had known nothing of the horrors of war for centuries, and were rich with the accumulated products of industry. According to Theophanes, some of the ravages even penetrated as far as Chalcedon, on the opposite side of the straits from Constantinople; but this is probably the anticipation of an event belonging to a later time. No movements of importance are assigned to A.D. 610; but in the May of the next year the Persians once more crossed the Euphrates, completely defeated and destroyed the Roman army which protected Syria, and sacked the two great cities of Apameia and Antioch.

Meantime a change had occurred at Constantinople. The double revolt of Heraclius, prefect of Egypt, and Gregory, his lieutenant, had brought the reign of the brutal and incapable Phocas to an end, and placed upon the imperial throne a youth of promise, innocent of the blood of Maurice, and well inclined to avenge it. Chosroes had to consider whether he should adhere to his original statement, that he took up arms to punish the murderer of his friend, and benefactor, and consequently desist from further hostilities now that Phocas was dead, or whether, throwing consistency to the winds, he should continue to prosecute the war, notwithstanding the change of rulers, and endeavor to push to the utmost the advantage which he had already obtained. He resolved on this latter alternative. It was while the young Heraclius was still insecure in his seat that he sent his armies into Syria, defeated the Roman troops, and took Antioch and Apameia. Following up blow with blow, he next year (A.D. 612) invaded Cappadocia a second time and captured Csesarea Mazaca. Two years later (A.D. 614) he sent his general Shahr-Barz, into the region east of the Antilibanus, and took the ancient and famous city of Damascus. From Damascus, in the ensuing year, Shahr-Barz advanced against Palestine, and, summoning the Jews to his aid, proclaimed a Holy War against the Christian misbelievers, whom he threatened to enslave or exterminate. Twenty-six thousand of these fanatics flocked to his standard; and having occupied the Jordan region and Galileee, Shahr-Barz in A.D. 615 invested Jerusalem, and after a siege of eighteen days forced his way into the town, and gave it over to plunder and rapine. The cruel hostility of the Jews had free vent. The churches of Helena, of Constantine, of the Holy Sepulchre, of the Resurrection, and many others, were burnt or ruined; the greater part of the city was destroyed; the sacred treasuries were plundered; the relics scattered or carried off; and a massacre of the inhabitants, in which the Jews took the chief part, raged throughout the whole city for some days. As many as seventeen thousand or, according to another account, ninety thousand, were slain. Thirty-five thousand were made prisoners. Among them was the aged Patriarch, Zacharius, who was carried captive into Persia, where he remained till his death.

The Cross found by Helena, and believed to be "the True Cross," was at the same time transported to Ctesiphon, where it was preserved with care and duly venerated by the Christian wife of Chosroes.

A still more important success followed. In A.D. 616 Shahr-Barz proceeded from Palestine into Egypt, which had enjoyed a respite from foreign war since the time of Julius Caesar. surprised Pelusium, the key of the country, and, pressing forward across the Delta, easily made himself master of the rich and prosperous Alexandria. John the Merciful, who was the Patriarch, and Nicetas the Patrician, who was the governor, had quitted the city before his arrival, and had fled to Cyprus. Hence scarcely any resistance was made. The fall of Alexandria was followed at once by the complete submission of the rest of Egypt. Bands of Persians advanced up the Nile valley to the very confines of Ethiopia, and established the authority of Chosroes over the whole country—a country in which no Persian had set foot since it was wrested by Alexander of Macedon from Darius Codomannus.

While this remarkable conquest was made in the southwest, in the north-west another Persian army under another general, Saina or Shahen, starting from Cappadocia, marched through Asia Minor to the shores of the Thracian Bosphorus, and laid siege to the strong city of Chalcedon, which lay upon the strait, just opposite Constantinople. Chalcedon made a vigorous resistance; and Heraclius, anxious to save it, had an interview with Shahen, and at his suggestion sent three of his highest nobles as ambassadors to Chosroes, with a humble request for peace. The overture was ineffectual. Chosroes imprisoned the ambassadors and entreated them cruelly; threatened Shahen with death for not bringing Heraclius in chains to the foot of his throne; and declared in reply that he would grant no terms of peace—the empire was his, and Heraclius must descend from his throne. Soon afterwards (A.D. 617) Chalcedon, which was besieged through the winter, fell; and the Persians established themselves in this important stronghold, within a mile of Constantinople. Three years afterwards, Ancyra (Angora), which had hitherto resisted the Persian arms, was taken; and Rhodes, though inaccessible to an enemy who was without a naval force, submitted.

Thus the whole of the Roman possessions in Asia and Eastern Africa were lost in the space of fifteen years. The empire of Persia was extended from the Tigris and Euphrates to the Egean and the Nile, attaining once more almost the same dimensions that it had reached under the first and had kept until the third Darius. It is difficult to say how far their newly acquired provinces wore really subdued, organized, and governed from Ctesiphon, how far they were merely overrun, plundered, and then left to themselves. On the one hand, we have indications of the existence of terrible disorders and of something approaching to anarchy in parts of the conquered territory during the time that it was held by the Persians; on the other, we seem to see an intention to retain, to govern, and even to beautify it. Eutychius relates that, on the withdrawal of the Romans from Syria, the Jews resident in Tyre, who numbered four thousand, plotted with their co-religionists of Jerusalem, Cyprus, Damascus, and Galilee, a general massacre of the Tyrian Christians on a certain day. The plot was discovered; and the Jews of Tyre were arrested and imprisoned by their fellow-citizens, who put the city in a state of defence; and when the foreign Jews, to the number of 26,000, came at the appointed time, repulsed them from the walls, and defeated them with great slaughter. This story suggests the idea of a complete and general disorganization. But on the other hand we hear of an augmentation of the revenue under Chosroes II., which seems to imply the establishment in the regions conquered of a settled government; and the palace at Mashita, discovered by a recent traveller, is a striking proof that no temporary occupation was contemplated, but that Chosroes regarded his conquests as permanent acquisitions, and meant to hold them and even visit them occasionally.

Heraclius was now well-nigh driven to despair. The loss of Egypt reduced Constantinople to want, and its noisy populace clamored for food. The Avars overran Thrace, and continually approached nearer to the capital. The glitter of the Persian arms was to be seen at any moment, if he looked from his palace windows across the Bosphorus. No prospect of assistance or relief appeared from any quarter. The empire was reduced to the walls of Constantinople, with the remnant of Greece, Italy, and Africa, and some maritime cities, from Tyre to Trebizond, of the Asiatic Coast. It is not surprising that under the circumstances the despondent monarch determined on flight, and secretly made arrangements for transporting himself and his treasures to the distant Carthage, where he might hope at least to find himself in safety. His ships, laden with their precious freight, had put to sea, and he was about to follow them, when his intention became known or was suspected; the people rose; and the Patriarch, espousing their side, forced the reluctant prince to accompany him to the church of St. Sophia, and there make oath that, come what might, he would not separate his fortunes from those of the imperial city.

Baffled in his design to escape from his difficulties by flight, Heraclius took a desperate resolution. He would leave Constantinople to its fate, trust its safety to the protection afforded by its walls and by the strait which separated it from Asia, embark with such troops as he could collect, and carry the war into the enemy's country. The one advantage which he had over his adversary was his possession of an ample navy, and consequent command of the sea and power to strike his blows unexpectedly in different quarters. On making known his intention, it was not opposed, either by the people or by the Patriarch. He was allowed to coin the treasures of the various churches into money, to collect stores, enroll troops, and, on the Easter Monday of A.D. 622, to set forth on his expedition.

His fleet was steered southward, and, though forced to contend with adverse gales, made a speedy and successful voyage through the Propontis, the Hellespont, the Egean, and the Cilician Strait, to the Gulf of Issus, in the angle between Asia Minor and Syria. The position was well chosen, as one where attack was difficult, where numbers would give little advantage, and where consequently a small but resolute force might easily maintain itself against a greatly superior enemy. At the same time it was a post from which an advance might conveniently be made in several directions, and which menaced almost equally Asia Minor, Syria, and Armenia. Moreover, the level tract between the mountains and the sea was broad enough for the manoeuvres of such an army as Heraclius commanded, and allowed him to train his soldiers by exercises and sham fights to a familiarity with the sights and sounds and movements of a battle. He conjectured, rightly enough, that he would not long be left unmolested by the enemy. Shahr-Barz, the conqueror of Jerusalem and Egypt, was very soon sent against him; and, after various movements, which it is impossible to follow, a battle was fought between the two armies in the mountain country towards the Armenian frontier, in which the hero of a hundred fights was defeated and the Romans, for the first time since the death of Maurice, obtained a victory. After this, on the approach of winter, Heraclius, accompanied probably by a portion of his army, returned by sea to Constantinople.

The next year the attack was made in a different quarter. Having concluded alliances with the Khan of the Khazars and some other chiefs of inferior power, Heraclius in the month of March embarked with 5000 men, and proceeded from Constantinople by way of the Black Sea first to Trebizond, and then to Mingrelia or Lazica. There he obtained contingents from his allies, which, added to the forces collected from Trebizond and the other maritime towns, may perhaps have raised his troops to the number of 120,000, at which we find them estimated. With this army, he crossed the Araxes, and invaded Armenia. Chosroes, on receiving the intelligence, proceeded into Azerbijan with 40,000 men, and occupied the strong city of Canzaca, the site of which is probably marked by the ruins known as Takht-i-Suleiman. At the same time he ordered two other armies, which he had sent on in advance, one of them commanded by Shahr-Barz, the other by Shahen, to effect a junction and oppose themselves to the further progress of the emperor. The two generals were, however, tardy in their movements, or at any rate were outstripped by the activity of Heraclius, who, pressing forward from Armenia into Azerbijan, directed his march upon Canzaca, hoping to bring the Great King to a battle. His advance-guard of Saracens did actually surprise the picquets of Chosroes; but the king himself hastily evacuated the Median stronghold, and retreated southwards through Ardelan towards the Zagros mountains, thus avoiding the engagement which was desired by his antagonist. The army, on witnessing the flight of their monarch, broke up and dispersed. Heraclius pressed upon the flying host and slew all whom he caught, but did not suffer himself to be diverted from his main object, which was to overtake Chosroes. His pursuit, however, was unsuccessful. Chosroes availed himself of the rough and difficult country which lies between Azerbijan and the Mesopotamian lowland, and by moving from place to place contrive to baffle his enemy. Winter arrived, and Heraclius had to determine whether he would continue his quest at the risk of having to pass the cold season in the enemy's country, far from all his resources, or relinquish it and retreat to a safe position. Finding his soldiers divided in their wishes, he trusted the decision to chance, and opening the Gospel at random settled the doubt by applying the first passage that met his eye to its solution. The passage suggested retreat; and Heraclius, retracing his steps, recrossed the Araxes, and wintered in Albania.

The return of Heraclius was not unmolested. He had excited the fanaticism of the Persians by destroying, wherever he went, the temples of the Magians, and extinguishing the sacred fire, which it was a part of their religion to keep continually burning. He had also everywhere delivered the cities and villages to the flames, and carried off many thousands of the population. The exasperated enemy consequently hung upon his rear, impeded his march, and no doubt caused him considerable loss, though, when it came to fighting, Heraclius always gained the victory. He reached Albania without sustaining any serious disaster, and even brought with him 50,000 captives; but motives of pity, or of self-interest, caused him soon afterwards to set these prisoners free. It would have been difficult to feed and house them through the long and severe winter, and disgraceful to sell or massacre them.

In the year A.D. 624 Chosroes took the offensive, and, before Heraclius had quitted his winter quarters, sent a general, at the head of a force of picked troops, into Albania, with the view of detaining him in that remote province during the season of military operations. But Sarablagas feared his adversary too much to be able very effectually to check his movements; he was content to guard the passes, and hold the high ground, without hazarding an engagement. Heraclius contrived after a time to avoid him, and penetrated into Persia through a series of plains, probably those along the course and about the mouth of the Araxes. It was now his wish to push rapidly southward; but the auxiliaries on whom he greatly depended were unwilling; and, while he doubted what course to take, three Persian armies, under commanders of note, closed in upon him, and threatened his small force with destruction. Heraclius feigned a disordered flight, and drew on him an attack from two out of the three chiefs, which he easily repelled. Then he fell upon the third, Shahen, and completely defeated him. A way seemed to be thus opened for him into the heart of Persia, and he once more set off to seek Chosroes; but now his allies began to desert his standard, and return to their homes; the defeated Persians rallied and impeded his march; he was obliged to content himself with a third, victory, at a place which Theophanes calls Salban, where he surprised Shahr-Barz in the dead of the night, massacred his troops, his wives, his officers, and the mass of the population, which fought from the flat roofs of the houses, took the general's arms and equipage, and was within a little of capturing Shahr-barz himself. The remnant of the Persian army fled in disorder, and was hunted down by Heraclius, who pursued the fugitives unceasingly till the cold season approached, and he had to retire into cantonments. The half-burnt Salban afforded a welcome shelter to his troops during the snows and storms of an Armenian winter.

Early in the ensuing spring the indefatigable emperor again set his troops in motion, and, passing the lofty range which separates the basin of Lake Van from the streams that flow into the upper Tigris, struck that river, or rather its large affluent, the Bitlis Chai, in seven days from Salban, crossed into Arzanene, and proceeding westward recovered Martyropolis and Amida, which had now been in the possession of the Persians for twenty years. At Amida he made a halt, and wrote to inform the Senate of Constantinople of his position and his victories, intelligence which they must have received gladly after having lost sight of him for above a twelvemonth. But he was not allowed to remain long undisturbed. Before the end of March Shahr-Barz had again taken the field in force, had occupied the usual passage of the Euphrates, and threatened the line of retreat which Heraclius had looked upon as open to him. Unable to cross the Euphrates by the bridge, which Shahr-barz had broken, the emperor descended the stream till he found a ford, when he transported his army to the other bank, and hastened by way of Samosata and Germanicaea into Cilicia. Here he was once more in his own territory, with the sea close at hand, ready to bring him supplies or afford him a safe retreat, in a position with whose advantages he was familiar, where broad plains gave an opportunity for skilful maneuvers, and deep rapid rivers rendered defence easy. Heraclius took up a position on the right bank of the Sarus (Syhuri), in the immediate vicinity of the fortified bridge by which alone the stream could be crossed. Shahr-Barz followed, and ranged his troops along the left bank, placing the archers in the front line, while he made preparations to draw the enemy from the defence of the bridge into the plain on the other side. He was so far successful that the Roman occupation of the bridge was endangered; but Heraclius, by his personal valor and by almost superhuman exertions, restored the day; with his own hand he struck down a Persian of gigantic stature and flung him from the bridge into the river; then pushing on with a few companions, he charged the Persian host in the plain, receiving undaunted a shower of blows, while he dealt destruction on all sides. The fight was prolonged until the evening and even then was undecided; but Shahr-Barz had convinced himself that he could not renew the combat with any prospect of victory. He therefore retreated during the night, and withdrew from Cilicia. Heraclius, finding himself free to march where he pleased, crossed the Taurus, and proceeded to Sebaste (Sivas), upon the Halys, where he wintered in the heart of Cappadocia, about half-way between the two seas. According to Theophanes the Persian monarch was so much enraged at this bold and adventurous march, and at the success which had attended it, that, by way of revenging himself on Heraclius, he seized the treasures of all the Christian churches in his dominions, and compelled the orthodox believers to embrace the Nestorian heresy. The twenty-fourth year of the war had now arrived, and it was difficult to say on which side lay the balance of advantage. If Chosroes still maintained his hold on Syria, Egypt, and Asia Minor as far as Chalcedon, if his troops still flaunted their banners within sight of Constantinople, yet on the other hand he had seen his hereditary dominions deeply penetrated by the armies of his adversary; he had had his best generals defeated, his cities and palaces burnt, his favorite provinces wasted; Heraclius had proved himself a most formidable opponent; and unless some vital blow could be dealt him at home, there was no forecasting the damage that he might not inflict on Persia by a fresh invasion. Chosroes therefore made a desperate attempt to bring the war to a close by an effort, the success of which would have changed the history of the world. Having enrolled as soldiers, besides Persians, a vast number of foreigners and slaves, and having concluded a close alliance with the Khan of the Avars, he formed two great armies, one of which was intended to watch Heraclius in Asia Minor, while the other co-operated with the Avars and forced Constantinople to surrender. The army destined to contend with the emperor was placed under the command of Shahen; that which was to bear a part in the siege of Constantinople was committed to Shahr-Barz. It is remarkable that Heraclius, though quite aware of his adversary's plans, instead of seeking to baffle them, made such arrangements as facilitated the attempt to put them into execution. He divided his own troops into three bodies, one only of which he sent to aid in the defence of his capital. The second body he left with his brother Theodore, whom he regarded as a sufficient match for Shahen. With the third division he proceeded eastward to the remote province of Lazica, and there engaged in operations which could but very slightly affect the general course of the war. The Khazars were once more called in as allies; and their Khan, Ziebel, who coveted the plunder of Tiflis, held an interview with the emperor in the sight of the Persians who guarded that town, adored his majesty, and received from his hands the diadem that adorned his own brow. Richly entertained, and presented with all the plate used in the banquet, with a royal robe, and a pair of pearl earrings, promised moreover the daughter of the emperor (whose portrait he was shown) in marriage, the barbarian chief, dazzled and flattered, readily concluded an alliance, and associated his arms with those of the Romans. A joint attack was made upon Tiflis, and the town was reduced to extremities; when Sarablagas, with a thousand men, contrived to throw himself into it, and the allies, disheartened thereby, raised the siege and retired.

Meanwhile, in Asia Minor, Theodore engaged the army of Shahen; and, a violent hailstorm raging at the time, which drove into the enemy's face, while the Romans were, comparatively speaking, sheltered from its force, he succeeded in defeating his antagonist with great slaughter. Chosroes was infuriated; and the displeasure of his sovereign weighed so heavily upon the mind of Shahen that he shortly afterwards sickened and died. The barbarous monarch gave orders that his corpse should be embalmed and sent to the court, in order that he might gratify his spleen by treating it with the grossest indignity.

At Constantinople the Persian cause was equally unsuccessful. Shahr-Barz, from Chalcedon, entered into negotiations with the Khan of the Avars, and found but little difficulty in persuading him to make an attempt upon the imperial city. From their seats beyond the Danube a host of barbarians—Avars, Slaves, Gepidas, Bulgarians, and others—advanced through the passes of Heemus into the plains of Thrace, destroying and ravaging. The population fled before them and sought the protection of the city walls, which had been carefully strengthened in expectation of the attack, and were in good order. The hordes forced the outer works; but all their efforts, though made both by land and sea, were unavailing against the main defences; their attempt to sap the wall failed; their artillery was met and crushed by engines of greater power; a fleet of Slavonian canoes, which endeavored to force an entrance by the Golden Horn, was destroyed or driven ashore; the towers with which they sought to overtop the walls were burnt; and, after ten days of constantly repeated assaults, the barbarian leader became convinced that he had undertaken an impossible enterprise, and, having burnt his engines and his siege works, he retired. The result might have been different had the Persians, who were experienced in the attack of walled places, been able to co-operate with him; but the narrow channel which flowed between Chalcedon and the Golden Horn proved an insurmountable barrier; the Persians had no ships, and the canoes of the Slavonians were quite unable to contend with the powerful galleys of the Byzantines, so that the transport of a body of Persian troops from Asia to Europe by their aid proved impracticable. Shahr-Barz had the annoyance of witnessing the efforts and defeat of his allies, without having it in his power to take any active steps towards assisting the one or hindering the other.

The war now approached its termination; for the last hope of the Persians had failed; and Heraclius, with his mind set at rest as regarded his capital, was free to strike at any part of Persia that he pleased, and, having the prestige of victory and the assistance of the Khazars, was likely to carry all before him. It is not clear how he employed himself during the spring and summer of A.D. 627; but in the September of that year he started from Lazica with a large Roman army and a contingent of 40,000 Khazar horse, resolved to surprise his adversary by a winter campaign, and hoping to take him at a disadvantage. Passing rapidly through Armenia and Azerbijan without meeting an enemy that dared to dispute his advance, suffering no loss except from the guerilla warfare of some bold spirits among the mountaineers of those regions, he resolved, notwithstanding the defection of the Khazars, who declined to accompany him further south than Azerbijan, that he would cross the Zagros mountains into Assyria, and make a dash at the royal cities of the Mesopotamian region, thus retaliating upon Chosroes for the Avar attack upon Constantinople of the preceding year, undertaken at his instigation. Chosroes himself had for the last twenty-four years fixed his court at Dastagherd in the plain country, about seventy miles to the north of Ctesiphon. It seemed to Heraclius that this position might perhaps be reached, and an effective blow struck against the Persian power. He hastened, therefore, to cross the mountains; and the 9th of October saw him at Chnaethas, in the low country, not far from Arbela, where he refreshed his army by a week's rest. He might now easily have advanced along the great post-road which connected Arbela with Dastagherd and Ctesiphon; but he had probably by this time received information of the movements of the Persians, and was aware that by so doing he would place himself between two fires, and run the chance of being intercepted in his retreat. For Chosroes, having collected a large force, had sent it, under Ehazates, a new general, into Azerbijan; and this force, having reached Canzaca, found itself in the rear of Heraclius, between him and Lazica. Heraclius appears not to have thought it safe to leave this enemy behind him, and therefore he idled away above a month in the Zab region, waiting for Ehazates to make his appearance. That general had strict orders from the Great King to fight the Romans wherever he found them, whatever might be the consequence; and he therefore followed, as quickly as he could, upon Heraclius's footsteps, and early in December came up with him in the neighborhood of Nineveh. Both parties were anxious for an immediate engagement, Rhazates to carry out his master's orders, Heraclius because he had heard that his adversary would soon receive a reinforcement. The battle took place on the 12th of December, in the open plain to the north of Nineveh. It was contested from early dawn to the eleventh hour of the day, and was finally decided, more by the accident that Rhazates and the other Persian commanders were slain, than by any defeat of the soldiers. Heraclius is said to have distinguished himself personally during the fight by many valiant exploits; but he does not appear to have exhibited any remarkable strategy on the occasion. The Persians lost their generals, their chariots, and as many as twenty-eight standards; but they were not routed, nor driven from the field. They merely drew off to the distance of two bowshots, and there stood firm till after nightfall. During the night they fell back further upon their fortified camp, collected their baggage, and retired to a strong position at the foot of the mountains. Here they were joined by the reinforcement which Chosroes had sent to their aid; and thus strengthened they ventured to approach Heraclius once more, to hang on his rear, and impede his movements. He, after his victory, had resumed his march southward, had occupied Nineveh, recrossed the Groat Zab, advanced rapidly through Adiabene to the Lesser Zab, seized its bridges by a forced march of forty-eight (Roman) miles, and conveyed his army safely to its left bank, where he pitched his camp at a place called Yesdem, and once more allowed his soldiers a brief repose for the purpose of keeping Christmas. Chosroes had by this time heard of the defeat and death of Rhazates, and was in a state of extreme alarm. Hastily recalling Shahr-Barz from Chalcedon, and ordering the troops lately commanded by Rhazates to outstrip the Romans, if possible, and interpose themselves between Heraclius and Dastaghord, he took up a strong position near that place with his own army and a number of elephants, and expressed an intention of there awaiting his antagonist. A broad and deep river, or rather canal, known as the Baras-roth or Barazrud, protected his front; while at some distance further in advance was the Torna, probably another canal, where he expected that the army of Rhazates would make a stand. But that force, demoralized by its recent defeat, fell back from the line of the Torna, without even destroying the bridge over it; and Chosroes, finding the foe advancing on him, lost heart, and secretly fled from Dastagherd to Ctesiphon, whence he crossed the Tigris to Guedeseer or Seleucia, with his treasure and the best-loved of his wives and children.

The army lately under Rhazates rallied upon the line of the Nahr-wan canal, three miles from Ctesiphon; and here it was largely reinforced, though with a mere worthless mob of slaves and domestics. It made however a formidable show, supported by its elephants, which numbered two hundred; it had a deep and wide cutting in its front; and, this time, it had taken care to destroy all the bridges by which the cutting might have been crossed. Heraclius, having plundered the rich palace of Dastagherd, together with several less splendid royal residences, and having on the 10th of January encamped within twelve miles of the Nahrwan, and learnt from the commander of the Armenian contingent, whom he sent forward to reconnoitre, that the canal was impassable, came to the conclusion that his expedition had reached its extreme limit, and that prudence required him to commence his retreat. The season had been, it would seem, exceptionally mild, and the passes of the mountains were still open; out it was to be expected that in a few weeks they would be closed by the snow, which always falls heavily during some portion of the winter. Heraclius, therefore, like Julian, having come within sight of Ctesiphon, shrank from the idea of besieging it, and, content with the punishment that he had inflicted on his enemy by wasting and devastation, desisted from his expedition, and retraced his steps. In his retreat he was more fortunate than his great predecessor. The defeat which he had inflicted on the main army of the Persians paralyzed their energies, and it would seem that his return march was unmolested. He reached Siazurus (Shehrizur) early in February, Barzan (Berozeh) probably on the 1st of March,176 and on the 11th of March Canzaca, where he remained during the rest of the winter.

Chosroes had escaped a great danger, but he had incurred a terrible disgrace. He had fled before his adversary without venturing to give him battle. He had seen palace after palace destroyed, and had lost the magnificent residence where he had held his court for the last four-and-twenty years. The Romans had recovered 300 standards, trophies gained in the numerous victories of his early years. They had shown themselves able to penetrate into the heart of his empire, and to retire without suffering any loss. Still, had he possessed a moderate amount of prudence, Chosroes might even now have surmounted the perils of his position, and have terminated his reign in tranquillity, if not in glory. Heraclius was anxious for peace, and willing to grant it on reasonable conditions. He did not aim at conquests, and would have been contented at any time with the restoration of Egypt, Syria, and Asia Minor. The Persians generally were weary of the war, and would have hailed with joy almost any terms of accommodation. But Chosroes was obstinate; he did not know how to bear the frowns of fortune; the disasters of the late campaign, instead of bending his spirit, had simply exasperated him, and he vented upon his own subjects the ill-humor which the successes of his enemies had provoked. Lending a too ready ear to a whispered slander, he ordered the execution of Shahr-Barz, and thus mortally offended that general, to whom the despatch was communicated by the Romans. He imprisoned the officers who had been defeated by, or had fled before Heraclius. Several other tyrannical acts are alleged against him; and it is said that he was contemplating the setting aside of his legitimate successor, Siroes, in favor of a younger son, Merdasas, his offspring by his favorite wife, the Christian Shirin, when a rebellion broke out against his authority. Gurdanaspa, who was in command of the Persian troops at Ctesiphon, and twenty-two nobles of importance, including two sons of Shahr-Barz, embraced the cause of Siroes, and seizing Chosroes, who meditated flight, committed him to "the House of Darkness," a strong place where he kept his money. Here he was confined for four days, his jailers allowing him daily a morsel of bread and a small quantity of water; when he complained of hunger, they told him by his son's orders, that he was welcome to satisfy his appetite by feasting upon his treasures. The officers whom he had confined were allowed free access to his prison, where they insulted him and spat upon him. Merdasas, the son whom he preferred, and several of his other children, were brought into his presence and put to death before his eyes. After suffering in this way for four days he was at last, on the fifth day from his arrest (February 28), put to death in some cruel fashion, perhaps, like St. Sebastian, by being transfixed with arrows. Thus perished miserably the second Chosroes, after having reigned thirty-seven years (A.D. 591-628), a just but tardy Nemesis overtaking the parricide.

The Oriental writers represent the second Chosroes as a monarch whose character was originally admirable, but whose good disposition was gradually corrupted by the possession of sovereign power. "Parviz," says Mirkhond, "holds a distinguished rank among the kings of Persia through the majesty and firmness of his government, the wisdom of his views, and his intrepidity in carrying them out, the size of his army, the amount of his treasure, the flourishing condition of the provinces during his reign, the security of the highways, the prompt and exact obedience which he enforced, and his unalterable adherence to the plans which he once formed." It is impossible that these praises can have been altogether undeserved; and we are bound to assign to this monarch, on the authority of the Orientals, a vigor of administration, a strength of will, and a capacity for governing, not very commonly possessed by princes born in the purple. To these merits we may add a certain grandeur of soul, and power of appreciating the beautiful and the magnificent, which, though not uncommon in the East, did not characterize many of the Sassanian sovereigns. The architectural remains of Chosroes, which will be noticed in a future chapter, the descriptions which have come down to us of his palaces at Dastagherd and Canzaca, the accounts which we have of his treasures, his court, his seraglio, even his seals, transcend all that is known of any other monarch of his line. The employment of Byzantine sculptors and architects, which his works are thought to indicate, implies an appreciation of artistic excellence very rare among Orientals. But against these merits must be set a number of most serious moral defects, which may have been aggravated as time went on, but of which we see something more than the germ, even while he was still a youth. The murder of his father was perhaps a state necessity, and he may not have commanded it, or have been accessory to it before the fact; but his ingratitude towards his uncles, whom he deliberately put to death, is wholly unpardonable, and shows him to have been cruel, selfish, and utterly without natural affection, even in the earlier portion of his reign. In war he exhibited neither courage nor conduct; all his main military successes were due to his generals; and in his later years he seems never voluntarily to have exposed himself to danger. In suspecting his generals, and ill-using them while living, he only followed the traditions of his house; but the insults offered to the dead body of Shahen, whose only fault was that he had suffered a defeat, were unusual and outrageous. The accounts given of his seraglio imply either gross sensualism or extreme ostentation; perhaps we may be justified in inclining to the more lenient view, if we take into consideration the faithful attachment which he exhibited towards Shirin. The cruelties which disgraced his later years are wholly without excuse; but in the act which deprived him of his throne, and brought him to a miserable end—his preference of Merdasas as his successor—he exhibited no worse fault than an amiable weakness, a partiality towards the son of a wife who possessed, and seems to have deserved, his affection.

The coins of the second Chosroes are numerous in the extreme, and present several peculiarities. The ordinary type has, on the obverse, the king's head in profile, covered by a tiara, of which the chief ornament is a crescent and star between two outstretched wings. The head is surrounded by a double pearl bordering, outside of which, in the margin, are three crescents and stars. The legend is Khusrui afzud, with a monogram of doubtful meaning. The reverse shows the usual fire altar and supporters, in a rude form, enclosed by a triple pearl bordering. In the margin, outside the bordering, are four crescents and stars. The legend is merely the regnal year and a mint-mark. Thirty-four mint-marks have been ascribed to Chosroes II. [PLATE XXIII., Fig. 4.]

A rarer and more curious type of coin, belonging to this monarch, presents on the obverse the front face of the king, surmounted by a mural crown, having the star and crescent between outstretched wings at top. The legend is Khusrui mallean malka—afzud. "Chosroes, king of kings—increase (be his)." The reverse has a head like that of a woman, also fronting the spectator, and wearing a band enriched with pearls across the forehead, above which the hair gradually converges to a point. [PLATE XXIV., Fig. 1.] A head very similar to this is found on Indo-Sassanian coins. Otherwise we might have supposed that the uxorious monarch had wished to circulate among his subjects the portrait of his beloved Shirin.

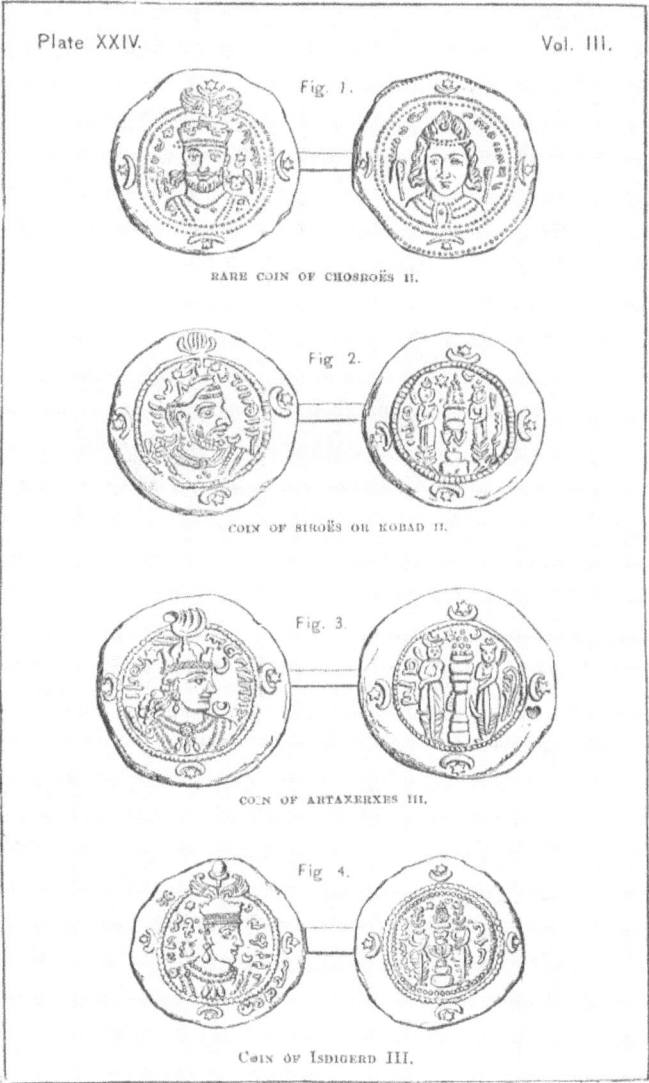

Plate XXIV.                    Vol. III.

Fig. 1.

RARE COIN OF CHOSROËS II.

Fig 2.

COIN OF SIROËS OR KOBAD II.

Fig. 3.

COIN OF ARTAXERXES III.

Fig 4.

COIN OF ISDIGERD III.

PLATE XXIV

CHAPTER XXV

*Accession of Siroe's, or Kobad II. His Letter to Heraclius. Peace made with Rome. Terms of the Peace. General Popularity of the new Reign. Dissatisfaction of Shahr-Barz. Kobad, by the advice of the Persian Lords, murders his Brothers. His Sisters reproach him with their Death. He falls into low spirits and dies. Pestilence in his Reign. His coins. Accession of Artaxerxes III. Revolt of Shahr-Barz. Reign of Shahr-Barz. His Murder. Reign of Purandocht. Rapid Succession of Pretenders. Accession of Isdigerd III.*

*"Kobades, regno prefectus, justitiam prae se tulit, et injuriam qua oppressa fuerat movit."*
—*Eutychius, Annales, vol, ii. p. 253.*

Siroes, or Kobad the Second, as he is more properly termed, was proclaimed king on the 25th of February, 2 A.D. 628, four days before the murder of his father. According to the Oriental writers, he was very unwilling to put his father to death, and only gave a reluctant consent to his execution on the representations of his nobles that it was a state of necessity. His first care, after this urgent matter had been settled, was to make overtures of peace to Heraclius, who, having safely crossed the Zagros mountains, was wintering at Canzaca. The letter which he addressed to the Roman Emperor on the occasion is partially extant; but the formal and official tone which it breathes renders it a somewhat disappointing document. Kobad begins by addressing Heraclius as his brother, and giving him the epithet of "most clement," thus assuming his pacific disposition. He then declares, that, having been elevated to the throne by the especial favor of God, he has resolved to do his utmost to benefit and serve the entire human race. He has therefore commenced his reign by throwing open the prison doors, and restoring liberty to all who were detained in custody. With the same object in view, he is desirous of living in peace and friendship with the Roman emperor and state as well as with all other neighboring nations and kings. Assuming that his accession will be pleasing to the emperor, he has sent Phaeak, one of his privy councillors, to express the love and friendship that he feels towards his brother, and learn the terms upon which peace will be granted him. The reply of Heraclius is lost; but we are able to gather from a short summary which has been preserved, as well as from the subsequent course of events, that it was complimentary and favorable; that it expressed the willingness of the emperor to bring the war to a close, and suggested terms of accommodation that were moderate and equitable. The exact formulation of the treaty seems to have been left to Eustathius, who, after Heraclius had entertained Phaeak royally for nearly a week, accompanied the ambassador on his return to the Persian court.

The general principle upon which peace was concluded was evidently the status quo ante bellum. Persia was to surrender Egypt, Palestine, Syria, Asia Minor, Western Mesopotamia, and any other conquests that she might have made from Rome, to recall her troops from them, and to give them back into the possession of the Romans. She was also to surrender all the captives whom she had carried off from the conquered countries; and, above all, she was to give back to the Romans the precious relic which had been taken from Jerusalem, and which was believed on all hands to be the veritable cross whereon Jesus Christ suffered death. As Rome had merely made inroads, but not conquests, she did not possess any territory to surrender; but she doubtless set her Persian prisoners free, and she made arrangements for the safe conduct and honorable treatment of the Persians, who evacuated Syria, Egypt, and Asia Minor, on their way to the frontier. The evacuation was at once commenced; and the wood of the cross, which had been carefully preserved by the Persian queen, Shirin, was restored. In the next year, Heraclius made a grand pilgrimage to Jerusalem, and replaced the holy relic in the shrine from which it had been taken.

It is said that princes are always popular on their coronation day. Kobad was certainly no exception to the general rule. His subjects rejoiced at the termination of a war which had always been a serious drain on the population, and which latterly had brought ruin and desolation upon the hearths and homes of thousands. The general emptying of the prisons was an act that cannot be called statesman-like; but it had a specious appearance of liberality, and was probably viewed with favor by the mass of the people. A still more popular measure must have been the complete remission of taxes with which Kobad inaugurated his reign—a remission which, according to one authority, was to have continued for three years, had the generous prince lived so long. In addition to these somewhat questionable proceedings, Kobad adopted also a more legitimate mode of securing the regard of his subjects by a careful administration of justice, and a mild treatment of those who had been the victims of his father's severities. He restored to their former rank the persons whom Chosroes had degraded or imprisoned, and compensated them for their injuries by a liberal donation of money.

Thus far all seemed to promise well for the new reign, which, though it had commenced under unfavorable auspices, bid fair to be tranquil and prosperous. In one quarter only was there any indication of coming troubles. Shahr-Barz, the great general, whose life Chosroes had attempted shortly before his own death, appears to have been dissatisfied with the terms on which Kobad had concluded peace with Rome; and there is even reason to believe that he contrived to impede and delay the full execution of the treaty. He held under Kobad the government of the western provinces and was at the head of an army which numbered sixty thousand men. Kobad treated him with marked favor; but still he occupied a position almost beyond that of a subject, and one which could not fail to render him an object of fear and suspicion. For the present, however, though he may have nurtured ambitious thoughts, he made no movement, but bided his time, remaining quietly in his province, and cultivating friendly relations with the Roman emperor.

Kobad had not been seated on the throne many months when he consented to a deed by which his character for justice and clemency was seriously compromised, if not wholly lost. This was the general massacre of all the other sons of Chosroes II., his own brothers or half-brothers—a numerous body, amounting to forty according to the highest estimate, and to fifteen according to the lowest. We are not told of any circumstances of peril to justify the deed, or even account for it. There have been Oriental dynasties, where such a wholesale murder upon the accession of a sovereign has been a portion of the established system of government, and others where the milder but little less revolting expedient has obtained of blinding all the brothers of the reigning prince; but neither practice was in vogue among the Sassanians; and we look vainly for the reason which caused an act of the kind to be resorted to at this conjuncture. Mirkhond says that Piruz, the chief minister of Kobad, advised the deed; but even he assigns no motive for the massacre, unless a motive is implied in the statement that the brothers of Kobad were "all of them distinguished by their talents and their merit." Politically speaking, the measure might have been harmless, had Kobad enjoyed a long reign, and left behind him a number of sons. But as it was, the rash act, by almost extinguishing the race of Sassan, produced troubles which greatly helped to bring the empire into a condition of hopeless exhaustion and weakness.

While thus destroying all his brothers, Kobad allowed his sisters to live. Of these there were two, still unmarried, who resided in the palace, and had free access to the monarch. Their names were Purandocht and Azermidocht, Purandocht being the elder. Bitterly grieved at the loss of their kindred, these two princesses rushed into the royal presence, and reproached the king with words that cut him to the soul. "Thy ambition of ruling," they said, "has induced thee to kill thy father and thy brothers. Thou hast accomplished thy purpose within the space of three or four months. Thou hast hoped thereby to preserve thy power forever. Even, however, if thou shouldst live long, thou must die at last. May God deprive thee of the enjoyment of this royalty!" His sisters' words sank deep into the king's mind. He acknowledged their justice, burst into tears, and flung his crown on the ground. After this he fell into a profound melancholy, ceased to care for the exercise of power, and in a short time died. His death is ascribed by the Orientals to his mental sufferings; but the statement of a Christian bishop throws some doubt on this romantic story. Eutychius, Patriarch of Alexandria, tells us that, before Kobad had reigned many months, the plague broke out in his country. Vast numbers of his subjects died of it; and among the victims was the king himself, who perished after a reign which is variously estimated at six, seven, eight, and eighteen months.

There seems to be no doubt that a terrible pestilence did afflict Persia at this period. The Arabian writers are here in agreement with Eutychius of Alexandria, and declare that the malady was of the most aggravated character, carrying off one half, or at any rate one third, of the inhabitants of the provinces which were affected, and diminishing the population of Persia by several hundreds of thousands. Scourges of this kind are of no rare occurrence in the East; and the return of a mixed multitude to Persia, under circumstances involving privation, from the cities of Asia Minor, Syria, and Palestine, was well calculated to engender such a calamity.

The reign of Kobad II. appears from his coins to have lasted above a year. He ascended the throne in February, A.D. 628; he probably died about July, A.D. 629. The coins which are attributed to him resemble in their principal features those of Ohosroes II. and Artaxerxes III., but are without wings, and have the legend Kavat-Firuz. The bordering of pearls is single on both obverse and reverse, but the king wears a double pearl necklace. The eye is large, and the hair more carefully marked than had been usual since the time of Sapor II. [PLATE XXIV., Figs. 2 and 3].

At the death of Kobad the crown fell to his son, Artaxerxes III., a child of seven, or (according to others) of one year only. The nobles who proclaimed him took care to place him under the direction of a governor or regent, and appointed to the office a certain Mihr-Hasis, who had been the chief purveyor of Kobad. Mihr-Hasis is said to have ruled with justice and discretion; but he was not able to prevent the occurrence of those troubles and disorders which in the East almost invariably accompany the sovereignty of a minor, and render the task of a regent a hard one. Shahr-Barz, who had scarcely condescended to comport himself as a subject under Kobad, saw in the accession of a boy, and in the near extinction of the race of Sassan, an opportunity of gratifying his ambition, and at the same time of avenging the wrong which had been done him by Chosroes. Before committing himself, however, to the perils of rebellion, he negotiated with Heraclius, and secured his alliance and support by the promise of certain advantages. The friends met at Heraclea on the Propontis. Shahr-Barz undertook to complete the evacuation of Egypt, Syria, and Asia Minor, which he had delayed hitherto, and promised, if he were successful in his enterprise, to pay Heraclius a large sum of money as compensation for the injuries inflicted on Rome during the recent war. Heraclius conferred on Nicetas, the son of Shahr-Barz, the title of "Patrican," consented to a marriage between Shahr-Barz's daughter, Nike, and his own son, Theodosius, and accepted Gregoria, the daughter of Nicetas, and grand-daughter of Shahr-Barz, as a wife for Constantine, the heir to the empire. He also, it is probable, supplied Shahr-Barz with a body of troops, to assist him in his struggle with Artaxerxes and Mihr-Hasis.

Of the details of Sharhr-Barz's expedition we know nothing. He is said to have marched on Ctesiphon with an army of sixty thousand men; to have taken the city, put to death Artaxerxes, Mihr-Hasis, and a number of the nobles, and then seized the throne. We are not told what resistance was made by the monarch in possession, or how it was overcome, or even whether there was a battle. It would seem certain, however, that the contest was brief. The young king was of course powerless; Mihr-Hasis, though well-meaning, must have been weak; Shahr-Barz had all the rude strength of the animal whose name he bore, and had no scruples about using his strength to the utmost. The murder of a child of two, or at the most of eight, who could have done no ill, and was legitimately in possession of the throne, must be pronounced a brutal act, and one which sadly tarnishes the fair fame, previously unsullied, of one of Persia's greatest generals.

It was easy to obtain the crown, under the circumstances of the time; but it was not so easy to keep what had been wrongfully gained. Shahr-Barz enjoyed the royal authority less than two months. During this period he completed the evacuation of the Roman provinces occupied by Chosroes II., restored perhaps some portions of the true cross which had been kept back by Kobad, and sent an expeditionary force against the Khazars who had invaded Armenia, which was completely destroyed by the fierce barbarians. He is said by the Armenians to have married Purandocht, the eldest daughter of Chosroes, for the purpose of strengthening his hold on the crown; but this attempt to conciliate his subjects, if it was really made, proved unsuccessful. Ere he had been king for two months, his troops mutinied, drew their swords upon him, and killed him in the open court before the palace. Having so done, they tied a cord to his feet and dragged his corpse through the streets of Ctesiphon, making proclamation everywhere as follows: "Whoever, not being of the blood-royal, seats himself upon the Persian throne, shall share the fate of Shahr-Barz." They then elevated to the royal dignity the princess Purandocht, the first female who had ever sat in the seat of Cyrus.

The rule of a woman was ill calculated to restrain the turbulent Persian nobles. Two instances had now proved that a mere noble might ascend the throne of the son of Babek; and a fatal fascination was exercised on the grandees of the kingdom by the examples of Bahram-Chobin and Shahr-Barz.

Pretenders sprang up in all quarters, generally asserting some connection, nearer or more remote, with the royal house, but relying on the arms of their partisans, and still more on the weakness of the government. It is uncertain whether Purandocht died a natural death; her sister, Azermidocht, who reigned soon after her, was certainly murdered. The crown passed rapidly from one noble to another, and in the course of the four or five years which immediately succeeded the death of Chosroes II. it was worn by nine or ten different persons. Of these the greater number reigned but a few days or a few months; no actions are ascribed to them; and it seems unnecessary to weary the reader with their obscure names, or with the still more obscure question concerning the order of their succession. It may be suspected that, in some cases two or more were contemporary, exercising royal functions in different portions of the empire at the same time. Of none does the history or the fate possess any interest; and the modern historical student may well be content with the general knowledge that for four years and a half after the death of Chosroes II. the government was in the highest degree unsettled; anarchy everywhere prevailed; the distracted kingdom was torn in pieces by the struggles of pretenders; and "every province, and almost each city of Persia, was the scene of independence, of discord, and of bloodshed."

At length, in June, A.D. 632, an end was put to the internal commotions by the election of a young prince, believed to be of the true blood of Sassan, in whose rule the whole nation acquiesced without much difficulty. Yezdigerd (or Isdigerd) the Third was the son of Shahriar and the grandson of Chosroes II. He had been early banished from the Court, and had been brought up in obscurity, his royal birth being perhaps concealed, since if known it might have caused his destruction. The place of his residence was Istakr, the ancient capital of Persia, but at this time a city of no great importance. Here he had lived unnoticed to the age of fifteen, when his royal rank having somehow been discovered, and no other scion of the stock of Chosroes being known to exist, he was drawn forth from his retirement and invested with the sovereignty.

But the appointment of a sovereign in whose rule all could acquiesce came too late. While Rome and Persia, engaged in deadly struggle, had no thought for anything but how most to injure each other, a power began to grow up in an adjacent country, which had for long ages been despised and thought incapable of doing any harm to its neighbors. Mohammed, half impostor, half enthusiast, enunciated a doctrine, and by degrees worked out a religion, which proved capable of uniting in one the scattered tribes of the Arabian desert, while at the same time it inspired them with a confidence, a contempt for death, and a fanatic valor, that rendered them irresistible by the surrounding nations.

Mohammed's career as prophet began while Heraclius and Chosroes II. were flying at each other's throats; by the year of the death of Chosroes (A.D. 628) he had acquired a strength greater than that of any other Arab chief; two years later he challenged Rome to the combat by sending a hostile expedition into Syria; and before his death (A.D. 632) he was able to take the field at the head of 30,000 men. During the time of internal trouble in Persia he procured the submission of the Persian governor of the Yemen; as well as that of Al Mondar, or Alamundarus, King of Bahrein, on the west coast of the Persian Gulf. Isdigerd, upon his accession, found himself menaced by a power which had already stretched out one arm towards the lower Euphrates, while with the other it was seeking to grasp Syria and Palestine. The danger was imminent; the means of meeting it insufficient, for Persia was exhausted by foreign war and internal contention; the monarch himself was but ill able to cope with the Arab chiefs, being youthful and inexperienced; we shall find, however, that he made a strenuous resistance. Though continually defeated, he prolonged the fight for nearly a score of years, and only succumbed finally when, to the hostility of open foes, was added the treachery of pretended friends and allies.

CHAPTER XXVI

*Death of Mohammed and Collapse of Mohammedanism. Recovery under Abu-bekr. Conquest of the Kingdom of Hira. Conquest of Obolla. Invasion of Mesopotamia. Battle of the Bridge—the Arabs suffer a Reverse. Battle of El Bow-eib—Mihran defeated by El Mothanna. Fresh Effort made by Persia—Battle of Cadesia—Defeat of the Persians. Pause in the War. March of Sa'ad on Ctesiphon. Flight of Isdigerd. Capture of Ctesiphon. Battle of Jalula. Conquest of Susiana and invasion of Persia Proper. Recall of Sa'ad. Isdigerd assembles an Army at Nehawend. Battle of Nehawend. Flight of Isdigerd. Conquest of the various Persian Provinces. Isdigerd murdered. Character of Isdigerd. Coins of Isdigerd.*

"*Yazdejird, Persarum rex.... Rostamum misit oppugnatum Saadum... neque unquam belloram et dissentionum expers fuit, donee oecideretur. Regnavit autem annos viginti.*"—Eutychius, Annales, vol. ii. pp. 295-6.

The power which Mohammed had so rapidly built up fell to pieces at his decease. Isdigerd can scarcely have been well settled upon this throne when the welcome tidings must have reached him that the Prophet was dead, that the Arabs generally were in revolt, that Al Mondar had renounced Islamism and resumed a position of independence. For the time Mohammedanism was struck down. It remained to be seen whether the movement had derived its strength solely from the genius of the Prophet, or whether minds of inferior calibre would suffice to renew and sustain the impulse which had proceeded from him, and which under him had proved of such wonderful force and efficacy.

The companions of Mohammed lost no time in appointing his successor. Their choice fell upon Abu-bekr, his friend and father-in-law, who was a person of an energetic character, brave, chaste, and temperate. Abu-bekr proved himself quite equal to the difficulties of the situation. Being unfit for war himself, as he was above sixty years of age, he employed able generals, and within a few months of his accession struck such a series of blows that rebellion collapsed everywhere, and in a short time the whole Arab nation, except the tribe of Gassan, acknowledged themselves his subjects. Among the rivals against whom he measured himself, the most important was Moseilama. Moseilama, who affected the prophetic character, had a numerous following, and was able to fight a pitched battle with the forces of Abu-bekr, which numbered 40,000 men. At the first encounter he even succeeded in repulsing this considerable army, which lost 1200 warriors; but in a second engagement the Mohammedans were victorious—Moseilama was slain—and Kaled, "the Sword of

God," carried back to Medina the news of his own triumph, and the spoils of the defeated enemy. Soon after the fall of Moseilama, the tribes still in rebellion submitted themselves, and the first of the Caliphs found himself at liberty to enter upon schemes of foreign conquest.

Distracted between the temptations offered to his arms by the East and by the West, Abu-bekr in his first year (A.D. 633) sent expeditions in both directions, against Syria, and against Hira, where Iyas, the Persian feudatory, who had succeeded Noman, son of Al Mondar, held his court, on the western branch of the Euphrates. For this latter expedition the commander selected was the irresistible Kaled, who marched a body of 2000 men across the desert to the branch stream,s which he reached in about latitude 30°. Assisted by Al Mothanna, chief of the Beni Sheiban, who had been a subject of Iyas, but had revolted and placed himself under the protection of Abu-bekr, Kaled rapidly reduced the kingdom of Hira, took successively Banikiya, Barasuilia, and El Lis, descended the river to the capital, and there fought an important battle with the combined Persian and Arab forces, the first trial of arms between the followers of Mohammed and those of Zoroaster. The Persian force consisted entirely of horse, and was commanded by a general whom the Arab writers call Asadsubeh. Their number is not mentioned, but was probably small. Charged furiously by Al Mothanna, they immediately broke and fled; Hira was left with no other protection than its walls; and Iyas, yielding to necessity, made his submission to the conqueror, and consented to pay a tribute of 290,000 dirhems.

The splendid success of his pioneer induced Abu-bekr to support the war in this quarter with vigor. Reinforcements joined Kaled from every side, and in a short time he found himself at the head of an army of 18,000 men. With this force he proceeded southwards bent on reducing the entire tract between the desert and the Eastern or real Euphrates. The most important city of the southern region was at the time Obolla which was situated on a canal or backwater derived from the Euphrates, not far from the modern Busrah. It was the great emporium for the Indian trade, and was known as the limes Indorum or "frontier city towards India." The Persian governor was a certain Hormuz or Hormisdas who held the post with 20,000 men. Kaled fought his second great battle with this antagonist, and was once more completely victorious, killing Hormuz, according to the Arabian accounts, with his own hands. Obolla surrendered; a vast booty was taken; and, after liberally rewarding his soldiers Kaled sent the fifth part of the spoils, together with a captured elephant, to Abu-bekr at Medina. The strange animal astonished the simple natives, who asked one another wonderingly "Is this indeed one of God's works, or did human art make it."

The victories of Kaled Over Asadsubeh and Hormuz were followed by a number of other successes, the entire result being that the whole of the fertile region on the right bank of the Euphrates from Hit to the Persian Gulf, was for the time reduced, made a portion of Ahu-bekr's dominions, and parcelled out among Mohammedan governors. Persia was deprived of the protection which a dependent Arab kingdom to the west of the river had hitherto afforded her, and was brought into direct contact with the great Mohammedan monarchy along almost the whole of her western frontier. Henceforth she was open to attack on this side for a distance of above four hundred miles, with no better barrier than a couple of rivers interposed between her enemy and her capital.

Soon after his conquest of the kingdom of Hira, Kaled was recalled from the Euphrates to the Syrian war, and was employed in the siege of Damascus, while Persia enjoyed a breathing-space. Advantage was taken of this interval to stir up disaffection in the newly-conquered province. Rustam appointed to the command against the Arabs by Isdigerd sent emissaries to the various towns of the Sawad, urging them to rise in revolt and promising to support such a movement with a Persian army. The situation was critical; and if the Mohammedans had been less tenacious, or the Persians more skilfully handled, the whole of the Sawad might have been recovered. But Rustam allowed his troops to be defeated in detail. Al Mothanna and Abu Obediah, in three separate engagements, at Namarik,

Sakatiya, and Barusma, overcame the Persian leaders, Jaban, Narses, and Jalenus, and drove their shattered armies back on the Tigris. The Mohammedan authority was completely re-established in the tract between the desert and the Euphrates; it was even extended across the Euphrates into the tract watered by the Shat-el-Hie; and it soon became a question whether Persia would be able to hold the Mesopotamian region, or whether the irrepressible Arabs would not very shortly wrest it from her grasp. But at this point in the history the Arabs experienced a severe reverse. On learning the defeat of his lieutenants, Rustam sent an army to watch the enemy, under the command of Bahman-Dsul-hadjib, or "Bahman the beetle-browed," which encamped upon the Western Euphrates at Kossen-natek, not far from the site of Kufa. At the same time, to raise the courage of the soldiers, he entrusted to this leader the sacred standard of Persia, the famous durufsh-kawani, or leathern apron of the blacksmith Kawah, which was richly adorned with silk and gems, and is said to have measured, eighteen feet long by twelve feet broad. Bahman had with him, according to the Persian tradition, 30,000 men and thirty elephants; the Arabs under Abu Obediah numbered no more than 9000, or at the most 10,000. Bahman is reported to have given his adversary the alternative of passing the Euphrates or allowing the Persians to cross it. Abu Obediah preferred the bolder course, and, in spite of the dissuasions of his chief officers, threw a bridge of boats across the stream, and so conveyed his troops to the left bank. Here he found the Persian horse-archers covered with their scale armor, and drawn up in a solid line behind their elephants. Galled severely by the successive flights of arrows, the Arab cavalry sought to come to close quarters; but their horses, terrified by the unwonted sight of the huge animals, and further alarmed by the tinkling of the bells hung round their necks, refused to advance. It was found necessary to dismount, and assail the Persian line on foot. A considerable impression had been made, and it was thought that the Persians would take to flight, when Abu Obediah, in attacking the most conspicuous of the elephants, was seized by the infuriated animal and trampled under his feet. Inspirited by this success, the Persians rushed upon their enemies, who, disheartened by the loss of their commander, began a retrograde movement, falling back upon their newly-made bridge. This, however, was found to have been broken, either by the enemy, or by a rash Arab who thought, by making retreat impossible, to give his own side the courage of despair. Before the damage done could be repaired, the retreating host suffered severely. The Persians pressed closely upon them, slew many, and drove others into the stream, where they were drowned. Out of the 9000 or 10,000 who originally passed the river, only 5000 returned, and of these 2000 at once dispersed to their homes. Besides Abu Obediah, the veteran Salit was slain; and Al Mothanna, who succeeded to the command on Abu Obediah's death, was severely wounded. The last remnant of the defeated army might easily have been destroyed, had not a dissension arisen among the Persians, which induced Bahman to return to Otesiphon.

The Arabs, upon this repulse, retired to El Lis; and Al Mothanna sent to Omar for reinforcements, which speedily arrived under the command of Jarir, son of Abdallah. Al Mothanna was preparing to resume the offensive when the Persians anticipated him. A body of picked troops, led by Mihran a general of reputation, crossed the Euphrates, and made a dash at Hira. Hastily collecting his men, who were widely dispersed, Al Mothanna gave the assailants battle on the canal El Boweib, in the near vicinity of the threatened town, and though the Persians fought with desperation from noon to sunset, succeeded in defeating them and in killing their commander. The beaten army recrossed the Euphrates, and returned to Otesiphon without suffering further losses, since the Arabs were content to have baffled their attack, and did not pursue them many miles from the field of battle. All Mesopotamia, however, was by this defeat laid open to the invaders, whose ravages soon extended to the Tigris and the near vicinity of the capital.

The year A.D. 636 now arrived, and the Persians resolved upon an extraordinary effort. An army of 120,000 men was enrolled, and Rustam, reckoned the best general of the day, was placed at its head. The Euphrates was once more crossed, the Sawad entered, its inhabitants invited to revolt, and the Arab force, which had been concentrated at Cadesia (Kadisiyeh), where it rested upon a fortified town, was sought out and challenged to the combat. The Caliph Omar had by great efforts contrived to raise his troops in the Sawad to the number of 30,000, and had entrusted the command of them to Sa'ad, the son of Wakas, since Al Mothanna had died of his wound. Sa'ad stood wholly on the defensive. His camp was pitched outside the walls of Cadesia, in a position protected on either side by a canal, or branch stream, derived from the Euphrates, and flowing to the south-east out of the Sea of Nedjef. He himself, prevented by boils from sitting on his horse, looked down on his troops, and sent them directions from the Cadesian citadel. Rustam, in order to come to blows, was obliged to fill up the more eastern of the branch streams (El Atik), with reeds and earth, and in this way to cross the channel. The Arabs made no attempt to hinder the operation; and the Persian general, having brought his vast army directly opposite to the enemy, proceeded to array his troops as he thought most expedient. Dividing his army into a centre and two wings, he took himself the position of honor in, the mid-line with nineteen elephants and three fifths of his forces, while he gave the command of the right wing to Jalenus, and of the left to Bendsuwan; each of whom we may suppose to have had 24,000 troops and seven elephants. The Arabs, on their side, made no such division. Kaled, son of Orfuta, was the sole leader in the fight, though Sa'ad from his watch-tower observed the battle and gave his orders. The engagement began at mid-day and continued till sunset. At the signal of Allah akbar, "God is great," shouted by Sa'ad from his tower, the Arabs rushed to the attack. Their cavalry charged; but the Persians advanced against them their line of elephants, repeating with excellent effect the tactics of the famous "Battle of the Bridge." The Arab horse fled; the foot alone remained firm; victory seemed inclining to the Persians, who were especially successful on either wing; Toleicha, with his "lions" failed to re-establish the balance; and all would have been lost, had not Assem, at the command of Sa'ad, sent a body of archers and other footmen to close with the elephants, gall them with missiles, cut their girths, and so precipitate their riders to the ground. Relieved from this danger, the Arab horse succeeded in repulsing the Persians, who as evening approached retired in good order to their camp. The chief loss on this, the "day of concussion," was suffered by the Arabs, who admit that they had 500 killed, and must have had a proportional number of wounded.

On the morning of the second day the site of the battle was somewhat changed, the Persians having retired a little during the night. Reinforcements from Syria kept reaching the Arab camp through most of the day; and hence it is known to the Arab writers as the "day of succors." The engagement seems for some time not to have been general, the Arabs waiting for more troops to reach them, while the Persians abstained because they had not yet repaired the furniture of their elephants. Thus the morning passed in light skirmishes and single combats between the champions of either host, who went out singly before the lines and challenged each other to the encounter. The result of the duels was adverse to the Persians, who lost in the course of them two of their best generals, Bendsuwan and Bahman-Dsulhadjib. After a time the Arabs, regarding themselves as sufficiently reinforced, attacked the Persians along their whole line, partly with horse, and partly with camels, dressed up to resemble elephants. The effect on the Persian cavalry was the same as had on the preceding day been produced by the real elephants on the horse of the Arabs; it was driven off the field and dispersed, suffering considerable losses. But the infantry stood firm, and after a while the cavalry rallied; Rustam, who had been in danger of suffering capture, was saved; and night closing in, defeat was avoided, though the advantage of the day rested clearly with the Arabs. The Persians had lost 10,000 in killed and wounded, the Arabs no more than 2000.

In the night which followed "the day of succors" great efforts were made by the Persians to re-equip their elephants, and when morning dawned they were enabled once more to bring the unwieldy beasts into line. But the Arabs and their horses had now grown more familiar with the strange animals; they no longer shrank from meeting them; and some Persian deserters gave the useful information that, in order to disable the brutes it was only necessary to wound them on the proboscis or in the eye. Thus instructed, the Arabs made the elephants the main object of their attack, and, having wounded the two which were accustomed to lead the rest, caused the whole body on a sudden to take to flight, cross the canal El Atik, and proceed at full speed to Ctesiphon. The armies then came to close quarters; and the foot and horse contended through the day with swords and spears, neither side being able to make any serious impression upon the other. As night closed in, however, the Persians once more fell back, crossing the canal El Atik, and so placing that barrier between themselves and their adversaries.

Their object in this manoeuvre was probably to obtain the rest which they must have greatly needed. The Persians were altogether of a frame less robust, and of a constitution less hardy, than the Arabs. Their army at Kadisiyeh was, moreover, composed to a large extent of raw recruits; and three consecutive days of severe fighting must have sorely tried its endurance. The Persian generals hoped, it would seem, by crossing the Atik to refresh their troops with a quiet night before renewing the combat on the morrow. But the indefatigable Arabs, perhaps guessing their intention, determined to frustrate it, and prevented the tired host from enjoying a moment's respite. The "day of embittered war," as it was called, was followed by the "night of snarling"—a time of horrid noise and tumult, during which the discordant cries of the troops on either side were thought to resemble the yells and barks of dogs and jackals. Two of the bravest of the Arabs, Toleicha and Amr, crossed the Atik with small bodies of troops, and under cover of the darkness entered the Persian camp, slew numbers, and caused the greatest confusion. By degrees a general engagement was brought on, which continued into the succeeding day, so that the "night of snarling" can scarcely be separated from the "day of cormorants"—the last of the four days' Kadisiyeh fight.

It would seem that the Persians must on the fourth day have had for a time the advantage, since we find them once more fighting upon the old ground, in the tract between the two canals, with the Atik in their rear. About noon, however, a wind arose from the west, bringing with it clouds of sand, which were blown into the faces and eyes of the Persians, while the Arabs, having their backs to the storm, suffered but little from its fury. Under these circumstances the Moslems made fresh efforts, and after a while a part of the Persian army was forced to give ground. Hormuzan, satrap of Susiana, and Firuzan, the general who afterwards commanded at Nehavend, fell back. The line of battle was dislocated; the person of the commander became exposed to danger; and about the same time a sudden violent gust tore away the awning that shaded his seat, and blew it into the Atik, which was not far off. Rustam sought a refuge from the violence of the storm among his baggage mules, and was probably meditating flight, when the Arabs were upon him. Hillal, son of Alkama, intent upon plunder, began to cut the cords of the baggage and strew it upon the ground. A bag falling severely injured Rustam, who threw himself into the Atik and attempted to swim across. Hillal, however, rushed after him, drew him to shore, and slew him; after which he mounted the vacant throne, and shouted as loudly as he could, "By the lord of the Kaaba, I have killed Rustam." The words created a general panic. Everywhere the Persian courage fell; the most part despaired wholly, and at once took to flight; a few cohorts alone stood firm and were cut to pieces; the greater number of the men rushed hastily to the Atik; some swam the stream others crossed where it had been filled up; but as many as 30,000 perished in the waves. Ten thousand had fallen on the field of battle in the course of the preceding night and day, while of the Mohammedans as many as 6000 had been slain. Thus the last day of the Kadisiyeh fight was stoutly contested; and the Persian defeat was occasioned by no deficiency of courage, but by the occurrence of a sand-storm and by the almost accidental death of the commander. Among the Persian losses in the battle that of the national standard, the durufsh-kawani was reckoned the most serious.

The retreat of the defeated army was conducted by Jalenus. Sa'ad, anxious to complete his victory, sent three bodies of troops across the Atik, to press upon the flying foe. One of these, commanded by Sohra, came up with the Persian rear-guard under Jalenus at Harrar, and slaughtered it, together with its leader. The other two seem to have returned without effecting much. The bulk of the fugitives traversed Mesopotamia in safety, and found a shelter behind the walls of Ctesiphon.

By the defeat of Kadisiyeh all hope of recovering the territory on the right bank of the Euphrates was lost; but Persia did not as yet despair of maintaining her independence. It was evident, indeed, that the permanent maintenance of the capital was henceforth precarious; and a wise forethought would have suggested the removal of the Court from so exposed a situation and its transference to some other position, either to Istakr, the ancient metropolis of Persia Proper, or to Hamadan, the capital city of Media. But probably it was considered that to retire voluntarily from the Tigris would be a confession of weakness, as fatal to the stability of the empire as to be driven back by the Arabs; and perhaps it may have been hoped that the restless nomads would be content with their existing conquests, or that they might receive a check at the hands of Rome which would put a stop to their aggressions elsewhere. It is remarkable that, during the pause of a year and a half which intervened between the battle of Kadisiyeh and the resumption of hostilities by the Arabs, nothing seems to have been done by Persia in the way of preparation against her terrible assailants.

In the year A.D. 637 the Arabs again took the offensive. They had employed the intervening year and a half in the foundation of Busrah and Kufam and in the general consolidation of their sway on the right bank of the Euphrates. They were now prepared for a further movement. The conduct of the war was once more entrusted to Sa'ad. Having collected an army of 20,000 men, this general proceeded from Kufa to Anbar (or Perisabor), where he crossed the Euphrates, and entered on the Mesopotamian region. Isdigerd, learning that he had put his forces in motion, and was bent upon attacking Ctesiphon, called a council of war, and asked its advice as to the best course to be pursued under the circumstances. It was generally agreed that the capital must be evacuated, and a stronger situation in the more mountainous part of the country occupied; but Isdigerd was so unwilling to remove that he waited till the Arabian general, with a force now raised to 60,000, had reached Sabat, which was only a day's march from the capital, before he could be induced to commence his retreat. He then abandoned the town hastily, without carrying off more than a small portion of the treasures which his ancestors had during four centuries accumulated at the main seat of their power, and retired to Holwan, a strong place in the Zagros mountain-range. Sa'ad, on learning his movement, sent a body of troops in pursuit, which came up with the rear-guard of the Persians, and cut it in pieces, but effected nothing really important. Isdigerd made good his retreat, and in a short time concentrated at Holwan an army of above 100,000 men. Sa'ad, instead of pushing forward and engaging this force, was irresistibly attracted by the reputed wealth of the Great Ctesiphon, and, marching thither, entered the unresisting city, with his troops, in the sixteenth year of the Hegira, the four hundred and eleventh from the foundation of the Sassanian kingdom by Artaxerxes, son of Babek.

Ctesiphon was, undoubtedly, a rich prize. Its palaces and its gardens, its opulent houses and its pleasant fields, its fountains and its flowers, are celebrated by the Arabian writers, who are never weary of rehearsing the beauty of its site, the elegance of the buildings, the magnificence and luxury of their furniture, or the amount of the treasures which were contained in them. The royal palace, now known as the Takht-i-Khosru, especially provoked their admiration. It was built of polished stone, and had in front of it a portico of twelve marble pillars, each 150 feet high. The length of the edifice was 450 feet, its breadth 180, its height 150. In the centre was the hall of audience, a noble apartment, 115 feet long and 85 high, with a magnificent vaulted roof, bedecked with golden stars, so arranged as to represent the motions of the planets among the twelve signs of the Zodiac, where the monarch was accustomed to sit on a golden throne, hearing causes and dispensing justice to his subjects. The treasury and the various apartments were full of gold and silver, of costly robes and precious stones, of jewelled arms and dainty carpets. The glass vases of the spice magazine contained an abundance of musk, camphor, amber, gums, drugs, and delicious perfumes. In one apartment was found a carpet of white brocade, 450 feet long and 90 broad, with a border worked in precious stones of various hues, to represent a garden of all kinds of beautiful flowers. The leaves were formed of emeralds, the blossoms and buds of pearls, rubies, sapphires, and other gems of immense value. Among the objects found in the treasury were a horse made entirely of gold, bearing a silver saddle set with a countless multitude of jewels, and a camel made of silver, accompanied by a foal of which the material was gold. A coffer belonging to Isdigerd was captured at the bridge over the Nahrwan canal as its guardians were endeavoring to carry it off. Among its contents were a robe of state embroidered with rubies and pearls, several garments made of tissue of gold, the crown and seal of Chosroes (Anushirwan?), and ten pieces of silk brocade. The armory of Chosroes also fell into the conqueror's hands. It contained his helmet, breastplate, greaves, and arm-pieces, all of solid gold adorned with pearls, six "cuirasses of Solomon," and ten costly scimitars. The works of art, and a fifth part of the entire booty, were set apart for the Caliph Omar, and sent by trusty messengers to Medina; the value of the remainder was so enormous that when Sa'ad divided it among his 60,000 soldiers the share of each amounted to 12,000 dirhems (L312.).

It is said that Sa'ad, after capturing Ctesiphon, was anxious to set out in pursuit of Isdigerd, but was restrained by dispatches received from Omar, which commanded him to remain at the Persian capital, and to employ his brother Hashem, and the experienced general, El Kakaa, in the further prosecution of the war. Hashem was, therefore, sent with 12,000 men, against the fugitive monarch, whose forces, said to have exceeded 100,000 men, and commanded by a Mihran, were drawn up at Jalula, not far from Holwan. The disparity of numbers forced Hashem to condescend to maneuvering; and it was six months before he ventured on a general engagement with his antagonist. Again the Mohammedans proved victorious; and this time the carnage was excessive; 100,000 Persians are said to have lain dead on the battle-field; the commander was himself among the slain. Jalula at once surrendered; and fresh treasures were obtained. Among other precious articles, a figure of a camel, with its rider, in solid gold, was found in one of the tents. Altogether the booty is reckoned at about four millions of our money—the share of each soldier engaged being 10,000 dirhems, or about L260. sterling.

Isdigerd, on learning the result of the battle of Jalula, quitted Holwan, and retired to Rei, a large town near the Caspian sea, at a short distance from the modern Teheran, thus placing the entire Zagros range between himself and his irresistible foes. A general named Khosru-sum was left behind with a large body of troops, and was bidden to defend Holwan to the last extremity. Instead of remaining, however, within the walls of the stronghold, Khosru-sum rashly led his force to meet that of El Kakaa, who defeated him at Kasr-i-Shirin and entirely dispersed his army. Holwan, being left without protection, surrendered; the conquest of Shirwan, Mahsabadan, and Tekrit followed; and by the close of the year A.D. 637 the banner of the Prophet waved over the whole tract west of Zagros, from Nineveh almost to Susa, or from the Kurnib to the Kuran river.

Another short pause in the Arabian aggressions upon Persia now occurred; but in the year A.D. 639 their attacks were resumed, and the Persians had to submit to further losses. Otba, governor of Busrah, sent an expedition across the Shat-el-Arab into. Susiana, and, supported by the Arab population of the province, which deserted the Persian side, engaged Horrmuzan, the satrap, in two battles, defeated him, and forced him to cede a portion of his territory, including the important city of Ahwaz. Soon afterwards, Ala, governor of Bahrein, conducted in person an expedition into Persia Proper, crossing the Gulf in the rude vessels of the time, and attacking Shehrek, the Persian satrap, who acknowledged the authority of Isdigerd. Here, the Arabs were for once unsuccessful. Shehrek collected a force which Ala was afraid to encounter; the Arab chief retreated to the coast, but found his fleet engulfed by the waves; and it was only with great difficulty that he made his escape by land from the country which he had ventured to invade. He owed his escape to Otba, who sent troops from Busrah to his aid, defeated Shehrek, and rescued his fellow governor from the peril which threatened, him.

In the next year (A.D. 640) Hormuzan, incited by Isdigerd, made a desperate attempt to recover the territory which he had been compelled to cede. Assisted by Shehrek, governor of Persia Proper, he attacked the Arabs unawares, but was speedily met, driven from Ram-Hormuz to Shuster, and there besieged for the space of six months. As many as eighty engagements are said to have taken place before the walls, with no decided advantage to either side. At length Al-Bera, son of Malik, one of the companions of the Prophet, and believed by many to possess the prophetic spirit, announced that victory was about to incline to the Moslems, but that he himself would be slain. A chance arrow having fulfilled one-half of the prediction, the Arabs felt an assurance that the other half would follow, and fought with such fanatic ardor that their expectations were soon fulfilled. The town was won; but Hormuzan retired into the citadel, and there successfully maintained himself, till Abu-Sabra, the Mohammedan general, consented to spare his life, and send him to Medina, where his fate should be determined by the Caliph. Hormuzan, on obtaining an audience, pretended thirst and asked for a cup of water, which was given him: he then looked suspiciously around, as if he expected to be stabbed while drinking. "Fear nothing," said Omar; "your life is safe till you have drunk the water." The crafty Persian flung the cup to the ground, and Omar felt that he had been outwitted, but that he must keep his word. Hormuzan became an Arab pensionary, and shortly afterwards embraced Islamism. His territories were occupied by the Moslems, whose dominions were thereby extended from the Kuran to the Tab river.

The Arab conquests on the side of Persia had hitherto been effected and maintained by the presiding genius of one of the ablest of the Mohammedan commanders, the victor of Kadi-siyeh, Sa'ad Ibn Abi Wakas. From Kufa, where he built himself a magnificent palace, which Omar however caused to be destroyed, this great general and skilful administrator directed the movements of armies, arranged the divisions of provinces, apportioned the sums to be paid to the revenue, dealt out justice, and generally superintended affairs throughout the entire region conquered by the Arabs to the east of the desert. A man in such a position necessarily made himself enemies; and complaints were frequently carried to Omar of his lieutenant's pride, luxury, and injustice. What foundation there may have been for these charges is uncertain; but it seems that Omar was persuaded, towards the close of A.D. 640, or very early in A.D. 641, that they were of sufficient weight to make it necessary that they should be investigated. He accordingly recalled Sa'ad from his government to Medina, and replaced him at Kufa by Ammar Ibn Yaser.

The news of this change was carried to Isdigerd at Rei, and caused him to conceive hopes of recovering his lost territory. The event shows that he attributed too much to the personal ability of his great antagonist; but the mistake was not unnatural; and it was a noble impulse which led him to seize the first promising occasion, in order to renew the struggle and make a last desperate effort to save his empire and repulse the barbarous nomads. The facts are not as the Arabian historians represent them. There was no intention on the part of the Mohammedans to be content with the conquests which they made, or to remain within the boundary line of the mountains that separate the Mesopotaraian region from the high plateau of Iran. Mohammedanism had an insatiable ambition, and was certain to spread itself in all directions until its forces were expended, or a bound was set to it by resistance which it could not overcome. Isdigerd, by remaining quiet, might perhaps have prolonged the precarious existence of Persia for half a dozen years, though even this is uncertain, and it is perhaps as probable that the tide of conquest would have flowed eastward in A.D. 641 or 642, even had he attempted nothing. What alone we can be sure of his, that no acquiescence on his part, no abstention from warlike enterprise, no submission short of the acceptance of Islamism, would have availed to save his country for more than a very brief space from the tramp of the hordes that were bent on enriching themselves with the plunder of the whole civilized world, and imposing on all the nations of the earth their dominion and their religion.

From the citadel of Rei, Isdigerd, in A.D. 641, sounded the call to battle with no uncertain note. His envoys spread themselves through Media, Azerbijan, Khorassan, Gurgan, Tabaristan, Merv, Bactria, Seistan, Kerman, and Farsistan (or Persia Proper), demanding contingents of troops, and appointing, as the place of rendezvous, the small town of Nehavend, which is in the mountain region, about fifty miles south of Hamadan. The call was responded to with zeal; and in a short time there was gathered together at the place named an army of 150,000 men. Firuzan, one of the nobles who had commanded at Kadisiyeh, was made general-in-chief. The design was entertained of descending on Holwan, and thence upon the lowland region, of re-taking Ctesiphon, crossing the great rivers, and destroying the rising cities of Kufa and Busrah. But the Arabs were upon the alert, and anticipated the intended invasion. Noman, son of Mokarrin, who commanded at Ahwaz, was hastily commissioned by Omar to collect the Arab troops stationed in Irak, Khuzistan, and the Sawad, to put himself at their head, and to prevent the outbreak by marching at once on Nehavend. He succeeded in uniting under his standard about 30,000 soldiers, and with this moderate force entered the mountain tract, passed Holwan and Merj, and encamped at Tur, where he expected the attack of the enemy. But Firuzan had now resolved to maintain the defensive. He had entrenched himself strongly in front of Nehavend and was bent on wearing out the patience of the Arabs by a prolonged resistance. Noman, finding himself unmolested, advanced from Tur to the immediate neighborhood of Nehavend, and endeavored to provoke his adversary to give battle, but without effect. For two months the two hosts faced each other without fighting. At last, the stores of the Arabs, as well as their patience, began to fail; and it was necessary to employ some device, or to give up the war altogether. Hereupon, Noman, by the advice of two of his captains, had recourse to a stratagem. He spread a report that Omar was dead, and breaking up from from his camp began a hasty retreat. The plan succeeded. Firuzan quitted his entrenchments, and led his army on the traces of the flying foe. It was two days before he reached them, and on the third day the battle began. Noman, having addressed his soldiers and made arrangements concerning the command in case of his own death, mounted a milk-white steed, and gave the signal for the fight by thrice shouting the famous tehbir, or battle-cry, "Allah akbar." The Arabs charged with fury, and for a while, amid the clouds of dust which rose beneath their feet, nothing was heard but the clash of steel. At length the Persians gave way; but, as Noman advanced his standard and led the pursuit, a volley of arrows from the flying foe checked his movement, and at the same time terminated his career. A shaft had struck him in a vital part, and he fell at the moment of victory. For his men, maddened by the loss of their commander, pressed on more furiously than before; the Persians were unable to rally; and a promiscuous flight began. Then followed a dreadful slaughter. The numbers of the Persians must have impeded their retreat; and in the defiles of the mountains a rapid flight was impossible. Firuzan himself, who, instead of falling back on Nehavend, took the road leading north to Hamadan, was overtaken by El Kakaa in a narrow pass, and put to the sword. More than 100,000 Persians are said to have perished.128 The victors, pressing onwards, easily took Nehavend. Hamadan surrendered to them shortly afterwards.120

The defeat of Nehavend terminated the Sassanian power. Isdigerd indeed, escaping from Rei, and flying continually from place to place, prolonged an inglorious existence for the space of ten more years—from A.D. 641 to A.D. 651; but he had no longer a kingdom. Persia fell to pieces on the occasion of "the victory of victories," and made no other united effort against the Arabs. Province after province was occupied by the fierce invaders; and, at length, in A.D. 651, their arms penetrated to Merv, where the last scion of the house of Babek had for some years found a refuge. It is said that during this interval he had made efforts to engage the Khan of the Turks and the Emperor of the Chinese to embrace his cause; but, if this were so, it was without success. Though they may have lent him some encouragement, no real effort was made by either potentate on his behalf. Isdigerd, at Merv, during his later years, experienced the usual fate of sovereigns who have lost their kingdoms. He was alternately flattered and coerced by pretended friends among his own people—induced to cherish vain hopes, and driven to despair, by the fluctuating counsels of the monarchs of neighboring nations. At last he was murdered by a subject for the sake of his clothes, when he was flying from a combined attack of treacherous subjects and offended foreigners.

It is difficult to form a decided opinion as to the character of Isdigerd III. He was but fifteen years of age at his accession, twenty-four at the time of the battle of Nehavend, and thirty-four at his decease, A.D. 651. It is in his favor that "history lays no crimes to his charge;" for this can be said of very few Sassanian sovereigns. It is also to his credit that he persevered so long in struggling against his fate, and in endeavoring to maintain, or restore, the independence of his nation. But, on the other hand, it must be confessed that there is little to be admired in the measures which he took to meet the perils of the time, and that personally he appears to have been weak and of luxurious habits. During the whole of his long struggle with the Arabs he seems never once to have placed himself at the head of his troops, much less to have crossed swords with the enemy. He intrusted the defence of Persia to generals, and did not even seek to inspire his soldiers with enthusiasm by his own presence in their camp. Always occupying some secure fortress far in the rear of his army, he fled from each as the enemy made a step in advance, quitting Ctesiphon for Holwan, Holwan for Rei, and Rei for Merv, never venturing upon a stand, never making an appeal to the loyalty which was amongst the best qualities of the Persians, and which would have caused them to fight with desperation in defence of a present king. Carrying with him in all his wanderings the miserable pageant of an Oriental court, he suffered his movements to be hampered and his resources crippled by a throng of 4000 useless retainers, whom he could not bring himself to dismiss. Instead of donning the armor which befitted one who was struggling for his crown, he wore to the last the silken robes, the jewelled belt, the rings and bracelets that were only suited for the quiet inmate of a palace, and by this incongruous and misplaced splendor he provoked, and, perhaps we may say, deserved his fate. A monarch who loses his crown for the most part awakens interest and sympathy; but no historian has a word of commiseration for the last of the Sassanidae, who is reproached with feebleness, cowardice, and effeminacy. It must certainly be allowed that he was no hero; but considering his extreme youth when his perils began, the efforts which he made to meet them, and the impossibility of an effective resistance in the effete and exhausted condition of the Persian nation, history is scarcely justified in passing upon the unfortunate prince a severe judgment.

The coins assigned to Isdigerd III. are neither numerous nor very remarkable. The head is in general very similar to that of Artaxerxes III. The pearl bordering around it is single, and in the margin are the usual stars and crescents of the later Sassanian kings. The margin, however, shows also in some instances a peculiar device behind the crown, and also a legend, which has been read, but very doubtfully, as "Ormazd." The king's name is given as Iskart or Iskarti. Among the regnal years marked on the reverse have been found the numbers "nineteen" and "twenty." Among the mint-marks are Azer-bijan, Abiverd, and Merv. [PLATE XXIV., Fig. 4]

CHAPTER XXVII

*Architecture of the Sassanians. Its Origin. Its Peculiarities. Oblong Square Plan. Arched Entrance Halls. Domes resting on Pendentives. Suites of Apartments. Ornamentation: Exterior, by Pilasters, Cornices, String-courses, and shallow arched Recesses, with Pilasters between them; Interior, by Pillars supporting Transverse Ribs, or by Door-ways and False Windows, like the Persopolitan. Specimen Palaces at Serbistan, at Firuzbad, at Ctesiphon, at Mashita. Elaborate Decoration at the last-named Palace. Decoration Elsewhere. Arch of Takht-i-Bostan. Sassanian Statuary. Sassanian*

***Bas-reliefs. Estimate of their Artistic Value. Question of the Employment by the Sassanians of Byzantine Artists. General Summary.***

*"With the accession of the Sassanians, Persia regained much of that power and stability to which she had been so long a stranger.... The improvement in the fine arts at home indicates returning prosperity, and a degree of security unknown since the fall of the Achaemenidae."—Fergusson, History of Architecture, vol. i. pp. 381-3, 3d edition.*

When Persia under the Sassanian princes shook off the barbarous yoke to which she had submitted for the space of almost five centuries, she found architecture and the other fine arts at almost the lowest possible ebb throughout the greater part of Western Asia. The ruins of the Achaemenian edifices, which were still to be seen at Pasargadae, Persopolis, and elsewhere, bore witness to the grandeur of idea, and magnificence of construction, which had once formed part of the heritage of the Persian nation; but the intervening period was one during which the arts had well-nigh wholly disappeared from the Western Asiatic world; and when the early sovereigns of the house of Sassan felt the desire, common with powerful monarchs, to exhibit their greatness in their buildings, they found themselves at the first without artists to design, without artisans to construct, and almost without models to copy. The Parthians, who had ruled over Persia for nearly four hundred years,' had preferred country to city life, tents to buildings, and had not themselves erected a single edifice of any pretension during the entire period of their dominion. Nor had the nations subjected to their sway, for the most part, exhibited any constructive genius, or been successful in supplying the artistic deficiencies of their rulers. In one place alone was there an exception to this general paralysis of the artistic powers. At Hatra, in the middle Mesopotamian region, an Arab dynasty, which held under the Parthian kings, had thought its dignity to require that it should be lodged in a palace, and had resuscitated a native architecture in Mesopotamia, after centuries of complete neglect. When the Sassanians looked about for a foundation on which they might work, and out of which they might form a style suitable to their needs and worthy of their power and opulence, they found what they sought in the Hatra edifice, which was within the limits of their kingdom, and at no great distance from one of the cities where they held their Court.

The early palaces of the Sassanians have ceased to exist. Artaxerxes, the son of Babek, Sapor the first, and their immediate successors, undoubtedly erected residences for themselves exceeding in size and richness the buildings which had contented the Parthians, as well as those in which their own ancestors, the tributary kings of Persia under Parthia, had passed their lives. But these residences have almost wholly disappeared. The most ancient of the Sassanian buildings which admit of being measured and described are assigned to the century between A.D. 350 and 450; and we are thus unable to trace the exact steps by which the Sassanian style was gradually elaborated. We come upon it when it is beyond the stage of infancy, when it has acquired a marked and decided character, when it no longer hesitates or falters, but knows what it wants, and goes straight to its ends. Its main features are simple, and are uniform from first to last, the later buildings being merely enlargements of the earlier, by an addition to the number or to the size of the apartments. The principal peculiarities of the style are, first, that the plan of the entire building is an oblong square, without adjuncts or projections; secondly, that the main entrance is into a lofty vaulted porch or hall by an archway of the entire width of the apartment; thirdly, that beside these oblong halls, the building contains square apartments, vaulted with domes, which are circular at their base, and elliptical in their section, and which rest on pendentives of an unusual character; fourthly, that the apartments are numerous and en suite, opening one into another, without the intervention of passages; and fifthly, that the palace comprises, as a matter of course, a court, placed towards the rear of the building, with apartments opening into it.

The oblong square is variously proportioned. The depth may be a little more than the breadth, or it may be nearly twice as much. In either case the front occupies one of the shorter sides, or ends of the edifice. The outer wall is sometimes pierced by one entrance only; but, more commonly, entrances are multiplied beyond the limit commonly observed in modern buildings. The great entrance is in the exact centre of the front. This entrance, as already noticed, is commonly by a lofty arch which (if we set aside the domes) is of almost the full height of the building, and constitutes one of its most striking, and to Europeans most extraordinary, features. From the outer air, we look; as it were, straight into the heart of the edifice, in one instance to the depth of 115 feet, a distance equal to the length of Henry VII.'s Chapel at Westminster. The effect is very strange when first seen by the inexperienced traveller; but similar entrances are common in the mosques of Armenia and Persia, and in the palaces of the latter country. In the mosques "lofty and deeply-recessed portals," "unrivalled for grandeur and appropriateness," are rather the rule than the exception; and, in the palaces, "Throne-rooms" are commonly mere deep recesses of this character, vaulted or supported by pillars, and open at one end to the full width and height of the apartment. The height of the arch varies in Sassanian buildings from about fifty to eighty-five feet; it is generally plain, and without ornament; but in one case we meet with a foiling of small arches round the great one, which has an effect that is not unpleasing.

The domed apartments are squares of from twenty-five to forty feet, or a little more. The domes are circular at their base; but a section of them would exhibit a half ellipse, with its longest and shortest diameters proportioned as three to two. The height to which they rise from the ground is not much above seventy feet. A single building will have two or three domes, either of the same size, or occasionally of different dimensions. It is a peculiarity of their construction that they rest, not on drums, but on pendentives of a curious character. A series of semi-circular arches is thrown across the angles of the apartment, each projecting further into it than the preceding, and in this way the corners are got rid of, and the square converted into the circular shape. A cornice ran round the apartment, either above or below the pendentives, or sometimes both above and below. The domes were pierced by a number of small holes, which admitted some light, and the upper part of the walls between the pendentives was also pierced by windows.

There are no passages or corridors in the Sassanian palaces. The rooms for the most part open one into the other. Where this is not the case, they give upon a common meeting-ground, which is either an open court, or a large vaulted apartment. The openings are in general doorways of moderate size, but sometimes they are arches of the full width of the subordinate room or apartment. As many as seventeen or eighteen rooms have been found in a palace.

There is no appearance in any Sassanian edifice of a real second story. The famous Takht-i-Khosru presents externally the semblance of such an arrangement; but this seems to have been a mere feature of the external ornamentation, and to have had nothing to do with the interior.

The exterior ornamentation of the Sassanian buildings was by pilasters, by arched recesses, by cornices, and sometimes by string-courses. An ornamentation at once simple and elegant is that of the lateral faces of the palace at Firuzabad, where long reed-like pilasters are carried from the ground to the cornice, while between them are a series of tall narrow doubly recessed arches. Far less satisfactory is the much more elaborate design adopted at Ctesiphon, where six series of blind arches of different kinds are superimposed the one on the other, with string-courses between them, and with pilasters, placed singly or in pairs, separating the arches into groups, and not regularly superimposed, as pillars, whether real or seeming, ought to be.

The interior ornamentation was probably, in a great measure, by stucco, painting, and perhaps gilding. All this, however, if it existed, has disappeared; and the interiors now present a bare and naked appearance, which is only slightly relieved by the occasional occurrence of windows, of ornamental doorways, and of niches, which recall well-known features at Persepolis. In some instances, however, the arrangement of the larger rooms was improved by means of short pillars, placed at some distance from the walls, and supporting a sort of transverse rib, which broke the uniformity of the roof. The pillars were connected with the side walls by low arches.

Such are the main peculiarities of Sassanian palace architecture. The general effect of the great halls is grand, though scarcely beautiful; and, in the best specimens, the entire palace has an air of simple severity which is striking and dignified. The internal arrangements do not appear to be very convenient. Too much is sacrificed to regularity; and the opening of each room into its neighbor must, one would think, have been unsatisfactory. Still, the edifices are regarded as "indicating considerable originality and power," though they "point to a state of society when attention to security hardly allowed the architect the free exercise of the more delicate ornaments of his art."

From this general account of the main features of the architecture it is proposed now to proceed to a more particular description of the principal extant Sassanian buildings—the palaces at Serbistan, Firuzabad, Ctesiphon, and Mashita.

The palace at Serbistan is the smallest, and probably the earliest of the four. It has been assigned conjecturally to the middle of the fourth century, or the reign of Sapor II. The ground plan is an oblong but little removed from a square, the length being 42 French metres, and the breadth nearly 37 metres. [PLATE XXV., Fig. 1.] The building faces west, and is entered by three archways, between which are groups of three semi-circular pilasters, while beyond the two outer arches towards the angles of the building is a single similar pilaster. Within the archways are halls or porches of different depths, the central one of the three being the shallowest. [PLATE XXV., Fig. 2.] This opens by an arched doorway into a square chamber, the largest in the edifice. It is domed, and has a diameter of about 42 feet or, including recesses, of above 57 feet. The interior height of the dome from the floor is 65 feet. Beyond the domed chamber is a court, which measures 45 feet by 40, and has rooms of various sizes opening into it. One of these is domed; and others are for the most part vaulted. The great domed chamber opens towards the north, on a deep porch or hall, which was entered from without by the usual arched portal. On the south it communicates with a pillared hall, above 60 feet long by 30 broad. There is another somewhat similar hall on the north side of the building, in width about equal, but in length not quite 50 feet. In both halls the pillars are short, not exceeding six feet. They support piers, which run up perpendicularly for a considerable height, and then become ribs of the vaulting.

Fig 1.

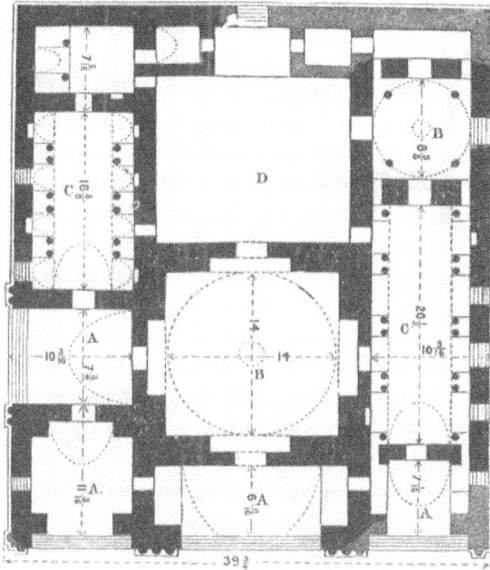

GROUND PLAN OF THE SERBISTAN PALACE (after Flandin).

N.B.—The dimensions are given in English yards.

A A A   Porches.              C C   Pillared Halls.
B B     Domed Halls.          D     Court,

Fig. 2.

FRONT VIEW OF SERBISTAN PALACE, RESTORED (after Flandin).

PLATE XXV

The Firuzabad palace has a length of above 390 and a width of above 180 feet. Its supposed date is A.D. 450, or the reign of Isdigerd I. As usual the ground plan is an oblong square. [PLATE XXVI.] It is remarkable that the entire building had but a single entrance. This was by a noble arch, above 50 feet in height, which faced north, and gave admission into a vaulted hall, nearly 90 feet long by 43 wide, having at either side two lesser halls of a similar character, opening into it by somewhat low semi-circular arches, of nearly the full width of the apartments. Beyond these rooms, and communicating with them by narrow, but elegant doorways, were three domed chambers precisely similar, occupying together the full width of the building, each about 43 feet square, and crowned by elliptical domes rising to the height of nearly 70 feet. [PLATE XXVII., Fig. 1.] The ornamentation of these chambers was by their doorways, and by false windows, on the Persepolitan model. The domed chambers opened into some small apartments, beyond which was a large court, about 90 feet square, surrounded by vaulted rooms of various sizes, which for the most part communicated directly with it. False windows, or recesses, relieved the interior of these apartments, but were of a less elaborate character than those of the domed chambers. Externally the whole building was chastely and tastefully ornamented by the tall narrow arches and reed-like pilasters already mentioned. [PLATE XXVII., Fig. 2.] Its character, however, was upon the whole "simple and severe;" nor can we quarrel with the judgment which pronounces it "more like a gigantic bastile than the palace of a gay, pavilion-loving people like the Persians."

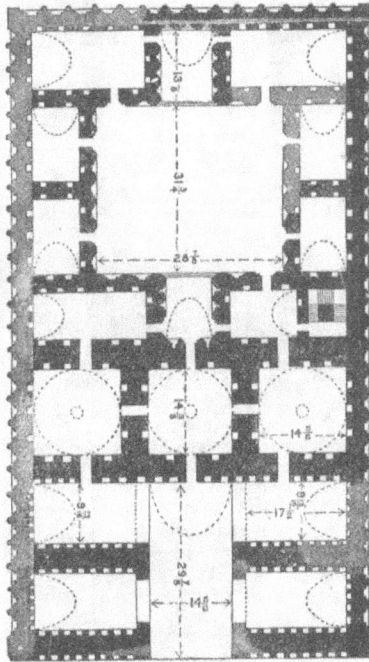

Plate XXVI.　　　　　　　　　　　　　　　Vol. III.

Ground Plan of the Palace at Firuzabad (after Flandin).
N.B.—The dimensions are in English yards.

PLATE XXVI

Vol. III.                                                                        Plate XXVII.

Fig. 1

Chosroës II. From a relief at Takht-i-Bostan (after Flandin).

Fig. 2.

Fig. 3.

Sassanian Chariot (from the bas-reliefs).

Fig. 4.

A Persian Guardsman (from the bas-reliefs).

PLATE XXVII

It is difficult to form any very decided opinion upon the architectural merits of the third and grandest of the Sassanian palaces, the well known "Takht-i-Ehosru," or palace of Chosroe's Anushirwan, at Ctesiphon. What remains of this massive erection is a mere fragment, which, to judge from the other extant Sassanian ruins, cannot have formed so much as one fourth part of the original edifice. [PLATE XXVIII., Fig. 1.] Nothing has come down to our day but a single vaulted hall on the grandest scale, 72 feet wide, 85 high, and 115 deep, together with the mere outer wall of what no doubt constituted the main facade of the building.

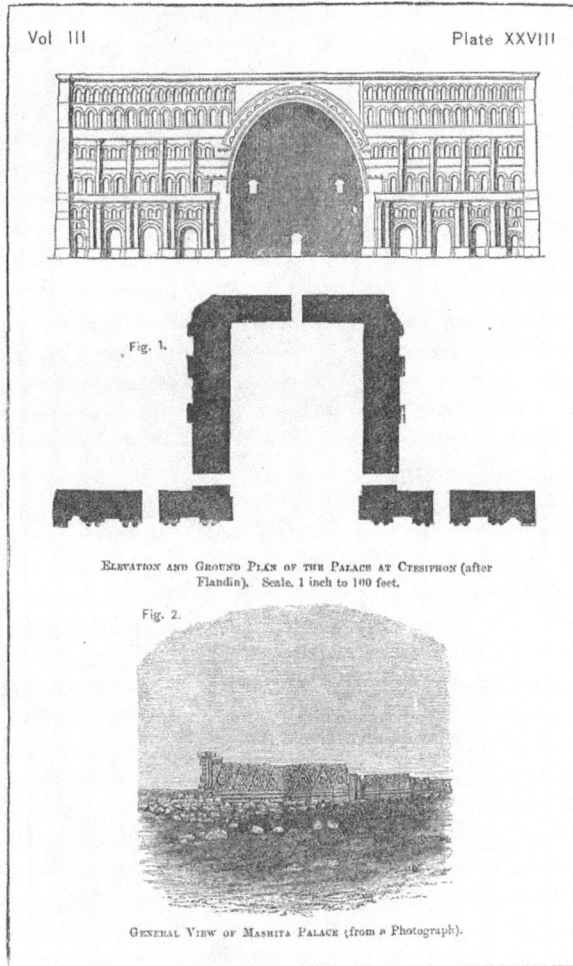

Vol III                                                                  Plate XXVIII

Fig. 1.

ELEVATION AND GROUND PLAN OF THE PALACE AT CTESIPHON (after Flandin). Scale. 1 inch to 100 feet.

Fig. 2.

GENERAL VIEW OF MASHITA PALACE (from a Photograph).

PLATE XXVIII

The apartments, which, according to all analogy, must have existed at the two sides, and in the rear, of the great hall, some of which should have been vaulted, have wholly perished. Imagination may supply them from the Firuzabad, or the Mashita palace; but not a trace, even of their foundations, is extant; and the details, consequently, are uncertain, though the general plan can scarcely be doubted. At each side of the great hall were probably two lateral ones, communicating with each other, and capable of being entered either from the hall or from the outer air. Beyond the great hall was probably a domed chamber, equalling it in width, and opening upon a court, round which were a number of moderate-sized apartments. The entire building was no doubt an oblong square, of which the shorter sides seem to have measured 370 feet. It had at least three, and may not improbably have had a larger number of entrances, since it belongs to tranquil times and a secure locality.

The ornamentation of the existing facade of the palace is by doorways, doubly-arched recesses, pilasters, and string-courses. These last divide the building, externally, into an appearance of three or four distinct stories. The first and second stories are broken into portions by pilasters, which in the first or basement stories are in pairs, but in the second stand singly. It is remarkable that the pilasters of the second story are not arranged with any regard to those of the first, and are consequently in many cases not superimposed upon the lower pilasters. In the third and fourth stories there are no pilasters, the arched recesses being here continued without any interruption. Over the great arch of the central hall, a foiling of seventeen small semicircular arches constitutes a pleasing and unusual feature.

The Mashita palace, which was almost certainly built between A.D. 614 and A.D. 627, while on a smaller scale than that of Ctesiphon, was far more richly ornamented. [PLATE XXVIII., Fig. 2.] This construction of Chosroes II. (Parwiz) consisted of two distinct, buildings (separated by a court-yard, in which was a fountain), extending each of them about 180 feet along the front, with a depth respectively of 140 and 150 feet. The main building, which lay to the north, was entered from the courtyard by three archways, semicircular and standing side by side, separated only by columns of hard, white stone, of a quality approaching to marble. These columns were surmounted by debased Corinthian capitals, of a type introduced by Justinian, and supported arches which were very richly fluted, and which are said to have been "not unlike our own late Norman work." [PLATE XXIX., Fig. 2.] The archways gave entrance into an oblong court or hall, about 80 feet long, by sixty feet wide, on which opened by a wide doorway the main room of the building. This was a triapsal hall, built of brick, and surmounted by a massive domed roof of the same material, which rested on pendentives like those employed at Serbistan and at Firuzabad. The diameter of the hall was a little short of 60 feet. On either side of the triapsal hall, and in its rear, and again on either side of the court or hall on which it opened, were rooms of a smaller size, generally opening into each other, and arranged symmetrically, each side being the exact counterpart of the other. The number of these smaller apartments was twenty-five. [PLATE XXIX., Fig. 1.]

The other building, which lies towards the south, and is separated from the one just described by the whole length of the court-yard, a distance of nearly 200 feet, appears to have been for the most part of an inferior character. It comprised one large hall, or inner court, but otherwise contained only small apartments, which, it is thought, may have been "intended as guard-rooms for the soldiers." Although, however, in most respects so unpretending, this edifice was adorned externally with a richness and magnificence unparalleled in the other remains of Sassanian times, and scarcely exceeded in the architecture of any age or nation. Forming, as it did, the only entrance by which the palace could be approached, and possessing the only front which was presented to the gaze of the outer world, its ornamentation was clearly an object of Chosroes' special care, who seems to have lavished upon it all the known resources of art. The outer wall was built of finely-dressed hard stone; and on this excellent material the sculptors of the time—whether Persian or Byzantine, it is impossible to determine—proceeded to carve in the most elaborate way, first a bold pattern of zigzags and rosettes, and then, over the entire surface, a most delicate tracery of foliage, animals, and fruits. The effect of the zigzags is to divide the wall into a number of triangular compartments, each of which is treated separately, covered with a decoration peculiar to itself, a fretwork of the richest kind, in which animal and vegetable forms are most happily intermingled.

 Plate XXIX.

Fig. 1.

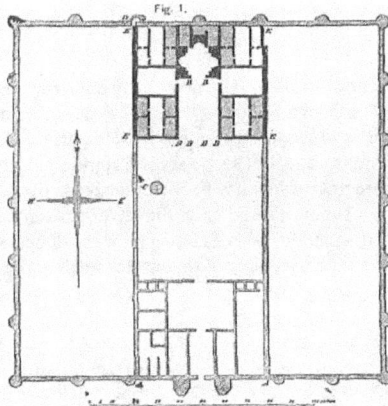

GROUND-PLAN OF PALACE AT MASHITA (after Tristram).
A A, Sculptured façade.   B B B B, Pillared entrances.   c, Well or fountain.   D, Tower with staircase.   E E E E, Main building of Palace.

Fig. 2.

INNER GATEWAY OF MASHITA PALACE (from a Photograph).

PLATE XXIX

Plate. XXX.　　　　　　　　Vol. III.

ELABORATE ORNAMENTATION OF PALACE AT MASHITA.

PLATE XXX

In one a vase of an elegant shape stands midway in the triangle at its base; two doves are seated on it, back to back; from between them rises a vine, which spreads its luxuriant branches over the entire compartment, covering it with its graceful curves and abundant fruitage; on either side of the vase a lion and a wild boar confront the doves with a friendly air; while everywhere amid the leaves and grapes we see the forms of birds, half revealed, half hidden by the foliage. Among the birds, peacocks, parrots, and partridges have been recognized; among the beasts, besides lions and wild boars, buffaloes, panthers, lynxes, and gazelles. In another panel a winged lion, the "lineal descendant of those found at Nineveh and Persepolis," reflects the mythological symbolism of Assyria, and shows how tenacious was its hold on the West-Asian mind. Nor is the human form wholly wanting. In one place we perceive a man's head, in close juxtaposition with man's inseparable companion, the dog; in another, the entire figure of a man, who carries a basket of fruit.

Besides the compartments within the zigzags, the zigzags themselves and the rosettes are ornamented with a patterning of large leaves, while the moulding below the zigzags and the cornice, or string-course, above them are covered with conventional designs, the interstices between them being filled in with very beautiful adaptations of lesser vegetable forms.

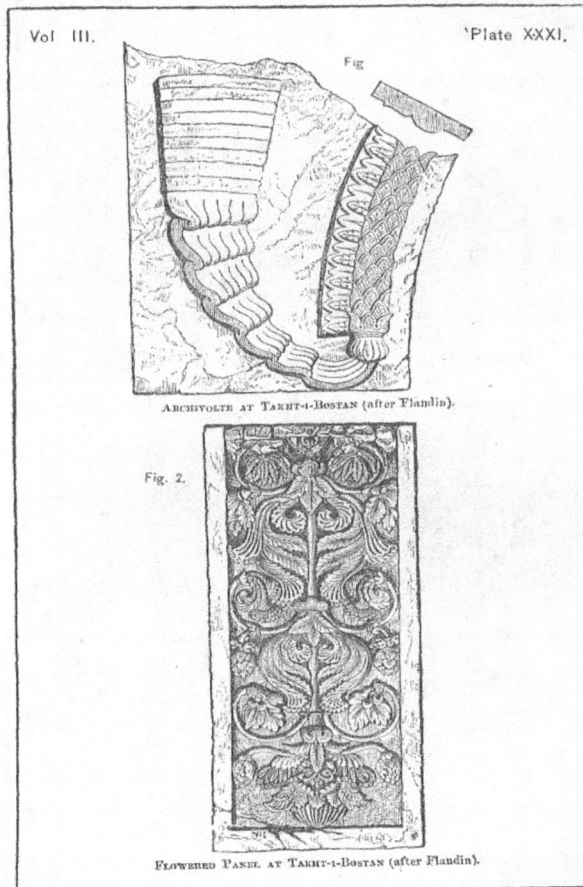

Vol III.                                                                 'Plate XXXI.

Fig

ARCHIVOLTE AT TAKHT-I-BOSTAN (after Flandin).

Fig. 2.

FLOWERED PANEL AT TAKHT-I-BOSTAN (after Flandin).

PLATE XXXI

Altogether, the ornamentation of this magnificent facade may be pronounced almost unrivalled for beauty and appropriateness; and the entire palace may well be called "a marvellous example of the sumptuousness and selfishness of ancient princes," who expended on the gratification of their own taste and love of display the riches which would have been better employed in the defence of their kingdoms, or in the relief of their poorer subjects.

The exquisite ornamentation of the Mashita palace exceeds anything which is found elsewhere in the Sassanian buildings, but it is not wholly different in kind from that of other remains of their architecture in Media and Persia Proper. The archivolte which adorns the arch of Takht-i-Bostan [PLATE XXXI., Fig. 1.] possesses almost equal delicacy with the patterned cornice or string-course of the Mashita building; and its flowered panels may compare for beauty with the Mashita triangular compartments. [PLATE XXXI., Fig. 2.] Sassarian capitals are also in many instances of lovely design, sometimes delicately diapered (A, B), sometimes worked with a pattern of conventional leaves and flowers [PLATE XXXII.], occasionally exhibiting the human form (D, E), or a flowery patterning, like that of the Takht-i-Bostan (F, Q). [PLATE XXXIII.] In the more elaborate specimens, the four faces—for the capitals are square—present designs completely different; in other instances, two of the four faces are alike, but on the other two the design is varied. The shafts of Sassanian columns, so far as we can judge, appear to have been fluted.

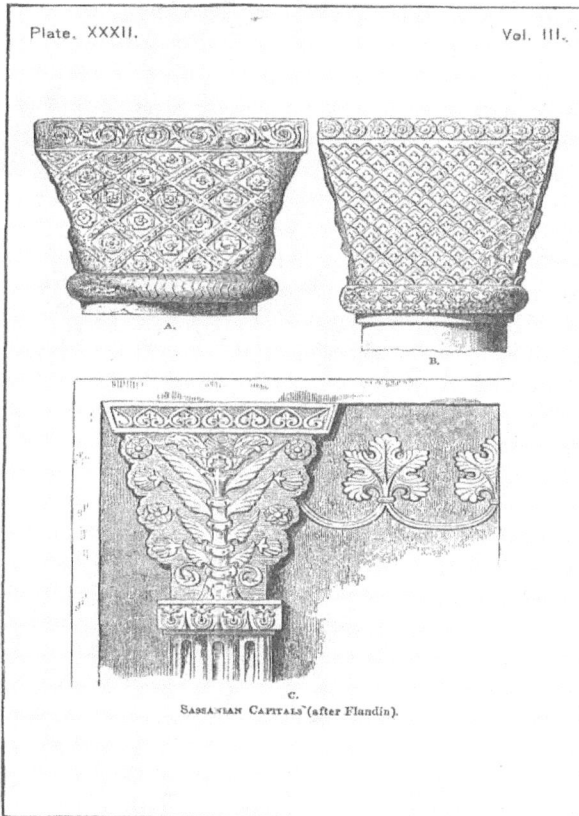

Plate. XXXII.                                        Vol. III.

C.

SASSANIAN CAPITALS (after Flandin).

PLATE XXXII

D.                                                    E.

F.

SASSANIAN CAPITALS (after Flandin)

PLATE XXXIII

A work not exactly architectural, yet possessing architectural features—the well-known arch of Chosroes II. above alluded to—seems to deserve description before we pass to another branch of our subject. [PLATE XXXIV., Fig. 1.] This is an archway or grotto cut in the rock at Takht-i-Bostan, near Kerman-shah, which is extremely curious and interesting. On the brink of a pool of clear water, the sloping face of the rock has been cut into, and a recess formed, presenting at its further end a perpendicular face. This face, which is about 34 feet broad, by 31 feet high, and which is ornamented at the top by some rather rude gradines, has been penetrated by an arch, cut into the solid stone to the depth of above 20 feet, and elaborately ornamented, both within and without. Externally, the arch is in the first place surmounted by the archivolte already spoken of, and then, in the spandrels on either side are introduced flying figures of angels or Victories, holding chaplets in one hand and cups or vases in the other, which are little inferior to the best Roman art. [PLATE XXXIV., Fig. 2.] Between the figures is a crescent, perhaps originally enclosing a ball, and thus presenting to the spectator, at the culminating point of the whole sculpture, the familiar emblems of two of the national divinities. Below the spandrels and archivolte, on either side of the arched entrance, are the flowered panels above-mentioned, alike in most respects, but varying in some of their details. Within the recess, its two sides, and its further end, are decorated with bas-reliefs, those on the sides representing Chosroes engaged in the chase of the wild boar and the stag, while those at the end, which are in two lines, one over the other, show the monarch, above, in his robes of state, receiving wreaths from ideal beings; below, in his war costume, mounted upon his favorite charger, Sheb-Diz, with his spear poised in his hand, awaiting the approach of the enemy. The modern critic regards this figure as "original and interesting." We shall have occasion to recur to it when we treat of the "Manners and Customs" of the Neo-Persian people.

Plate XXXIV.                                        Vol. III.

Fig. 1

Arch of Chosroës II. at Takht-i-Bostan (after Flandin).

Fig. 2

Figure of Victory, from the Arch at Takht-i-Bostan (after Flandin).

PLATE XXXIV

The glyptic art of the Sassanian is seen chiefly in their bas-reliefs; but one figure "in the round" has come down to us from their times, which seems to deserve particular description. This is a colossal statue of Sapor I., hewn (it would seem) out of the natural rock, which still exists, though overthrown and mutilated, in a natural grotto near the ruined city of Shapur. [PLATE XXXV.] The original height of the figure, according to M. Texier, was 6 metres 7 centimetres, or between 19 and 20 feet. It was well proportioned, and carefully wrought, representing the monarch in peaceful attire, but with a long sword at his left side, wearing the mural crown which characterizes him on the bas-reliefs, and dressed in a tunic and trousers of a light and flexible material, apparently either silk or muslin. The hair, beard, and mustachios, were neatly arranged and well rendered. The attitude of the figure was natural and good. One hand, the right, rested upon the hip; the other touched, but without grasping it, the hilt of the long straight sword. If we may trust the representation of M. Texier's artist, the folds of the drapery were represented with much skill and delicacy; but the hands and feet of the figure, especially the latter, were somewhat roughly rendered.

Vol. III.                                    Plate XXXV

STATUE OF SAPOR I. AT SHAPUR (RESTORED).

PLATE XXXV

The bas-reliefs of the Sassanians are extremely numerous, and though generally rude, and sometimes even grotesque, are not without a certain amount of merit. Some of the earlier and coarser specimens have been already given n this volume; and one more of the same class is here appended [PLATE XXXVI., Fig. 1.] but we have now to notice some other and better examples, which seem to indicate that the Persians of this period attained a considerable proficiency in this branch of the glyptic art. The reliefs belonging to the time of Sapor I. are generally poor in conception and ill-executed; but in one instance, ur less the modern artist has greatly flattered his original, a work of this time is not devoid of some artistic excellence. This is a representation of the triumph of Sapor over Valerian, comprising only four figures—Sapor, an attendant, and two Romans—of which the three principal are boldly drawn, in attitudes natural, yet effective, and in good proportion. [PLATE XXXVII.] The horse on which Sapor rides is of the usual clumsy description, reminding us of those which draw our brewers' wains; and the exaggerated hair, floating ribbons and uncouth head-dress of the monarch give an outre and ridiculous air to the chief figure; but, if we deduct these defects, which are common to almost all the Sassanian artists, the representation becomes pleasing and dignified. Sapor sits his horse well, and thinks not of himself, but of what he is doing. Cyriades, who is somewhat too short, receives the diadem from his benefactor with a calm satisfaction. But the best figure is that of the captive emperor, who kneels on one knee, and, with outstretched arms, implores the mercy of the conqueror. The whole representation is colossal, the figures being at least three times the size of life; the execution seems to have been good; but the work has been considerably injured by the effects of time.

PLATE XXXVI

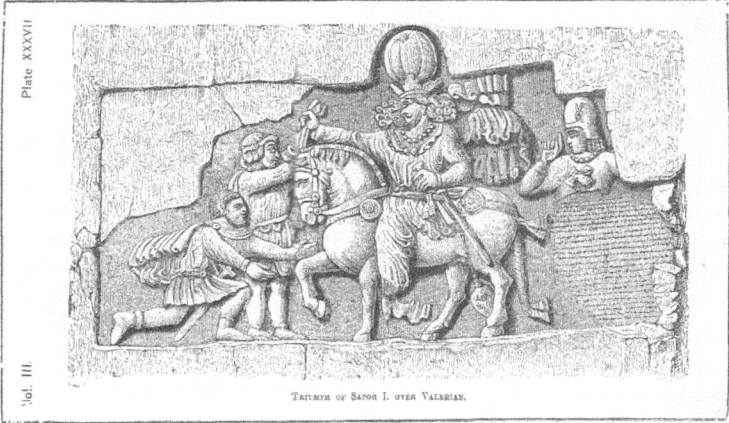

PLATE XXXVII

Another bas-relief of the age of Sapor I. is on too large a scale, and too complicated, to be represented here; but a description may be given of it, and a specimen subjoined, from which the reader may judge of its character. On a surface of rock at Shapur, carefully smoothed and prepared for sculpture, the second Sassanian monarch appears in the centre of the tablet, mounted on horseback, and in his usual costume, with a dead Roman under his horse's feet, and holding another (Cyriades?), by the hand. In front of him, a third Roman, the representative of the defeated nation, makes submission; and then follow thirteen tribute-bearers, bringing rings of gold, shawls, bowls, and the like, and conducting also a horse and an elephant. Behind the monarch, on the same line, are thirteen mounted guardsmen. Directly above, and directly below the central group, the tablet is blank; but on either side the subject is continued, above in two lines, and below in one, the guardsmen towards the left amounting in all to fifty-six, and the tribute-bearers on the right to thirty-five. The whole tablet comprises ninety-five human and sixty-three animal figures, besides a Victory floating in the sky. The illustration [PLATE XXXVIII.] is a representation of the extreme right-hand portion of the second line.

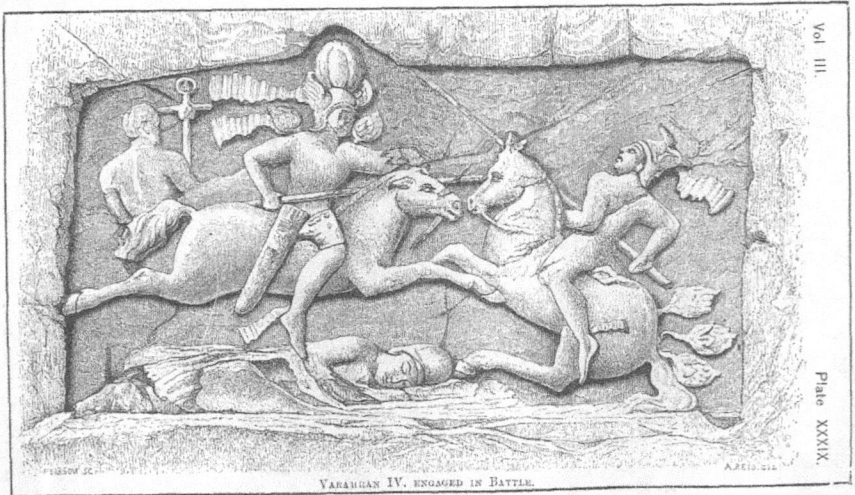

VARAHRAN IV. ENGAGED IN BATTLE.

PLATE XXXVIII

After the time of Sapor I. there is a manifest decline in Sassanian art. The reliefs of Varahran II. and Varahran III., of Narses and Sapor III., fall considerably below those of Sapor, son of Artaxerxes. It is not till we arrive at the time of Varahran IV. (A.D. 388-399) that we once more have works which possess real artistic merit. Indications have already appeared in an earlier chapter of this monarch's encouragement of artists, and of a kind of art really meriting the name. We saw that his gems were exquisitely cut, and embodied designs of first-rate excellence. It has now to be observed further, that among the bas-reliefs of the greatest merit which belong to Sassanian times, one at least must be ascribed to him; and that, this being so, there is considerable probability that two others of the same class belong also to his reign. The one which must undoubtedly be his, and which tends to fix the date of the other two, exists at Nakhsh-i-Kustam, near Persepolis, and has frequently been copied by travellers. It represents a mounted warrior, with the peculiar head-dress of Varahran IV., charging another at full speed, striking him with his spear, and bearing both horse and rider to the ground. [PLATE XXXIX.] A standard-bearer marches a little behind; and a dead warrior lies underneath Varahran's horse, which is clearing the obstacle in his bound. The spirit of the entire composition is admirable; and though the stone is in a state of advanced decay, travellers never fail to admire the vigor of the design and the life and movement which characterize it.

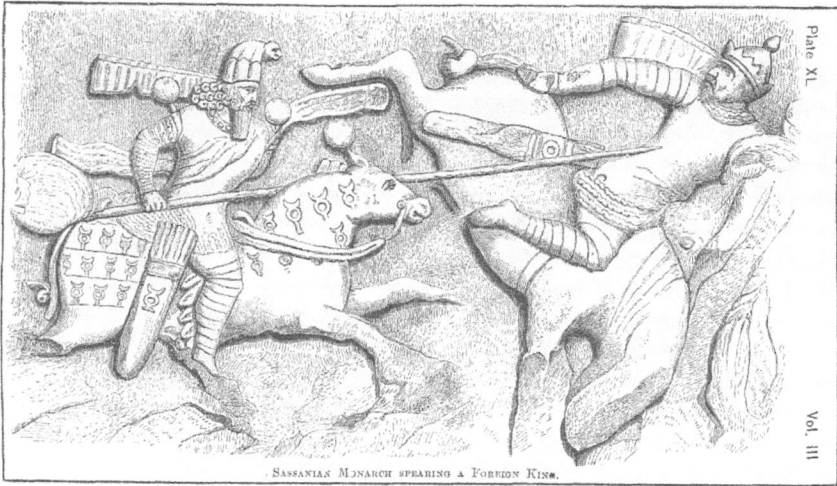

SASSANIAN MONARCH SPEARING A FOREIGN KING.

PLATE XXXIX

The other similar reliefs to which reference has been made exist, respectively, at Nakhsh-i-Eustam and at Firuzabad. The Nakhsh-i-Rustam tablet is almost a duplicate of the one above described and represented, differing from it mainly in the omission of the prostrate figure, in the forms of the head-dresses borne by the two cavaliers, and in the shape of the standard. It is also in better preservation than the other, and presents some additional details. The head-dress of the Sassanian warrior is very remarkable, being quite unlike any other known example. It consists of a cap, which spreads as it rises, and breaks into three points, terminating in large striped balls. [PLATE XXVI., Fig. 2.] His adversary wears a helmet crowned with a similar ball. The standard, which is in the form of a capital T, displays also five balls of the same sort, three rising from the cross-bar, and the other two hanging from it. Were it not for the head-dress of the principal figure, this sculpture might be confidently assigned to the monarch who set up the neighboring one. As it is, the point must be regarded as undecided, and the exact date of the relief as doubtful. It is, however, unlikely to be either much earlier, or much later, than the time of Varahran IV.

The third specimen of a Sassanian battle-scene exists at Firuzabad, in Persia Proper, and has been carefully rendered by M. Flandin. It is in exceedingly bad condition, but appears to have comprised the figures of either five or six horsemen, of whom the two principal are a warrior whose helmet terminates in the head of a bird, and one who wears a crown, above which rises a cap, surmounted by a ball. [PLATE XL.] The former of these who is undoubtedly a Sassanian prince, pierces with his spear the right side of the latter, who is represented in the act of falling to the ground. His horse tumbles at the same time, though why he does so is not quite clear, since he has not been touched by the other charger. His attitude is extravagantly absurd, his hind feet being on a level with the head of his rider. Still more absurd seems to have been the attitude of a horse at the extreme right, which turns in falling, and exposes to the spectator the inside of the near thigh and the belly. But, notwithstanding these drawbacks, the representation has great merit. The figures live and breathe—that of the dying king expresses horror and helplessness, that of his pursuer determined purpose and manly strength. Even the very horses are alive, and manifestly rejoice in the strife. The entire work is full of movement, of variety, and of artistic spirit.

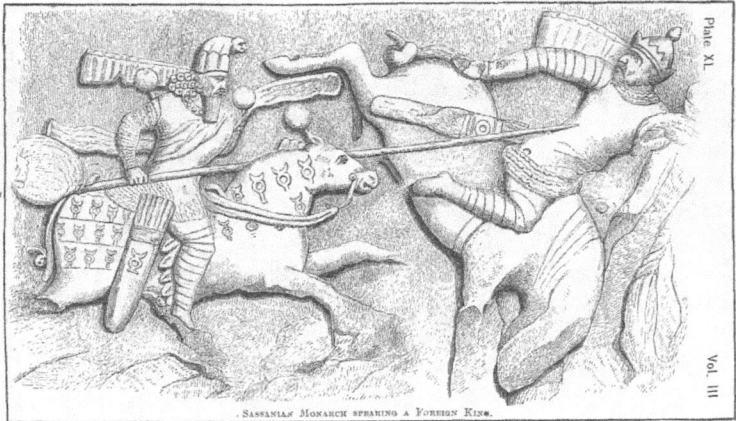

SASSANIAN MONARCH SPEARING A FOREIGN KING.

PLATE XL

If we have regard to the highest qualities of glyptic art, Sassanian sculpture must be said here to culminate. There is a miserable falling off, when about a hundred and fifty years later the Great Chosroes (Anushirwan) represents himself at Shapur, seated on his throne, and fronting to the spectator, with guards and attendants on one side, and soldiers bringing in prisoners, human heads, and booty, on the other. [PLATE XLI.] The style here recalls that of the tamer reliefs set up by the first Sapor, but is less pleasing. Some of the prisoners appear to be well drawn; but the central figure, that of the monarch, is grotesque; the human heads are ghastly; and the soldiers and attendants have little merit. The animal forms are better—that of the elephant especially, though as compared with the men it is strangely out of proportion.

CHOSROËS I. RECEIVING TRIBUTE FROM THE ROMANS.

PLATE XLI

With Chosroes II. (Eberwiz or Parviz), the grandson of Anushirwan, who ascended the throne only twelve years after the death of his grandfather, and reigned from A.D. 591 to A.D. 628, a reaction set in. We have seen the splendor and good taste of his Mashita palace, the beauty of some of his coins, and the general excellence of his ornamentation. It remains to notice the character of his reliefs, found at present in one locality only, viz., at Takht-i-Bostan, where they constitute the main decorations of the great triumphal arch of this monarch. [PLATE XLII.]

Plate XLII     Vol. III.

CHOSROËS II. AND EMBLEMATIC FIGURES UNDER ARCH AT TAKHT-I-BOSTAN.

PLATE XLII

These reliefs consist of two classes of works, colossal figures and hunting-pieces. The colossal figures, of which some account has been already given, and which are represented in PLATE XLI., have but little merit. They are curious on account of their careful elaboration, and furnish important information with respect to Sassanian dress and armature, but they are poor in design, being heavy, awkward, and ungainly. Nothing can well be less beautiful than the three overstout personages, who stand with their heads nearly or quite touching the crown of the arch, at its further extremity, carefully drawn in detail, but in outline little short of hideous. The least bad is that to the left, whose drapery is tolerably well arranged, and whose face, judging by what remains of it, was not unpleasing. Of the other two it is impossible to say a word in commendation.

The mounted cavalier below them—Chosroes himself on his black war horse, Sheb-Diz—is somewhat better. The pose of horse and horseman has dignity; the general proportions are fairly correct, though (as usual) the horse is of a breed that recalls the modern dray-horse rather than the charger. The figure, being near the ground, has suffered much mutilation, probably at the hands of Moslem fanatics; the off hind leg of the horse is gone; his nose and mouth have disappeared; and the horseman has lost his right foot and a portion of his lower clothing. But nevertheless, the general effect is not altogether destroyed. Modern travellers admire the repose and dignity of the composition, its combination of simplicity with detail, and the delicacy and finish of some portions. It may be added that the relief of the figure is high; the off legs of the horse were wholly detached; and the remainder of both horse and rider was nearly, though not quite, disengaged from the rock behind them.

The hunting-pieces, which ornament the interior of the arched recess on either side, are far superior to the colossal figures, and merit an exact description. On the right, the perpendicular space below the spring of the arch contains the representation of a stag hunt, in which the monarch and about a dozen other mounted horsemen take part, assisted by some ten or twelve footmen, and by a detachment mounted on elephants. [PLATE XLIII.] The elephants, which are nine in number, occupy the extreme right of the tablet, and seem to be employed in driving the deer into certain prepared enclosures. Each of the beasts is guided by three riders, sitting along their backs, of whom the central one alone has the support of a saddle or howdah. The enclosures into which the elephants drive the game are three in number; they are surrounded by nets; and from the central one alone is there an exit. Through this exit, which is guarded by two footmen, the game passes into the central field, or main space of the sculpture, where the king awaits them. He is mounted on his steed, with his bow passed over his head, his sword at his side, and an attendant holding the royal parasol over him. It is not quite clear whether he himself does more than witness the chase. The game is in the main pursued and brought to the ground by horsemen without royal insignia, and is then passed over into a further compartment—the extreme one towards the left, where it is properly arranged and placed upon camels for conveyance to the royal palace. During the whole proceeding a band of twenty-six musicians, some of whom occupy an elevated platform, delights with a "concord of sweet sounds" the assembled sportsmen.

Plate XLIII

CHOSROES II. ENGAGED IN A STAG-HUNT.

PLATE XLIII

On the opposite, or left-hand, side of the recess, is represented a boar-hunt. [PLATE XLIV.] Here again, elephants, twelve in number, drive the game into an enclosure without exit. Within this space nearly a hundred boars and pigs may be counted. The ground being marshy, the monarch occupies a boat in the centre, and from this transfixes the game with his arrows. No one else takes part in the sport, unless it be the riders on a troop of five elephants, represented in the lower middle portion of the tablet. When the pigs fall, they are carried into a second enclosure, that on the right, where they are upturned, disembowelled, and placed across the backs of elephants, which convey them to the abode of the monarch. Once more, the scene is enlivened by music. Two bands of harpers occupy boats on either side of that which carries the king, while another harper sits with him in the boat from which he delivers his arrows. In the water about the boats are seen reeds, ducks, and numerous fishes. The oars by which the boats are propelled have a singular resemblance to those which are represented in some of the earliest Assyrian sculptures. Two other features must also be noticed. Near the top of the tablet, towards the left, five figures standing in a boat seem to be clapping their hands in order to drive the pigs towards the monarch; while in the right centre of the picture there is another boat, more highly ornamented than the rest, in which we seem to have a second representation of the king, differing from the first only in the fact that his arrow has flown, and that he is in the act of taking another arrow from an attendant In this second representation the king's head is surrounded by a nimbus or "glory." Altogether there are in this tablet more than seventy-five human and nearly 150 animal forms. In the other, the human forms are about seventy, and the animal ones about a hundred.

Plate XLIV.

CHOSROES II. ENGAGED IN A BOAR HUNT.

PLATE XLIV

The merit of the two reliefs above described, which would require to be engraved on a large scale, in order that justice should be done to them, consists in the spirit and truth of the animal forms, elephants, camels, stags, boars, horses, and in the life and movement of the whole picture. The rush of the pigs, the bounds of the stags and hinds, the heavy march of the elephants, the ungainly movements of the camels, are well portrayed; and in one instance, the foreshortening of a horse, advancing diagonally, is respectably rendered. In general, Sassanian sculpture, like most delineative art in its infancy, affects merely the profile; but here, and in the overturned horse already described, and again in the Victories which ornament the spandrels of the arch of Chosroes, the mere profile is departed from with good effect, and a power is shown of drawing human and animal figures in front or at an angle. What is wanting in the entire Sassanian series is idealism, or the notion of elevating the representation in any respects above the object represented; the highest aim of the artist is to be true to nature; in this truthfulness is his triumph; but as he often falls short of his models, his whole result, even at the best, is unsatisfactory and disappointing.

Such must almost necessarily be the sentence of art critics, who judge the productions of this age and nation according to the abstract rules, or the accepted standards, of artistic effort. But if circumstances of time and country are taken into account, if comparison is limited to earlier and later attempts in the same region, or even in neighboring ones, a very much more favorable judgment will be passed. The Saseanian reliefs need not on the whole shrink from a comparison with those of the Achaemenian Persians. If they are ruder and more grotesque, they are also more spirited and more varied; and thus, though they fall short in some respects, still they must be pronounced superior to the Achaemenian in some of the most important artistic qualities. Nor do they fall greatly behind the earlier, and in many respects admirable, art of the Assyrians. They are less numerous and cover a lees variety of subjects; they have less delicacy; but they have equal or greater fire. In the judgment of a traveller not given to extravagant praise, they are, in some cases at any rate, "executed in the most masterly style." "I never saw," observes Sir R. Kerr Porter, "the elephant, the stag, or the boar portrayed with greater truth and spirit. The attempts at detailed human form are," he adds, "far inferior."

Before, however, we assign to the Sassanian monarchs, and to the people whom they governed, the merit of having produced results so worthy of admiration, it becomes necessary to inquire whether there is reason to believe that other than native artists wore employed in their production. It has been very confidently stated that Chosroes the Second "brought Roman artists" to Takht-i-Bostan, and by their aid eclipsed the glories of his great predecessors, Artaxerxes, son of Babek, and the two Sapors. Byzantine forms are declared to have been reproduced in the moldings of the Great Arch, and in the Victories. The lovely tracery of the Mashita Palace is regarded as in the main the work of Greeks and Syrians.06 No doubt it is quite possible that there may be some truth in these allegations; but we must not forget, or let it be forgotten, that they rest on conjecture and are without historical foundation. The works of the first Chosroes at Ctesiphon, according to a respectable Greek writer, were produced for him by foreign artists, sent to his court by Justinian. But no such statement is made with respect to his grandson. On the contrary, it is declared by the native writers that a certain Ferhad, a Persian, was the chief designer of them; and modern critics admit that his hand may perhaps be traced, not only at Takht-i-Bostan, but at the Mashita Palace also. If then the merit of the design is conceded to a native artist, we need not too curiously inquire the nationality of the workmen employed by him.

At the worst, should it be thought that Byzantine influence appears so plainly in the later Sassanian works, that Rome rather than Persia must be credited with the buildings and sculptures of both the first and the second Chosroes, still it will have to be allowed that the earlier palaces—those at Serbistan and Firuzabad—and the spirited battle-scenes above described, are wholly native; since they present no trace of any foreign element. But, it is in these battle-scenes, as already noticed, that the delineative art of the Sassanians culminates; and it may further be questioned whether the Firuzabad palace is not the finest specimen of their architecture, severe though it be in the character of its ornamentation; so that, even should we surrender the whole of the later works enough will still remain to show that the Sassanians, and the Persians of their day, had merit as artists and builders, a merit the more creditable to them inasmuch as for five centuries they had had no opportunity of cultivating their powers, having been crushed by the domination of a race singularly devoid of artistic aspirations. Even with regard to the works for which they may have been indebted to foreigners, it is to be remembered that, unless the monarchs had appreciated high art, and admired it, they would not have hired, at great expense, the services of these aliens. For my own part, I see no reason to doubt that the Sassanian remains of every period are predominantly, if not exclusively, native, not excepting those of the first Chosroes, for I mistrust the statement of Theophylact.

CHAPTER XXVIII

ON THE RELIGION, MANNERS, CUSTOMS, ETC., OF THE LATER PERSIANS.

*Religion of the later Persians, Dualism of the extremest kind. Ideas entertained with respect to Ormazd and Ahriman. Representations of them. Ormazd the special Guardian of the Kings. Lesser Deities subject to Ormazd: Mithra, Serosh, Vayu, Airyanam, Vitraha, etc. The six Amshash-pands: Bahman, Ardibehesht, Shahravar, Isfand-armat, Khordad, and Amerdat. Religion, how far idolatrous. Worship of Anaitis. Chief Evil Spirits subject to Ahriman: Alcomano, Indra, Caurva, Naonhaitya, Taric, and Zaric. Position of Man between the two Worlds of Good and Evil. His Duties: Worship, Agriculture, Purity. Nature of the Worship. Hymns, Invocations, the Homa Ceremony, Sacrifice. Agriculture a part of Religion. Purity required: 1, Moral; 2, Legal. Nature of each. Man's future Prospects. Position of the Magi under the Sassanians; their Organization, Dress, etc. The Fire-temples and Altars. The Barsom. The Khrafcthraghna. Magnificence of the Sassanian Court; the Throne-room, the Seraglio, the Attendants, the Ministers. Midttude of Palaces. Dress of the Monarch: 1, in Peace; 2, in War, Favorite Pastimes of the Kings. Hunting. Maintenance of Paradises. Stag and Boar-hunts. Music. Hawking. Games. Character of the Persian Warfare under the Sassanians. Sassanian Chariots. The Elephant Corps. The Cavalry. The Archers. The ordinary Infantry. Officers. Standards. Tactics. Private Life of the later Persians. Agricultural Employment of the Men. Non-seclusion of the Women. General Freedom from Oppression of all Classes except the highest.*

Πέρσας οἶδα νόμοισι τοῖσδε χρεωμένους.—Herod. i. 131.

The general character of the Persian religion, as revived by the founder of the Sassanian dynasty, has been described in a former chapter; but it is felt that the present work would be incomplete if it failed to furnish the reader with a tolerably full account of so interesting a matter; more especially, since the religious question lay at the root of the original rebellion and revolution which raised the Sassanidae to power, and was to a considerable extent the basis and foundation of their authority. An access of religious fervor gave the Persians of the third century after Christ the strength which enabled them to throw off the yoke of their Parthian lords and recover the sceptre of Western Asia. A strong—almost fanatical—religious spirit animated the greater number of the Sassanian monarchs. When the end of the kingdom came, the old faith was still flourishing; and, though its star paled before that of Mohammedanism, the faith itself survived, and still survives at the present day.

It has been observed that Dualism constituted the most noticeable feature of the religion. It may now be added that the Dualism professed was of the most extreme and pronounced kind. Ormazd and Ahriman, the principles of Good and Evil, were expressly declared to be "twins." They had "in the beginning come together to create Life and Death, and to settle how the world was to be." There was no priority of existence of the one over the other, and no decided superiority. The two, being coeval, had contended from all eternity, and would, it was almost certain, continue to contend to all eternity, neither being able to vanquish the other. Thus an eternal struggle was postulated between good and evil; and the issue was doubtful, neither side possessing any clear and manifest advantage.

The two principles were Persons. Ormazd was "the creator of life, the earthly and the spiritual," he who "made the celestial bodies, earth, water, and trees." He was "good," "holy," "pure," "true," "the Holy God," "the Holiest," "the Essence of Truth," "the father of all truth," "the being best of all," "the master of purity." He was supremely "happy," being possessed of every blessing, "health, wealth, virtue, wisdom, immortality." From him came every good gift enjoyed by man; on the pious and the righteous he bestowed, not only earthly advantages, but precious spiritual gifts, truth, devotion, "the good mind," and everlasting happiness; and, as he rewarded the good, so he also punished the bad, though this was an aspect in which he was but seldom represented.

While Ormazd, thus far, would seem to be a presentation of the Supreme Being in a form not greatly different from that wherein it has pleased him to reveal Himself to mankind through the Jewish and Christian scriptures, there are certain points of deficiency in the representation, which are rightly viewed as placing the Persian very considerably below the Jewish and Christian idea. Besides the limitation on the power and freedom of Ormazd implied in the eternal co-existence with him of another and a hostile principle, he is also limited by the independent existence of space, time, and light, which appear in the Zenda vesta as "self-created," or "without beginning," and must therefore be regarded as "conditioning" the Supreme Being, who has to work, as best he may, under circumstances not caused by himself. Again, Ormazd is not a purely spiritual being. He is conceived of as possessing a sort of physical nature. The "light," which is one of his properties, seems to be a material radiance. He can be spoken of as possessing health. The whole conception of him, though not grossly material, is far from being wholly immaterial. His nature is complex, not simple. He may not have a body, in the ordinary sense of the word; but he is entangled with material accidents, and is far from answering to the pure spirit, "without body, parts, or passions," which forms the Christian conception of the Deity.

Ahriman, the Evil Principle, is of course far more powerful and terrible than the Christian and Jewish Satan. He is uncaused, co-eternal with Ormazd, engaged in a perpetual warfare with him. Whatever good thing Ormazd creates, Ahriman corrupts and ruins it. Moral and physical evils are alike at his disposal. He blasts the earth with barrenness, or makes it produce thorns, thistles, and poisonous plants; his are the earthquake, the storm, the plague of hail, the thunderbolt; he causes disease and death, sweeps off a nation's flocks and herds by murrain, or depopulates a continent by pestilence; ferocious wild beasts, serpents, toads, mice, hornets, mosquitoes, are his creation; he invented and introduced into the world the sins of witchcraft, murder, unbelief, cannibalism, sodomy; he excites wars and tumults, stirs up the bad against the good, and labors by every possible expedient to make vice triumph over virtue. Ormazd can exercise no control over him; the utmost that he can do is to keep a perpetual watch on his rival, and seek to baffle and defeat him. This he is not always able to do. Despite his best endeavors, Ahriman is not unfrequently victorious.

In the purer times of the Zoroastrian religion it would seem that neither Ormazd nor Ahriman was represented by sculptured forms. A symbolism alone was permitted, which none could mistake for a real attempt to portray these august beings. But by the date of the Sassanian revival, the original spirit of the religion had suffered considerable modification; and it was no longer thought impious, or perilous, to exhibit the heads of the Pantheon, in the forms regarded as appropriate to them, upon public monuments. The great Artaxerxes, probably soon after his accession, set up a memorial of his exploits, in which he represented himself as receiving the insignia of royalty from Ormazd himself, while Ahriman, prostrate and seemingly, though of course not really, dead, lay at the feet of the steed on which Ormazd was mounted. In the form of Ormazd there is nothing very remarkable; he is attired like the king, has a long beard and flowing locks, and carries in his left hand a huge staff or baton, which he holds erect in a slanting position. The figure of Ahriman possesses more interest. The face wears an expression of pain and suffering; but the features are calm, and in no way disturbed. They are regular, and at least as handsome as those of Artaxerxes and his divine patron. He wears a band or diadem across the brow, above which we see a low cap or crown. From this escape the heads and necks of a number of vipers or snakes, fit emblems of the poisonous and "death-dealing" Evil One.

Some further representations of Ormazd occur in the Sassanian sculptures; but Ahriman seems not to be portrayed elsewhere. Ormazd appears on foot in a relief of the Great Arta-xerxes, which contains two figures only, those of himself and his divine patron. He is also to be seen in a sculpture which belongs probably to Sapor I., and represents that monarch in the act of receiving the diadem from Artaxerxes, his father. In the former of these two tablets the type exhibited in the bas-relief just described is followed without any variation; in the latter, the type is considerably modified. Ormazd still carries his huge baton, and is attired in royal fashion; but otherwise his appearance is altogether new and singular. His head bears no crown, but is surrounded by a halo of streaming rays; he has not much beard, but his hair, bushy and abundant, flows down on his two shoulders; he faces the spectator, and holds his baton in both his hands; finally, he stands upon a blossom, which is thought to be that of a sim-flower. Perhaps the conjecture is allowable that here we have Ormazd exhibited to us in a solar character, with the attributes of Mithra, from whom, in the olden time, he was carefully distinguished.

Ormazd seems to have been regarded by the kings as their special guardian and protector. No other deity (unless in one instance) is brought into close proximity with them; no other obtains mention in their inscriptions; from no other do they allow that they receive the blessing of offspring. Whatever the religion of the common people, that of the kings would seem to have been, in the main, the worship of this god, whom they perhaps sometimes confused with Mithra, or associated with Anaitis, but whom they never neglected, or failed openly to acknowledge.

Under the great Ormazd were a number of subordinate deities, the principal of whom were Mithra and Serosh, Mithra, the Sun-God, had been from a very early date an object of adoration in Persia, only second to Ormazd. The Achaemenian kings joined him occasionally with Ormazd in their invocations. In processions his chariot, drawn by milk-white horses, followed closely on that of Ormazd. He was often associated with Ormazd, as if an equal, though a real equality was probably not intended. He was "great," "pure," "imperishable," "the beneficent protector of all creatures," and "the beneficent preserver of all creatures." He had a thousand ears and ten thousand eyes. His worship was probably more widely extended than that of Ormazd himself, and was connected in general with a material representation.

In the early times this was a simple disk, or circle; but from the reign of Artaxerxes Mnemon, a human image seems to have been substituted. Prayer was offered to Mithra three times a day, at dawn, at noon, and at sunset; and it was usual to worship him with sacrifice. The horse appears to have been the victim which he was supposed to prefer.

Sraosha, or Serosh, was an angel of great power and dignity. He was the special messenger of Ormazd, and the head of his celestial army. He was "tall, well-formed, beautiful, swift, victorious, happy, sincere, true, the master of truth." It was his office to deliver revelations, to show men the paths of happiness, and to bring them the blessings which Ormazd had assigned to each. He invented the music for the five most ancient Gathas, discovered the barsom or divining-rod, and first taught its use to mankind. From his palace on the highest summit of the Elburz range, he watched the proceedings of the evil genii, and guarded the world from their attempts. The Iranians were his special care; but he lost no opportunity of injuring the Powers of Darkness, and lessening their dominion by teaching everywhere the true religion. In the other world it was his business to conduct the souls of the faithful through the dangers of the middle passage, and to bring them before the golden throne of Ormazd.

Among minor angelic powers were Vayu, "the wind," who is found also in the Vedic system; Airyanam, a god presiding over marriages; Vitraha, a good genius; Tistrya, the Dog Star, etc. The number of the minor deities was not, however, great; nor do they seem, as in so many other polytheistic religions, to have advanced in course of time from a subordinate to a leading position. From first to last they are of small account; and it seems, therefore, unnecessary to detain the reader by an elaborate description of them.

From the mass, however, of the lower deities or genii must be distinguished (besides Mithra and Serosh) the six Amesha Spentas, or Amshashpands, who formed the council of Ormazd, and in a certain sense reflected his glory. These were Vohu-mano or Bahman, Ashavahista or Ardibehesht, Khsha-thra-vairya or Shahravar, Spenta-Armaiti or Isfandarmat, Haurvatat or Khordad, and Ameretat or Amerdat. Vohu-mano, "the Good Mind," originally a mere attribute of Ormazd, came to be considered a distinct being, created by him to be his attendant and his councillor. He was, as it were, the Grand Vizier of the Almighty King, the chief of the heavenly conclave. Ormazd entrusted to him especially the care of animal life; and thus, as presiding over cattle, he is the patron deity of the agriculturist. Asha-vahista, "the best truth," or "the best purity," is the Light of the universe, subtle, pervading, omnipresent. He maintains the splendor of the various luminaries, and presides over the element of fire. Khsha-thra-vairya, "wealth," has the goods of this world at his disposal, and specially presides over metals, the conventional signs of wealth; he is sometimes identified with the metal which he dispenses. Spenta-Armaiti, "Holy Armaiti," is at once the genius of the Earth, and the goddess of piety. She has the charge of "the good creation," watches over it, and labors to convert the desolate and unproductive portions of it into fruitful fields and gardens. Together with Vohu-mano, she protects the agriculturist, blessing his land with increase, as Vohu-mano does his cattle. She is called "the daughter of Ormazd," and is regarded as the agent through whom Ormazd created the earth. Moreover, "she tells men the everlasting laws, which no one may abolish," or, in other words, imparts to them the eternal principles of morality. She is sometimes represented as standing next to Ormazd in the mythology, as in the profession of faith required of converts to Zoroastrianism. The two remaining Amshashpands, Haurvatat and Ameretat, "Health" and "Immortality," have the charge of the vegetable creation; Haurvatat causes the flow of water, so necessary to the support of vegetable life in countries where little rain falls; Ameretat protects orchards and gardens, and enables trees to bring their fruits to perfection.

Another deity, practically perhaps as much worshipped as Ormazd and Mithra, was Anaitis or Anahit. Anaiitis was originally an Assyrian and Babylonian, not a Zoroastrian goddess; but her worship spread to the Persians at a date anterior to Herodotus, and became in a short time exceedingly popular. It was in connection with this worship that idolatry seems first to have crept in, Artaxerxes Mnemon (ab. B.C. 400) having introduced images of Anaitis into Persia, and set them up at Susa, the capital, at Persepolis, Ecbatana, Bactra, Babylon, Damascus, and Sardis. Anaitis was the Babylonian Venus; and her rites at Babylon were undoubtedly of a revolting character. It is to be feared that they were introduced in all their grossness into Persia, and that this was the cause of Anahitis great popularity. Her cult "was provided with priests and hieroduli, and connected with mysteries, feasts, and unchaste ways."

The Persian system was further tainted with idolatry in respect of the worship of Mithra, and possibly of Vohu-mano (Batman) and of Amerdat; but on the whole, and especially as compared with other Oriental cults, the religion, even of the later Zoroastrians, must be regarded as retaining a non-materialistic and anti-idolatrous character, which elevated it above other neighboring religions, above Brahminism on the one hand and Syro-Chaldaean nature-worship on the other.

In the kingdom of Darkness, the principal powers, besides Ahriman, were Ako-mano, Indra, Qaurva, Naonhaitya, Taric, and Zaric. These six together formed the Council of the Evil One, as the six Amshashpands formed the council of Ormazd. Ako-mano, "the bad mind," or (literally) "the naught mind," was set over against Vohu-mano, "the good mind," and was Ahriman's Grand Vizier. His special sphere was the mind of man, where he suggested evil thoughts, and prompted to bad words and wicked deeds. Indra, identical with the vedic deity, but made a demon by the Zoroastrians, presided over storm and tempest, and governed the issues of war and battle  Qaurva and Naonhaitya were also Vedic deities turned into devils. It is difficult to assign them any distinct sphere. Taric and Zaric, "Darkness" and "Poison," had no doubt occupations corresponding with their names. Besides these chief demons, a countless host of evil genii (divs) and fairies (pairicas) awaited the orders and executed the behests of Ahriman.

Placed between the two contending worlds of good and evil, man's position was one of extreme danger and difficulty. Originally set upon the earth by Ormazd in order to maintain the good creation, he was liable to the continual temptations and seductions of the divs or devas, who were "wicked, bad, false, untrue, the originators of mischief, most baneful, destructive, the basest of all things." A single act of sin gave them a hold upon him, and each subsequent act increased their power, until ultimately he became their mere tool and slave. It was however possible to resist temptation, to cling to the side of right, to defy and overcome the deltas. Man might maintain his uprightness, walk in the path of duty, and by the help of the asuras, or "good spirits," attain to a blissful paradise.

To arrive at this result, man had carefully to observe three principal duties. These were worship, agriculture, and purity. Worship consisted in the acknowledgment of the One True God, Ormazd, and of his Holy Angels, the Amesha Spentas or Amshashpands, in the frequent offering of prayers, praises, and thanksgivings, in the recitation of set hymns, the performance of a certain ceremony called the Homa, and in the occasional sacrifice of animals. The set hymns form a large portion of the Zendavesta, where they occur in the shape of Gathas, or Yashts, sometimes possessing considerable beauty. They are sometimes general, addressed to Ormazd and the Amesha Spentas in common, sometimes special, containing the praises of a particular deity. The Homa ceremony consisted in the extraction of the juice of the Homa plant by the priests during the recitation of prayers, the formal presentation of the liquor extracted to the sacrificial fire, the consumption of a small portion of it by one of the officiating priests, and the division of the remainder among the worshippers. As the juice was drunk immediately after extraction and before fermentation had set in, it was not intoxicating. The ceremony seems to have been regarded, in part, as having a mystic force, securing the favor of heaven; in part as exerting a beneficial effect upon the body of the worshipper through the curative power inherent in the Homa plant. The animals which might be sacrificed were the horse, the ox, the sheep, and the goat, the horse being the favorite victim. A priest always performed the sacrifice, slaying the animal, and showing the flesh to the sacred fire by way of consecration, after which it was eaten at a solemn feast by the priest and people.

It is one of the chief peculiarities of Zoroastrianism that it regarded agriculture as a religious duty. Man had been placed upon the earth especially "to maintain the good creation," and resist the endeavors of Ahriman to injure, and if possible, ruin it. This could only be done by careful tilling of the soil, eradication of thorns and weeds, and reclamation of the tracts over which Ahriman had spread the curse of barrenness. To cultivate the soil was thus incumbent upon all men; the whole community was required to be agricultural; and either as proprietor, as farmer, or as laboring man, each Zoroastrian was bound to "further the works of life" by advancing tillage.

The purity which was required of the Zoroastrian was of two kinds, moral and legal, Moral purity comprised all that Christianity includes under it—truth, justice, chastity, and general sinlessness. It was coextensive with the whole sphere of human activity, embracing not only words and acts, but even the secret thoughts of the heart. Legal purity was to be obtained only by the observance of a multitude of trifling ceremonies and the abstinence from ten thousand acts in their nature wholly indifferent. Especially, everything was to be avoided which could be thought to pollute the four elements—all of them sacred to the Zoroastrian of Sassanian times—fire, water, earth, and air.

Man's struggle after holiness and purity was sustained in the Zoroastrian system by the confident hope of a futurity of happiness. It was taught that the soul of man was immortal, and would continue to possess for ever a separate conscious existence. Immediately after death the spirits of both good and bad had to proceed along an appointed path to "the bridge of the gatherer" (chinvat peretu). This was a narrow road conducting to heaven or paradise, over which the souls of the pious alone could pass, while the wicked fell from it into the gulf below, where they found themselves in the place of punishment. The steps of the good were guided and supported by the angel Serosh—the "happy, well-formed, swift, tall Serosh"—who conducted them across the difficult passage into the heavenly region. There Bahman, rising from his throne, greeted them on their entrance with the salutation, "Happy thou who art come here to us from the mortality to the immortality!" Then they proceeded joyfully onward to the presence of Ormazd, to the immortal saints, to the golden throne, to paradise. As for the wicked, when they fell into the gulf, they found themselves in outer darkness, in the kingdom of Ahriman, where they were forced to remain and to feed on poisoned banquets.

The priests of the Zoroastrians, from a time not long subsequent to Darius Hystaspis, were the Magi. This tribe, or caste, originally perhaps external to Zoroastrianism, had come to be recognized as a true priestly order; and was intrusted by the Sassanian princes with the whole control and direction of the religion of the state. Its chief was a personage holding a rank but very little inferior to the king. He bore the title of Tenpet, "Head of the Religion," or Movpetan Movpet, "Head of the Chief Magi." In times of difficulty and danger he was sometimes called upon to conduct a revolution; and in the ordinary course of things he was always reckoned among the monarch's chief counsellors. Next in rank to him were a number of Movpets, or "Chief Magi," called also destoors or "rulers," who scarcely perhaps constituted an order, but still held an exalted position. Under these were, finally, a large body of ordinary Magi, dispersed throughout the empire, but especially congregated in the chief towns.

The Magi officiated in a peculiar dress. This consisted of a tall peaked cap of felt or some similar material, having deep lappets at the side, which concealed the jaw and even the lips, and a long white robe, or cloak, descending to the ankles. They assembled often in large numbers, and marched in stately processions, impressing the multitude by a grand and striking ceremonial. Besides the offerings which were lavished upon them by the faithful, they possessed considerable endowments in land, which furnished them with an assured subsistence. They were allowed by Chosroes the First a certain administrative power in civil matters; the collection of the revenue was to take place under their supervision; they were empowered to interfere in cases of oppression, and protect the subject against the tax-gatherer.

The Zoroastrian worship was intimately connected with fire-temples and fire-altars. A fire-temple was maintained in every important city throughout the empire; and in these a sacred flame, believed to have been lighted from heaven, was kept up perpetually, by the care of the priests, and was spoken of as "unextinguishable." Fire-altars probably also existed, independently of temples; and an erection of this kind maintained from first to last an honorable position on the Sassanian coins, being the main impress upon the reverse. It was represented with the flame rising from it, and sometimes with a head in the flame; its stem was ornamented with garlands or fillets; and on either side, as protectors or as worshippers, were represented two figures, sometimes watching the flame, sometimes turned from it, guarding it apparently from external enemies.

Besides the sacerdotal, the Magi claimed to exercise the prophetical office. From a very early date they had made themselves conspicuous as omen-readers and dream-expounders; but, not content with such occasional exhibitions of prophetic power, they ultimately reduced divination to a system, and, by the help of the barsom or bundle of divining rods, undertook to return a true answer on all points connected with the future, upon which they might be consulted. Credulity is never wanting among Orientals; and the power of the priesthood was no doubt greatly increased by a pretension which was easily made, readily believed, and not generally discredited by failures, however numerous.

The Magian priest was commonly seen with the barsom in his hand; but occasionally he exchanged that instrument for another, known as the khrafgihraghna. It was among the duties of the pious Zoroastrian, and more especially of those who were entrusted with the priestly office, to wage perpetual war with Ahriman, and to destroy his works whenever opportunity offered. Now among these, constituting a portion of "the bad creation," were all such animals as frogs, toads, snakes, newts, mice, lizards, flies, and the like. The Magi took every opportunity of killing such creatures; and the Jchrafgthraghna was an implement which they invented for the sake of carrying out this pious purpose.

The court of the Sassanian kings, especially in the later period of the empire, was arranged upon a scale of almost unexampled grandeur and magnificence. The robes worn by the Great King were beautifully embroidered, and covered with gems and pearls, which in some representations may be counted by hundreds. [PLATE XLV.] The royal crown, which could not be worn, but was hung from the ceiling by a gold chain exactly over the head of the king when he took his seat in his throne-room, is said to have been adorned with a thousand pearls, each as large as an egg. The throne itself was of gold, and was supported on four feet, each formed of a single enormous ruby. The great throne-room was ornamented with enormous columns of silver, between which were hangings of rich silk or brocade. The vaulted roof presented to the eye representations of the heavenly bodies, the sun, the moon, and the stars;no while globes, probably of crystal, or of burnished metal, hung suspended from it at various heights, lighting up the dark space as with a thousand lustres.

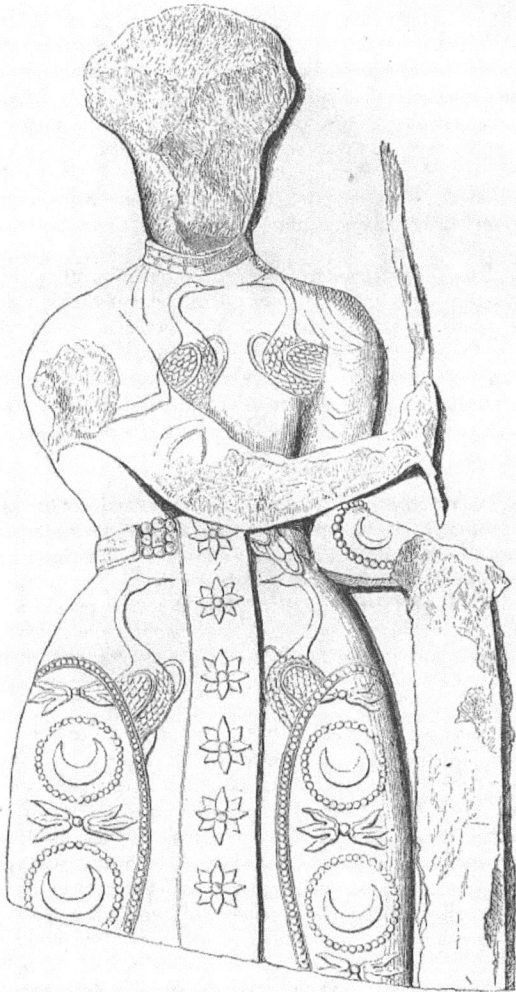

ROBED FIGURE, SHOWING SASSANIAN EMBROIDERY.

PLATE XLV

The state observed at the court resembled that of the most formal and stately of the Oriental monarchies. The courtiers were organized in seven ranks. Foremost came the Ministers of the crown; next the Mobeds, or chief Magi; after them, the hirbeds, or judges; then the sipehbeds, or commanders-in chief, of whom there were commonly four; last of all the singers, musicians, and men of science, arranged in three orders. The king sat apart even from the highest nobles, who, unless summoned, might not approach nearer than thirty feet from him.

A low curtain separated him from them, which was under the charge of an officer, who drew it for those only with whom the king had expressed a desire to converse.

An important part of the palace was the seraglio. The polygamy practised by the Sassanian princes was on the largest scale that has ever been heard of, Chosroes II. having maintained, we are told, three thousand concubines. The modest requirements of so many secondary wives necessitated the lodging and sustenance of twelve thousand additional females, chiefly slaves, whose office was to attend on these royal favorites, attire them, and obey their behests. Eunuchs are not mentioned as employed to any large extent; but in the sculptures of the early princes they seem to be represented as holding offices of importance, and the analogy of Oriental courts does not allow us to doubt that the seraglio was, to some extent at any rate, under their superintendence. Each Sassanian monarch had one sultana or principal wife, who was generally a princess by birth, but might legally be of any origin. In one or two instances the monarch sets the effigy of his principal wife upon his coins; but this is unusual, and when, towards the close of the empire, females were allowed to ascend the throne, it is thought that they refrained from parading themselves in this way, and stamped their coins with the head of a male.

In attendance upon the monarch were usually his parasol-bearer, his fan-bearer, who appears to have been a eunuch, the Senelcapan, or "Lord Chamberlain," the Maypet, or "Chief Butler," the Andertzapet, or "Master of the Wardrobe," the Alchorapet, or "Master of the Horse," the Taharhapet or "Chief Cupbearer," the Shahpan, or "Chief Falconer," and the Krhogpet, or "Master of the Workmen." Except the parasol-bearer and fan-bearer, these officials all presided over departments, and had under them a numerous body of subordinates. If the royal stables contained even 8000 horses, which one monarch is said to have kept for his own riding, the grooms and stable-boys must have been counted by hundreds; and an equal or greater number of attendants must have been required for the camels and elephants, which are estimated m respectively at 1200 and 12,000. The "workmen" were also probably a corps of considerable size, continually engaged in repairs or in temporary or permanent erections.

Other great officials, corresponding more nearly to the "Ministers" of a modern sovereign, were the Vzourkhramanatar, or "Grand Keeper of the Royal Orders," who held the post now known as that of Grand Vizier; the Dprapet Ariats, or "Chief of the Scribes of Iran," a sort of Chancellor; the Hazarapet dran Ariats, or "Chiliarch of the Gate of Iran," a principal Minister; the Hamarakar, a "Chief Cashier" or "Paymaster;" and the Khohrdean dpir, or "Secretary of Council," a sort of Privy Council clerk or registrar. The native names of these officers are known to us chiefly through the Armenian writers of the fifth and seventh centuries.

The Sassanian court, though generally held at Ctesiphon, migrated to other cities, if the king so pleased, and is found established, at one time in the old Persian capital, Persepolis, at another in the comparatively modern city of Dastaghord. The monarchs maintained from first to last numerous palaces, which they visited at their pleasure and made their residence for a longer or a shorter period. Four such palaces have been already described; and there is reason to believe that many others existed in various parts of the empire. There was certainly one of great magnificence at Canzaca; and several are mentioned as occupied by Heraclius in the country between the Lower Zab and Ctesiphon. Chosroes II. undoubtedly built one near Takht-i-Bostan; and Sapor the First must have had one at Shapur, where he set up the greater portion of his monuments. The discovery of the Mashita palace, in a position so little inviting as the land of Moab, seems to imply a very general establishment of royal residences in the remote provinces of the empire.

The costume of the later Persians is known to us chiefly from the representations of the kings, on whose figures alone have the native artists bestowed much attention. In peace, the monarch seems to have worn a sort of pelisse or long coat, partially open in front, and with close-fitting sleeves reaching to the wrist, under which he had a pair of loose trousers descending to the feet and sometimes even covering them. A belt or girdle encircled his waist. His feet were encased in patterned shoes, tied with long flowing ribbons. Over his pelisse he wore occasionally a long cape or short cloak, which was fastened with a brooch or strings across the breast and flowed over the back and shoulders. The material composing the cloak was in general exceedingly light and flimsy. The head-dress commonly worn seems to have been a round cap, which was perhaps ornamented with jewels. The vest and trousers were also in some cases richly jewelled. Every king wore ear-rings, with one, two, or three pendants. A collar or necklace was also commonly worn round the neck; and this had sometimes two or more pendants in front. Occasionally the beard was brought to a point and had a jewel hanging from it. The hair seems always to have been worn long; it was elaborately curled, and hung down on either shoulder in numerous ringlets. When the monarch rode out in state, an attendant held the royal parasol over him.

In war the monarch encased the upper part of his person in a coat of mail, composed of scales or links. Over this he wore three belts; the first, which crossed the breast diagonally, was probably attached to his shield, which might be hung from it; the second supported his sword; and the third his quiver, and perhaps his bow-case. A stiff, embroidered trouser of great fulness protected the leg, while the head was guarded by a helmet, and a vizor of chain mail hid all the face but the eyes. The head and fore-quarters of the royal charger were also covered with armor, which descended below the animal's knees in front, but was not carried back behind the rider. The monarch's shield was round, and carried on the left arm; his main offensive weapon was a heavy spear, which he brandished in his right hand.

One of the favorite pastimes of the kings was hunting. The Sassanian remains show us the royal sportsmen engaged in the pursuit of the stag, the wild boar, the ibex, the antelope, and the buffalo. To this catalogue of their beasts of chase the classical writers add the lion, the tiger, the wild ass, and the bear. Lions, tigers, bears, and wild asses were, it appears, collected for the purpose of sport, and kept in royal parks or paradises until a hunt was determined on. The monarchs then engaged in the sport in person, either singly or in conjunction with a royal ambassador, or perhaps of a favorite minister, or a few friends. The lion was engaged hand to hand with sword or spear; the more dangerous tiger was attacked from a distance with arrows. Stags and wild boars were sufficiently abundant to make the keeping of them in paradises unnecessary. When the king desired to hunt them, it was only requisite to beat a certain extent of country in order to make sure of finding the game. This appears to have been done generally by elephants, which entered the marshes or the woodlands, and, spreading themselves wide, drove the animals before them towards an enclosed space, surrounded by a net or a fence, where the king was stationed with his friends and attendants. If the tract was a marsh, the monarch occupied a boat, from which he quietly took aim at the beasts that came within shot. Otherwise he pursued the game on horseback, and transfixed it while riding at full speed. In either case he seems to have joined to the pleasures of the chase the delights of music. Bands of harpers and other musicians were placed near him within the enclosure, and he could listen to their strains while he took his pastime.

The musical instruments which appear distinctly on the Sassanian sculptures are the harp, the horn, the drum, and the flute or pipe. The harp is triangular, and has seven strings; it is held in the lap, and played apparently by both hands. The drum is of small size. The horns and pipes are too rudely represented for their exact character to be apparent. Concerted pieces seem to have been sometimes played by harpers only, of whom as many as ten or twelve joined in the execution. Mixed bands were more numerous. In one instance the number of performers amounts to twenty-six, of whom seven play the harp, an equal number the flute or pipe, three the horn, one the drum, while eight are too slightly rendered for their instruments to be recognized. A portion of the musicians occupy an elevated orchestra, to which there is access by a flight of steps.

There is reason to believe that the Sassanian monarchs took a pleasure also in the pastime of hawking. It has been already noticed that among the officers of the court was a "Head Falconer," who must have presided over this species of sport. Hawking was of great antiquity in the East, and appears to have been handed down uninterruptedly from remote times to the present day. We may reasonably conjecture that the ostriches and pheasants, if not the peacocks also, kept in the royal preserves, were intended to be used in this pastime, the hawks being flown at them if other game proved to be scarce.

The monarchs also occasionally amused themselves in their leisure hours by games. The introduction of chess from India by the great Chosroes (Anushirwan) has already been noticed; and some authorities state that the same monarch brought into use also a species of tric-trac or draughts. Unfortunately we have no materials for determining the exact form of the game in either case, the Sassanian remains containing no representation of such trivial matters.

In the character of their warfare, the Persians of the Sassanian period did not greatly differ from the same people under the Achaemenian kings. The principal changes which time had brought about were an almost entire disuse of the war chariot, [PLATE XLVI. Fig. 3.] and the advance of the elephant corps into a very prominent and important position. Four main arms of the service were recognized, each standing on a different level: viz. the elephants, the horse, the archers, and the ordinary footmen. The elephant corps held the first position. It was recruited from India, but was at no time very numerous. Great store was set by it; and in some of the earlier battles against the Arabs the victory was regarded as gained mainly by this arm of the service. It acted with best effect in an open and level district; but the value put upon it was such that, however rough, mountainous, and woody the country into which the Persian arms penetrated, the elephant always accompanied the march of the Persian troops, and care was taken to make roads by which it could travel. The elephant corps was under a special chief, known as the Zend-hapet, or "Commander of the Indians," either because the beasts came from that country, or because they were managed by natives of Hindustan.

Plate XLVI

Vol. III

Fig.

Section of Central Domed Chamber, Firuzabad (after Flandin).

Fig 2.

External Ornamentation of Palace at Firuzabad.

PLATE XLVI

The Persian cavalry in the Sassanian period seems to have been almost entirely of the heavy kind. [PLATE XLVI., Fig. 4.] We hear nothing during these centuries of those clouds of light horse which, under the earlier Persian and under the Parthian monarchy, hung about invading or retreating armies, countless in their numbers, agile in their movements, a terrible annoyance at the best of times, and a fearful peril under certain circumstances. The Persian troops which pursued Julian were composed of heavily armed cavalry, foot archers, and elephants; and the only light horse of which we have any mention during the disastrous retreat of his army are the Saracenic allies of Sapor. In these auxiliaries, and in the Cadusians from the Caspian region, the Persians had always, when they wished it, a cavalry excellently suited for light service; but their own horse during the Sassanian period seems to have been entirely of the heavy kind, armed and equipped, that is, very much as Chosroes II. is seen to bo at Takht-i-Bostan. The horses themselves wore heavily armored about their head, neck, and chest; the rider wore a coat of mail which completely covered his body as far as the hips, and a strong helmet, with a vizor, which left no part of the face exposed but the eyes. He carried a small round shield on his left arm, and had for weapons a heavy spear, a sword, and a bow and arrows. He did not fear a collision with the best Roman troops. The Sassanian horse often charged the infantry of the legions with success, and drove it headlong from the field of battle. In time of peace, the royal guards were more simply accoutred. [See PLATE XLVI.]

The archers formed the elite of the Persian infantry. They were trained to deliver their arrows with extreme rapidity, and with an aim that was almost unerring. The huge wattled shields, adopted by the Achaemenian Persians from the Assyrians, still remained in use; and from behind a row of these, rested upon the ground and forming a sort of loop-holed wall, the Sassanian bowmen shot their weapons with great effect; nor was it until their store of arrows was exhausted that the Romans, ordinarily, felt themselves upon even terms with their enemy. Sometimes the archers, instead of thus fighting in line, were intermixed with the heavy horse, with which it was not difficult for them to keep pace. They galled the foe with their constant discharges from between the ranks of the horsemen, remaining themselves in comparative security, as the legions rarely ventured to charge the Persian mailed cavalry. If they were forced to retreat, they still shot backwards as they fled; and it was a proverbial saying with the Romans that they were then especially formidable.

The ordinary footmen seem to have been armed with swords and spears, perhaps also with darts. They were generally stationed behind the archers, who, however, retired through their ranks when close fighting began. They had little defensive armor; but still seem to have fought with spirit and tenacity, being a fair match for the legionaries under ordinary circumstances, and superior to most other adversaries.

It is uncertain how the various arms of the service were organized internally. We do not hear of any divisions corresponding to the Roman legions or to modern regiments; yet it is difficult to suppose that there were not some such bodies. Perhaps each satrap of a province commanded the troops raised within his government, taking the actual lead of the cavalry or the infantry at his discretion. The Crown doubtless appointed the commanders-in-chief—the Sparapets, Spaha-pets, or Sipehbeds, as well as the other generals (arzbeds), the head of the commissariat (hambarapet or hambarahapet), and the commander of the elephants (zendkapet). The satraps may have acted as colonels of regiments under the arzbeds, and may probably have had the nomination of the subordinate (regimental) officers.

The great national standard was the famous "leathern apron of the blacksmith," originally unadorned, but ultimately covered with jewels, which has been described in a former chapter. This precious palladium was, however, but rarely used, its place being supplied for the most part by standards of a more ordinary character. These appear by the monuments to have been of two kinds. Both consisted primarily of a pole and a cross-bar; but in the one kind the crossbar sustained a single ring with a bar athwart it, while below depended two woolly tassels; in the other, three striated balls rose from the cross-bar, while below the place of the tassels was taken by two similar balls. It is difficult to say what these emblems symbolized, or why they were varied. In both the representations where they appear the standards accompany cavalry, so that they cannot reasonably be assigned to different arms of the service. That the number of standards carried into battle was considerable may be gathered from the fact that on one occasion, when the defeat sustained was not very complete, a Persian army left in the enemy's hands as many as twenty-eight of them.

During the Sassanian period there was nothing very remarkable in the Persian tactics. The size of armies generally varied from 30,000 to 60,000 men, though sometimes 100,000, and on one occasion as many as 140,000, are said to have been assembled. The bulk of the troops were footmen, the proportion of the horse probably never equalling one third of a mixed army. Plundering expeditions were sometimes undertaken by bodies of horse alone; but serious invasions were seldom or never attempted unless by a force complete in all arms; comprising, that is, horse, foot, elephants, and artillery. To attack the Romans to any purpose, it was always necessary to engage in the siege of towns; and although, in the earlier period of the Sassanian monarchy, a certain weakness and inefficiency in respect of sieges manifested itself, yet ultimately the difficulty was overcome, and the Persian expeditionary armies, well provided with siege trains, compelled the Roman fortresses to surrender within a reasonable time. It is remarkable that in the later period so many fortresses were taken with apparently so little difficulty—Daras, Mardin, Amida, Carrhse, Edessa, Hierapolis, Berhasa, Theodosiopolis, Antioch, Damascus, Jerusalem, Alexandria, Caesaraea Mazaca, Chalcedon; the siege of none lasting more than a few months, or costing the assailants very dear. The method used in sieges was to open trenches at a certain distance from the walls, and to advance along them under cover of hurdles to the ditch, and fill it up with earth and fascines. Escalade might then be attempted; or movable towers, armed with rams or balistae, might be brought up close to the walls, and the defences battered till a breach was effected. Sometimes mounds were raised against the walls to a certain height, so that their upper portion, which was their weakest part, might be attacked, and either demolished or escaladed. If towns resisted prolonged attacks of this kind, the siege was turned into a blockade, lines of circumvallation being drawn round the place, water cut off, and provisions prevented from entering. Unless a strong relieving army appeared in the field, and drove off the assailants, this plan was tolerably sure to be successful.

Not much is known of the private life of the later Persians. Besides the great nobles and court officials, the strength of the nation consisted in its dilchans or landed proprietors, who for the most part lived on their estates, seeing after the cultivation of the soil, and employing thereon the free labor of the peasants. It was from these classes chiefly that the standing army was recruited, and that great levies might always be made in time of need. Simple habits appear to have prevailed among them; polygamy, though lawful, was not greatly in use; the maxims of Zoroaster, which commanded industry, purity, and piety, were fairly observed. Women seem not to have been kept in seclusion, or at any rate not in such seclusion as had been the custom under the Parthians, and as again became usual under the Arabs. The general condition of the population was satisfactory. Most of the Sassanian monarchs seem to have been desirous of governing well; and the system inaugurated by Anushirwan, and maintained by his successors, secured the subjects of the Great King from oppression, so far as was possible without representative government. Provincial rulers were well watched and well checked; tax-gatherers were prevented from exacting more than their due by a wholesale dread that their conduct would be reported and punished; great pains were taken that justice should be honestly administered; and in all cases where an individual felt aggrieved at a sentence an appeal lay to the king. On such occasions the cause was re-tried in open court, at the gate, or in the great square; the king, the Magi, and the great lords hearing it, while the people were also present. The entire result seems to have been that, so far as was possible under a despotism, oppression was prevented, and the ordinary citizen had rarely any ground for serious complaint.

But it was otherwise with the highest class of all. The near relations of the monarch, the great officers of the court, the generals who commanded armies, were exposed without defence to the monarch's caprice, and held their lives and liberties at his pleasure. At a mere word or sign from him they were arrested, committed to prison, tortured, blinded, or put to death, no trial being thought necessary where the king chose to pronounce sentence. The intrinsic evils of despotism thus showed themselves even under the comparatively mild government of the Sassanians; but the class exposed to them was a small one, and enjoyed permanent advantages, which may have been felt as some compensation to it for its occasional sufferings.

ROYAL HOUSE OF THE SASSANIANS.

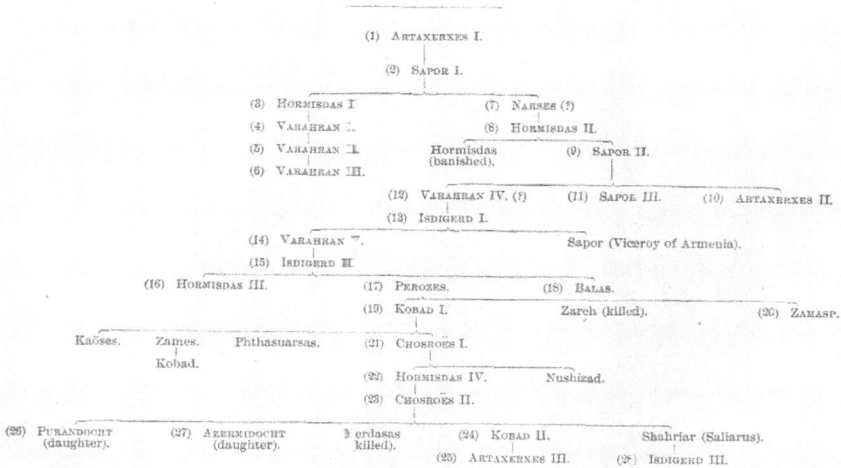

FAMILY-TREE